India's and China's Recent Experience
with Reform and Growth

Also by Wanda Tseng

CHINA: Competing in the Global Economy (co-editor M. Rodlauer)

India's and China's Recent Experience with Reform and Growth

Edited by

Wanda Tseng

and

David Cowen

International Monetary Fund

© International Monetary Fund 2005

All rights reserved. No reproduction, copy or transmission of this publication may be made without written permission.

No paragraph of this publication may be reproduced, copied or transmitted save with written permission or in accordance with the provisions of the Copyright, Designs and Patents Act 1988, or under the terms of any licence permitting limited copying issued by the Copyright Licensing Agency, 90 Tottenham Court Road, London W1T 4LP.

Any person who does any unauthorized act in relation to this publication may be liable to criminal prosecution and civil claims for damages.

The authors have asserted their rights to be identified as the authors of this work in accordance with the Copyright, Designs and Patents Act 1988.

First published in hardcover 2005
First published in paperback 2007 by
PALGRAVE MACMILLAN
Houndmills, Basingstoke, Hampshire RG21 6XS and
175 Fifth Avenue, New York, N.Y. 10010
Companies and representatives throughout the world.

PALGRAVE MACMILLAN is the global academic imprint of the Palgrave Macmillan division of St. Martin's Press, LLC and of Palgrave Macmillan Ltd. Macmillan® is a registered trademark in the United States, United Kingdom and other countries. Palgrave is a registered trademark in the European Union and other countries.

ISBN-13: 978–1–4039–4351–4 hardback
ISBN-10: 1–4039–4351–6   hardback
ISBN-13: 978–0–230–54281–5 paperback
ISBN-10: 0–230–54281–6   paperback

This book is printed on paper suitable for recycling and made from fully managed and sustained forest sources. Logging, pulping and manufacturing processes are expected to conform to the environmental regulations of the country of origin.

A catalogue record for this book is available from the British Library.

Library of Congress Cataloging-in-Publication Data

India's and China's recent experience with reform and growth / edited by Wanda Tseng and David Cowen.
    p. cm.
Includes bibliographical references and index.
ISBN 1–4039–4351–6 (cloth) ISBN 0–230–54281–6 (paper)
    1. India—Economic policy. 2. India—Economic conditions. 3. China—Economic policy. 4. China—Economic conditions. I. Tseng, Wanda. II. Cowen, David, 1960–
HC435.3.I53 2005
338.951'009'045—dc22   2005047037

Printed and bound in Great Britain by
CPI Antony Rowe, Chippenham and Eastbourne

Contents

List of Tables	viii
List of Figures	xi
List of Boxes	xiii
List of Abbreviations	xiv
Acknowledgments	xvii
Preface	xviii
Notes on Contributors	xxi

1 India and China: An Essay in Comparative Political Economy   **1**
Meghnad Desai

1.1	Introduction	1
1.2	Historical legacies	3
1.3	Development paths	8
1.4	Speculations and counterfactuals	14
1.5	Can China combine capitalism with one party rule?	15
1.6	Can India catch up with China?	17
1.7	Conclusion	19

2 India's Growth Experience   **23**
Kanhaiya Singh and Suman Bery

2.1	Introduction	23
2.2	India in the global context	24
2.3	Growth over half a century: an overview	27
2.4	Structural shifts in output: a closer look	33
2.5	Sources of growth: analysis of the aggregate data	44
2.6	Overall assessment and concluding remarks	53

3 China's Economic Growth and Poverty Reduction (1978–2002)   **59**
Hu Angang, Hu Linlin, and Chang Zhixiao

3.1	Introduction	59
3.2	Trends in and evaluation of poverty reduction (1978–2002)	59

3.3 Slowing poverty reduction in the 1990s: an analysis 69
3.4 New strategies for poverty reduction (2003–15) 83

4 Reform Strategies in the Indian Financial Sector 91
Saugata Bhattacharya and Urjit R. Patel

4.1 Introduction 91
4.2 Reform in the financial sector 95
4.3 Deconstructing the reform strategy 103
4.4 A good beginning, but . . . aspects of financial intermediation 116
4.5 Conclusion 125

5 Financial System Reform and Economic Development in China 132
Chen Yuan

6 Bank Financing in India 138
Abhijit Banerjee, Shawn Cole, and Esther Duflo

6.1 Introduction 138
6.2 Is there underlending? 139
6.3 Lending practice in India 142
6.4 Understanding lending practices 146
6.5 Conclusion—policy responses 153

7 Trade Liberalization and Its Role in Chinese Economic Growth 158
Nicholas R. Lardy

7.1 Introduction 158
7.2 Trade liberalization in China 159
7.3 Effects of competitiveness on openness 163
7.4 Conclusion 166

8 India in the 1980s and the 1990s: A Triumph of Reforms 170
Arvind Panagariya

8.1 Introduction 170
8.2 The fragility of growth in the 1980s 174
8.3 Connection to liberalization 178
8.4 Unsustainable public expenditure and external borrowing 186
8.5 A brief look at the 1990s 188
8.6 Looking ahead: why India lags behind China 193
8.7 Conclusion 195

9   Effects of Financial Globalization on Developing
    Countries: Some Empirical Evidence   201
    Eswar Prasad, Kenneth Rogoff, Shang-Jin Wei, and M. Ayhan Kose

    9.1   Overview   201
    9.2   Basic stylized facts   202
    9.3   Financial integration and economic growth   207
    9.4   Financial globalization and macroeconomic volatility 214
    9.5   Select factors in the benefits and risks of
          globalization   221
    9.6   Conclusion   224

10 Understanding India's Services Revolution   229
    James Gordon and Poonam Gupta

    10.1 Introduction   229
    10.2 Growth and sectoral shares: cross-country experiences 231
    10.3 Which services have grown rapidly?   237
    10.4 Explaining services sector growth   243
    10.5 Empirical tests of competing hypotheses   254
    10.6 Summary and conclusion   258

11 Capital Account Controls and Liberalization:
    Lessons for India and China   264
    Jonathan Anderson

    11.1 Capital controls in emerging markets   264
    11.2 Do capital controls "work"?   266
    11.3 The lessons of liberalization   270
    11.4 The experiences of China and India   271
    11.5 China versus India—who wins?   272
    11.6 Summary lessons for China and India   273

12 Capital Account Liberalization: The Indian
    Experience   275
    Narendra Jadhav

    12.1 Introduction   275
    12.2 Costs and benefits, preconditions and sequencing   276
    12.3 Cross-country perspective   279
    12.4 The Indian approach   287
    12.5 Conclusion   303

List of Tables

1.1   Share of world output and population   2
1.2   Human development indices, 1950–2000   10
2.1   Select economic indictors of major economies   25
2.2   Evolving economic structure of India and select
      comparator countries   27
2.3   India: GDP growth and outliers, 1951/52–2002/03   28
2.4   India: terms of prime ministers and years of general elections 30
2.5   India: average growth rates and real GDP shares by sectors,
      1951/52–2002/03   34
2.6   India: unorganized economy in GDP by sectors,
      1971/72–2000/01   35
2.7   India: saving and investment rates, 1951/52–2002/03   37
2.8   India: gross fixed capital formation, 1951/52–2001/02   39
2.9   Cereal yield in India and select parts of the world   40
2.10 India: agricultural sector indicators, 1971/72–2002/03   41
2.11 India: industrial output, 1981/82–2003/04   43
2.12 India: services GDP, 1981/82–2002/03   45
2.13 India: decomposition of growth, 1961/62–2001/02   48
2.14 India: alternate models of total factor productivity growth   50
2.15 India: distributed lag model of TFP and real GDP growth   51
2.16 Granger-Block non-causality test   52
3.1   China: growth, poverty reduction, and farmers' welfare,
      1978–2002   60
3.2   China: rural poverty population and poverty rates,
      1978–2002   61
3.3   Number of persons living on less than US$1 per day   62
3.4   Poverty population in select Asian countries   62
3.5   World poverty population and poverty rates, 1950–99   63
3.6   China: rural households grouped by annual per
      capita net income, 1978–2001   64
3.7   China: population and labor force movement from
      rural to urban areas, 1982–2000   65
3.8   China: basic human capital indicators   67
3.9   China: national antipoverty fund, 1986–2000   68
3.10 China: official poverty line, 1978–2002   70
3.11 China: internal agricultural trade and losses, 1996–2000   79
3.12 China: total and transfer income of urban and rural residents 81
3.13 China: estimates of income distribution in rural areas,
      1978–2000   82

3.14	China: average income and taxes and fees paid by income group in 1999	83
4.1	India: comparative profile of financial intermediaries and markets	97
4.2	India: decadal indicators of financial deepening	97
4.3	India: cost of bank rescues	99
4.4	India: segment-wise distribution of gross nonperforming assets	100
4.5	India: volume of activity in cash and derivatives markets in 2002/03	102
4.6	India: institutional processes in the reform strategy of the financial sector	105
4.7	India: portfolio allocation of lendable resources of scheduled commercial banks	105
4.8	Reserve Bank of India: prompt corrective action framework	108
4.9	Reserve Bank of India norms on exposure limits for banks and financial institutions	111
4.10	India: loan classification of scheduled commercial banks	117
6.1	Are firms credit constrained?	141
6.2	Bank financing—granted, maximum, and previous limits of a PSB	144
6.3	Determinants of the working capital limit and interest rate	145
6.4	Summary statistics for corruption study	148
6.5	Effect of vigilance activity on credit	149
6.6	Interest rate spreads, bank credit, and state growth	152
6.7	Nonperforming assets of priority sector borrowers at a public sector bank	153
7.1	China's and India's shares of global trade	159
8.1	India: real GDP growth, 1951/52–2002/03	176
8.2	India: average real GDP growth in select periods	177
8.3	India: variance of GDP growth rates, 1980s and 1990s	178
8.4	India: average growth rates of non-oil merchandise trade in select periods	180
8.5	India: non-oil merchandise exports and imports, 1970/71–1989/90	185
8.6	India: changes in protection and growth in productivity by industry classification	186
8.7	India: fiscal indicators, 1980/81–1989/90	188
8.8	India: composition of GDP	194
9.1	Fastest and slowest growing economies during 1980–2000 and financial openness	210
9.2	Volatility of annual growth rates of select variables	215
10.1	India: sectoral growth rates	230

10.2	Global averages of sectoral shares of GDP in 2001	232
10.3	India: sectoral shares of GDP, 1950–2003	234
10.4	India: share of services sector in employment and capital formation	237
10.5	India: services growth rates and sectoral shares	238
10.6	India: evolution of input–output coefficients	245
10.7	India: private final consumption of services	247
10.8	India: growth of services value added and final consumption and GDP	247
10.9	India: explaining services growth using time series data, 1952–2000	256
10.10	India: explaining services growth using panel data, 1970–2000	258
10.11	Sources of data and construction of variables	261
12.1	Type of capital transactions that could be subject to controls	283
12.2	India: purpose of capital controls	284
12.3	Three proposals for "sand in the wheels" capital controls, and how they differ	288
12.4	India: current position and preconditions suggested for capital account convertibility	290
12.5	India: pattern of capital flows and their use	302

List of Figures

2.1	India: real GDP at factor cost, 1951/52–2003/04	28
2.2	India: ICOR and real gross fixed capital formation, 1955/56–2001/02	38
2.3	India: factor decomposition of real GDP growth, 1961/62–2001/02	47
2.4	India: factor shares of real GDP growth, 1961/62–2001/02	48
3.1	China: rural employment in nonagricultural sectors, 1978–2001	65
3.2	China: farmers' wage income	66
3.3	China: purchase price index of agricultural products, 1985–2000	68
3.4	Human poverty index	74
3.5	China: illiterate and semi-illiterate persons in select provinces	75
3.6	China: per capita GDP and consumption, 1978–2001	76
3.7	China: agricultural labor and output, 1978–2001	76
3.8	China: sources of farmers' per capita net income	77
3.9	China: status of agriculture in the national economy, 1978–2002	78
3.10	China: rural employment trends, 1978–2001	79
3.11	China: per capita disposable income and consumption	80
4.1	India: concentration of banking sector	98
4.2	India: banks' investment in government securities	107
4.3	Cross-country comparison of government ownership of banks	114
7.1	China: average import tariff rate, 1982–2005	161
7.2	China: openness of the economy, 1990–2003	164
7.3	China: state employment, 1978–2002	165
7.4	China: inventory accumulation, 1990–2002	166
7.5	China: profitability of state-owned manufacturers, 1978–2002	167
8.1	India: real GDP, pre- and post-reform	177
9.1	Measures of financial integration	204
9.2	Channels through which financial integration can raise economic growth	208
9.3	Correlation between financial openness and real per capita GDP growth 1982–97	211

10.1	India: sectoral shares in GDP, 1950–2000	233
10.2	Cross-country comparison of per capita income and services share in GDP	234
10.3	Cross-country comparison of services output and employment share in 2001	237
10.4	India: growth of services sector, 1953/54–2000/01	240
10.5	India: fast growing services subsectors, 1952/53–1998/99	241
10.6	India: contribution of fast growers to services growth	244
10.7	India: output of fast growers, 1950/51–1999/2000	248
10.8	India: ratio of services price deflator to GDP deflator, 1990/91–1999/2000	249
10.9	India: export of services, 1980–2001	250
10.10	India: composition of export of services, 1990 and 2000	251
10.11	India: cumulative FDI and average growth in the 1990s	253
10.12	India: private sector's share of output and average growth in the 1990s	253
10.13	India: contributing factors to services growth in the 1990s	254
11.1	Capital account restrictiveness index in emerging market economies	265
11.2	Capital account restrictiveness index in Asian economies	266
11.3	Capital volatility in Asia	267
11.4	China: balance of payments flows, 1987–2003	268
11.5	India: balance of payments flows, 1987–2003	268
11.6	Japan: balance of payments flows, 1987–2003	269
11.7	Balance of payments flows for Asia ex-Japan, 1987–2003	269
11.8	Capital openness versus peak FDI inflows for Asia	272

List of Boxes

3.1   Overview of China's poverty line   70
4.1   Salient features of the SARFAESI Act 2002   119
4.2   Investment patterns of large financial institutions   121
10.1   Services sector in China   235
12.1   Types of capital controls   281

List of Abbreviations

ADR	American Depository Receipt
AMP	Asiatic Mode of Production
ARC	asset reconstruction company
ARCIL	Asset Reconstruction Company of India Limited
AREAER	Annual Report on Exchange Arrangements and Exchange Restrictions
BIFR	Board for Industrial and Financial Reconstruction
BJP	Bharatiya Janata Party
CAC	Capital account convertibility
CCP	Chinese Communist Party
CDR	corporate debt restructuring
CMIE	Centre for Monitoring Indian Economy
CRAR	capital to risk-weighted assets ratio
CRR	cash reserve requirement
CSO	Central Statistical Organization
CVC	Central Vigilance Commission
DART	Debt Recovery Appellate Tribunal
DCA	Department of Company Affairs
DICGC	Deposit Insurance and Credit Guarantee Corporation
DRT	Debt Recovery Tribunal
ECB	external commercial borrowing
EPF	Employees' Provident Fund
EPFO	Employees' Provident Fund Organisation
ERM	exchange rate mechanism
FDI	foreign direct investment
FIs	financial institutions
FIIs	foreign institutional investors
FIPB	Foreign Investment Promotion Board
FPI	foreign portfolio investment
FSA	Financial Services Authority
GDP	gross domestic product
GNP	gross national product
HDFC	Housing Development Finance Corporation
HDI	Human Development Index
HDR	Human Development Report
HPI	Human Poverty Index
IDBI	Industrial Development Bank of India
IDBs	India development bonds

IFR	investment fluctuation reserve
IIP	Index of industrial production
IMF	International Monetary Fund
IRDA	Insurance Regulatory and Development Authority
IT	information technology
JVs	joint ventures
LFI	Less financially integrated
LIC	Life Insurance Corporation of India
MFI	more financially integrated
MOF	Ministry of Finance
MRTP	Monopolies and Restrictive Trade Practices
MSCI	Morgan Stanley Capital International Inc.
NBFC	Nonbanking financial companies
NBS	National Bureau of Statistics
NCAER	National Council of Applied Economic Research
NCLT	National Company Law Tribunal
NDP	net domestic product
NDTL	net demand and time liabilities
NPAs	nonperforming assets
NRI	non-resident Indian
NRNRD	nonrepatriable rupee denominated
OGL	Open General Licensing
OTS	one-time settlements
PCA	prompt corrective action
PLR	prime lending rate
PPP	purchasing power parity
PSB	public sector bank
PSU	public sector undertaking
RBI	Reserve Bank of India
REER	real effective exchange rate
RIBs	Resurgent India Bonds
S&P	Standard and Poor's
SAR	Special Administrative Region
SARFAESI	Securitization and Reconstruction of Financial Assets and Enforcement of Security Interest
SBI	State Bank of India
SCB	Scheduled commercial banks
SCRA	Securities Contracts (Regulation) Act
SEB	State Electricity Board
SEBI	Securities and Exchange Board of India
SEZs	Special Economics Zones
SLR	statutory liquidity ratio
SSI	small scale industry

TFP   total factor productivity
TOT   terms of trade
UPSC   Union Public Service Commission
UTI   Unit Trust of India
WDIs   World Development Indicators
WTO   World Trade Organization

Acknowledgments

The editors acknowledge each author's contribution to this volume, as well as his or her participation at the November 2003 conference *A Tale of Two Giants: India's and China's Experience with Reforms and Growth* in New Delhi. The conference was co-sponsored by the International Monetary Fund (IMF) and India's National Council of Applied Economic Research (NCAER).

We would like to recognize the special efforts of several people in the IMF's Asia and Pacific Department who provided support to the production of this volume and the associated conference. We are most indebted to Nong Jotikasthira for her excellent editorial work and for her untiring and efficient assistance in organizing and running the conference. We also thank Pihuan Cormier for her assistance in the early phase of the conference's organization, and Fritz Pierre-Louis and Corinne Danklou for their work on the volume.

We would like to give special thanks to Kalpana Kochhar in the IMF's Research Department, who played a key role in bringing the conference together, and Hiroyuki Hino of the IMF's Regional Office for Asia and the Pacific (OAP), whose support for the conference and volume was essential. From the same office, we are further grateful to Belinda Ruch for working with the conference organizers and to Kumiko Tanaka for assisting with finalizing this volume.

We would also like to recognize Suman Bery of the NCAER, whose organization made a very significant contribution as a conference partner. He and his colleague Kanhaiya Singh are also authors of one of the papers in this volume, for which we are grateful. We would further thank Michael Wattleworth (and his predecessor Jim Gordon), Sudip Mohapatra, and, especially, Alex Jaini of the IMF Resident Representative Office in India for their vital support in organizing the conference. They were assisted by Brig. Narinder Sapra, Balwant Singh, and their colleagues at the NCAER.

Finally, the editors would like to acknowledge the work done by Sean Culhane in the IMF's External Relations Department in advising and arranging publication. The patience and advice of Amanda Hamilton at Palgrave also are very much appreciated.

Preface

India and China have each been growing rapidly for at least the last twenty years; China has on average grown considerably faster than India. Indian scholars such as Amartya Sen and T.N. Srinivasan have been studying the Chinese experience in areas such as agriculture, international trade, and human development for many years, and drawing implications for India's policies and performance. But interest in comparing the two countries has spread to the financial press, investment banks, and investor conferences only relatively recently.

It is interesting to speculate on what lies behind this enhanced interest in the two countries. Since China's torrid growth has been an accepted fact for some time, what may be new is a reassessment of India's performance and potential. Such a reassessment at this particular moment is, in some ways, surprising, since the first years of the new century were not particularly stellar for Indian growth, and India's coalition politics have, if anything, become even more messy and confused. What seems to have changed India's image is its success as an offshore provider to the industrial countries of such skill-based services as software development, industrial research, and business services.

This success has created visibility and a political uproar in some host countries, particularly the United States. This is despite the small scale of the phenomenon relative to both the host and home countries' economies, and the view of most analysts that this form of trade is no different from trade in goods, and should be just as welfare-enhancing and growth-promoting. Instead, as with the North American Free Trade Agreement (NAFTA) in the 1990s, politicians and the media have once again raised the specter of a 'giant sucking sound' of jobs fleeing the United States, only this time it is the American middle class that is fearful.

Lord Desai's essay in this volume reminds us of how fickle and volatile such international perceptions can be. As recently as the 1960s, India and China were the poster children of world poverty, unable to feed themselves, and certainly no threat to the confident North which was then in the high noon of its own post-war recovery. Long-term projections made at that time would inevitably have been Malthusian in their gloom. Mechanical projections made of the prospects of Australia and Argentina (or even Brazil and Russia) at the beginning of the twentieth century would have been equally wide of the mark.

Such precedents should provoke some skepticism toward the breathless tone of recent growth projections for the two countries over the next half century. While such projections usefully describe the limits of what might be, they should not deflect attention from the fact that these are both poor, populous, substantially rural societies attempting to manage the stresses of modernization within political frameworks that are still evolving. The sheer scale of what is needed is unprecedented in human history. The international environment is also hugely different from that of the nineteenth century, in the gap between rich and poor nations, and in the absence of empty lands.

While applauding the distance both societies have come, we should not lose sight of the enormous challenges still ahead. Indeed, the focus on the absolute size of the two economies, measured at purchasing power parity, can be something of a trap: while it is helpful for certain diplomatic goals, it can also be used as a device to demand commitments. An example of this is the pressure on the two countries to make commitments in respect of the Kyoto protocol, despite their low income.

The attention therefore needs to be on the nearer term, on the policy and institutional lessons to be learned from each country's experience so that the growth momentum can be sustained. The papers in this volume help illuminate the experience of each country. Implicitly, and sometimes explicitly, they draw comparisons between the two; only occasionally do they touch upon their fast-growing economic linkages.

Lord Desai's essay further draws attention to the fundamentally different historical and political context that shapes economic policy in the two countries. China has historically been unified, with a successful tradition of great public works, so as to command legitimacy, but with, according to him, an abiding distrust of foreigners.

By contrast, India's identity over the millennia has been more cultural, rather than political or geographic. The challenge facing the Indian state remains one of accommodating regional identities (and economic and sectional interests) within a coherent whole. Even as both countries progress in their efforts at economic development, their models could emerge to become as dissimilar as those of the US and France today.

Within these different political traditions as pointed out by Desai (and detailed for India in the papers by Singh and Bery and by Panagariya, and for China by Lardy), both societies made significant and similar shifts in strategy at the end of the 1970s. Looking to the future they will continue to grapple with similar problems. Here, I would mention only three.

The first is shifting labor out of agriculture into higher productivity activities. Here, China has had much greater success through its export-oriented light manufacturing, and through the institutional innovation of town and village enterprises. However, as the paper by Hu Angang and associates points out, significant challenges remain for China. The Indian picture is more confused, with wages rising but employment apparently stagnant in both agriculture and large-scale manufacturing, and disappointing even in the fast-growing services sector, as pointed out in the paper by Gordon and Gupta.

In both countries the challenge is to put in place the kind of investment climate that fosters the growth of small entrepreneurial firms. In India, the main impediment is overregulation and a dysfunctional bureaucracy, as well as the political power of entrenched monopolistic lobbies in both the public and private sectors. In China it is continued uncertainty on the political implications of a growing domestic private sector. On balance, China may have further to go than India in this area.

A second challenge is integrating with the international economy. The papers by Panagariya and Lardy describe the very different experiences of the two countries in integration on the real side, while those of Prasad and associates, Anderson, and Jadhav describe their approaches to financial integration. There is no question that China has been bolder, and more successful, on the real side, with a cleaner trade policy regime, and greater success in attracting export-oriented foreign direct investment. India is probably further ahead on the financial side, although both countries remain cautious liberalizers.

The third and perhaps most difficult challenge is to improve domestic structures for financial intermediation and risk assessment. Chen Yuan's paper provides a realistic account of the issues and difficulties faced by China in its transition from budgetary allocation to a greater reliance on banks and securities markets, while Bhattacharya and Patel and Banerjee and associates describe similar challenges facing India.

In neither country are banks ready to take on the job that they are being asked to do; indeed, China's reliance on foreign direct investment at a time of massive reserve accumulation in part reflects this failure of domestic intermediation. More broadly, China pays too high a price in foregone consumption for the growth it enjoys, partly because of poor intermediation. Indian banks also fail in scouting out promising investment opportunities largely because of the incentives embedded in public ownership. Reform of the financial sector is therefore a crucial challenge facing managers in both economies.

In conclusion, I would like to thank the International Monetary Fund for partnering with the National Council of Applied Economic Research for the conference on India's and China's experience with reform and growth from which this publication has emerged, and for according me the opportunity to contribute this preface. The conference marks an excellent use of the Fund's knowledge of issues and resource persons in key emerging markets, and its capacity to draw them together both in Washington and in locations around the globe. I trust that this initiative will lead to many others like it.

SUMAN BERY
Director-General
National Council of Applied Economic Research, New Delhi

Notes on Contributors

Jonathan Anderson   Chief Economist, Asia, UBS Investment Bank.

Abhijit Banerjee   Ford International Professor, Department of Economics, Massachusetts Institute of Technology.

Suman Bery   Director General, National Council of Applied Economic Research (NCAER).

Saugata Bhattacharya   Hindustan Lever Limited (Unilever India).

Chang Zhixiao   Associate Professor, School of Government, Peking University.

Chen Yuan   Governor, China Development Bank.

Shawn Cole   Department of Economics, Massachusetts Institute of Technology.

Meghnad Desai   Emeritus Professor of Economics, London School of Economics; Founder-Director, Centre for the Study of Global Governance; and Member of the House of Lords, The United Kingdom Parliament.

Esther Duflo   Professor, Department of Economics, Massachusetts Institute of Technology; Research Associate, National Bureau of Economic Research; and Research Fellow, Center for Economic and Policy Research.

James Gordon   Chief of Division 3 in the IMF's Asia and Pacific Department and was previously IMF Senior Resident Representative for India (at the time this paper was written).

Poonam Gupta   Economist in the Macroeconomic Studies Division in the IMF's Research Department and was previously an Economist in the Resident Representative Office for India (also when this paper was written).

Hu Angang   Professor, Director of Center for China Study, Chinese Academy of Science and Tsinghua University.

Hu Linlin   PhD student, School of Public Policy and Management, Tsinghua University.

Narendra Jadhav   Principal Adviser and Chief Economist, Department of Economic Analysis and Policy, Reserve Bank of India.

M. Ayhan Kose   Economist in the Economic Modeling Division in the IMF's Research Department.

Nicholas R. Lardy   Senior Fellow, Institute for International Economics, Washington, DC.

Arvind Panagariya   Bhagwati Professor of Indian Political Economy and Professor of Economics, Columbia University.

Urjit R. Patel   Infrastructure Development Finance Company Limited (IDFC).

Eswar Prasad   currently Chief of the Financial Studies Division in the IMF's Research Department; previously, he was Chief of the China Division in the IMF's Asia and Pacific Department.

Kenneth Rogoff   Professor at Harvard University and was the Director of the IMF's Research Department and Economic Counselor.

Shang-Jin Wei   Head of the Trade Unit in the IMF's Research Department.

Kanhaiya Singh   Senior Economist, National Council of Applied Economic Research (NCAER).

1
India and China: An Essay in Comparative Political Economy

Meghnad Desai[1]

1.1 Introduction

India and China are two of the oldest and still extant civilizations. For Europeans, they were legendary seats of immense wealth and wisdom right up to the eighteenth century. Somewhere between the mid-eighteenth century and early nineteenth centuries, both of these countries became, in the European eyes, bywords for stagnant, archaic, and weak nations. For China, this happened between the adulation of Voltaire and the cooler judgment of Montesquieu; in India's case, it was the contrast between Sir William Jones's desire to learn things Indian and James Mill's dismissal of Indian history as nothing but darkness.

The twentieth century brought nothing but a deepening of the perception of the two countries as bywords for misery and the perceptions were not too far behind actual conditions of the two countries. For one thing they were, and remain, the two most populous countries. In 1820, they had a combined population in excess of half a billion and by 1900, it reached 700 million. Within the twentieth century, their population had trebled. But they were also two of the poorest countries, typically thought of as locations of famine, disease, backwardness and superstition, of women with bound feet and men with long pony-tails in China, untouchables beyond the pale and myriads of gods with many heads and limbs in India.

In the mid-twentieth century, particularly in the 1960s, the fortunes of these two countries seemed to have reached their nadir. They were independent republics supposedly launched on their path of development, but both suffered devastating famines. China's famine was hidden, perhaps more from China's own ruling classes than from its people or the world, but it had followed swiftly upon the debacle of the Great Leap Forward, a memorable piece of policymaking by fantasy. A double harvest failure in 1965 and 1966 brought India to its proverbial knees in terms of foreign policy and dependence on US food aid. These two countries were "basket cases" in the then fashionable terms of international diplomacy.

1

In the span of less than forty years, we are discussing China and India not as failures nor for their ancient wisdoms, but as dynamic modern economies. The *Economist* has to write editorials to tell the world not to be afraid of China's economic power. American legislators pass laws to prevent their businesses from outsourcing work to India's software and telecommunication services. China ranks as the second largest economy in terms of gross domestic product (GDP) in purchasing power parity (PPP) dollars. Together the two countries account for 19.2 percent of gross world product—China 11.5 percent and India 7.7 percent. This is still below their share of world population 37.5 percent—with China 21 percent and India 16.5 percent.

National income estimates covering a long period are, by their nature, broadly indicative rather than precise.[2] Angus Maddison, to whom the profession is indebted for making these calculations his lifetime work, gives the shares of gross world product and population of China and India for two earlier dates in the twentieth century as follows:

Table 1.1 succinctly describes the course of the two economies over the twentieth century. They start with the share of income below that of population. Over the previous century they had slightly different trajectories. India's per capita income is estimated to have grown from M$533 in 1820 (Maddison dollars [M$] or 1990 international dollars) to M$673 in 1913 while China's per capita income declined from M$600 in 1820 to M$552 in 1913. But during the first half of the twentieth century, both countries saw a decline in their per capita incomes—India from M$673 in 1913 to M$619 in 1950 and China from M$552 in 1913 to M$439 in 1950.[3]

Table 1.1 says two things: India and China both suffered a declining per capita income and a rising population during the first half of the twentieth century, but India was slightly better off than China between 20 percent[4] and 40 percent.[5] By 1998 this was reversed. Both countries were better off, but China was much better off than India. China's per capita income was M$3117 while India's was M$1760. Thus, while India roughly trebled its income, China increased it sevenfold. In earlier periods, China, while more populous than India, was not noticeably richer. In terms of GDP, the two

Table 1.1 Share of world output and population (in percent)

Year	Share of gross world product		Share of world population	
	China	India	China	India
1913	8.9	7.5	26.4	17.0
1950	4.5	4.2	21.1	14.2
1998	11.5	7.7	21.0	16.5

Source: Maddison (2001).

economies were of roughly similar size. The ratio of China's GDP to India's was 1.18 in 1918; 1.08 in 1950; but in 1998, it was 2.28.

Therefore, one theme of this chapter is the contrast between the economic performance of China and India and its proximate causes. But there are also a lot of similarities between the two, both in the path to modernization and, as we shall see later, the future prospects for their economies. There are also political similarities and contrasts between the two, both as to their twentieth-century history and twenty-first century challenges.

1.2   Historical legacies

1.2.1   Political legacy

While both India and China have a long history, their histories are very different. China has been by and large a stable, centrally run state throughout its history with limited periods of instability and lack of a single authority. India's history has been exactly the reverse. The periods when a single king or political authority ruled over even the major part of India's territory can be counted on the fingers of one hand. In China's case there was a deep desire for unification of the country as a driving force of nationalism in the twentieth century. But it was called reunification. Thus at the onset of the Second World War, China was divided, and Jonathan Spence (1999) expresses the drive for nationalists as follows:

> The solidification of such a group of new states, that is, war lords, KMT [Kuomintang], communists and Japanese enclaves, would return China to the situation that had prevailed before the Qin conquests of 221 B.C., during the so-called Warring States period when ten major regimes controlled the country among them; or it might bring a recurrence of the shifting patterns of authority and alliances that typified China's history from the third to sixth century A.D., and again from tenth to the thirteenth.[6]

In India's case, there never was any authority which has ruled over all of India; indeed, not even the British or even the present Indian government. India has been an idea in world culture for millennia, but its borders had been fixed only in the late nineteenth century sometime after the British gave up on Afghanistan and drew the Durand line. Kings have ruled over much of North India—the Maurya and Gupta dynasties just before and after the BC/AD division. The Mughals could be said to have ruled over much of India between the years of Akbar's maturity in 1570 and Aurangzeb's death in 1707. Their empire extended to Kabul but did not take in all of South India. The British could be said to have ruled over two-thirds of India between 1857 and 1947, with the remaining third being ruled by native princes under their paramountcy but not direct rule. In 1947, India was partitioned and thus even what is now called India is not what Nehru in 1946 wrote about in *The Discovery of India*.[7] Indian system of kingly power was not so much like a pyramid, but like a multitiered cake. It was flatter and while there was a top and a bottom plus layers in between, the power of the top king over his vassals below was not absolute. Loyalty, though owed by the lower tiers to the top, was always negotiable and there had to be some give and take.[8] The British were perhaps the first rulers to try a more absolute and hierarchical structure of power under the limitation of oversight by a democratic Parliament back in London.

Yet in one sense it was British rule which gave India its definitive territorial extent, fixed its boundaries and gave it a structure of provinces and central government with an administrative "steel frame." The British gave India their language, which facilitates even today India's access to global markets, as do the legal system of property rights and Western orientation of its elite. India's independence movement was critical of the economic ruin the British had caused—deindustrialization, drain of treasure, deskilling and diversion of agriculture into commercial crops away from food crops, and so on. But India began to acquire railroads and modern industry in the 1850s—a quarter of a century earlier than China. More foreign capital per capita was poured into India than in China; in 1913 India had US$6.9 per capita foreign capital while China had US$3.7.[9]

There is however another much less-mentioned benefit that India derived from British rule. Of course, it might have been better for India to have never suffered foreign rule, but to have been united under a native king or republic. But between 1500 and 1800, India had several foreign trading companies vying for control—the Portuguese, the Dutch, the French, the Danes, and of course, the English. As a counterfactual of history, it is possible to imagine what we call India today and take it for granted as a single country being made up of several different "countries" in the west, south, east, and north with different foreign languages being spoken along with local languages. Thus the Tamils could have been French speaking and the Maharashtrians Portuguese speaking and so on. Thanks to the religious wars of Europe in the seventeenth century and British victories in European wars in the eighteenth century, India ended up with a single foreign power, and thus the idea of India as a single country developed with its modern nationalism. This is not entirely fanciful since Southeast Asia with a population and extent not dissimilar to India's was ruled by the Dutch (Indonesia), the French (Indochina) and the British (Burma, Malaysia, and Singapore) with Thailand being independent. What is more, the hegemonic political ideology of the nationalist movement—liberal democracy—was also borrowed from the foreign rulers. The India we talk of today is a nineteenth century product in more than one sense.

China, by contrast, never suffered foreign rule over majority of its territory. There were foreign concessions in ports and later in interior towns extracted by several foreign powers in circumstances that the Chinese found humiliating.

But it had not suffered classic imperial rule until 1931 when the Japanese invaded Manchuria and later in 1937 when they occupied large chunks of eastern and central China.[10] Yet China's attitude to foreigners was and is much more hostile than India's. The removal of foreigners, especially the reversal of concessions, became a driving force for China. For India, the hostility to things foreign, except perhaps for foreign private capital, melted like snow in spring soon after independence. If anything, India in its early days after independence sought foreign capital from public rather than private sources and from a variety of countries rather than merely its old colonial masters. China after 1949 relied on one country, the USSR, and soon came to regret its connection. China's problem, unlike that of India, was the multiplicity of foreign powers gnawing at its sides with no single hegemonic ruling ideology as India had had with liberal democracy from Britain. It had the Germans, Japanese, Americans, French, and the British jostling not so much for rule over Chinese minds as over their cash boxes. There was some missionary input, more than in India, but eventually China had to forge its own ideology of modernity. It had to struggle to confront Confucianism against Western ideologies—liberalism, Fascism, and Communism.

These historical legacies shaped both the politics and economics of the two countries. For India, the problem was in achieving unity in diversity and in accommodating various languages and religions in a political structure, so as to give its center enough power to maintain its territorial integrity but its regions enough room to develop their diversities. India had a problem of articulating a single vision of Indian nationhood since it had been a nation only since the mid-nineteenth century and even this was asserted against by the foreign rulers who saw India not as a single nation but a motley collection of races and religions.[11] India thus chose a federal polity with a strong center able to alter state boundaries, split up states or create new ones. India even so is a soft state in Myrdal's famous description where the government has to work consensually and exert control sparingly and, that too, only against serious threats to national integrity.[12] India's fear is a break up of its territorial unity as had happened in the Partition.[13]

China has always had a vision of itself as a nation. Through much of its history, there has been a strong central power, and China has been run as a unitary polity. Indeed, Sun Yat Sen and his Communist supporters viewed the prospect of federalism as akin to feudalism.[14] The theme of reunification in early twentieth century China meant recentralization of authority. China has its minorities, but it is viewed and indeed views itself as a country of the Han people—a solid homogenous mass. While there are differences between Mandarin and Cantonese, the language is the same for an overwhelming majority of the Chinese. China is thus a unitary hard state which can pursue a single goal with determination and mobilize maximal resources in its achievement. It has ever been thus, be it in building the Great Wall or the system of grand canals, or in recent times in the Great Leap Forward.

There was a further advantage of being a unitary state which has often not been recognized. As Kent Deng has said in a recent survey of Chinese economic history:

> a basic structural factor—namely, that for most of the time most of China had a nationwide market, a single government (which was active in maintaining food supply, famine relief, and price control), a standard-ized written language, a uniform calendar and a system of weights and measures, a dominant Confucian code of conduct, a nationwide transport network, and the mechanisms for social mobility and inter-regional migration ... China could claim to have been a proto industrialized coun-try by the 13th century and indeed has been considered by many schol-ars to have been a prime candidate for a capitalist revolution which it missed.[15]

But anticipating somewhat later themes, strong states can also be brittle states, while soft states are difficult to smash and break since they are pliable. India has through its history been ruled by many authorities and sometimes none, but it has had a social stability which is remarkable. In India's case the enveloping unity was provided by the Hindu social structure, especially the caste system, which determined the basis on which interre-gional mobility could be conducted. Indeed the caste system proved to be so powerful that even among the Muslims and Christians a caste hierarchy took root and developed. While the concept of the Asiatic Mode of Production (AMP) is much derided nowadays, its essence was about a society in which the state was epiphenomenal and the peasant society went on impervious to changing rulers. India was throughout its history like that.[16] China, on the other hand strong as it was, became subject to spasmodic breakdowns which lasted several years. Within the modern period, we have had the Taiping Rebellion (1851–64), the Boxer Uprising (1900) which eventually led to end of empire (1911) and four decades of warlordism, and more recently the Cultural Revolution (1966–76). Even the Tiananmen incidents of 1989 are more a sign of brittleness than of strength.

1.2.2   Economic legacy

Both India and China were a highly urban civilization by the eighteenth century, though of course the bulk of the population lived in rural areas. China was much advanced in science and technology, with gunpowder, printing, paper, and paper currency as its inventions. China's scientific and technological achievements are known to us thanks to the monumental efforts of Joseph Needham.[17] India was known for its mathematics and its philosophy. The Chinese gave the world the wheelbarrow and bureaucracy; India gave the world the zero, decimals and Buddhism. Both were major exporters of fine textiles, silks and muslins; their ships sailed around the world and indeed dominated the seas till 1500. After that the Chinese withdrew from the seas and while the Indians continued, the powers that be in Delhi or Agra had no need for a navy. It was the kingdoms in South India which were maritime adventurers. As they declined in power under the Mughals, Indian shipping began to be conducted increasingly on a private basis rather than a state sponsored one. The control of the seas passed to a series of Western European countries. Yet China and India remained economically vibrant till the late eighteenth century.

China had a higher productivity in its agriculture, the iron tipped plough having been in use at least half a millennium before it made its appearance in India. Thus Needham attributes the animal drawn plough to the period of the Warring states, while Habib says that the iron plough came to India in the first century AD.[18] Chinese irrigation systems were bigger and better than any in India.[19] Thus Maddison's estimate of M\$600 per capita income for China and M\$533 for India in 1820 is roughly the right sort of relative difference.

The difference was made up in the next 130 years. By 1950, India had caught up with China, as we saw earlier, in the per capita as well as total income estimates. In output per person employed, Maddison shows India at M\$1377 in 1950 and China at M\$1297. The story is that in the nineteenth century India did enjoy a rising per capita income. This is not uncontroversial, as everything else about British impact on India. But it is consistent with much data.[20] India was a land surplus rather than a labor surplus country in the nineteenth century with a population of about 200–230 million, that is, one-fifth of the current level, and much the same amount of land. It became for a while an agricultural exporter rather than industrial exporter, but still managed a trade surplus. By the late nineteenth century, India began to acquire modern infrastructure and industry, not large relative to its population, but large relative to other countries. India is in this sense an early industrializing country. In 1945, it was the seventh largest industrial country by volume of output.

But their history drove both China and India to define industrialization rather than economic development as their prime goal. Even within industrialization, the strategy was one of concentrating on basic goods such as steel and machinery—"Department I goods" in Marxian terminology—rather than consumer and low-tech goods. Both countries were inspired by the example of the USSR and its planning achievements. They both sought independence of foreign capital and self-sufficiency.

The contrast between the two was most stark in agriculture. Being vast territories there is a similar diversity in the eco-agricultural make up of regions in both countries. But China's central rule meant that a uniform revenue collection system and land ownership pattern prevailed especially while the central power was effective. India by contrast had different legal patterns of revenue collection and different land tenures as a result of a lack of central authority reinforced by British experimentation with Ryotwari, Zamindari, Mahalwari, and the like. Land reform was a straightforward issue of changing ownership of large landholdings across China as far as the Communists were concerned. They were also committed to it as soon as they could become the sole powers. In India land reform was a maze of regional complexity and the Congress Party was not a revolutionary organization. Land reform thus became a state/provincial subject rather than a union/central policy issue. Thus India added legal and economic variation to the eco-agricultural one.

1.3   Development paths

Differences between China and India appear much greater from the current vantage point than they would have in 1973 or even 1983. Each has gone through two broad phases, which I characterize in this section.

1.3.1   Taking nationalism seriously—mistakes and learning

Both countries feared foreign domination and considered development as synonymous with industrialization. Both considered the State as the engine and the driver of growth and suspected the private sector's initiatives. The ideology forged during the long march to independence—Marxism, Leninism, Maoism in China and Gandhism in India, plus an amalgam of social and liberal democracy in India shaped the response more than economic realities warranted. One man ruled the roost though his closest associates did not share his beliefs as much as they said they did while he was still around. Mao for China and Nehru for India laid down the path from which each country had to deviate, if only because the path led to a blind alley.

For China the first period lasted from 1949 to 1978; for India from 1947 to 1980. China learned quickly thanks to Deng Xiao Ping. India did not have a Deng. Blood proved much thicker than pragmatism in matters of economic ideology. India began a halfhearted change in 1980 when Mrs Gandhi abandoned self-sufficiency as an ideal and took a big loan from the international monetary fund (IMF). But that loan and subsequent hard currency borrowing were frittered away. India could be said to have wasted ten years in a halfhearted liberalization, which hit the buffers in 1991 when the country nearly went bankrupt.

1.3.2   Living in the modern world and adapting to it

In the second phase, each country forgot the lessons it had thought it had learned from its history, xenophobia, fear of foreign trade and foreign capital, distrust of private initiative and decentralization. Each adapted to the rhythm of the world economy rather than sail against the wind. Being large vessels, they have a bit more freedom of maneuver than small countries. They misused the freedom in the first phase and corrected themselves in the second phase. Their comparators would be two smaller countries both with a colonial past—South Korea and Taiwan who did not go through a two-phase path. After 1960, South Korea single-mindedly pursued growth with spectacular results. Taiwan had a similar colonial background to Korea's but it also had the influx of the Guomindang elite, which transformed property rights in Taiwan and achieved what it could not on the mainland—a successful growth strategy.

The comparison between the two pairs of countries is revealing. In 1950 China and India had per capita incomes of M$439 and M$619, while South Korea and Taiwan had M$770 and M$936. By 1999, the numbers were: China M$3259, India M$1818, South Korea M$13,317 and Taiwan M$15,720. Let me examine the two phases in some detail.

The first phase

Both China and India saw a development of Department I goods—steel, cement, machine-making equipment—as pivotal to their growth strategies. India had at this time a viable world-class textile industry which it chose to stifle in its search for an employment-intensive growth strategy meant to favor small-scale and low-tech firms over large-scale industrialized firms. India diverted resources from the production of domestic consumption goods, especially of the machine-produced variety, to the production of investment goods by the industrial sector and consumer goods by small-scale industries. However, its savings rate was not significantly raised and the growth rate remained modest. China seems to have concentrated its industrial efforts also on the basic goods sector initially, but after the first three or four years switched to an all-round emphasis on heavy as well as light industries. Apart from the aberration of backyard steel furnaces in the Great Leap Forward phase, it was not saddled with a small-scale industry strategy. But China had a more successful resource mobilization strategy than India did. India's Second Five-Year Plan (1956–61) ran into a resource constraint by 1958. China on the other hand ran into the evils of overweening ambition in launching the Great Leap Forward. There seems to have been a slowdown in China in the 1960–65 period, whereas in India it came in the second half of the 1960s after the Third Five-Year Plan (1961–66).

China managed its agrarian reform better than India. Starting from a higher level of productivity, China went on to transform not only the tenurial relations in agriculture but also the production conditions. Thus abolishing of landlords and forming cooperatives and then communes changed not only the distribution of surplus, but also its size. India concentrated on changing the tenurial relations by abolishing zamindari and intermediaries and redistributing the surplus. Reform was of course different across regions as the polity dictated. But India did little to change production conditions—land pooling, technology used, or labor deployed. These changed in India in the 1960s with the advent of the Green Revolution, where a combination of foreign knowledge, domestic subsidies, and rural private initiative brought a

Table 1.2   Human development indices, 1950–2000

	1950	1960	1973	1980a	1980b	1992	2000
China	0.163	0.248	0.407	0.475	0.554	0.594	0.726
India	0.160	0.206	0.289	0.296	0.434	0.439	0.577

Sources: Crafts (1997) for 1950, 1973, and 1992; United Nations Development Programme, *Human Development Report* (HDR) (1997) for 1960 and 1980a; and *HDR* (2002) for 1980b and 2000.

capitalist revolution to the Indian countryside. Despite this, China's lead in agricultural productivity remained to the end of the first phase and indeed increased, when in the second phase, China moved to a more private initiative system.

But above all, China did very well by human development. Long-run calculations of Human Development Index (HDI) have been made by Nicholas Crafts. For China and India he has estimates for 1950, 1973, and 1992 (Table 1.2). The World Bank's Human Development Report (HDR) has over the various years published trends in countries' HDIs from 1960 onward. Its methodology has evolved over the years and so the estimates have also been revised even for earlier years. Using the 1997 HDR and the 2002 HDR we can see the trend up to 2002. The HDR estimates start in 1960 and are not strictly comparable to Crafts's estimates, but they are close enough.

Thus we see that despite having similar HDIs in 1950, China had left India behind by 1973, even with similar per capita incomes. Over the 50-year period, while the HDIs are not strictly comparable, China enhanced its HDI four-and-a-half times while India did so only three-and-a-half times. Taking the estimates for 1950, 1980b, and 2000, we see that in the first 30 years, China advanced much faster—by three-and-a-half times—than in the last 20 years—only by a third more. India on the other hand took its HDI up two and three-quarter times between 1950 and 1980 and again by a third in the next 20 years. Some writers have argued that the slowing down of China's advance in human development was due to the disbanding of the communes and with it the downgrading of the health care facilities available to all.[21] On the other hand, the closer a country's HDI comes to the limit of 1.0, the harder each step becomes. Whichever way we look at it, China has done much better in human development than India.

While there may be an argument about the state of health care facilities in China after the Deng reforms were launched, it is in other dimensions that China kept on doing well. Its emphasis on education for all from early on paid handsome dividends, while education remains a blot on India's record. Here again the centralist versus federal polity makes a lot of difference. Social conditions differ immensely across India in terms of caste structures, religious influence, and superstitions. Hinduism is not an egalitarian religion even in theory and Islam at least in India is not so in practice.[22] It is only when you go south where the influence of Christian missions was felt and social movements against the caste system were successful in early twentieth century that you witness an improvement in human development statistics. India continues to pay a heavy price for its neglect of education, especially as it concerns women.[23]

The first phase, despite the differences in approach to agrarian transformation and human development, altered the relative positions of China and India from what they were in 1950, but not by much. By 1978, per capita income of China was M\$979 and of India M\$966. China had caught up with India over the thirty years, but not dramatically surpassed it. Agricultural productivity per worker was almost identical in 1975 in the two countries—China 2.3 and India 1.9 (relative to the United States = 100).[24] One may ask why this was so. Why is it that China did not do much better than India despite its revolutionary effort in industry and agriculture and its immense achievements in education and poverty reduction. There are two responses to that question.

One, of course, is that it did. China's income doubled while India's only went up by 50 percent. Of course, China had suffered from the ravages of foreign and civil war through the 15 years since Japan's invasion of Manchuria in 1933. So its per capita income in 1950 was below its potential. But even then we must acknowledge that China's growth was not smooth. While it was rapid, China's growth suffered from the tendency of Mao to take immense risks and plunge the economy into catastrophes. I am personalizing the problem because Mao was a dominant influence in China to an extent that Nehru never was. This is where a totalitarian system can differ from a democratic one. It can accelerate growth and mobilize immense resources, but if the direction is wrong it can also crash and waste an awful lot of resources in a short period of time. But added to that, the political culture of China has been long used to such imperial power, while India has been a much less commandable polity. Thus Mao plunged China into the Great Leap Forward as well as the Great Proletarian Cultural Revolution (GPCR), with the structure of centralized and personalized power which led to the catastrophic famine of 1962. China paid a price for this in terms of death, starvation, and wasted resources in abandoned projects. Much human capital, of both university teachers and students, was revalorized during the GPCR.

India, by comparison, had its muddle and mess but no great discontinuities in its development experience. It had a multiparty system and even within the Congress Party had antagonistic factions, which could mobilize opposition to Nehru. Even before his death, Nehru was forced to abandon his preferred policy of cooperatives in agriculture by the farmers' leader Charan Singh, but then besides Nehru no one else in the Congress took cooperative agriculture seriously and had done nothing about it since the Agrarian Reforms Committee of the Congress proposed it in 1949. The Second Five-Year Plan had to be modified due to resource shortages, but the Third Five-Year Plan kept to the same basic strategy. During the 1960s, India went through what was known (in a Maoist parody) as the Three Twos—death of two prime ministers, two harvest failures and two wars. There was a policy reversal in agriculture when the High Yield Variety program was adopted. In addition, rural and regional political bosses asserted their hold over the Congress Party and displaced the urban Westernized elite after Nehru's death, but they in turn were displaced after 1969 when Mrs Gandhi regained control of the Congress. India also had to devalue its currency and felt the heat of the US and World Bank disapproval. Yet the economic strategy did not (sadly) change. The crisis of slow growth came in 1975 when in face of popular unrest, Mrs Gandhi was driven to suspend democracy and declare the Emergency. But that did not last long, proving yet again that India cannot be commanded by centralized and personalized power.[25]

The second phase

It was China, after 1978 under the influence of Deng, that accelerated, leaving India far behind. In the next 35 years China's per capita income more than trebled while that of India merely doubled. The logic of compound growth rates is pitiless, and China's per capita income is now almost double that of India. How did China do this?

China did this paradoxically by adopting a much more "capitalist road" or Bukharinist strategy[26] than any other communist regime (the former Yugoslavia included). What is more, China adopted a road that India could always have adopted; indeed, this was possible right after independence except that no one, not even the Indian capitalists, were advocating greater import of foreign capital, opening up the economy to an export orientation, with Special Export Zones (SEZs).[27] While India went on restricting its large native capitalist class after independence, China had to practically reinvent its own bourgeoisie after 1978. Indeed according to a newspaper story cited by Dharma Kumar,[28] China, which had invented an examination system for the selection of bureaucrats in the mists of time, approached India in the 1980s to seek its guidance about conducting examinations for its civil servants on the lines of the Union Public Service Commission (UPSC) exams in India.

Of course, China's policy revolution was not seamless and Deng had to struggle to establish his hegemony. There is a debate among China scholars about the fang/shou (stop-go) cycle in Deng's reforms between 1978 and 1989.[29] But once established, his control over policy was absolute; the political culture's habit of obedience to emperors helped.[30] Deng transformed agriculture by introducing the Family Responsibility System—privatization Chinese Communist style. He then took on the industrial sector and opened it up to foreign capital while making room for the growth of village and local enterprises. He left the public sector enterprises untouched but slowly brought modern methods of fiscal and financial control to China. China had to introduce property rights and contract laws which India has had since Macaulay in British times.

India meanwhile also started to jettison some of its own orthodoxies, but the personality in power was still the same. Mrs Gandhi abandoned the fetish of national self-sufficiency and began to borrow abroad, from the IMF to begin with. She, however, changed little else in the dirigiste logic of Indian economic policy. The collapse of India's textile industry was symptomatic of the malaise. Within 35 years of independence, India had managed to bankrupt its once globally competitive industry. Freed from the constraint of food grain availability thanks to the Green Revolution, India did not manage to apply to its industrial sector the lessons learnt in its agricultural revolution—that is, to use foreign knowledge, rely on the dynamic private sector and deploy subsidies selectively. Instead, foreign borrowing was used to ease the consumption constraint in the public sector and to cushion loss-making public enterprises. Ian Little and Vijay Joshi (1994) argue in their book on Indian economic reforms that Indian policymaking alternates between five-year spurts of radicalism then quiescence, flaring up under political or economic pressures.[31]

India really changed course only after the shock of 1991 when it was nearly bankrupt and had foreign reserves which would cover only two weeks' imports. But in changing the same personalities were involved as in the old dirigiste regime. Manmohan Singh as Finance Minister was crucial to the reform, but he was no Deng and neither was Narasimha Rao, who was Prime Minister 1991–96. Indeed, by 1994, India began to reveal its reluctance about economic liberalization. Ever since, India has been reforming its economy, but in a much more embattled way than China. Given the nature of the political culture, reform can only be introduced by broad consent, and all the potential losers (many of whom are in power) have to be bribed (sometime literally so) to advance matters.

Thus, while China has received a lot of foreign capital, India has not. By 1998, Maddison's calculations show that foreign direct investment (FDI) per capita in China was US$183 and in India US$14. Even if a lot of China's FDI was due to the Chinese diaspora, it only shows the failure of India to attract its own diaspora to invest, in spite of a lot of trying. Indeed, India has sought portfolio capital more than FDI since suspicion of foreigners remains strong, not only among India's politicians but even more among its capitalists. There has been some change for the better in the five years under the government of the Bharatiya Janata Party (BJP) and its National Democratic Alliance, but there is a long way to go.[32] There are other more usual reasons for the difference in economic performance. For one, China's savings rate is almost 50 percent of GDP, nearly twice that of India. Indeed given the higher savings rate in China plus the FDI influx, the growth rates are less far apart than should be the case. India averaged 5.5 percent in the 1980s and around 6.5 percent in the 1990s. Even at 7–9 percent, China's growth rate implies inefficient use of capital barring gross measurement errors. Or it could indicate sharply diminishing returns to capital, but I doubt that given that a lot of FDI embodies the latest knowledge.

The reason may be that in both countries there is a large public sector where enterprises are seriously loss making. Both countries are wedded to Soviet-style emphasis on inputs rather than outputs and accumulation for its own sake. India had begun to shed some of these traits and has always had a smaller public sector than China. So the waste of resources by mal-investment[33] is larger in China. In both countries, there is also a budget deficit which is out of control; perhaps more so in India due to the exigencies of democratic and coalitional politics, as well as weak central control over provincial budgets.

The two countries have mobilized savings through their financial structures, but the mobilization has left the financial sectors in fragile states. Nonperforming assets in the banking systems as well as the nonbank financial sector (international trade and investment corporations in China) indicate a problem ahead. India has failed to impose arm's-length regulatory regimes free of politics and the result has been fraud and corruption in equity market-related activities—Unit Trust of India (UTI), stock market scams of Harshad Mehta, and so on.

It is difficult to predict whether a combination of budget deficits, domestic debt, and financial sector weakness will cause a major crisis in either country. Both have managed to run their external accounts fairly well. Their reserve positions are healthy, exchange rate policy—pegged to the dollar in China and a dirty float in India—are prudent. India has moved faster to full capital convertibility in recent years while financial sector reforms have yet to be fully undertaken. China has not moved as far with convertibility but its peg to the dollar may cause problems if the dollar weakens to any significant extent. India's foreign liabilities are more weighted toward the short run and portfolio end, while China has a larger FDI flow. The Asian crisis reminded us that even sound macroeconomic performance is no guarantee against a run on the currency if the markets suspect a mismatch between internal and external balance. Here it is India which is more fragile than China.

1.4   Speculations and counterfactuals

I now turn to some very broad and highly speculative considerations. Having looked at China and India over the years since 1820 against a longer background, it is worth exploring a longer future. What follows is even more my own view than what has been said so far. In a *long duree* perspective, the present strong relative position of China can be attributed to the radical changes there since 1978, thanks to Deng. Of course the foundations laid in the first phase wherein China doubled its per capita income obviously helped. But the similarities in their respective per capita incomes in 1980 merely reflects the longer history of the two countries. *A priori*, there is no reason why China should have opened such a large distance in such a short period of time. This is especially so because as I have already remarked earlier, China adopted a policy which it was always possible for India to adopt. Indeed anyone looking at the two countries at any time between 1950 and 1975 could have thought that India had a better capitalist infrastructure as well as commercial culture than China had. The diasporas of both China and India have always been adept at commercial activity so there is nothing in Chinese or Indian culture as such which could make a difference. The difference arises out of the political and institutional differences inside the country and these are very much short run and changeable.

1.5   Can China combine capitalism with one party rule?

China appears to have been able to separate the political institutions of a Leninist state with single party dominance from its economic imperative of state ownership of all means of production. This is unique in the political economy of modern times. The transition is not yet fully complete as there is still a lot of central control over economic life and a large state-owned sector. It would be a bold person who could predict how far China could go in this separation. Thus could one have a fully capitalist or even a largely capitalist economy with a Leninist state? This is not the same as market socialism but more like state capitalism, although the word has now been much maligned in the polemics on the left. When Lenin spoke of state capitalism, he had the German war economy during the First World War in mind—a private ownership economy run in a centralized fashion.[34] The Chinese version of state capitalism could in the limit amount to private diffuse ownership with single party monopoly of political power. Is this feasible or likely?

Normally we associate rise of democracy with a prosperous middle class with plenty of "bourgeois" elements. A private ownership economy is bound to require a lot of economic freedom and as we are all crude materialists in this matter, we associate economic freedom with political liberties. While there is some opening out in the direction of separation of powers in some local jurisdictions,[35] it is difficult to envisage separation of powers in the absence of multiparty democracy with free elections and a possibility of change of the party in power. China's experiment is thus one of the most interesting episodes in modern political economy. Will China be able to sustain one-party rule with a private enterprise economy? Is state capitalism feasible in peaceful post-revolutionary times?

The implicit Chinese answer seems to be that if the Chinese Communist Party (CCP) delivers on fast and sustained economic growth while restructuring the economy continuously in a capitalist direction, then the CCP monopoly on political power will become feasible with limited concessions such as separation of powers but no party competition. Marxian and every other political economy says that this is not easy, even not possible.[36] Economic freedom will spill over into demands for political freedom. Even authoritarian governments—that is, noncommunist dictatorships—have been unable to sustain a monopoly on political power with developed capitalism. Leninist state formations in Europe collapsed along with their economic forms. Apart from China, only North Korea and Cuba remain as major non-capitalist economies and non-liberal democratic polities. Can China defy the so-called laws of historical materialism (or even cross section growth regressions of new political economy) and avoid the transition to democracy?

One particular problem in this respect relates to the legal framework. While civil and political liberties can be curtailed, once you grant property rights certain liberalizing consequences inevitably follow, as any eighteenth-century political economist will tell you. Thus, the Communist Party *qua* contractor or buyer and seller of property cannot be above the law. There has to be accountability and auditing, legal sanctions and punishments for non-delivery or nonperformance. From this requirement follows the need to have law courts and a legal profession which enjoy a certain degree of immunity from the perennial habits of communist parties to bully if not liquidate all those who disagree with them. An independent legal profession needs further freedoms of speech and association and so on. It is this compulsion to establish a rule of law which will be crucial for China. In a fascinating and detailed study of the growth of the rule of law in China, Peerenboom makes the following observation:

> In the end, however, a transition to democracy is likely to be necessary to overcome the [Communist] Party's legitimacy deficiencies, to address accountability issues, and to reduce growing social cleavages. It is possible that over time the Party could stave off extinction by transforming itself into a Social Democratic party. The Party could well gain support of its citizenry if in the next decade it is able to reduce corruption to a tolerable level and to sustain economic growth while dealing with such pressing problems as SOE [state-owned enterprise] reforms, reform of the banking and financial sectors, and the need to establish a social security system and to clean up the environment. It could further broaden its appeal by gradually relaxing its grip on society and allowing citizens greater, albeit still limited, freedom of speech, assembly, and association. In short, it could adopt a more communitarian approach. If it does not, and elections are held, it could very well lose out to the party that does adopt such an approach, all else being equal.[37]

This is a tall order for any country much less China. Indeed India itself has not eliminated corruption nor reformed its banking and financial sectors.

But people will tolerate corruption if they can throw the corrupt out of office, even if this exit is only through a revolving door. Democracies coexist with all sorts of imperfections and can indeed even withstand a lot of misery unlike authoritarian regimes, as the fate of the USSR in face of the stagflation crisis of the 1970s showed in contrast to Western economies. What Mrs Thatcher could do to the British economy, Brezhnev, Chernenko or Gorbachev could not. So China does not have to make things perfect if it can only grant bourgeois freedoms to its people. If not it has to be better than the most perfect democracy. Can China find its way out of this paradox?

My interim answer to this is that the odds are stacked against China being able to do this. Not that it is impossible or even unlikely but the odds are not favorable. There is one major reason for this, for which I appeal to Chinese history. This is China's inability to handle dissent and defiance of central rule without a lot of damage. The episodes of the Taiping and Boxer Rebellions in the Imperial era and GPCR, as well as the 1989 troubles which were not confined just to Tiananmen, show that China is fragile if not brittle when it comes to dissent. In the next ten years, China will be adjusting to economic restructuring in response to the demands of the World Trade Organization (WTO), as well as facing up to global media exposure due to the 2008 Olympic Games. It will be an open invitation to human rights movements and Falung Gong to expose the regime to international scrutiny. Moscow's experience of the 1980 Olympic Games proved crucial in the way the Soviet Union collapsed. What about China?

I expect China to survive as a powerful economy, but after a short period of political turbulence on the lines of the Taiping Rebellion or GPCR. China will be forced to make a political transition as profound as the Eastern European states did with their economies. The final shape will be a more democratic China, but it may not necessarily be a liberal democratic Western-type regime. There are after all living examples of "less-than-liberal" democracies—Singapore, Taiwan, Malaysia—which China can follow. You can have a multiparty democracy with a single party dominance as in Mexico and Japan, and India till 1989. One can also have dual power as in Iran, with the Ayatollahs vying for control with a democratically elected power. There are many choices on the way to a full transition to liberal democracy.

1.6   Can India catch up with China?

India has problems about delivering strong, focused government pursuing a single objective with total commitment. Its great achievement is to have constructed the world's most populous democracy against all the odds— illiteracy, multiple languages and religions, racial and social heterogeneity. There have been spurts of committed action—in the mid-1950s when the Second Five-Year Plan was formulated, in the early 1970s when Mrs Gandhi pursued her anti-poverty program, in the mid-1980s when Rajiv Gandhi pushed the import liberalization policy harder, the early 1990s with Narasimha Rao and Manmohan Singh liberalizing the economy, and finally in the last five years when the reform process has been kept up rather than reversed as many had feared. The average growth rate has gone up from 3.5 percent in the 1970s to 5.5 percent in the 1980s and now to 6.5 percent in the past decade.

India has also achieved another miracle relative to many post-colonial societies. It has maintained its territorial integrity, unlike for example Pakistan. It has not had a civil war, unlike Nigeria or Sri Lanka, and while multiethnic federations such as the former Yugoslavia and the USSR have broken up, India has not. This has absorbed resources as India has had to fight subnationalisms in the northeast Nagaland, in Panjab with Khalistan, and in Kashmir with international subversion added to internal dissension. It has had communal strife between Hindus and Muslims, Hindus and Sikhs, between caste Hindus and Untouchables/Dalits and so on. It has also faced class-based revolts in Telangana in the 1940s, in West Bengal, Andhra Pradesh, and Bihar with the Naxalites. Through all this it has survived as a democratic open society based on consensus and debate. Life is about more than per capita income and its growth.

For India any hope of growing faster depends on less government rather than more, on harnessing the private sector entrepreneurial talent which has always been there but was stifled for a long time. This requires a less interventionist government but also a better regulatory regime. India's bane is the politicization of all aspects of economic life and the difficulty of constructing an arm's-length regulatory regime free of political interference. This is because of and despite its democratic politics.[38] Thus even after a major stock market fraud or the mishandling of Unit Trust of India (UTI) customers' investments, there has been little by way of punishment. Indeed, a large number of financial scandals have thousands of victims but no culprits convicted.[39] One cannot expect a flourishing private enterprise culture in the absence of trust and effective regulation. Thus a black economy, smuggling, and criminalization of financial markets flourish. Depoliticization of the economy, therefore, remains a challenge. This is the same challenge as the more frequent complaint about control of the budget deficit, because the deficit is due to the compulsions of consensual politics with a coalition government and weak powers over regions.

What then are the chances for India that we may see a strong effective government emerge at the Center with effective fiscal control over its own budget as well as the budgets of states and an ability to depoliticize regulatory structures? Herein lies the deep dilemma of the Indian polity. India was set up after Independence as a federal polity because of the awareness of the first generation of leaders of the difficulty of holding the various linguistic and religious groups together. Indian nationhood was defined as unity in diversity. But lately a new, more unitarian construction of Indian nationhood has been advanced by the forces of Hindutva nationalism. Thus far, it has been muted in its approach, but is also quite successful. If in the forthcoming months and years the Unitarian approach were to be pursued harder and if it was to be electorally successful, then India may emerge simultaneously as a nonsecular, majority Hindu polity with single party dominance by the BJP and its parivar. The advocates of Hindutva often cite Israel as their ideal example.

Historically, modernity in India was supposed to come with a secular and perhaps even socialist society. This was certainly Nehru's ideal, as well as practice, and at least the rhetoric if not practice for the two Gandhis. But the events of the last ten years or so raise the serious possibility that modernity in India will come with a Hindu or religious rather than secular as well as a capitalist dispensation. It is conceivable that such a Unitarian nationalism may accelerate growth by following a more liberal policy. But it is also likely to lead to greater social disharmony. Of course a majoritarian rule of the largest religious group is possible with nondiscrimination of the minorities, but in the Indian context and given the history, it is not very likely.

1.7   Conclusion

My own view is that India will remain a soft state, a consensual polity, and it will not be capable of sustained growth at the sort of rates which China has attained. To stay a stable, peaceful society, India has to be a muddle and a mess. It is a miracle that proceeding in the way it has done, it has come as far as it has done, trebling its per capita income. But there will not be growth convergence between China and India.[40] India and China will both remove poverty in their midst and cease to be bywords for misery that they had become for 150 years after 1820. China will again become a viable Great Power; India may become just a Great Democracy.

Notes

1. Emeritus Professor of Economics, London School of Economics; Founder-Director, Centre for the Study of Global Governance; and Member of the House of Lords, The United Kingdom Parliament.
2. Beyond this vague assertion I do not intend to go into statistical measurement problems.
3. Dharma Kumar (1998), who independently made comparative estimates of India and China over the early twentieth century, arrives at not dissimilar estimates. She puts India's per capita income as US$60 in 1952 and China's as US$50 (at current prices).
4. Kumar (1998).
5. Maddison (2001).
6. Spence *et al.* (1999, p. 426).
7. Nehru (1946) and Keay (2001).
8. Inden (1999).

9. Maddison (2001, p. 99).
10. I am treating the Manchus as not being foreign, though many Chinese at the beginning of the twentieth century emphasized that they wanted to remove the Manchu empire and establish a Chinese republic.
11. Desai (2000).
12. I have learned a lot about federal structures and federalism in India while co-supervising Katherine Adeney (see Adeney (2003)).
13. Myrdal (1968).
14. Spence *et al.* (1999).
15. Deng (2000, p. 6) surveys this literature. There has been a similar though less extensive discussion among Indian historians as to whether India could have had its own capitalist revolution (see Habib (1971)).
16. See O'Leary (1989) for a critique of the Asiatic Mode of Production (AMP). Also see Habib (1983) for a sympathetic account of Marx's views on India, and Deng (2000), who sees the AMP as a useful concept.
17. Needham *et al.* (1954).
18. Needham *et al.* (1954) and Habib (1995).
19. Oriental Despotism, a notion begotten by Wittfogel from Marx and Engels's AMP, was supposed to be good at hydraulic projects. Be that as it may, the abandoned city of Fatehpur Sikri is a monument to how a Mughal king built a city where he failed to provide water supplies.
20. See Heston in Kumar and Desai (1983).
21. Dreze and Sen (1989).
22. The distinguished French anthropologist Louis Dumont has celebrated India's inegalitarianism in his *Homo Hierarichicus* as well as other books (see Dumont (1980)).
23. The usual exception in India is of course Kerala, which shows what can be achieved even in a democratic society by committed public action. Kerala has had the benefit of a democratically elected Communist government ever since the mid-1950s. But historically Travancore Cochin, which was the native state in what became Kerala, had a higher literacy rates even by the 1940s than its surrounding British India districts. Matriarchy and Christianity plus an enlightened ruler played their role here.
24. Maddison *et al.* (2002).
25. Desai (1975).
26. For those old enough to recall these arcane labels.
27. In China's case, the SEZs are not all that different from the foreign concessions in ports which were so much resented before 1949.
28. Kumar (1998)
29. See Baum (1994) and Shirk (1993).
30. After all, the establishment of Imperial authority had to go through such transition periods throughout Chinese history, but to support that claim will take me too far away from my theme as well as my competence.
31. Joshi and Little (1994).
32. For recent restructuring efforts in the organized private sector in India, see Forbes, N. (2002) in *Doing Business in India: What Has Liberalisation Changed?* (ed. by Krueger, 2002).
33. An old fashioned Hayekian word.
34. Desai (2002a).
35. For example, SEZs in China such as Shenzen.

36. See Moore (1971) and Desai (2002a).
37. Peerenboom (2002, p. 5723).
38. Desai (2002b).
39. See *India Today* (2003) for a recent list.
40. Except unless China has a long breakdown in its transition to democracy.

References

Adeney, Katherine, 2003, "Federal Formations and Consociational Stabilisation: The Politics of Identity Articulation and Ethnic Conflict Regulation in India and Pakistan" (Ph.D. dissertation; London: University of London).

Baum, Richard, 1994, *Burying Mao* (Princeton, NJ: Princeton University Press).

Crafts, Nicholas, 1997, "The Human Development Index and Changes in Standards of Living: Some Historical Comparisons," *European Review of Economic History*, Vol. 1, pp. 299–322.

Deng, Kent G., 2000, "A Critical Survey of Recent Research in Chinese Economic History," *Economic History Review*, Vol. LIII, No. 1 (February).

Desai, Meghnad, 2002a, *Marx's Revenge: The Resurgence of Capitalism and the Death of State Socialism* (London: Verso).

——, 2002b, "Democracy and Development: India 1947–2002," presented at the K.R. Narayanan Lecture (Canberra: Australia South Asia Research Centre, The Australian National University).

——, 2000, "Communalism, Secularism and the Dilemma of Indian Nationhood," in *Asian Nationalism*, ed. by Michael Leifer (London: Routledge).

——, 1975, "Contradictions of Slow Capitalist Development," in *Explosion in a Sub-Continent*, ed. by Robin Blackburn (London: Viking Penguin).

Dreze, Jean, and Amartya Kumar Sen, 1989, *Hunger and Public Action* (Oxford: Oxford University Press).

Dumont, Louis, 1980, *Homo Hierarchicus* (Chicago: University of Chicago Press).

Forbes, Naushad, 2002, "Doing Business in India: What Has Liberalization Changed?" in *Economic Policy Reforms and the Indian Economy*, ed. by Anne O. Krueger (Chicago: The University of Chicago Press).

Habib, Irfan, 1995, *Essays in Indian History: Towards a Marxist Perception* (New Delhi: Tulika).

——, 1983, "Marx's Perception of India," *The Marxist*, Vol. 1, No. 1 (July–September) and reprinted in Irfan Habib, 1995, *Essays in Indian History: Towards a Marxist Perception* (New Delhi: Tulika).

——, 1971, "Potentialities of Capitalist Development in the Economy of Mughal India," *Enquiry*, New Series (Winter).

Heston, Alan, 1983, "National Income," in *The Cambridge Economic History of India, Volume 2, c.1757–c.1970*, ed. by Dharma Kumar and Meghnad Desai (Cambridge: Cambridge University Press).

Inden, Ronald B., 2000, *Imagining India* (London: Hurst, 2nd edn).

Joshi, Vijay, and I.M.D. Little, 1994, *India: Macroeconomics and Political Economy, 1964–1991* (New Delhi: Oxford University Press).

Keay, John, 2001, *India: A History* (London: HarperCollins).

Krueger, Anne O., ed., 2002, *Economic Policy Reforms and the Indian Economy* (Chicago: The University of Chicago Press).

Kumar, Dharma, 1998, "The Chinese and Indian Economies, 1914–1949," in *Colonialism, Property and the State*, ed. by Dharma Kumar (New Delhi: Oxford University Press).

Kumar, Dharma, and Meghnad Desai, eds, 1983, *The Cambridge Economic History of India, Volume 2: c.1757–c.1970* (Cambridge: Cambridge University Press).

Maddison, Angus, 2001, *The World Economy: A Millennial Perspective* (Paris: Development Centre Studies, Organization for Economic Cooperation and Development).

——, D.S. Prasada Rao, and W.F. Shepherd, eds, 2002, *The Asian Economies in the Twentieth Century* (Cheltenham, UK: Edward Elgar Publishing).

Moore, Barrington Jr, 1971, *Social Origins of Dictatorship and Democracy* (London: Allen Lane).

Myrdal, Gunnar, 1968, *Asian Drama: An Inquiry into the Poverty of Nations* (New York: Pantheon).

Needham, Joseph *et al.*, 1954, *Science and Civilisation in China* (various volumes) (Cambridge: Cambridge University Press).

Nehru, Jawaharlal, 1946, *The Discovery of India* (Calcutta: Signet Press, 1st edn).

O'Leary, Brendan, 1989, *The Asiatic Mode of Production: Oriental Despotism, Historical Materialism, and Indian History* (Oxford and New York: Basil Blackwell).

Peerenboom, Randall, 2002, *China's Long March Toward Rule of Law* (Cambridge: Cambridge University Press).

Shirk, Susan L., 1993, *The Political Logic of Economic Reform in China* (Berkeley: University of California Press).

Spence, Jonathan *et al.*, 1999, *The Search for Modern China: A Documentary Collection* (New York: W.W. Norton and Company, 2nd edn).

United Nations Development Programme, *Human Development Report* (various years) (New York and Oxford: Oxford University Press).

Wittfogel, Karl A., 1957, *Oriental Despotism: A Comparative Study of Total Power* (New Haven, CT: Yale University Press).

2
India's Growth Experience

Kanhaiya Singh and Suman Bery[1]

2.1 Introduction

Perceptions of India's economic growth are shifting. In the first three decades after independence in 1947, the economy was known for its steady "Hindu" rate of growth of 3.5 percent. It is now apparent that India moved onto a higher growth trajectory in the 1980s, and that this underlying momentum lasted through the 1990s, notwithstanding some deceleration at the end of the decade. As many other fast-growing economies succumbed to financial crisis in the 1980s and the 1990s, the steadiness of India's growth performance began to attract greater attention abroad, as did India's reform program launched in 1991. In the eyes of many observers, by the end of the 1990s India had moved to being a "six percent growth" economy—not a "miracle" perhaps, but certainly respectable. This steady growth has produced predictable consequences. Sales of 10,000 motorcycles a day and more than one million new mobile phone subscriptions each month are some reflections of this momentum (Waldman (2003)). After fierce academic debate, there is also consensus that significant progress has been made in poverty reduction, but without a significant change in the personal distribution of income.[2]

Yet, puzzles remain. There are several peculiarities in India's growth experience. Saving and investment rates have been, at best, moderate. Manufacturing has remained stunted. Fiscal deficits have remained high. At the same time inflation has been declining, and the balance of payments strengthening. Infrastructure provision has been erratic, of poor quality, and bedeviled by problems of cost recovery. Agricultural growth has also been slowing. Most of the recent growth is in the poorly documented and understood services sector. While, at the time of writing, India is in an optimistic mood, with the goal of sustained 8 percent growth widely accepted, the uncomfortable fact is that the rapid growth of fiscal year 2003/04 (April 1– March 31) follows several years of sub-par growth, with government estimates of gross domestic product (GDP) growth in 2002/03 at just 4.4 percent.

Resolving these controversies is beyond the scope of this chapter. Its goals are more modest; it tries to present the basic factual information on India's growth experience over the half century since independence in 1947, with a particular focus on the 1990s. There are several existing papers which have already attempted such a retrospective.[3] The present chapter builds on these in three ways: it updates the story into the new century; it provides a broader range of international comparisons; and it gives some fresh estimates of growth in total factor productivity (TFP) in India using aggregate data. The purpose is to provide the context for the other chapters on India in this volume, as well as to provide a foil for the discussion of China's growth and poverty reduction experience. As might be expected, in the medium-term analysis of what remains a low-income developing country, the bulk of the attention is on supply-side issues. Only in the 1990s have issues of demand management started to become salient, and policy challenges more complex. These issues are accordingly treated toward the end of the chapter.

The rest of the chapter is organized as follows. Section 2.2 presents the Indian economy in the global context. Section 2.3 provides a brief overview of economic performance from independence to the present. Section 2.4 looks more closely at the sources of growth in the 1990s, examining supply side of the economy (sectoral developments). Section 2.5 presents an analysis of the sources of growth using a model of factor decomposition, while Section 2.6 builds upon the analysis in the previous sections to discuss policy implications and presents concluding remarks.

2.2   India in the global context

By most measures, India's growth performance has been reasonably strong over the last two decades in relation to the rest of the world. This follows a prolonged period of slow growth, when India was less open to the global economy, had a low level of industrialization, and lagged in human capital development. Nonetheless, even with the upturn in the 1980s and the 1990s, India's economy continued to lose ground with much of the Asia region. In 1980, China and India were the nineteenth and twentieth largest economies in the world (measured by GDP in constant 1995 US dollars at market exchange rates). By 2001, they ranked sixth and eleventh, respectively, with China's economy having grown almost sixfold over the past two decades, and India's economy having approximately doubled in size. In terms of GDP on a purchasing power parity (PPP) basis, the two economies ranked second and fourth, respectively, in 2001 (Table 2.1). During this period, the population grew by 29.6 percent in China and 63.2 percent in India. The combination of faster output growth with slower population growth in China as compared to India over the past 20 years has led to a dramatic divergence in per capita incomes between the two countries, whether measured at market exchange rates or on a PPP basis.

Table 2.1 Select economic indictors of major economies[a]

| | Gross Domestic Product (GDP)[b] | | | | Gross National Income per capita[b] (in US dollars) | | GDP (Annual percentage change)[c] 1990–2001 | Exports (in billions of US dollars) 2000 | Infant mortality (per 1000 births) 2000 | Life expectancy at birth (in years) 2000 | Population (percentage change)[c] 1990–2001 |
| | In billions of US dollars | | In constant 1995 US dollars | | | | | | | | |
	1980	2001	1980	2001	1980	2001					
United States	2,957	9,792	4,772	9,014	13,020	34,280	3.0	1,103	7	77	1.2
China	421	5,111	164	1,117	430	3,950	9.9	280	31	70	1.0
Japan	1,085	3,193	3,304	5,648	9,290	25,550	1.2	513	3	81	0.3
India	529	2,930	157	492	770	2,820	5.5	64	67	63	1.8
Germany	803	2,087	1,829	2,702	10,270	25,240	1.6	630	4	77	0.3
Italy	544	1,430	823	1,225	9,670	24,530	1.6	304	4	79	0.2
United Kingdom	498	1,420	799	1,335	8,690	24,340	2.3	402	6	77	0.4
France	518	1,420	1,154	1,805	9,660	24,080	1.9	373	4	79	0.4
Brazil	467	1,269	518	799	3,710	7,070	2.6	64	31	68	1.4
Canada	274	843	407	717	10,860	26,530	2.7	325	5	79	1.0
Mexico	288	838	222	372	4,130	8,240	3.2	180	24	73	1.6
Korea, Republic of	96	714	149	639	2,490	15,060	6.0	207	5	73	1.0
Indonesia	122	615	75	216	790	2,830	4.3	64	—	65	1.5
World	13,536	45,619	19,409	34,490	3,060	7,370	2.5	7,856	—	—	—

[a] Top nine countries in terms of size of GDP in 2001. Other countries are presented as competators.
[b] On a purchasing power parity basis.
[c] Simple averages for the period.

Sources: World Bank, *World Development Indicators CD ROM 2003, and World Development Report 2003;* and United Nations Development Programme, *Human Development Report 2002.*

Growth theory posits initial conditions as an important determinant of growth. Poor countries are predicted to grow faster than rich countries as they have a wider shelf of technological opportunities available to them. This basic hypothesis has been further enriched by such concepts as increasing returns to scale[4] and conditional convergence.[5] In addition, the structure of the economy and its endowments are pertinent. Countries with abundant natural resources also have been found to perform more poorly than those that are more industrialized.

In Table 2.2, we compare India's growth performance during 1961–2001 with that of China and other major emerging markets, as well as the United States. In 1961, India was somewhat richer than China, a little poorer than Indonesia, but already much poorer than Malaysia and the Republic of Korea (henceforth Korea). Over the next few decades, India's experience did not bear out the convergence hypothesis: countries richer than it (and poorer, in the case of China) grew faster, although in general the lower income countries grew faster than the United States. What is particularly striking is the differential performance of manufacturing in India over this period against its comparators. Manufacturing had a low share in India at the beginning of the period; while the share of manufacturing increased in Indonesia and Korea, in India it stagnated. Also of interest is the continued high share of agriculture in GDP even when compared to the other two large, populous Asian economies of China and Indonesia. Over the 40-year period, therefore, the structural composition of India's economy has on balance changed somewhat slower than in its closest comparators. The sluggishness of manufacturing growth has been a continuing focus of policy over the entire post-independence period and remains so even today.

Two other key differences appear in India's performance vis-à-vis other major emerging markets. First, the level of human capital development was lower in India, with illiterate persons accounting for 67 percent of the population in 1961, compared to 47 percent in China and 13 percent in Korea. In addition to the initial difference being large, the pace at which other countries approached full literacy has been much more rapid than in India. Second, the level of industrialization was initially lower in Korea, Malaysia, and Indonesia than in India in the early 1960s. However, with greater exposure to foreign trade in the latter three countries, in particular imports, they eventually surpassed India, with rapidly rising industrialization also fueling exports. As Romer (1993, p. 543) notes: "The source of growth in a few Asian economies was their ability to extract relevant technological knowledge from industrial economies and utilize it productively within the domestic economy." Owing to its highly regimented import substitution policy, India could not harness this advantage despite the fact that it had a higher share in world exports in 1970.

Table 2.2 Evolving economic structure of India and select comparator countries[a]

Parameter and years	India	China	Brazil	Indonesia	Korea	Malaysia	United States	World
Real per capita GDP (1961)								
(in 1995 US dollars)	187.0	70.0	1,864.0	258.8	1,351.0	1,015.0	13,258.0	2,696.0
GDP growth (1970–1990)[b]	4.4	8.4	5.3	7.2	8.1	6.9	3.1	3.5
GDP growth (1980–2001)[b]	5.7	9.5	2.5	5.5	6.8	6.4	2.9	2.7
GDP growth (1990–2001)[b]	5.4	9.4	2.0	4.7	6.2	6.8	2.9	2.5
Industry share in GDP								
1961 or earliest	19.5	32.6	41.7	16.3	20.1	21.3	33.4	—
2001 or latest	26.5	51.1	33.9	46.5	41.4	49.1	24.9	29.8
Manufacturing share in GDP								
1961 or earliest	14.1	40.5	31.4	10.9	13.5	7.9	—	—
2001 or latest	15.5	35.4	21.0	26.1	30.0	30.6	17.2	20.1
Services share in GDP								
1961 or earliest	36.1	31.9	38.8	37.9	41.0	43.1	63.8	55.5
2001 or latest	48.4	33.6	56.8	37.1	54.1	42.4	73.5	66.3
Agriculture share in GDP								
1961 or earliest	44.4	35.5	19.5	45.8	38.9	35.6	2.9	6.5
2001 or latest	25.1	15.2	9.3	16.4	4.4	8.5	1.6	3.9
External trade								
(in percent of GDP)								
1961 or earliest	8.1	3.7	14.6	23.6	20.3	87.0	9.3	—
2001 or latest	29.1	49.2	27.8	73.7	83.5	214.3	26.2	58.2
Export of goods and services								
(in percent of GDP)								
1961 or earliest	3.6	1.8	7.3	10.7	5.3	46.1	5.1	—
2001 or latest	13.7	25.8	13.4	41.1	42.9	116.3	11.2	29.9
Export of manufacture								
(in percent of total exports)								
1961 or earliest	43.0	47.7	3.1	0.3	19.6	5.2	62.9	58.8
2001 or latest	76.5	88.6	54.3	56.4	90.7	80.1	82.1	78.0
High technology export								
(in percent of manufactured								
exports)								
1990 or earliest	3.9	6.1	6.1	1.4	17.8	36.1	32.3	15.7
2001 or latest	5.7	20.4	17.9	13.4	29.1	56.9	32.1	23.3
Total exports								
(in percent of world exports)								
1970	0.5	0.4	0.7	0.3	0.3	0.4	14.8	—
2001 or latest	0.9	3.9	0.9	0.8	2.4	1.3	14.0	—
Adult illiteracy rate (in percent)								
1961 or earliest	66.9	47.1	31.6	43.9	13.2	41.9	—	—
2001 or latest	42.0	14.2	12.7	12.7	2.1	12.1	—	—

[a] Data for the United States and the world pertain to 1980 and 2000.
[b] Annual averages for the period.

Source: World Bank, *World Development Indicators 2003*.

2.3 Growth over half a century: an overview

India has experienced sharp variations in growth performance since Independence, in part reflecting drought and crisis periods (Figure 2.1). Notwithstanding these events, India's economic performance has picked up since the 1980s (Table 2.3), with the convergent view associating this positive outcome with the reform process. Where controversy arises is about the efficacy of different waves of reforms introduced at different periods of time and their sustainability. Most of these discussions hover around periods

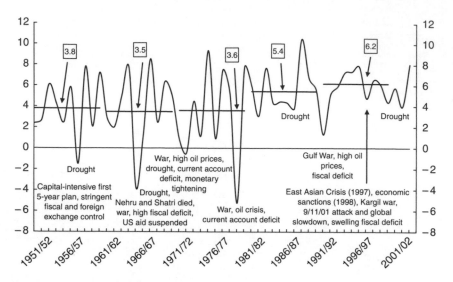

Figure 2.1   India: real GDP at factor cost, 1951/52–2003/04[a] (annual percentage change)
[a] Figures in boxes represent rate of trend real GDP growth for the respective decade.
Source: Central Statistical Organization.

Table 2.3   India: GDP growth and outliers, 1951/52–2002/03 (annual percentage change, unless otherwise indicated)[a]

	1951/52 to 1960/61	1961/62 to 1970/71	1971/72 to 1980/81	1981/82 to 1990/91	1991/92 to 2000/01	1996/97 to 2002/03
Average growth	3.93	3.74	3.14	5.64	5.65	5.62
Average growth without outliers	4.53	4.57	4.64	5.64	6.30	6.12
Year(s) of the outliers	1957/58	1965/66	1972/73, 1979/80		1991/92, 1997/98	1997/98, 2002/03

[a] Annual averages for the period.
Sources: Central Statistical Organization, *National Accounts Statistics* (various years) and authors' estimates.

associated with leadership of former Prime Ministers Rajiv Gandhi (1984–89) and Narasimha Rao (1991–96).[6] Some of these discussions, however, fail to note the wide-ranging trade reforms introduced during the late 1970s and the industrial policy reforms introduced during the early 1980s when Morarji Desai and Indira Gandhi were respectively the prime ministers. Further, the debate misses the extent to which reform has been institutionalized and efforts made to change attitudes and perceptions both from within and outside the economy under the former Prime Minister A.B. Vajpayee. In addition, while measuring the effect of a given regime, it is important that the outcome of a suitably extended period (following the reform) is taken into consideration and the effects of non-policy circumstances are sufficiently discounted.

India's early development strategy formally started with the Industrial Policy Resolution in 1948 and the Planning Commission's establishment in 1950. Following extensive debate in the period leading up to independence, as well as the experience of the Soviet Union in the 1930s and that of India with heavy intervention during the Second World War, India's First Five-Year Plan (1951–56) set the stage for an interventionist framework, and the Second Plan (1956–61) provided the analytical foundation for a development strategy that continued substantially unaltered till the end of the 1980s. Indeed, the impulse towards economic autarky and state intervention gained momentum after 1969 and through the 1970s. The strategy was based on promoting import substitution and developing indigenous capability through massive investments in the public sector, thus eliminating competition against public sector industries, and controlling private investment through a licensing process.[7] However, this strategy was also accompanied by institutional development, particularly in higher education.

The 1960s managed to achieve a trend growth rate of only 3.5 percent, despite a substantial increase in public sector investment. Growth was held down by extreme drought (1965–66), which reduced agricultural production by 17 percent and food grain production by 20 percent that year.[8] This period also encompasses the 1965 war with Pakistan and the death of two important leaders, Jawaharlal Nehru and Lal Bahadur Shastri, in quick succession (Table 2.4). When Indira Gandhi took over as prime minister in January 1966, she vigorously followed the economic paradigm of her father and in addition adopted a new program of "green revolution" to neutralize frequent drought. In order to facilitate implementation of these policies and as a populist move, major commercial banks were nationalized in 1969.[9] In part this was also to retaliate against the private sector, which had initiated a challenge to her office in the 1967 elections.

The 1970s can be categorized as a period of technology absorption and the golden age of the public sector, with increased control over the private sector. Public sector employment increased from 11.1 million in 1970/71 to 15.5 million in 1980/81, as compared to the private sector, where employment increased from 6.7 million to 7.4 million during the same period (Reserve Bank of India, 2003b). In addition, public sector investment rose, averaging 8.4 percent of GDP a year in the 1970s compared to 4.8 percent and 6.9 percent a year in the 1950s and the 1960s, respectively. However, this was also a period of external shocks and political uncertainties associated with an influx of refugees from Bangladesh (erstwhile East Pakistan) and subsequently the 1971 war with Pakistan, with severe droughts in 1972 and

Table 2.4   India: terms of prime ministers and years of general elections

Prime Minister	Period of service			Year(s) of election
	From	To	Days	
Pandit Jawaharlal Nehru	August 15, 1947	May 27, 1964	6,131	1951, 1957, 1962
Guljari Lal Nanda	May 27, 1964	June 9, 1964	14	
Lal Bahadur Shastri	June 9, 1964	January 11, 1966	582	
Guljari Lal Nanda	January 11, 1966	January 24, 1964	14	
Indira Gandhi	January 24, 1966	March 24, 1977	5,831[a]	1967, 1971
Morarji Desai	March 24, 1977	July 28, 1979	857	1977
Charan Singh	July 28, 1979	January 14, 1980	171	
Indira Gandhi	January 14, 1980	October 31, 1984	5,831[a]	1980
Rajiv Gandhi	October 31, 1984	December 1, 1989	1,857	1985
V.P. Singh	December 1, 1989	November 10, 1990	344	1989
Chandra Shekhar	November 10, 1990	June 21, 1991	224	
P.V. Narasimha Rao	June 21, 1991	May 10, 1996	1,785	1991
A.B. Vajpayee	May 16, 1996	June 1, 1996	16	1996
H.D. Deve Gowda	June 1, 1996	April 1, 1997	325	
I.K. Gujral	April 1, 1997	November 8, 1997	223	
A.B. Vajpayee	March 19, 1998	May 13, 2004	2,254	1998, 1999
Manmohan Singh	May 13, 2004	Present	—	2004

[a] Includes all terms.

Source: Government of India, Press Information Bureau.

1974, and with the hike in international oil prices in 1973. The result was huge current account deficits, fiscal deterioration, and declining terms of trade. Inflation rose to an all-time high of 25 percent. In 1975, a political emergency was declared. Stricter monetary management and general macroeconomic discipline brought the economy back on track. Major steps were also taken to allow increases in the licensed capacities of existing plants based on their past performances through the Industrial Policy, 1975/76.

A new industrial policy was introduced in December 1977 under the leadership of Morarji Desai, following general elections in 1977, which saw the Congress Party thrown out of power at the center for the first time. The concept of District Industry Centre was ushered in, giving greater priority to the small-scale industries (SSIs). Nevertheless, the import–export policy for 1977/78 was by far the most liberal of its kind in widening the scope of Open General Licenses (OGL), imports by SSIs and end-users, and exemptions from custom duties on advance license facility. In addition, the concept of absolutely prohibited items was introduced instead of permissible items. Special measures were also taken to boost exports. In particular, differential treatment between public and private sector and between merchant and manufacturer exporters in respect of Replenishment (REP) Licenses was abolished. Nonetheless, the period between 1975 and 1980 saw extreme political uncertainty, exemplified by a number of changes in government in quick succession. In combination with declining labor productivity, growth averaged only 3.2 percent a year during 1971/72–1980/81—the lowest average growth rate for a decade since independence.

The 1980s started with relatively low inflation and high growth, but the period also witnessed the emergence of the twin deficits. The current account deficit was 25 percent of exports (1.7 percent of GDP), and the combined fiscal deficit of the centre and the states was 7.6 percent of GDP in 1980/81. Prompted by the balance of payments problems, the 1980/81 import–export policy reversed several measures aimed at liberalizing imports under the government headed by Morarji Desai. In addition, formula-based capacity expansion for industrial firms was introduced. Some liberalizing steps were eventually taken in the form of the 1984/85 industrial policy, which allowed broad banding for generic industries, mostly automobiles. In addition, special consideration was given to requests for setting up 100 percent export-oriented units, including proposals for single point clearance and tax holidays. Exporters also enjoyed several new benefits not available to others aimed at improving capacity utilization.

At the time, the government headed by Rajiv Gandhi (1984–89) was credited with also introducing some "quasi-Southeast Asian style" economic reforms, which were mostly directed to promoting exports. However, controls on imports continued. Some further liberalization in industrial activity also took place. In 1987/88, a system of memoranda of understanding between the central government and public sector undertakings (PSUs) was introduced to enhance PSUs' performance. The policy of allowing select firms that attained high capacity utilization to expand overall capacity to specified limits was continued. In addition, more firms were allowed broad banding. More importantly, the regime for industrial licensing was eased, removing some industries, and a system of negative lists for licensing was created for the rest. These reforms, though limited in nature, helped firms to harness some benefits of scale economies.

In view of the above developments and coupled with a bumper crop, agricultural GDP growth reached 16 percent in 1988/89 and overall growth achieved a record high of 10 percent, compared to an average of 4 percent during the previous four years. However, this high growth proved to be unsustainable, as the three consecutive years following 1988/89 showed declines in growth rates. This drop-off in performance partly arose from gross negligence in macroeconomic management during the second half of the 1980s. The current account deficit and fiscal deficit kept increasing throughout the period and foreign exchange reserves dropped sharply. Subsidies also increased, and by the end of the period (1990/91), the current account deficit was about 52 percent of exports (3.1 percent of GDP) and the overall fiscal deficit reached 10 percent of GDP. The collapse of the Soviet Union, an important trading partner, added to the problem. Foreign exchange reserves were sufficient to meet just a month's imports. This led to the 1991 financial crisis, which was further exacerbated by the surge in oil prices due to the 1990 Gulf War.[10] Between 1988/89 and 1991/92, GDP growth fell from 10 percent to almost nil. Nonetheless, the 1980s ended with the highest average growth rate in a decade since Independence at 5.6 percent. This performance was aided by reforms to industrial policy throughout the 1980s and into the early 1990s to make it more cost-efficient and investment-friendly—a process that withstood a rapid succession of three governments between late 1989 and mid-1991.[11]

By mid-1991, India's economy was in full-blown crisis. The last of these governments, headed by P.V. Narasimha Rao (with the then, Finance Minister and now, Prime Minister Manmohan Singh), undertook emergency measures of far-reaching importance, including the devaluation of the rupee, cuts in the fiscal deficit, and other wide-ranging economic reforms, assisted by loans from the International Monetary Fund (IMF) and the World Bank. The "license raj" that had guided industrial development for many years was sought to be abolished, and measures were taken to liberalize the external sector. The economy responded positively to these changes and GDP growth crossed the 7 percent mark once again in 1994/95. However, by the end of the Rao regime, growth started to decline. India entered another period of political uncertainty between May 1996 and March 1998, with three changes in governments. Nonetheless, the direction of economic reforms remained positive and roadmaps were charted to undertake major financial sector reforms, including capital account convertibility. However, in response to the East Asian crisis starting in mid-1997, economic reforms slowed down and capital account convertibility was postponed till certain pre-conditions were met, including the strengthening of the financial sector.

A renewed effort was made to reinvigorate the reform process by a new government headed by A.B. Vajpayee, which took over in March 1998. As part of this effort, a series of legislative changes of far-reaching economic importance were undertaken. After initial hesitations, the Vajpayee government demonstrated the resolve to carry forward reforms, in terms of accelerating privatization, rationalizing the regulatory framework, and further liberalizing the trade and financial sectors. Overall, growth averaged 5.7 percent in the 1990s (and 5.5 percent inclusive through 2002/03)—slightly higher than the 1980s, but dragged down by several crises.[12] In summary, economic performance in India since Independence can be divided into three general parts.

- The period 1950s–70s is characterized by a public sector-led and socialistic pattern of growth. It resulted in an economy that was fragile and suscep-tible to external shocks. There was hardly any competitive democracy that might have spurred reforms. The economy, in fact, experienced four episodes of negative growth. After 1977, there was the beginning of democratic competition. This generated new ideas which led ultimately to liberalization.

- The second period is the 1980s, which saw industry capacity limits eased and export-promoting measures adopted, but under a fragile policy regime. Licensing procedures were simplified, but the basic paradigm of Industrial Policy Resolution of 1956 was largely maintained.
- The third period, or roughly the 1990s, saw a further range of economic reforms, in part in response to the balance of payments crisis in 1990/91 and the need to spur growth. Democracy became even more competitive, and the rules of the game were further changed in favor of market forces.

The reform process, in turn, has yielded more benefits in recent years, as external shocks have not been able to pull the economy severely down for prolonged periods owing to greater resiliency than earlier. This change is evident in the coefficient of variation of growth numbers, which went from a high of 138 percent during the 1970s to a low 23 percent during 1996–2002.

2.4   Structural shifts in output: a closer look

2.4.1   Structural shifts

India's economy has also experienced major structural shifts in the sources of output since Independence. The share of agriculture in GDP, which averaged 55 percent in the 1950s, was down to 29 percent in the 1990s and 22 percent by 2002/03 (Table 2.5). This has reduced the vulnerability of economic performance to monsoon rains. However, most of the shift from agriculture has gone to services instead of industry. The share of industry in GDP has moved up only marginally from an average of 21 percent in the 1960s to 27 percent in the 1990s, where it stood in 2002/03. Thus, the public sector-based model of growth did not deliver the expected growth in manufacturing. On the other hand, the services sector—as the major source of growth and contributor to output in India—accounted for almost 51 percent of GDP in 2002/03. Its size and growth have helped in maintaining the overall resiliency of India's economy, most importantly by creating employment opportunities for skilled people, as evidenced by massive gains in the field of information technology (IT) in recent years.

It is also worth noting that the contribution of the unorganized sector, broadly defined as production units without power and having fewer than seven workers, in net domestic product (NDP) has remained dominant, with only a marginal decrease during 30 years (Table 2.6). Agriculture, hotels, and restaurants are almost completely in the unorganized sector, with at least half of the income in manufacturing, construction, transport, and financial services and real estate also generated by it. The downside of a huge unorganized sector is that a large part of the economy still experiences poor economies of scale, less effort in research and development, and low productivity and quality, and generates less tax revenue for the government than would otherwise be expected. However, the advantage of a large

Table 2.5 India: average growth rates and real GDP shares by sectors, 1951/52–2002/03[a] (in percent, unless otherwise indicated)

Period	Agriculture and allied products		Industry		Services		GDP growth at factor cost	Per capita GDP growth	Wholesale price index[b]
	Growth	Share of GDP	Growth	Share of GDP	Growth	Share of GDP			
1951/52–1960/61	3.1	55.4	6.3	16.3	4.3	28.1	3.9	2.0	—
1961/62–1970/71	2.6	47.0	5.5	21.4	4.8	31.6	3.8	1.5	—
1971/72–1980/81	1.8	42.1	4.1	23.0	4.4	34.9	3.2	0.8	10.3
1981/82–1990/91	3.5	35.7	7.1	25.4	6.7	39.0	5.6	3.4	7.2
1991/92–2000/01	2.6	28.2	5.7	27.1	7.6	44.7	5.7	3.6	8.1
1991/92–1995/96	2.5	30.4	6.1	26.9	7.1	42.7	5.4	3.3	10.1
1996/97–2000/01	2.7	26.0	5.3	27.3	8.2	46.2	5.9	4.0	5.1
2001/02	5.7	23.9	3.3	26.7	6.8	49.5	5.6	3.7	3.6
2002/03	−3.2	22.1	6.1	27.1	7.1	50.8	4.4	2.6	3.4

[a] On fiscal year (April–March) basis, with GDP in constant 1993/94 prices. Agriculture and allied activities include agriculture, forestry, and fishing. Industry includes mining and quarrying; manufacturing; electricity, gas, and water supply; and construction. Services includes trade, hotels, and restaurants; transport, and storage.
[b] Percentage change.

Source: Reserve Bank of India, *Handbook of Statistics on the Indian Economy* (various years).

Table 2.6 India: unorganized economy in GDP by sectors, 1971/72–2000/01 (in percent of total)

	Agriculture and allied products	Industry				Services				Total NDP at factor cost
		Mining and quarrying	Manufacturing	Electricity, gas, and water supply	Construction	Trade, hotels, and restaurants	Transport, storage, and communications	Finance, insurance, real estate, and business services	Community, social, and personal services	
1971/72–1980/81	97.7	7.9	57.5	0.9	54.3	90.7	38.4	51.5	18.4	68.4
1981/82–1990/91	95.4	6.5	37.3	5.6	48.2	90.2	48.8	50.5	21.6	65.1
1991/92–1995/96	96.4	8.2	36.9	5.0	52.4	88.0	47.9	43.0	19.6	62.5
1996/97–2000/01	96.6	7.3	37.6	5.8	55.6	82.6	49.8	42.2	17.7	60.3

Source: Central Statistical Organization, *National Accounts Statistics* (various years).

unorganized sector lies in the decentralization of the production process, which makes it more adaptable to realigning product type, quality, and price, and thus less susceptible to external shocks. This may be one reason why economic crises in India have tended to be less painful and why the inflation rate has never reached high levels.

Also noteworthy is the dominant position the public sector still holds in the organized sector. Currently, the organized public sector accounts for 26 percent of NDP, compared to the organized private sector's less than 14 percent of NDP. It is well known that India's informal sector is more market-driven than its formal sector because of the rigid labor laws that apply to the latter, which force firms to keep employment above minimum regulated levels and distort their investment decisions.

2.4.2   Saving and investment

The inward looking policies followed from the 1950s through the 1980s were mostly aimed at increasing domestic savings and investing it in public sector enterprises (Table 2.7). Investment by the bigger private business houses was effectively limited and prices for most of their products were mostly administered. Prices of most public sector products were fixed on the basis of cost plus formula with little emphasis on efficiency improvements.

Public sector investment began to wane in the 1990s, with the lifting of budgetary support to PSUs and shifting in priorities of the government. On the other hand, private sector investment almost doubled (as a share of GDP) during the first half of the 1990s as compared to the 1980s. However, it has been sluggish since the second half of the 1990s. Part of this change may reflect increased competition in recent years brought on by trade reform and industrial liberalization, which has made private businesses more cautious in their investment decisions following the initial flush of exuberance in the 1980s and in the first half of the 1990s. For India's corporate sector, in fact, profits after tax as a percentage of gross sales fell gradually from 4.0 percent in 1994/95 to 0.5 percent in 2001/02.[13] However, they recovered to 2.4 percent during 2002/03. Owing to uncertain market demand, firms have been consolidating production processes without much increase in their capacity. At the same time, domestic financial institutions have been under sustained regulatory pressure to clean up their balance sheets and attain stricter capital adequacy norms, which has prompted them to become more careful in credit expansion. Nonetheless, India seems well-poised for another investment spurt, given the recent pickup in demand for consumer durables, most notably for automobiles, a renewal in corporate profitability, especially in the manufacturing sector, and backing of financial institutions with new securitization legislation aimed at strengthening creditor rights.

2.4.3   Capital absorption

Focusing on the relation between capital formation and economic growth, economic reforms should be expected to raise investment efficiency and

Table 2.7 India: saving and investment rates, 1951/52–2002/03 (in percent of GDP)[a]

Sector	1951/52 to 1960/61	1961/62 to 1970/71	1971/72 to 1980/81	1981/82 to 1990/91	1991/92 to 2000/01	1991/92 to 1995/96	1996/97 to 2000/01	2001/02 to 2002/03
Domestic saving rate	10.2	12.9	17.9	19.8	23.2	23.3	23.1	23.8
Public sector	1.9	2.8	3.8	2.8	0.7	1.6	−0.3	−2.4
Private corporate sector	1.1	1.5	1.6	1.9	3.9	3.5	4.2	4.1
Household sector	7.3	8.7	12.6	15.2	18.7	18.2	19.2	22.1
Domestic investment rate	11.7	14.8	18.1	21.8	24.3	24.4	24.2	24.0
Public sector	4.8	6.9	8.4	10.1	7.6	8.4	6.7	6.4
Private corporate sector	1.9	2.7	2.5	4.4	6.8	6.8	6.8	4.9
Household sector	5.0	5.2	7.3	7.4	10.0	9.2	10.7	12.7
Foreign saving rate	1.5	1.8	0.2	2.0	1.1	1.2	1.1	0.2

[a] Annual averages for the period.

Sources: Central Statistical Organization, *National Accounts Statistics* and Reserve Bank of India, *Handbook of Statistics on the Indian Economy* and *Annual Report* (various years).

improve absorptive capacity in India's economy over the long run. We examine this by calculating (i) the ratio of incremental capital (gross capital formation as a percentage of GDP) to real GDP growth, or incremental capital-output ratio (ICOR), for aggregate sectors, and (ii) the growth in real gross fixed capital formation (RGFCF).[14] If additional capital is not fully absorbed in the economy, the ICOR will increase and vice versa.

In this respect, our results suggest that reforms implemented during the late 1970s and the early 1980s were more effective than those during the second half of the 1980s. While there was little growth in RGFCF, the ICOR remained moderate in the second half of the 1980s, but went up by almost 50 percent in the first half of the 1990s given the investment spurt brought by renewed reforms (Figure 2.2). However, since 1996/97, the ICOR has fallen below 4 despite reasonable growth in RGFCF at least until 1999/2000, supporting the view that domestic producers have consolidated efficiency.

Capital formation has been weakest in sectors where the government still has a large role, most notably agriculture, construction, mining, power, and transport (Table 2.8). Although most of these sectors come under infrastructure development, of late government has focused its interest in developing roads, ports, and telecommunications. At the same time, coal mines need to be privatized and rail network improved, and above all, power shortages

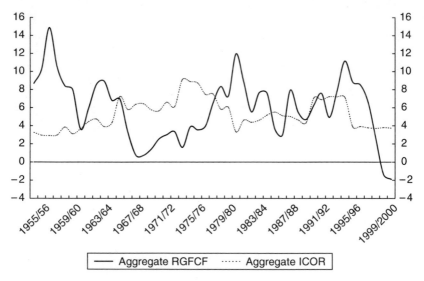

Figure 2.2 India: ICOR and real gross fixed capital formation, 1955/56–2001/02[a] (annual percentage change; 5-year moving average)

[a] Periods of negative growth are considered outliers and are not used to calculate the ICOR shown here.

Source: Central Statistical Organization.

Table 2.8 India: gross fixed capital formation, 1951/52–2001/02[a] (annual percentage change)[b]

	1951/52 to 1955/56	1956/57 to 1960/61	1961/62 to 1965/66	1966/67 to 1970/71	1971/72 to 1975/76	1976/77 to 1980/81	1981/82 to 1985/86	1986/87 to 1990/91	1991/92 to 1995/96	1996/97 to 2000/01	2001/02
Agriculture and allied activities	5.2	2.0	7.5	2.6	2.6	9.3	-0.9	4.5	1.5	1.3	8.3
Industry	12.0	12.9	9.5	2.4	10.4	3.6	14.1	3.7	14.9	-4.0	-7.1
Mining and quarrying	21.5	36.1	8.1	11.7	26.9	13.9	24.9	2.8	9.2	-10.6	-19.2
Manufacturing	7.1	15.5	8.6	2.7	10.5	1.5	17.0	4.0	21.8	-5.0	-6.6
Electricity, gas, and water supply	43.2	2.6	23.2	2.0	11.1	8.5	8.2	7.3	0.8	3.7	-4.2
Construction	67.3	32.9	11.0	-1.6	1.7	12.5	2.5	13.1	19.4	10.8	-19.4
Services	8.7	6.7	5.9	0.7	2.8	6.3	3.8	6.7	8.8	2.1	-2.6
Trade, hotels, and restaurants	1.0	4.7	24.3	27.8	-1.9	3.6	5.5	7.0	13.2	-3.5	0.5
Transport, storage, and communications	11.4	12.1	7.5	-1.8	5.4	2.7	4.9	6.6	10.0	4.2	-21.6
Financing, insurance, real estate, and business services	2.8	3.6	1.5	1.1	4.8	6.5	2.3	12.9	9.6	-1.2	-2.9
Community, social, and personal services	18.5	5.7	5.3	-3.2	2.7	12.8	4.6	2.5	5.4	8.0	19.3
Total gross fixed capital formation	8.7	7.4	7.2	1.4	5.5	5.4	7.6	4.7	11.2	-1.4	-4.0

[a] In constant 1993/94 prices.
[b] Annual averages for the period, except for 2001/02.

Source: Central Statistical Organization, National Account Statistics (various years).

reduced. Otherwise, a key bottleneck in raising productivity in industrial sector will remain, which, if not corrected, runs the risk of dampening private investment despite the recent optimism shown.

2.4.4   Agriculture

India, with almost 13 percent of the world's arable land, has increased agricultural output substantially since the Green Revolution in the 1960s, but among major crop producers average yield still lags that in China and the developed countries. Nonetheless, average yield in India has risen more than twofold, from 977 kilogram per hectare in the 1960s to 2318 kilogram per hectare by 2001/02, almost twice the average of low-income countries (Table 2.9). However, growth in real agricultural output has slowed over the past decade, with real value added in agriculture increasing by an average rate of 2.6 percent in the 1990s, as against 3.5 percent during the 1980s (Table 2.10).

This slowdown in agriculture's growth in India reflects a lack of capital investment (especially in water and irrigation), as well as the underdeveloped state of scientific research and a serious lack of farm education. These problems are compounded by relatively low levels of fertilizer use and farm mechanization.[15] The growth of yield-enhancing inputs was also significantly more subdued in the 1990s than in the previous decade, with the annual average growth rates of fertilizer use per hectare and gross irrigated area lower in the 1990s than in the previous decade. The relatively large food stock that is maintained by the government coupled with the price support mechanism also appears to distort the prices faced and production decisions made by farmers. Acharya (2002b) argues that the financial burden arising from pay awards granted by the Fifth Pay Commission (1997) has acted to hamper the government's ability to provide adequate resources for maintenance and operation of irrigation system, research and development, and

Table 2.9   Cereal yield in India and select parts of the world (in kilograms per hectare)[a]

	1961–70	1971–80	1981–90	1991–95	1996–2000	2001
India[b]	977	1,220	1,622	2,053	2,270	2,318
China	1,733	2,532	3,823	4,468	4,881	4,904
Low-income countries	930	1,050	1,162	1,195	1,315	1,311
Middle-income countries	1,257	1,586	1,949	2,134	2,287	2,291
High-income countries	2,652	3,151	3,746	4,163	4,372	4,315
World	1,241	1,469	1,768	1,924	2,079	2,171

[a] Annual averages for the period, except 2001.
[b] On a fiscal year basis.

Source: World Bank, *World Development Indicators 2003*.

Table 2.10 India: agricultural sector indicators, 1971/72–2002/03 (average annual percentage change, unless otherwise indicated)

	1971/72 to 1980/81	1981/82 to 1990/91	1991/92 to 1995/96	1996/97 to 2000/01	2001/02	2002/03
Real value added from agriculture	1.8	3.5	2.5	2.7	-0.6	5.7
Real value of output						
Crops	2.6	3.3	2.0	2.2	-2.8	5.7
Total (crops, livestock, fishery, and forestry)	2.4	3.4	2.5	2.5	-0.9	5.1
Yield						
Food grains	2.0	3.2	1.6	1.9	-4.6	6.9
All crops yield index	1.4	2.8	0.9	0.8	-3.5	6.1
Prices						
All crops		8.2	12.3	6.6	-1.2	4.3
Fertilizer consumption per hectare of gross sown area						
Nitrogenous	7.5	4.0	1.7	-7.2	2.0	—
Phosphatic	9.5	-1.9	8.3	-13.5	2.4	—
Potassic	7.2	-0.7	7.3	-8.0	4.8	—
Total	7.9	2.0	3.5	-8.9	2.4	—
Land use statistics						
Net irrigated area	2.2	2.2	2.3	1.8	0.3	—
Gross irrigated area	2.7	2.3	2.7	3.2	1.2	—
Area sown						
Net area sown	0.0	0.2	-0.1	-0.1	-0.9	—
Gross area sown	0.4	0.8	0.2	0.5	-1.7	—
Institutional credit (in rupees per hectare)	10.2	19.8	18.5	12.2	19.6	—
Average number of tractors per 1,000 hectares of gross sown area	16.7	10.0	9.5	4.4[a]	7.6	—

[a] For 1996/97–1999/2000.

Sources: Department of Agriculture and Cooperation, Agriculture Statistics at a Glance; Central Statistical Organization, National Accounts Statistics; Ministry of Finance, Economic Survey; and Fertilizer Association of India, Fertilizer Statistics (all various years).

rural roads and state highways, although a recent drive has been made to connect highly populated villages by all season roads and sparsely populated villages by unpaved roads. Srinivasan (2000) notes that agriculture in India is still very far from being integrated into world markets, which will require more upgrades to infrastructure and better promotion and facilitation of traditional and nontraditional agricultural exports. Thus, the trends in the agricultural sector are not particularly encouraging in terms of output growth. Although private investment is rising, there is still a need to reduce dependency on rains. A second green revolution is also required, aimed at applying scientific research to the new opportunities, together with a massive improvement in rural infrastructure and a complete rethinking of direct subsidies and price supports.

2.4.5   Industry

As noted earlier, industrial growth picked up substantially in the 1980s, with the annual growth rate of the general index of industrial production (IIP) exceeding 8 percent in seven out of ten years, and averaging about 8 percent a year for the period as a whole (Table 2.11). In the mid-1990s, average growth reached in the order of 9 percent, with the maximum contribution coming from the manufacturing sector. Whereas the rise in industrial growth in the 1980s appears related to the easing of capacity constraints, developments in the mid-1990s owe more to an investment surge and sweeping reforms earlier in the decade. For the 1990s as a whole, however, average performance looks inferior to the 1980s. The downturn in industrial production since the mid-1990s has been concentrated in electricity, mining and quarrying, machinery and equipment, and cotton textiles. What went wrong in these sectors? Simply put, investment has not taken place, a point made earlier.[16] In the past, the government supported industry through public investment, trade barriers, and budgetary allocations.

Focusing on the power sector, recent investment has been contingent upon the guarantee of timely payment by the electricity purchasers, mostly the state electricity boards (SEBs). The record of the SEBs in this respect is dismal. Most of them are still surviving on subsidies and yet only a few are making profits. Unless power reforms take place and the health of electricity boards is restored, other industries will also suffer, most notably coal, whose main customer is power plants. Fortunately, after a decade of back and forth in power sector reforms, Parliament passed the much-awaited Electricity Bill in May 2003. With this, the government has dispensed with the licensing requirement for setting up generating facilities and has allowed new entrants to seek licenses for supplying power to areas that are already under license.

However, bringing higher growth to the industrial sector as a whole will require more than reliable and affordable power. Careful attention is needed to promote scale economies and to enlarge the domestic consumption base for two reasons. First, it will help make Indian firms become more competitive

Table 2.11 India: industrial output, 1981/82–2003/04 (average annual percentage change, unless otherwise indicated)

	Key industries				Use-based classification				Consumer goods	
	General	Manufacturing	Mining	Electricity	Basic goods	Capital goods	Intermediate goods	Consumer goods	Durables	Nondurables
1981/82–1990/91	7.8	7.6	8.3	9.0	7.9	11.5	5.9	6.7	13.9	5.5
1991/92–1995/96	6.2	6.1	4.8	7.5	7.8	0.3	7.9	6.3	9.3	5.8
1996/97–2000/01	5.7	6.2	1.8	5.7	4.2	7.7	7.1	5.5	9.4	4.3
2000/01	5.1	5.4	3.7	4.0	3.9	1.7	4.7	8.0	14.6	5.8
2001/02	2.6	2.9	0.4	3.1	2.4	−3.4	1.6	6.0	11.5	4.1
2002/03	5.8	6.0	5.8	3.2	4.8	10.4	3.8	7.2	−6.4	12.2
2003/04 (April–August)	5.6	6.2	4.4	2.4	4.3	7.7	3.3	8.9	4.8	10.2
Weight in index of industrial production	100.0	79.4	10.5	10.2	35.6	9.3	26.5	28.7	5.4	23.3

Source: Central Statistical Organization.

abroad and second, in the event of weak external demand, it will provide backstop support. In this context, it becomes imperative to rationalize the tax regime and to de-reserve production processes, in particular those reserved for small-scale operations. Bankruptcy laws and associated regulations also need to be strengthened, as the current regime severely limits the flexibility of labor markets and resolution of failed firms and increases transaction costs associated with administrative hurdles. Some changes are already proposed through the enactment of Companies (Amendment and Second Amendment) Act 2002 and Competition Act 2002.[17] However, the pace of industrial restructuring needs to pick up, including a comprehensive modernization of Companies Act 1956, to make the whole system and business environment compatible with the dynamics of globalization.

2.4.6   Services

Unlike industry, services witnessed an uptick in activity in the second half of the 1990s, when annual sector growth averaged 8 percent growth, compared to 7 percent in the first half of the 1990s and 6.7 percent in the 1980s. Within the services sector, communications; trade, hotel and restaurants; other (non-rail) transport; and banking, insurance and business services (including the IT sector) have experienced the highest growth rates (Table 2.12). There was also a steep increase in the growth of public administration and defense during the second half of the 1990s, likely reflecting the hefty salary increase for civil servants with subsequent implementation of the Fifth Pay Commission's award. However, in more recent years, growth in this component has declined under fiscal pressure.

There are several reasons why the services sector has performed better in the 1990s versus the 1980s, unlike agriculture and industry. First, there is less intervention from the government in this sector, which is predominantly unorganized in nature. Second, the absence of a structured tax system for this sector makes services more lucrative. Third, a number of reforms have been introduced in the services area covering banking, insurance, and ports and roads operations, which have likely given a further boost to growth in the services sector and helped spread efficiency gains economy-wide. Lastly, the emergence of vibrant IT, telecommunications, biotechnology, and electronics sectors has created a whole new demand for skills and application of processes, which has given a boost to the economy as a whole as well as to the services sector.

2.5   Sources of growth: analysis of the aggregate data

In this section, we analyze the sources of growth in India's economy through a factor decomposition of growth, providing explanations for the growth in factor productivity in order to highlight the importance of underlying macroeconomic variables discussed earlier. Given the fact that a major part

Table 2.12 India: services GDP, 1981/82–2002/03[a]

	Trade, hotels, and restaurants			Transport, storage, and communications					Banking, insurance, real estate and business services			Community, social, and personal services			Total services
	Total	Trade	Hotels and restaurants	Total	Railways	Transport by other means	Storage	Communications	Total	Banking and insurance	Real estate[b]	Total	Public administration and defence	Other services	
Average annual percentage change															
1981/82–1990/91	5.9	5.9	6.5	5.6	4.8	5.9	3.4	6.1	9.9	12.1	8.5	6.1	6.5	5.8	6.7
1991/92–1995/96	7.8	7.7	9.7	7.8	2.7	7.9	2.9	13.5	9.0	11.8	6.7	4.3	3.5	5.1	7.1
1996/97–2000/01	6.8	6.7	9.2	9.6	4.4	6.4	1.0	20.2	8.0	9.7	6.4	9.2	9.0	9.4	8.2
2000/01	4.1	3.9	6.9	12.2	4.3	6.6	3.1	26.8	3.5	-1.2	9.2	5.6	2.5	8.1	5.6
2001/02	8.8	8.7	11.2	8.5	6.0	3.9	-0.8	17.0	4.5	3.4	5.7	5.6	2.9	7.7	6.8
2002/03	12.1	—	—	0.1	—	—	—	—	6.1	—	—	6.8	—	—	7.1
In percent of total services GDP															
1981/82–1990/91	12.5	11.8	0.7	6.3	1.4	3.7	0.1	1.0	8.2	3.2	5.0	12.0	5.6	6.3	39.0
1991/92–1995/96	13.0	12.2	0.8	6.6	1.3	4.0	0.1	1.2	11.2	5.2	6.0	11.9	5.5	6.4	42.7
1996/97–2000/01	14.4	13.5	1.0	7.4	1.1	4.3	0.1	2.0	12.2	6.4	5.8	12.6	5.7	6.9	46.7
2000/01	14.6	13.6	1.0	8.2	1.1	4.3	0.1	2.7	12.6	6.6	6.0	13.5	6.0	7.5	48.9
2001/02	15.1	14.0	1.1	8.4	1.1	4.3	0.1	3.0	12.5	6.5	6.0	13.5	5.9	7.6	49.5
2002/03	16.2	—	—	8.1	—	—	—	—	12.7	—	—	13.8	—	—	50.8

[a] Based on constant 1993/94 prices.
[b] Includes ownership of dwellings and business services.

Source: Central Statistical Organization, *National Accounts Statistics* (various years).

of the domestic product originates from the unorganized sector, where data are not separately available, it is considered appropriate to examine output at the aggregate level.

2.5.1 Decomposition of the sources of growth

The growth accounting literature attributes growth to increases in factor supply and residual productivity, the latter of which reflects changes in efficiency with which factors are used. There are a number of modified versions of what are known as Solow's residuals used to calculate growth in TFP.[18] However, we follow a fairly simple method for our purpose. Consider the standard Cobb–Douglas production function:

$$Y_t = A\, K_t^{\alpha}\, L_t^{(1-\alpha)} \tag{2.1}$$

where Y is output, K is capital, L is labor, and A can be considered to represent other variables, which can affect output either independently or through their effect on factor efficiency. Differentiating (2.1) with respect to time after taking logs and rearranging terms, growth in total factor productivity (GTFP) can be expressed as:

$$\text{GTFP} = \frac{\dot{A}}{A} = \frac{\dot{Y}}{Y} - \alpha\left(\frac{\dot{K}}{K}\right) - (1 - \alpha)\left(\frac{\dot{L}}{L}\right) \tag{2.2}$$

where α is the share of factor payments in total product, or the elasticity with respect to capital in equation (2.2). Knowing the value of α and the rates of growth in factors K and L, the rate of growth in factor productivity A can be easily calculated. However, it is important that GTFP, which is calculated as a residual, be stationary in order to draw sensible conclusions. Intuitively, productivity growth measures shift in the production function, which may be caused by economic as well as non-economic factors.

In the present analysis, two exercises are done. First, GTFP is calculated for the aggregate economy, for which data are readily available. The second exercise is carried out to explain GTFP using macroeconomic variables through a general to specific model search process. For calculating aggregate GTFP, the total labor force, as shown in the World Bank's *World Development Indicators*, is taken to proxy labor in the above equation, while the real capital stock is taken from the Central Statistical Organization's National Accounts. Considering the shares of factor income generated by capital and labor in NDP over previous years, α is assumed to be approximately 0.60.[19]

The decomposition of real GDP growth calculated for the full sample years is plotted in Figure 2.3. The results clearly indicate that most of the growth is obtained from capital accumulation and factor productivity growth. In fact, most of the variation can be attributed to variations in factor

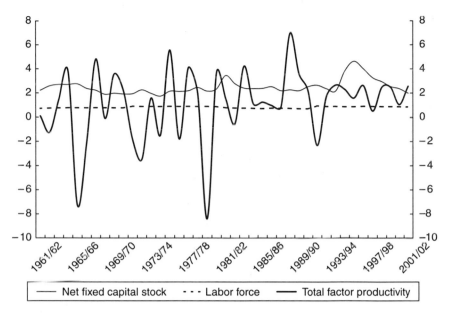

Figure 2.3 India: factor decomposition of real GDP growth, 1961/62–2001/02 (in percent)

Source: Authors' estimates.

productivity over time. This finding is consistent with some of the earlier studies such as Guha-Khasnobis and Bari (2003), which argue that growth in the South Asian region is mostly driven by capital accumulation and factor productivity. Nonetheless, the results must be interpreted carefully. A sudden inflow of capital in the economy is likely to lower productivity growth if it does not translate into real output growth in the same year. Therefore, positive values of productivity growth are more important than negative values. Negative values can be obtained in the above methodology both due to adverse external shocks as well as sudden capital inflows. Since outflows of fixed capital stock are rare and usually only happen in extreme conditions, it can be assumed for most of the time that the positive values of factor productivity growth so obtained represent technical gains for the economy as a whole.

We summarize the period-wise averages of the decomposition of growth due to capital, labor and factor productivity in Figure 2.4 and Table 2.13. The decade of the 1970s was most adversely affected in terms of factor productivity. Two severe droughts, oil price inflation, and external crises drastically curtailed productivity in the economy. On the other hand, the 1980s registered the highest productivity growth. This period is characterized by

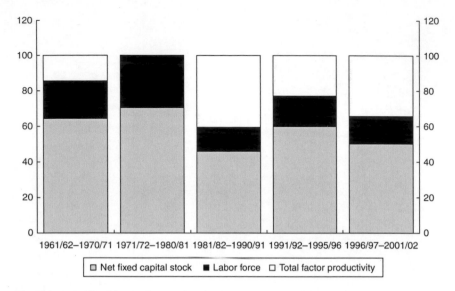

Figure 2.4   India: factor shares of real GDP growth, 1961/62–2001/02 (in percent of total)

Source: Authors' estimates.

Table 2.13   India: decomposition of growth, 1961/62–2001/02 (annual percentage change)[a]

| Period | Real GDP growth | Due to a change in | | |
		Fixed capital stock	Total labor force	Total factor productivity
1961/62–1970/71	3.63	2.34	0.77	0.52
1971/72–1980/81	3.03	2.14	0.90	0.00
1981/82–1990/91	5.47	2.51	0.74	2.21
1991/92–1995/96	5.22	3.13	0.90	1.19
1996/97–2001/02	5.74	2.85	0.88	1.95

[a] Annual averages for the period.

Sources: Central Statistical Organization, *National Accounts Statistics* (various years), and authors' estimates.

generally stable macroeconomic conditions (including low inflation) and initiatives to decontrol industrial capacity restrictions. However, the effects of macroeconomic mismanagement in the 1980s weigh heavily on the first half of the 1990s. While this period witnessed an investment spurt following economic reforms, the changes could only be partially absorbed in the economy. Nevertheless, the first half of the 1990s showed employment increases and ushered in significant changes in the macroeconomic environment.

The opening up of the economy and the increased competition it brought have paid dividends in recent years. Despite a low level of investment and a series of external and natural shocks in the second half of the 1990s, growth did not suffer much. Productivity growth increased significantly, almost to the level of the 1980s. Thus, a GTFP of nearly 2 percent per year is significant in its own right and gives more confidence about future growth prospects.

2.5.2 Factor productivity growth and macroeconomic factors

Relatively few studies have been conducted to explain factor productivity growth, as most cross country analyses restrict their focus on output growth. Fischer (1993) provides one of the early studies attempting to explain TFP growth using macroeconomic variables. In his analysis, the inflation rate, standard deviation of inflation, and black market premium on the exchange rate were found to be negatively related to productivity growth, while the government budget surplus and improvement in terms of trade were found to be positively related. More importantly, the significant relationship was found to exist in panel regressions but not in cross-sectional regressions. This implies that time series variations between productivity and TFP growth are significantly important.

With the above motive, we attempt to explain the GTFP for India's economy using various macroeconomic, social, and climate indicators as explanatory variables. This exercise is important in many ways and particularly from the point of view of macroeconomic policy formulation. The estimation starts with a number of variables using a distributed lag specification. The results are reported in Table 2.14 for those specifications with robust variables only. Significant variables that are found to explain GTFP include the deviation of rain from normal (DRAIN), rate of inflation (ΔP), and change in literacy rate (ΔLIT)—all in percents; the level of the terms of trade (TOT), where 1993/94 = 1; and the change in the current account balance as a percentage of GDP (ΔCAB).

Four different variants of the model are presented in order to demonstrate the statistical robustness of the explanatory variables. The model residuals are rigorously tested for consistency, and the test results are also presented. The diagnostic tests are important as the model contains a nonstationary variable TOT. All other variables are stationary. The explanatory power as indicated by the R^2 values is sufficiently large for making important conclusions. The nonlinear effect of inflation is also introduced in the model following the works of Sarel (1996) and Singh and Kalirajan (2003).

Table 2.14   India: alternate models of total factor productivity growth[a]

	GTFP-1 1973–2000	GTFP-2 1972–2000	GTFP-3 1972–2000	GTFP-4 1972–2000
Variables[b]				
Intercept	−0.100 (0.128)[e]	−0.237 (0.114)[c]	−0.321 (0.102)[d]	0.200 (0.110)[e]
DRAIN	0.145 (0.035)[c]	0.137 (0.033)[c]	0.134 (0.027)[c]	0.135 (0.025)[c]
DRAIN(−1)	−0.060 (0.031)[e]	−0.071 (0.032)[d]	−0.077 (0.027)[c]	−0.087 (0.025)[c]
ΔP	−0.222 (0.069)[c]	−0.165 (0.063)[d]	−0.242 (0.058)[c]	0.156 (0.194)
ΔP(−1)	0.215 (0.066)[c]	0.184 (0.063)[c]	0.232 (0.056)[c]	0.261 (0.053)[c]
ΔP(−2)	−0.121 (0.071)[e]			
ΔLIT(−1)	15.76 (15.276)	30.877 (13.770)[d]	36.551 (11.644)[c]	21.041 (12.987)
D92ON		0.009 (0.007)		
TOT(−1)			0.053 (0.020)[d]	0.036 (0.200)[e]
ΔCAB(−1)			0.480 (0.252)[e]	0.495 (0.233)[d]
PIDE55				−0.514 (0.240)[d]
R^2	0.76	0.77	0.84	0.87
Adjusted R^2	0.69	0.70	0.79	0.82
Standard error of regression	0.016	0.016	0.013	0.012
F-statistic, $F(k − 1, n − k)$, $n = 29$, k = number of regressors, including the intercept	11.016 [0.00]	12.11 [0.00]	15.80 [0.00]	16.75 [0.00]
Diagnostic tests				
LM (1) serial correlation	1.58 [0.21]	1.34 [0.25]	0.10 [0.75]	1.32 [0.25]
ARCH (1) test chi-square (1)	3.26 [0.07]	0.73 [0.39]	0.00 [0.99]	0.37 [0.54]
Functional form chi-square (1)	4.33 [0.04]	2.60 [0.11]	2.58 [0.11]	0.65 [0.42]
Normality chi-square (2)	1.26 [0.53]	1.06 [0.59]	1.20 [0.55]	3.26 [0.20]
Residual unit root				
Test statistics (Dickey–Fuller)[f]	−4.24	−4.52	−5.19	−4.33

[a] Values in parentheses ( ) are standard errors, and values in square brackets [ ] are *p*-values.
[b] DRAIN = deviation of rain from normal, ΔP = wholesale price inflation, ΔLIT = change in literacy rate of people above age 15 (all in percents); D92ON = intercept dummy for period of 1993 and beyond; TOT = terms of trade (1993/94 = 1); ΔCAB = change in current account balance (in percent of GDP); and PIDE55 = inflation dummy, which is equal to 0 if the annual inflation rate is less than 5.5 percent and is equal to the value of actual inflation less 5.5 percent if annual inflation is greater than or equal to 5.5 percent.
[c] Significant at the 1 percent level.
[d] Significant at the 5 percent level.
[e] Significant at the 10 percent level.
[f] Unit root test statistics are presented corresponding to the Schwarz Bayesian Criterion model selection criteria of second-order augmented Dickey–Fuller test of unit roots.
Source: Authors' estimates.

We subsequently estimate the factors explaining GTFP for the period 1972/73 to 2000/01 and examine the forecasting ability of the model for 2001/02. After assuming plausible values of the explanatory variables, we simulate GTFP and hence real GDP growth from the model for the period 2001/02–2004/05. The estimated values of the explanatory variables and simulated values of GTFP are presented in Table 2.15. Using them, we calculate real GDP growth after assuming the same growth of labor as in 2001/02, but allowing a slight increase in the growth of capital in 2003/04, for which data are available.[20] The slight increase in the growth of capital stock is justified on the basis of leading indicators such as credit from banks and performance of the capital market compared to the previous year.

Among the variables examined, we find the following set to be most plausible in explaining GTFP.

Table 2.15   India: distributed lag model of TFP and real GDP growth

	DRAIN	ΔP	ΔLIT	TOT	CAB	ΔCAB	GTFP-3	GTFP-4
1. Estimated values of the explanatory variables in distributed lag model of growth in total factor productivity (GTFP) for 1972/73–2000/01								
1999/2000	−0.010	0.033	0.008	0.926	−0.001	0.000	—	—
2000/01	−0.085	0.071	0.008	0.884	0.003	0.016	−0.002	0.001
2001/02	−0.079	0.036	0.008	0.865	0.009	0.000	0.019	0.020
2002/03	−0.175	0.034	0.008[a]	0.784	0.006	0.000	−0.005	−0.003
2003/04	0.030	0.055	0.008[a]	0.780[a]	0.006	0.000	0.028	0.036
2004/05	−0.140[a]	0.065[a]	—	—	—	0.010	−0.009	−0.003

2. Simulated values of GTFP and calculated values of real GDP growth

		Growth in GDP due to			GDP growth	
Period	Growth in capital stock	Fixed capital stock	Total labor force	GTFP (using GTFP-4 model)	Calculated	Actual
2001/02	0.037	2.216	0.858	1.977	5.1	5.4
2002/03	0.038	2.298	0.858	−0.336	2.8	4.3
2003/04	0.040	2.400	0.858	3.614	6.9	8.2
2004/05	0.045	2.700	0.858	−0.292	3.3	

[a] Assumed values.

Source: Authors' estimates.

- *Deviation from normal rainfall*: GTFP increases with good rainfall in India, which has a direct impact on farm productivity and an indirect one on other sectors via expected demand in industry and services.
- *Inflation rate*: In the long run, inflation has been found to reduce growth by lowering the efficiency of capital investment in productivity growth. This relationship has been confirmed in several recent studies using cross-country and panel regressions, including by Fischer (1993), Gregorio (1993), Barro (1995), Fry *et al.* (1996), Ambler and Cardia (1997), and Ghosh and Phillips (1998). Corden (1996) observed that one of the strong features of the newly industrialized economies like Singapore, Taiwan, Malaysia, and Thailand was very low levels of inflation over a long period (1961–91). In our model, GTFP is negatively affected by inflation at least in the short run. In order to confirm the causal relationship, between the inflation rate and productivity growth, we use a Granger-Block non-causality test and report the results in Table 2.16. There is clear unidirectional causality from inflation to GTFP, and therefore the model estimated in Table 2.14 is consistent. When nonlinearity is introduced in the model GTFP-4, the explanatory power of the model increases substantially and clearly the total effect of contemporaneous inflation is significantly negative when it is above 5.5 percent.[21]
- *Literacy rate*: There is a large literature supporting positive effects of education on growth.[22] Most growth related studies in particular have examined effects of human capital on growth in one form or the other. In

Table 2.16   Granger-Block non-causality test[a,b]

	Test variable (lagged x)	GTFP	ΔP
VAR(-1)	Dependent (y) CHSQ (1)	ΔP 0.11 [0.742]	GTFP 8.995 [0.003]

[a] Test between per capita income growth and inflation in a bi-variate vector autoregression (VAR). The direction of non-causality being tested is from x to y for the period 1971–98.
[b] p-values for Chi-Square statistics are shown in square brackets. Using a Wald test, null hypothesis is that the coefficients of the explanatory variables in Table 2.15 are zero. A lower p-value means rejection of the null hypothesis and therefore existence of a causal direction.
Source: Authors' estimates.

the present analysis also, a rise in the literacy rate increases productivity growth with a lag. Clearly, investment in education has positive returns. Unfortunately, the current pace and level of investment in India, particularly in primary education, are too low to meet the projected requirements for growth.

• *Terms of trade*: An improvement in the terms of trade can lead to an increase in productivity growth in several ways. It can also be argued that such an improvement in and of itself is equivalent to a rise in productivity growth.[23] With relatively lower import prices, domestic producers are able to afford better technology, capital goods, and intermediate products, which may improve overall productivity. Further, with relatively higher export prices, domestic producers are better motivated to increase total output and thus may realize scale economies. The estimated models in Table 2.14 indicate such positive effects of the terms of trade exist in India with a lag. To the extent improvements in the terms of trade also arise from sectoral shifts in output, India stands to benefit from further industrialization.

• *Current account balance*: The channel of improvement in current account balance to GTFP is considered to be more direct than that of the terms of trade, the changes which are typically restricted to the merchandise trade balance. An increase in foreign receipts over payments could allow domestic firms to invest in more productive technologies and processes, which in turn could improve GTFP. This relationship holds in the model estimated in Table 2.14. However, it can be argued that through the "Laursen–Metzler effect," the terms of trade and current account balance are linked,[24] and therefore some multicollinearity may exist in the model. A simple test reveals very low correlation of 0.2 between changes in TOT and in CAB. Further, since both variables are statistically significant and have the expected signs, the model is consistent.

2.6 Overall assessment and concluding remarks

Policy formulation has come under increasing strain as India has become a more open economy in the 1990s, even though openness still has a long way to go.[25] India has demonstrated the capability to grow faster and the resilience to cope better with an adverse environment. Economic reforms have given it a chance to demonstrate its competitiveness and it has done so. The reforms have improved overall factor productivity, which has raised the base-level growth path. The best is yet to come. In fact, India is viewed as among the few countries with the potential for long-term sustained growth of above 5 percent a year.[26]

Several fronts are open for action to bring sustained growth. Reform is one. While all of the suggested reforms will ultimately support faster growth, it is also the case that they will in turn be facilitated by growth itself. Most notably, growth would boost government revenues; which in turn could reduce the fiscal deficit and the debt level (at least as a percent of GDP). This could lead to a rise in domestic saving, particularly if government non-developmental expenditure is kept in check. The easiest and least costly way of administering a positive confidence shock to jump-start the growth and investment cycle would be through a major commitment to privatization, industrialization, and administrative reforms. It would also be advantageous to move farther on external trade and financial sector liberalization and to allow greater exchange rate flexibility.

In the foregone analysis, several important points emerge that provide a clearer direction to policymakers for ensuring higher and sustained growth. They can be summarized as follows:

- Industrial growth helps both agriculture and services sector growth through demand and supply effects. Therefore, recognizing the benefits of a more open economy and needing policies for great scale economies, far and wide industrialization in India will depend on lowering the tax burden, eliminating the reservation system, and enacting flexible and easy laws for firm entry and exit. An increase in industry's contribution to overall GDP should help counter the growth volatility arising from weather conditions, particularly monsoon effects. Moreover, increasing industrialization, and efficiency therein, could improve India's terms of trade vis-à-vis the rest of the world, which in turn could stimulate TFP growth at an aggregate level.
- A revival in agricultural growth will hinge on expanding infrastructure projects (extending the rural road network, promoting water harvesting and storage, and adopting more efficient irrigation methods such as drip irrigation) and investing in new crop varieties.
- The analysis of factors explaining growth in TFP in India suggests that inflation negatively affects growth by reducing the efficiency of investment

and lowering the level of productivity—at least above a threshold rate of 5.5 percent. A higher literacy rate also appears beneficial to growth in TFP, suggesting that education policy needs to be a top priority in stimulating growth.

- Finally, our results suggest that an improvement in the current account balance positively affects growth, more directly than through the terms of trade. Specifically, the improved balance suggests a lessening of constraints on the ability to generate foreign exchange to purchase necessary imports for improving productivity.

Notes

1. Senior Economist and Director General, National Council of Applied Economic Research (NCAER), respectively. The standard disclaimer applies and the contents are in no way opinions of the NCAER. The authors are thankful to the Canadian International Development Agency, which has supported this research through its grant to the NCAER. The authors are also thankful to Ms. Rachna Sharma for her excellent research assistance.
2. Deaton and Drèze (2002) and Bhalla (2002).
3. Acharya (2002a), Acharya (2002b), and Virmani (2004).
4. See Romer (1986).
5. Countries will have different steady-state income levels. But after controlling for the determinants of the steady-state level, the poorer countries should grow faster. See Sachs and Warner (1995), Barro and Sala-i-Martin (1995).
6. See DeLong (2001), Panagariya (2003), and Rodrik (2002).
7. Industrial Policy Resolution of 1956.
8. Joshi and Little (1994).
9. For an early history of banking in India, see Tandon (1989).
10. The first sign of the payment crisis was evident in the second half of 1990/91, when default on payment of external debt became a serious possibility. Twenty tons of gold were pledged against external liabilities in May 1991 and another 47 tons of gold were pledged in July 1991.
11. The first of three governments during this period lasted for less than a year under V.P. Singh. It gained fame by implementing the Mandal Commission recommendation for government job reservation for backward castes, which led to widespread violence in north India. The second (minority) government, headed by Chandra Shekhar, stayed in power for just more than eight months, despite support from a much larger Congress Party. General elections were held in mid-1991 and while campaigning, Congress leader Rajiv Gandhi was assassinated. Despite the wave of sympathy for the Congress Party, the electorate chose a minority government led by P.V. Narasimha Rao.
12. India's economy has faced a number of challenges since 1997, not only arising from the East Asian crisis, but also from renewed tensions with Pakistan in 1999, the global slowdown following the events of September 11, 2001, and a severe drought in 2002. Excluding the crisis periods, growth in the 1990s would have averaged 6.3 percent.
13. Centre for Monitoring Indian Economy (CMIE), *Corporate Sector* (April 2004).

14. The Central Statistical Organization reports two measures of capital formation: one by economic sector as shown in Table 2.5, and another by industry use. The latter, which is based on expenditure, is used here because it can be related more easily to data in Table 2.6 on gross fixed capital formation. The two measures of capital formation result in errors and omissions and therefore do not match exactly.

15. By international standards, India's fertilizer use per hectare (103.4 kilograms in 2000) and farm mechanization measured by the number of tractors per hectare (0.94 in 1999) are both low. On the other hand, China uses more fertilizers (279.1 kilograms in 2000) than most other developing countries, with developed countries relying on other means for ensuring high yields. In addition, almost 60 percent of India's gross cropped area is not irrigated; this varies from 91 percent in Mizoram to 8 percent in Punjab.

16. It should be noted that the electricity and mining sectors are large consumers of manufactured goods and therefore, despite their relatively low weights in the IIP, a slowdown in these sectors may have large second-order effects on industrial output.

17. The Companies (Amendment) Act 2002 provides primary producers a new form of company organization, that is, one that allows them to produce and market the product in a modern and professional manner at par with other types of producers. The Companies (Second Amendment) Act 2002 establishes a National Company Law Board Tribunal (NCLT), replacing the Board of Industrial and Financial Reconstruction (BIFR), which, among other things, provides better protection to creditors by limiting a company's recourse to delay debt settlement. The Sick Industrial Companies (Special Provisions) Act 1985 was repealed alongside. The Competition Act of 2002 replaces the MRTP Act of 1969. It aims to prohibit a range of anticompetitive practices, including abuse of dominance.

18. See Hulton (2000) and Hulton and Srinivasan (1999).

19. In India's national accounts, employees' contribution to factor income falls in the range of 32–37 percent. However, this excludes income from self-employment and rent from agriculture, which are reported in the national accounts as surpluses and mixed income. Therefore, we take this exclusion into account and assume the contribution of labor to factor income to be approximately 40 percent. As there is little variation in the fully employed labor force, this approximation is not expected to affect the conclusions.

20. Several institutions, including the NCAER, predicted real GDP growth of 6.5–7.0 percent for 2003/04. Due to severe drought, the NCAER's prediction for GDP growth is about 6.0 percent for 2004/05, although this may be on the high side given inflationary pressure on the economy.

21. This result appears consistent with Kannan and Joshi (1998), who calculate an inflation rate of 6 percent as the threshold level before output growth is adversely affected. In a more elaborate model, Singh and Kalirajan (2003) show that negative effects prevail for any inflation rate. Rangarajan (1998) has also stressed the need for maintaining low inflation in India.

22. For example, see *inter alia* Levine and Renelt (1992) and Sala-i-Martin (1997a and 1997b).

23. Laursen and Metzler (1950).

24. See also Obstfeld (1982).

25. Bery (2004).

26. Most recently, this view has been shared by Wilson and Purushothaman (2003) and Rodrik and Subramanian (2004).

References

Acharya, S. 2002a, "Macroeconomic Management in the Nineties," *Economic and Political Weekly* (April 20), pp. 1515–38.

——, 2002b, "India's Medium-Term Growth Prospects," *Economic and Political Weekly* (July 13), pp. 2897–906.

Ambler, S. and E. Cardia, 1997, "Testing the Link Between Inflation and Growth," in proceedings of the Bank of Canada conference on *Price Stability, Inflation Targets and Monetary Policy*, Ottawa.

Barro, R.J., 1995, "Inflation and Economic Growth," NBER Working Paper No. 5326 (Cambridge, MA: National Bureau of Economic Research).

Barro, R.J. and X. Sala-i-Martin, 1995, *Economic Growth* (New York: McGraw Hill).

Bery, S., 2004, "The Next Wave," *Business Standard* (India) (April 13).

Bhalla, S.S., 2002, "Imagine There's No Country: Poverty, Inequality and Growth in the Era of Globalization," (Washington, DC: Institute of International Economics).

Centre for Monitoring Indian Economy, 2004, *Corporate Sector* (April) (Mumbai).

Corden, W.M., 1996, *Pragmatic Orthodoxy: Macroeconomic Policies in Seven East Asian Economies* (San Francisco: International Center for Economic Growth).

Deaton, A. and J. Drèze, 2002, "Poverty and Inequality in India, A Re-Examination," *Economic and Political Weekly* (September 7), pp. 3729–48.

DeLong, J.B., 2001, "India Since Independence: An Analytic Growth Narrative," available via the Internet: http://www.j-bradford-delong.net.

Department of Agriculture and Cooperation (various years), *Agricultural Statistics at a Glance* (New Delhi).

Fertilizer Association of India (various years), *Fertilizer Statistics* (New Delhi).

Fischer, S., 1993, "The Role of Macroeconomic Factors in Growth," *Journal of Monetary Economics*, Vol. 32, pp. 485–512.

Fry, M., C. Goodhart, and A. Almeida, 1996, *Central Banking in Developing Countries: Objectives, Activities and Independence* (London and New York: Routledge).

Ghosh, A. and S. Phillips, 1998, "Inflation, Disinflation, and Growth," IMF Working Paper 98/68 (Washington, DC: International Monetary Fund).

Government of India, Press Information Bureau (New Delhi).

Gregorio, J.D., 1993, "Inflation, Taxation, and Long-Run Growth," *Journal of Monetary Economics*, Vol. 31, pp. 271–98.

Guha-Khasnobis, B. and F. Bari, 2003. "Sources of Growth in South Asian Countries," in *The South Asian Experience with Growth*, ed. by I.J. Ahluwalia and J. Williamson (New Delhi: Oxford University Press).

Hulton, C.R., 2000, "Total Factor Productivity: A Short Biography," NBER Working Paper No. 7471 (Cambridge, MA: National Bureau of Economic Research).

Hulton, C.R. and S. Srinivasan, 1999, "Indian Manufacturing Industry: Elephant or Tiger? Near Evidence on the Asian Miracle," NBER Working Paper No. 7441 (Cambridge, MA: National Bureau of Economic Research).

Joshi, Vijay and I.M.D. Little, 1994, *India: Macroeconomics and Political Economy, 1964–1991* (New Delhi: Oxford University Press).

Kannan, R. and H. Joshi, 1998, "Growth–Inflation Trade-Off: Estimating Threshold Rate of Inflation for India," *Economic and Political Weekly* (October 17–23 and 24–30), pp. 2724–8.

Laursen, S. and L.A. Metzler, 1950, "Flexible Exchange Rates and The Theory of Employment," *The Review of Economics and Statistics*, Vol. 32, No. 4, pp. 281–8.

Levine, R. and D. Renelt, 1992, "A Sensitivity Analysis of Cross-Country Growth Regressions," *The American Economic Review*, Vol. 82, No. 4, pp. 942–63.

Ministry of Finance (various years), *Economic Survey* (New Delhi).

Ministry of Statistics and Programme Implementation (various years), *National Accounts Statistics* (New Delhi: Central Statistical Organization).

Obstfeld, M., 1982, "Aggregate Spending and the Terms of Trade: Is There a Laursen–Metzler Effect?" *Quarterly Journal of Economics*, Vol. 97 (May), pp. 251–70.

Panagariya, A., 2003, "India in the 1980s and the 1990s: A Triumph of Reforms," paper presented at the International Monetary Fund and National Council for Applied Economic Research conference on *A Tale of Two Giants: India's and China's Experience with Reform and Growth*, New Delhi (November 14–16).

Rangarajan, C., 1998, *Indian Economy: Essays on Money and Finance* (New Delhi: UBS Publishers' Distributors Ltd).

Reserve Bank of India, 2003a, *Annual Report* (Mumbai).

——, 2003b, *Handbook of Statistics on the Indian Economy 2002–03* (Mumbai).

——, (various years), *Handbook of Statistics on the Indian Economy* (Mumbai).

——, (various years), *Report on Currency and Finance* (Mumbai).

Rodrik, D. 2002, "Institutions, Integration, and Geography: In Search of the Deep Determinants of Economic Growth," available via the Internet: http://ksghome. harvard.edu/~drodrik/growthintro.pdf.

——, and A. Subramanian, 2004, "Why India Can Grow at 7 Percent a Year or More: Projections and Reflections," *Economic and Political Weekly* (April 17), pp. 1591–6.

Romer, P.M., 1993, "Idea Gaps and Object Gaps in Economic Development," *Journal of Monetary Economics*, Vol. 32, No. 3, pp. 543–73.

——, 1986, "Increasing Returns and Long-Run Growth," *Journal of Political Economy*, Vol. 94, No. 5, pp. 1002–37.

Sachs, J.D. and A.M. Warner, 1995, "Economic Convergence and Economic Policies," NBER Working Paper No. 5039 (Cambridge, MA: National Bureau of Economic Research).

Sala-i-Martin, X.X., 1997a, "I Just Ran Four Million Regressions," NBER Working Paper No. 6252 (Cambridge, MA: National Bureau of Economic Research).

——, 1997b, "I Just Ran Two Million Regressions," *The American Economic Review*, Vol. 87, No. 2, pp. 178–83.

Sarel, M., 1996, "Nonlinear Effects of Inflation on Economic Growth," *International Monetary Fund Staff Papers*, Vol. 43, No. 1, pp. 199–215.

Singh, K. and K.P. Kalirajan, 2003, "The Inflation-Growth Nexus in India: An Empirical Analysis," *Journal of Policy Modeling*, Vol. 25, pp. 377–96.

Srinivasan, T.N., 2000, *Eight Lectures on India's Economic Reforms* (New Delhi: Oxford University Press).

Tandon, P., 1989, *Banking Century: A Short History of Banking in India* (New Delhi: Viking).

United Nations Development Programme, 2002, *Human Development Report* (New York).

Virmani, A., 2004, "India's Economic Growth: From Socialistic Rate of Growth to Bhartiya Rate of Growth," Indian Council for Research on International Economic Relations (ICRIER) Working Paper No. 122 (New Delhi: ICRIER).

Waldman, A., 2003, "All Eyes Now on India as It Rides the Fast Growth Track," *Business Standard* (India) (October 21).

Wilson, D. and Purushothaman, R., 2003, "Dreaming With BRICs: The Path to 2050," Goldman Sachs Global Economics Paper No. 99 (New York: Goldman Sachs).

World Bank, 2003, *World Development Indicators CD ROM 2003* (Washington, DC).

—— (various years), *World Development Report* (Washington, DC).

3
China's Economic Growth and Poverty Reduction (1978–2002)

Hu Angang, Hu Linlin, and Chang Zhixiao[1]

3.1 Introduction

This chapter summarizes and evaluates trends of China's poverty reduction in the period 1978–2002. China has obtained great achievements in poverty reduction since 1978 and made a major contribution to world poverty reduction. However, poverty reduction in China has not always come with economic growth, and its pace has slowed since the mid-1980s. In addition, some new forms of poverty have arisen.

In the following sections, we analyze the main reasons for the above phenomenon, namely the decline in the quality of the economic growth and the rise in the degree of inequality. The final section asserts that a new strategy to reduce poverty (2003–15) should be worked out, including adjusting the national poverty line, identifying three types of poverty (income poverty, human poverty, and knowledge poverty), and attaching importance to increasing the opportunities for the disadvantaged groups to participate in and experience the benefits of social activities. In addition, the new strategy would involve designing an effective and comprehensive antipoverty framework so as to make antipoverty policies correspond with macroeconomic and regional development policies.

3.2 Trends in and evaluation of poverty reduction (1978–2002)

3.2.1 Progress in poverty reduction

China's economy has been in the take off stage since 1978, with an average growth rate of per capita gross domestic product (GDP) of 8.1 percent. Just as Amartya Sen has analyzed, in the past two decades, China's economy has developed very rapidly. The growth of China's per capita income is much faster than that of any other region in the world, which is rather terrific for such a large country. The experience of China has been totally different from that of well-known countries or regions with rapid economic growth such as Hong Kong and

Singapore. Unlike China, which has a very large rural population, Hong Kong and Singapore are actually cities. It is an extraordinary achievement for such a large country with such great regional differences to obtain such a high growth rate.[2]

Over the same period, there has been a large decrease in China's rural poverty population. According to China's national poverty line, the rural poverty population dropped from 250 million in 1978 to 28 million in 2002, decreasing by 88.7 percent or an average of 9.2 million per year (Table 3.1). According to the international poverty line, currently a daily per capita cost of living of below US$1, the World Bank estimates that China's rural poverty population dropped from 280 million in 1990 to 124 million in 1999, decreasing by 55.7 percent or an average of 22.3 million per year (Table 3.2). These different estimates demonstrate that China, as the country with the world's largest overall and poverty population, is making unprecedented achievements in poverty reduction.

China's achievements in poverty reduction also have made a huge contribution to the world poverty reduction. The World Bank estimates that the number of people living below the international poverty line in China dropped from 542 million to 375 million in the 1980s. In the corresponding period, the poverty population of the entire world (mainly referring to developing areas) decreased by 98 million. Thus, China accounted for 167 percent of world poverty reduction. In the 1990s, China's poverty population decreased by 115 million and thus was attributable for 123 percent of world poverty reduction. It is also estimated by the World Bank that China's poverty population will drop to 74 million by 2015, representing a net decrease of 150 million compared with 1999 (Table 3.3), or accounting for 42 percent of projected world poverty reduction. In 1990, China's poverty population accounted for 29 percent of that of the world, but only around 19 percent in 1999. This number is expected to fall to 9 percent by 2015.

Table 3.1   China: growth, poverty reduction, and farmers' welfare, 1978–2002 (average annual percentage change, unless otherwise indicated)

Period	Annual poverty reduction[a]	Real per capita GDP	Farmers' per capita consumption	Farmers' per capita net income
1978–85	17.9	8.3	10.0	15.1
1985–90	8.0	6.2	2.5	3.0
1990–97	5.0	9.9	8.0	5.0
1997–2002	4.4	7.7	3.4	3.8
1978–2002	9.2	8.1	5.6	7.2

[a] Government estimate, in millions.

Sources: National Bureau of Statistics, *China Statistical Abstract* (2002) and *The Statistical Communiqué of China's National Economy and Social Development in 2003* (March).

Table 3.2 China: rural poverty population and poverty rates, 1978–2002

Year	Rural population	Poverty population (in millions)		Poverty rate (in percent)	
		Official	World Bank	Official	World Bank
1978	790	250	—	33.1	—
1984	803	128	—	15.9	—
1985	808	125	—	15.5	—
1986	811	131	—	16.1	—
1987	816	122	—	14.9	—
1988	824	96	—	11.7	—
1989	832	106	—	12.7	—
1990	841	85	280	10.1	33.3
1991	853	94	287	11.0	33.6
1992	848	80	274	9.4	32.3
1993	852	80	266	9.3	31.2
1994	855	70	237	8.2	27.7
1995	859	65	200	7.6	23.3
1996	864	60	138	6.9	16.0
1997	866	50	124	5.8	14.3
1998	869	42	—	4.8	—
1999	870	34	—	3.7	—
2000	808	22	—	—	—
2001	796	27	—	—	—
2002	—	28	—	—	—

Sources: National Bureau of Statistics (NBS), *China Statistical Abstract* (2002) for rural population; NBS, *A Monitoring Report of China's Rural Poverty* (2000, p. 7) for official poverty data for 1978–2000; NBS, *The Statistical Communiqué of China's National Economic and Social Development in 2003* for official poverty data for 2001 and 2002; and World Bank, *World Development Indicators 2003*.

Asia as a whole contains the world's largest and most condensed poverty population. Among the five Asian countries with the most condensed poverty population (China, India, Pakistan, Indonesia, and Bangladesh), the ratio of the poverty to total population is the lowest in China (Table 3.4). Comparing China with India—the two countries in the world with the largest poverty populations—the share of people in China living on less than US$1 a day is 25.7 percentage points lower than that of India, while the share of people in China living on less than US$2 a day is 32.5 percentage points lower than in India. In broader terms, the ratio between China's and India's per capita GDP (on a purchasing power parity basis) is currently 1.6 to 1.0.

These statistics demonstrate that China has experienced a profound period in history with its large decrease in the poverty population over the past two decades. Based on data for 1999, it has brought a reversal of the

Table 3.3 Number of persons living on less than US$1 per day

Region	1990	1999	2015[a]
Poverty population (in millions)			
East Asia and the Pacific	486	279	80
(excluding China)	110	57	7
Europe and Central Asia	6	24	7
Middle East and North Africa	48	57	47
Latin America and Caribbean region	5	6	8
South Asia	506	488	264
Sub-Saharan Africa	241	315	404
Total	1,292	1,169	809
(excluding China)	917	945	635
China	375	224	74
Poverty population (in percent of total)			
East Asia and the Pacific	37.6	23.9	9.9
(excluding China)	8.5	4.9	0.9
Europe and Central Asia	0.5	2.1	0.9
Middle East and North Africa	3.7	4.9	5.8
Latin America and Caribbean region	0.4	0.5	1.0
South Asia	39.2	41.7	32.6
Sub-Saharan Africa	18.7	26.9	49.9
Total	100.0	100.0	100.0
(excluding China)	71.0	80.8	90.9
China	29.0	19.2	9.1

[a] Projected.

Source: World Bank, *Global Economic Prospects and the Development Countries* (2003, Table 1.9).

Table 3.4 Poverty population in select Asian countries[a] (in percent of total population, unless otherwise indicated)

Region	GDP per capita (1998)[b]	Population living below national poverty line		Share of population living on	
				Less than US$1 per day	Less than US$2 per day
Bangladesh	1,423	42.7 (1991/92)	35.6 (1995/96)	29.1 (1996)	77.8 (1996)
China	3,356	6.0 (1996)	4.6 (1998)	18.5 (1998)	53.7 (1998)
India	2,101	40.9 (1992)	35.0 (1994)	44.2 (1997)	86.2 (1997)
Indonesia	2,806	15.7 (1996)	27.1 (1999)	7.7 (1999)	55.3 (1999)
Pakistan	1,794	34.0 (1991)	— —	31.0 (1996)	84.7 (1996)

[a] Figures in parentheses represent year of observation.
[b] In US dollars on a purchasing power parity basis.

Source: World Bank, *World Development Report 2000/2001* (p. 64).

Table 3.5 World poverty population and poverty rates, 1950–99

	1950	1960	1970	1980	1992	1999
Poverty population (in millions)[a]	1,806	1,947	2,201	2,427	2,800	2,320
Population in extreme poverty (in millions)[b]	1,376	1,330	1,305	1,390	1,294	1,169
Poverty rate (in percent)		71.9	64.3	60.1	55.0	51.3	38.1
Extreme poverty rate (in percent)		54.8	44.0	35.6	31.5	23.7	13.3

[a] Refers to persons whose cost of living per day is less than US$2.
[b] Refers to persons whose cost of living per day is less than US$1.

Sources: Bourguignom and Morrisso (2002) for 1950–92 and World Bank, *Global Economic Prospects and the Development Countries* (2003, Table 1.9) for 1999.

trend rise in the world poverty population over the past five decades and has resulted in an absolute decrease in the poverty population for the first time (Table 3.5). That is to say, without China's efforts of poverty reduction, or excluding China's poverty population, the poverty population of the world would have increased from 848 million in 1980 to 917 million in 1990 and 945 million in 1999.

3.2.2   Factors explaining the large poverty decrease

The primary reasons for China's achievements in poverty reduction are as follows:

• The continuous high economic growth is the main basis for poverty reduction. The average annual growth rate of per capita GDP of China was 8.1 percent in the period 1978–2002 (see Table 3.1). The period represents the longest lasting time with the highest growth rate of per capita GDP and the largest population that benefited from it. It corresponds to a doubling of per capita GDP every 8.6 years and is 5.4 times the average annual growth rate of global per capita output in the same period (1.5 percent). According to World Bank estimates, it took Britain 58 years to double its per capita income (1780–1838), the United States 47 years (1839–86), Japan 34 years (1885–1919), and South Korea 11 years (1966–77). In China during the period 1978–2002, the annual growth rate of rural population's consumption level (the majority of China's population) was 5.6 percent and the annual growth rate of per capita net income of farmers was 7.2 percent, corresponding to a doubling of their per capita income every 9.7 years (see Table 3.1) and a major reason for China's great strides in rural poverty reduction. In 1978, nearly 100 percent of peasant households had a per capita net income below 500 yuan (Y); in 1985 it was 78 percent; in 1990 it was 35 percent; and in 2001 only 2.5 percent. In 1985, nearly 98 percent of peasant

Table 3.6   China: rural households grouped by annual per capita net income, 1978–2001 (in percent of total rural households)

	1978	1985	1990	1995	2001
Grouping by net income					
Less than 100 yuan	33.3	1.0	0.3	0.2	—
100–300	64.3	36.9	8.3	1.1	—
300–500	2.4[a]	39.8	26.4	3.8	2.5[b]
More than 500 yuan	—	22.3	65.0	95.0	97.5
More than 1,000 yuan	—	2.3	22.8	69.8	86.8

[a] For 1978, more than 300 yuan.
[b] For 2001, less than 500 yuan.

Sources: State Statistical Bureau, *China Social Statistics* (1990) for 1978 and 1985; National Bureau of Statistics, *China Statistical Yearbook* (2000) for 1990 and 1995; and *China Statistical Abstract* (2002) for 2001.

households had a per capita net income of less than Y1000, but by 2001 this was down to around 13 percent (Table 3.6), which shows that the extremely poor and the poor have decreased sharply.

•   A great deal of rural labor force has transferred to nonagricultural industries. More and more people are employed in village and township enterprises, rising from 28.3 million in 1978 to 130.9 million in 2001 (9.2 percent and 26.7 percent of total rural work force, respectively). In addition, 38.2 million people worked in private rural enterprises or were self-employed in 2001, accounting for 7.7 percent of the total rural work force (Figure 3.1).

•   China has experienced a speeding up of urbanization, resulting in the largest population movement in the world since its reform policies and opening up began. This includes population migration and population floating. Population migration refers to the change of one's permanent residence. In China's case, it refers to changing one's household register, resulting in a transformation from an agricultural population to a nonagricultural population by directly recruiting personnel for employment from rural areas, such as graduates of junior college and technical secondary school, demobilized servicemen, professional personnel, and the like. Population floating refers to a person's residence remaining permanent, but the person himself (or herself) leaving that place and straddling across a given administrative region, temporarily staying there and engaging in various activities. The activity of rural laborers going to cities to work is considered a type of population floating. In the period 1982–2000, 206.8 million people moved from rural to urban areas, equal to 45.0 percent of the average urban population in the same period and 84.6 percent of the net increase in the urban population (Table 3.7). In the same period, 109.6 million rural laborers moved to cities, equal to 45.8 percent of total town labor force and 94.3 percent of newly

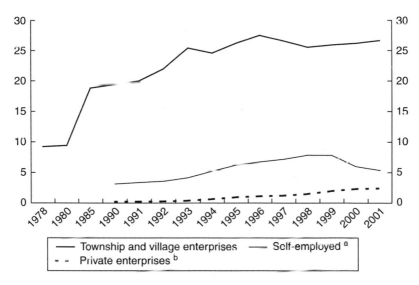

Figure 3.1   China: rural employment in nonagricultural sectors, 1978–2001[a] (in percent of total rural employment)

[a] Annual data from 1990 onward.
[b] From 1990.

Source: National Bureau of Statistics, *China Statistical Yearbook* (2002, p. 121).

Table 3.7   China: population and labor force movement from rural to urban areas, 1982–2000 (in millions)

Period	Change in the size of the total urban population	Size of the moving population	Size of the moving labor force	Average moving population per year	Average moving labor force per year
1982–90	87.2	65.1	32.1	8.1	4.0
1990–95	49.8	39.0	20.2	7.8	4.0
1996–2000	107.3	102.4	57.3	20.3	11.5
1990–2000	157.1	141.4	77.5	14.1	7.8
1982–2000	244.3	206.8	109.6	11.5	6.1

Sources: Ren (2003) and National Bureau of Statistics, *China Statistical Abstract 2002* (urban population only).

increased town labor force. From the above, we can see that the scales of moving population and labor force are enlarging rapidly. In the 1980s, the moving population was 8.1 million and moving labor force was 4.0 million, while in the 1990s, the numbers were 14.1 million and 7.8 million,

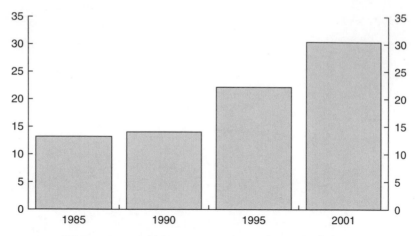

Figure 3.2 China: farmers' wage income (in percent of total income)

Source: National Bureau of Statistics, *China Statistical Abstract* (2002, p. 97).

respectively. Some were agricultural population who transformed into non-agricultural population, while the majority of the others were rural laborers who went to cities for work. As a result, wage income has become one of the most important sources of farmers' income. The ratio of farmers' wage income to their total income rose to 30.4 percent in 2001 from 13.2 percent in 1985 (Figure 3.2), which shows that peasants have partly enjoyed the benefits brought by urbanization and nonagricultural industries.

- Export-orientation and opening up policies have been implemented in China, with total export volume increasing rapidly, especially labor-intensive products, which has played an important role in expanding employment opportunities and poverty reduction. The total value of exports was US$325.6 billion in 2002—an increase of 32 times that in 1978. The share of exports in GDP has also increased rapidly, from 4.6 percent in 1978 to 23.0 percent in 2001. In addition, China has attracted considerable foreign investment and actively pursued economic globalization. These factors have contributed to poverty reduction, especially the foreign investment in Guangdong and Zhejiang, which attracts large quantities of surplus agricultural labor force in different areas. The floating labor force of Guangdong alone accounts for 39 percent of that of the whole country.

- The quality of human capital has been greatly improved since reform, as evident by the attainment of higher education levels and improved health conditions. Human capital accumulation has played an important role in improving people's living standard and aiding poverty reduction. As shown in Table 3.8, average schooling years of the population above age 15 has increased from 4.64 years in 1982 to 7.11 years in 2000. The illiterate population

Table 3.8 China: basic human capital indicators

	Year of observation[a]			
	1982	1990	1995	2000
Average schooling years (for population above age 15)	4.6	5.5	6.1	7.1
Illiterate people in total population (in percent)	22.8	15.9	12.0	6.7
Illiterate and semiliterate rural people in total population (in percent)	27.9 (1985)	20.7	13.5	9.0 (1999)
Infant mortality rate (in percent)	37.6 (1981)	32.9	33.0 (1996)	28.4
Average life expectancy (in years)	67.8 (1981)	68.6	70.8 (1996)	71.4

[a] Unless otherwise indicated in parentheses.

Sources: National Bureau of Statistics, *China Statistical Abstract 2002* and Li Chunbo (2001) for average schooling years only.

as a share of the total population has decreased largely, falling from 22.8 percent in 1982 to 6.7 percent in 2002; over the same period, the absolute illiterate population has decreased from 231.8 million to 84.9 million, with the rural illiterate and semiliterate population also falling. In addition, the infant mortality rate has decreased from 37.6 percent in 1982 to 28.4 percent in 2000, while the average life expectancy has increased from 67.8 years in 1981 to 71.4 years in 2000. This demonstrates the important progress in the area of education and medical care, and the complementary relationship between economic and social progress.[3]

• Antipoverty actions have been adopted by the government of China. The government made a political commitment to reduce poverty in the early 1980s and has reflected poverty reduction goals and plans in the national economic plans. With economic development, the central government's willingness to aid the poor has become stronger and stronger, and resources for helping them have increased (Table 3.9). In order to protect the livelihoods of the farmers, the government adjusted agricultural policies through a gradual increase and loosening of the prices of agricultural products. As a result, the purchase prices of agricultural products greatly increased in the 1980s and the middle of the 1990s. By 1996, the price index of agricultural products was 5.5 times higher than in 1978, with an average annual growth rate of 9.9 percent (Figure 3.3). In the corresponding period, the retail price index of rural industrial products was up 2.9 times, with an average annual growth rate of 6.1 percent. The growth rate of farmers' actual earnings per year (the growth rate of the price index of agricultural products minus that of industrial products) was 3.8 percent.

Table 3.9 China: national antipoverty fund, 1986–2000

	Interest-subsidized loans[a]	Work instead of relief[a]	Developing fund[a]	Total		
Year				In millions of yuan	In percent of GDP	In yuan per capita[b]
1986	230	90	100	420	0.41	32
1990	300	60	100	460	0.25	54
1991	350	180	100	630	0.29	67
1992	410	160	100	670	0.25	83
1993	350	300	110	760	0.22	101
1994	450	400	120	970	0.21	194
1995	450	400	130	980	0.17	151
1996	550	400	130	1,080	0.16	180
1997	850	400	280	1,530	0.21	306
1998	1,000	500	330	1,830	0.23	436
1999	1,500	650	430	2,580	0.31	756
2000	—	—	—	2,600	0.29	1,182

[a] Values are in millions of yuan.
[b] For poverty population.

Sources: Jiang and Gao, *The Financial Aid to the Poor by the Central Government* (1998) for 1986–97; National Bureau of Statistics, *A Monitoring Report on China's Rural Poverty* (2000) for 1998–99; and authors' estimates for 2000.

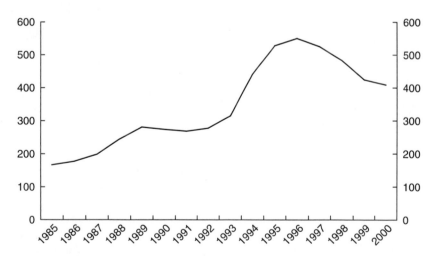

Figure 3.3 China: purchase price index of agricultural products, 1985–2000 (1978 = 100)

Source: National Bureau of Statistics, *China Statistical Yearbook* (2001, p. 282).

3.3 Slowing poverty reduction in the 1990s: an analysis

3.3.1 Background on slowing poverty reduction

China's per capita output and income greatly improved in the first several years of economic reform (1978–85), and income poverty correspondingly decreased by a large margin. According to the official poverty line, the rural poverty population decreased by 200 million in the period 1978–2002, half of which occurred in the period 1978–85. In this period, the total poverty population decreased annually by an average of 17.9 million, and the average annual growth rate of per capita GDP was 8.3 percent. The growth rate of farmers' per capita consumption level and per capita income was up to 10.0 percent and 15.1 percent, respectively. The rural population, especially the poverty population, was the main beneficiary of rapid economic growth in this period. However, in the second half of the 1980s, although China maintained a fairly high rate of economic growth, there are some indications that the pace of poverty reduction in rural areas slowed considerably. The average annual decrease in the poverty population fell by half to 8 million. In addition, the average growth rate of farmers' consumption level per year was only 2.5 percent, and the average growth rate of farmers' per capita net income was only 3.0 percent (see Table 3.1).

In the 1990s (referring specifically to the period 1990–97), China's annual growth rate of per capita GDP averaged 9.9 percent, greatly higher than that of the early period reform (1978–85). Despite rapid growth, the decline in rural poverty population slowed to 5 million annually, less than a third of that in the period 1978–85. The growth rate of farmers' consumption was also far lower than GDP growth rate (see Table 3.1). During the period 1997–2002, the average annual growth rate of per capita GDP remained high at 7.7 percent, but the average annual decrease in the rural poverty population slowed to 4.4 million. The average annual growth rate of farmers' per capita net income was 3.8 percent in the period 1998–2002, lower than the 7.2 percent in the reform period as a whole (1978–2002).

The decrease of China's rural poverty population in the 1990s has come as a result of a fall in the poverty line. Compared internationally, the income poverty line prescribed by the Chinese government is low. Currently, it is defined as per capita net income below Y300 (the fixed price in 1990), only corresponding to 66 percent of the international standard. Using the Chinese standard, the ratio of farmers' per capita net income to the official poverty line has decreased rapidly, from 43.7 percent in 1990 to 26.3 percent in 2002; its ratio to per capita GDP also has declined significantly, from 18.4 percent in 1990 to 7.9 percent in 2002 (Table 3.10). Based on this standard, the poverty population estimated by the government is much less than China's real poverty population, thus antipoverty achievements are overstated (Box 3.1). According to the official poverty line, there were still 22 million people stricken by poverty in rural areas at the end of 2000 (see Table 3.2).

Table 3.10   China: official poverty line, 1978–2002

Year	Official poverty line[a] In yuan per capita, at current prices	Official poverty line[a] In percent of per capita GDP	Ratio of official poverty line to farmers' per capita income (in percent)
1978	100	33.0	74.9
1985	205	24.0	51.6
1990	300	18.4	43.7
1991	304	16.2	42.9
1992	317	13.9	40.4
1993	350	11.9	38.0
1994	440	11.2	36.0
1995	530	10.9	33.6
1996	580	10.4	30.1
1997	600	9.9	28.7
1998	625	9.9	28.9
1999	625	9.5	28.3
2000	625	9.5	27.7
2001	630	8.8	25.4
2002	627	7.9	25.3

[a] China's current rural poverty line was calculated based on a survey of 67,000 farm inhabitants' income and expenditure by the Rural Research Office of the NBS in 1986. The rural poverty line was measured as an annual per capita net income of Y205 in 1985. The standard has been adjusted each year since then according to the price index.

Sources: State Statistical Bureau, *Rural Residents Survey Yearbook* (1986) and National Bureau of Statistics, *China Statistical Abstract* (2002, pp. 15, 91).

Box 3.1   Overview of China's poverty line

China currently has a broader gap than any other country between its national poverty line and the international poverty line. The poverty population in 1998 was estimated according to China's national poverty line (per capita annual income of less than Y650). At the time, it accounted for 4.6 percent of China's total population. The poverty-stricken population was estimated for the same year according to the international poverty line (daily per capita living cost of less that US$1) and accounted for 18.5 percent of the total population—a difference of about 14 percentage points.[a] Based on international standards, the poverty-stricken and other low-income population is likely underestimated by at least 100 million in China.

The following table shows China's rural poverty-stricken population estimated according to different schemes. Scheme A is the current national poverty line; Scheme B sets the poverty line at per capita annual income of Y1000; and

Scheme C sets it at Y1500. The result is that if Scheme B is adopted, the estimation is between that of the World Bank and the national poverty line; if Scheme C is adopted, the estimation of the poverty population is close to that made by the World Bank.

The national poverty line	Poverty line/per capita GDP (in percent)	The estimated rural poverty-stricken population (10,000)	Rural poverty-stricken population/ total rural population (in percent)	Rural poverty-stricken population/ total population (in percent)
Scheme A: Y650	8.6	2,713	3.40	2.1
Scheme B: Y1,000	13.2	10,518	13.22	8.2
Scheme C: Y1,500	19.9	24,044	30.22	18.8

We also show the proportion of poverty households in total households. According to the *China Statistical Abstract of 2002*, households with income below Y1000 accounted for 13.3 percent of investigated households in 2001. Based on new population data, which estimated the total number of rural households at 79.6 million in 2001, the number of households living on less than Y1000 can be worked out, as can the number of households living on less than Y1500.

2001			
Per capita income (in yuan)	Accounting for per capita GDP (in percent)	Proportion of poverty population (in percent)	Total poverty population (10,000)
100–600	1.3–8.0	3.87	3,078
600–800	8.0–10.6	3.88	3,087
800–1,000	10.6–13.3	5.47	4,352
Sub-total		13.22	10,518
1,000–1,200	13.3–15.9	6.30	5,012
1,200–1,300	15.9–17.2	3.45	2,745
1,300–1,500	17.2–19.9	7.25	5,786
Total (sum)		30.22	24,044

[a] In other places, country or regional estimates of the poverty line in fact exceed the international poverty line. In Brazil, for example, the poverty population accounts for 22 percent of its total population according to its national poverty line, but accounts for only 9 percent of its total population according to the international poverty line; in West Bengal (India), the two proportions are 35.6 percent and 29.1 percent, respectively; and in Indonesia, they are 27.1 percent and 7.7 percent, respectively.

The objective of providing 80 million poor people with adequate food and clothing promised in "The Eight-Seven Anti-Poverty Plan" set down in 1994 has not been met.

In China's urban areas, the poverty rate gradually increased in the 1990s, especially the extreme poverty rate and dire poverty rate. According to Khan's (1999) estimation, the extreme poverty rate increased from 2.2 percent in 1988 to 4.1 percent in 1995, and dire poverty rate from 1.3 percent to 2.7 percent. Khan estimates that the poorest population exceeded 10 million in 2001.[4] According to our estimation, the urban poverty population has risen to 24 million, which along with the rest of the population with low income (defined as per capita income of less than Y2497 a year) accounts for 5 percent of total (formal) urban population. To one's fear, the number of laid-off workers and unemployed people has sharply increased and the amount of defaulted payments to employees and retirees has also risen, leading to a rapid increase in the poverty population and resulting in the marginalization of these people. This phenomenon does not only cause serious economic problems, but also imposes grim challenges on China's society in the future.

3.3.2   Analysis of the characteristics of poverty since the 1990s

Urban–rural distribution of poverty population

Most of the poverty population lives in rural areas, where the degree of poverty is much deeper than in urban areas. One of the major reasons for this disparity is that there is a great gap between per capita income of urban residents and that of rural residents, which surpasses that in common developing countries. In addition, poor residents in urban areas enjoy a small amount of living insurance provided by the government, while most of rural poverty population has no other living insurance besides their own land.

Regional distribution of poverty population

Since the 1990s, China's rural poverty has begun to demonstrate regional and marginal characteristics. The poverty rate is highest in the western areas of China, where poverty population is the most concentrated and the degree of poverty the most acute in the country. According to the data given by the Rural Research Office of National Bureau of Statistics (NBS) of China in *A Monitoring Report on China's Rural Poverty* (2000), about two-thirds of the total poverty population resided in eastern and middle provinces in 1986 (based on 592 national poverty counties prescribed that year). Since then, the poverty population of these regions has decreased rapidly. By 2000, only 10 percent of poverty population resided in the eastern regions and 28 percent in the middle provinces. On the other hand, 62 percent of the poverty population resided in 12 western provinces in 2002, representing an increase of

590,000 poor households and a further regional condensing of China's poverty population. According to official poverty line, poverty rate in the west is far higher than that in the east. In 2000, poverty rate in middle-west provinces such as Heilongjiang, Shanxi, Inner Mongolia, Shaanxi, Gansu, Yunnan, Tibet, Guizhou, Qinghai, Ningxia was greater than 10 percent, while poverty rate in the eight eastern provinces (Shanghai, Beijing, Tianjin, Zhejiang, etc.) was less than 1 percent. Extreme poverty has been thoroughly diminished in all regions. However, the overall rate of poverty occurrence in the west is about 30 percent higher than in other parts of the country. Likewise, per capita income of poverty farmers in the west is also far lower than in the east. The poverty rates in poor regions are especially high when these regions have been struck by natural disasters and suffered overall economic decline.

The multidimensional characteristic of poverty

In the past two decades, the strategies of poverty reduction of the Chinese government have been mainly focused on eliminating income poverty, especially that in the national poverty counties. It is a reasonable policy choice, and it is a very necessary one, too. However, in entering the new century, the problems of new types of poverty such as human poverty and knowledge poverty are increasingly extruding; the affected population of which is far much larger than that of income poverty. Such types of poverty have gradually become major types of poverty. Human poverty refers to the lack of basic human ability, such as illiteracy, malnutrition, short life expectancy, low level of maternal and infant health and the harms caused by preventable diseases, and so on.[5] Knowledge poverty is a new form of poverty as the human race enters the knowledge-based society in the twenty-first century, defined as the problems caused by people's universal lack of the abilities to obtain information, communicate with each other, utilize and create knowledge and information, or the lack of basic rights and chances to obtain these abilities. These three types of poverty are not independent of one another, but interrelated. The poverty population is not always faced with only one type of poverty, but can face the problems of multidimensional and interdependent poverty. One of the indices used to measure human poverty is Human Poverty Index (HPI),[6] as shown in Figure 3.4 for China and several other countries. In addition, literacy rates across regions in China demonstrate the great gap in knowledge poverty (Figure 3.5).

3.3.3 Factors affecting poverty reduction since the 1990s

The relationship between economic growth and poverty reduction is not simplistic. It is not the speed of economic growth but the quality of economic growth that actually plays an important role. Since the 1990s, the economic development of many developing countries, especially those of East Asia, demonstrates that although economic growth plays an important supporting role in social development, rapid economic growth can have

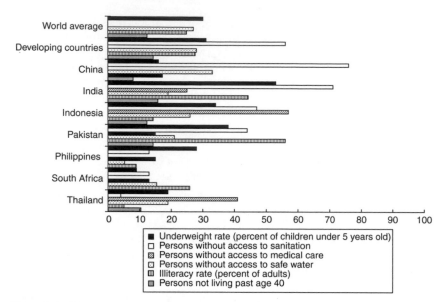

Figure 3.4   Human poverty index[a] (in percent of total population, unless otherwise indicated)

[a] Latest available observation prior to 2000.

Source: United Nations Development Programme, *Overcoming Human Poverty* (2000).

destructive effects on the environment and resources. Moreover, if economic growth is not based on a good system environment, various market distortions, inefficient investment and prevailing corruption will come into being; the public, especially the poverty population will be deprived of the chance and ability to participate in market activities and political decision making. Therefore, we must comprehensively survey the complex relationship between economic growth and poverty reduction.

Although China's economy has been growing very rapidly since the 1990s, the quality of the economic growth is declining and income inequality rising, which still results in decreased proportion of the benefits of growth being obtained by the poverty population. This is an important reason for the slowdown in the pace of poverty reduction in China.

Quality of growth and degree of poverty reduction

The growth rate of per capita GDP in China in the 1990s is the highest in recorded history, so why is the achievement of poverty reduction so limited? This is mainly because as the quality of economic growth has declined, China's poverty stratum has not directly benefited from the high overall growth rate, which can be shown by the following points.

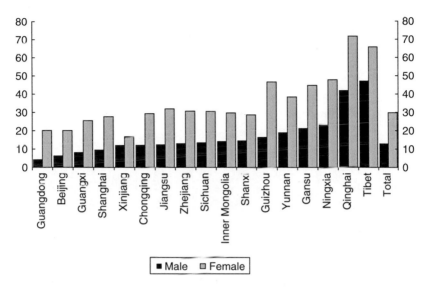

Figure 3.5 China: illiterate and semi-illiterate persons in select provinces (in percent of total male or female adult population over age 15)

Source: National Bureau of Statistics, *China Population Statistics Yearbook* (1998, p. 39).

The growth of per capita income and consumption lags far behind the growth of GDP per capita. In the past two decades, a rather complex relationship has emerged between China's growth rate of per capita income and that of per capita GDP (Figure 3.6). In the period 1978–85, the average annual growth rate of per capita GDP was 8.4 percent. During the same period, the growth rates of per capita consumption level and per capita net income of rural residents were 9.7 percent and 15.1 percent, respectively, higher than the growth rate of per capita GDP. They were also much higher than the growth rate of per capita consumption level of urban residents (1.3 percent), which demonstrates that the broad masses of farmers directly benefited from the economic growth in the early stage of reform. In the period 1985–2001, the growth rate of per capita GDP "separated from" that of per capita income; the growth rate of per capita consumption level of both rural and urban residents and the growth rate of per capita income of the rural population are obviously lower than that of per capita GDP (except during the period 1997–2001 when the growth rate of per capita income of urban population is slightly higher than that of per capita GDP).

The share of agricultural output in GDP has also greatly declined. Calculated at current prices, the share of agriculture in GDP fell from 28.4 percent in 1985 to 18.1 percent in 2002 (Figure 3.7). Along with this,

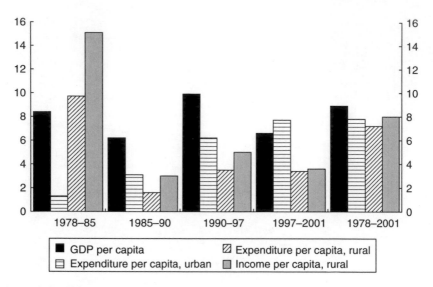

Figure 3.6 China: per capita GDP and consumption, 1978–2001 (average annual percentage change)

Sources: National Bureau of Statistics, *China Statistical Yearbook* (2002) and *Comprehensive Statistical Data and Materials on 50 Years of New China* (1999).

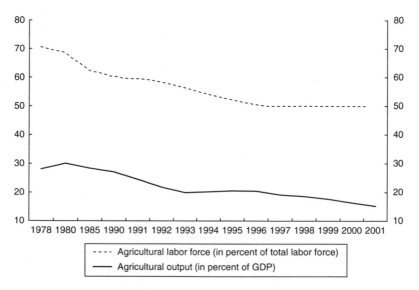

Figure 3.7 China: agricultural labor and output, 1978–2001[a]

[a] Annual data from 1990 onward.

Source: National Bureau of Statistics, *China Statistical Yearbook* (2002).

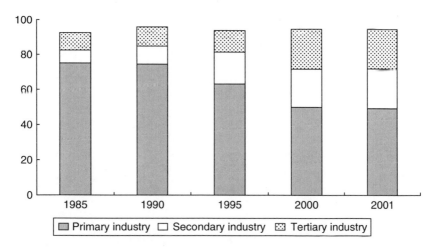

Figure 3.8   China: sources of farmers' per capita net income[a] (in percent of total)

[a] The sum is less than 100 percent due to unidentified components.

Source: National Bureau of Statistics, *China Statistical Yearbook* (2002).

the proportion of farmers' agricultural income in their total income has declined continuously, from 75 percent in 1985, and the proportion decreased to 50 percent in 2000 (Figure 3.8). Furthermore, the share of per capita farmers' income to per capita GDP has fallen steadily, from a high of 46.5 percent in 1985 to 31.1 percent in 1994, a level near which it has since stayed (see Figure 3.9). The proportion of agricultural labor force in total labor force also decreased continuously until 1995, but since then has remained at about 50 percent (see Figure 3.7). This has led to a rapid decrease in the ratio of agricultural labor productivity to national average labor productivity since 1985 (with the exception of a slight increase in the mid-1990s).

The opportunities for employment in rural areas are declining. Since the 1990s, the growth in employment opportunities has been greater for urban areas than in rural areas. In the period 1990–2001, the urban employment grew by 40.5 percent, while rural employment grew by only 2.9 percent. The development of village and township enterprises has also undergone serious setback. The number of people who were employed in rural areas increased by 21 percent in the period 1978–85 (Figure 3.10), but then decreased by 6 percent in the period 1990–2001. In 1996–98 alone, rural employment declined by 8 million, as a large number of workers were laid off and lost their jobs. At the same time, limits were imposed on rural laborers entering cities, which have had a very serious effect on rural poverty reduction in two important ways. First, the pressure of employment competition will become larger, and second, the income remitted from urban to rural areas will decline. Since many cities set limits on rural labor inflows or adopt

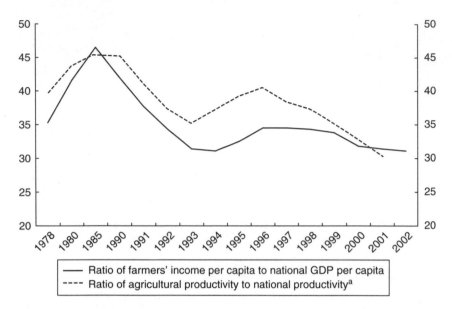

Figure 3.9   China: status of agriculture in the national economy, 1978–2002 (in percent)
ª To 2001.
Source: National Bureau of Statistics, *China Statistical Yearbook* (2002).

discriminative policies such as the requirement of formal residential identity, wage income of these workers will be directly influenced; in addition,
the living expenses of migrant families in cities will increase.

A large decrease in the prices of agricultural products in recent years has
reduced rural purchasing power. Farmers' incomes have also suffered from
natural disasters. Based on 1996 prices, the decrease in the purchase price
index for national agricultural products averaged 7 percent a year during the
period 1997–2000, representing a cumulative total loss of Y301.3 billion
(Table 3.11). This shows that the broad masses of farmers have been the most
serious victims of deflation, with price fluctuations in the overall economy
having a negative impact on farmers' income.

The increasing inequality in income distribution

Factors affecting poverty rates include not only income growth but also
income distribution. Even though the growth rate of per capita income is
lower than that of per capita GDP, if the degree of income inequality does
not worsen, rapid economic growth can still play a positive role in poverty
reduction. Since 1985, the degree of inequality between urban and rural
areas, among different regions, and even within urban areas has increased,
which has exerted a large negative impact on poverty reduction.

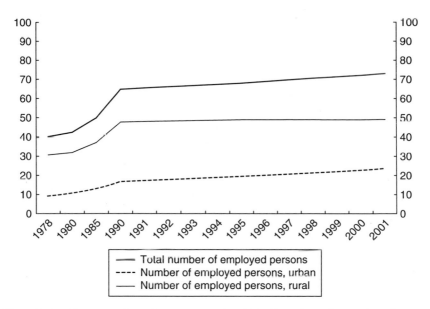

Figure 3.10   China: rural employment trends, 1978–2001[a] (in millions of workers)
[a] Annual data from 1990 onward.
Source: National Bureau of Statistics, *China Statistical Yearbook* (2002).

Table 3.11   China: internal agricultural trade and losses, 1996–2000

Year	Volume of internal trade (in millions of metric tons)	Purchase price of agricultural products (annual percentage change)	Annual losses from agricultural products sold (in billions of yuan)
1996	7,600	—	—
1997	9,136	−4.5	41.1
1998	10,123	−8.0	81.0
1999	11,018	−12.2	134.4
2000	12,443	−3.6	44.8

Source: National Bureau of Statistics, *China Statistical Yearbook* (2001).

A large gap exists between urban residents and rural residents in terms of per capita income, per capita consumption, tax transfer payments, and public services. The gap in per capita income between urban and rural residents first decreased but then increased under the policy of reform. Income inequality between urban areas and rural areas has also deteriorated, which to a large extent has directly resulted in the increase of the poverty rate. The urban to

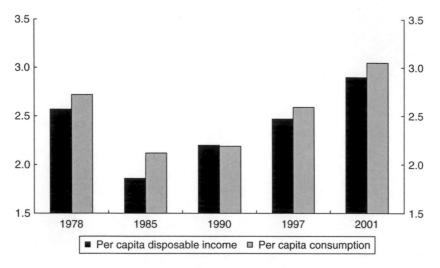

Figure 3.11 China: per capita disposable income and consumption (ratio between urban and rural residents)

Source: National Bureau of Statistics, *Comprehensive Statistical Data and Materials on 50 Years of New China* (1999).

rural proportions of per capita disposable income and per capita consumption (calculated at current prices) are shown in Figure 3.11 demonstrating the large gap. For per capita disposable income, urban households exceeded rural households by 2.57 times in 1978, falling down to 1.85 times in 1985, but increasing to 2.90 times in 2001 (71 percent higher than that in 1978 in constant prices). The ratio of per capita income in urban areas to that in rural areas increased from 1.53 times in 1985 to 2.12 times in 2001.

The fiscal distribution system, with highly unequal effects, has sharpened income inequality between the urban and rural populations. Per capita income of rural households is approximately two-fifths of that of urban households; however, in the total income of rural residents, the proportion of transfer income acquired from the state and the collective is far lower than that of urban residents (Table 3.12). Moreover, rural residents have to pay tax revenue that far exceeds fiscal transfers. By comparison, urban households can obtain various types of fiscal allowances and become beneficiaries of net subsidies. A large gap also exists between urban and rural residents in terms of access to public services. The Chinese government adopts public service policies that are preferable to cities. The rural population accounts for two-thirds of the total population now, but as little as one-tenth of the government's fiscal spending is directly on the rural population, which results in rural areas lagging far behind urban areas in provision of public services such as basic education and medical care and family planning, and in the

Table 3.12   China: total and transfer income of urban and rural residents[a]

Year	Urban residents			Rural residents		
	Annual per capita total income (in yuan)	Annual per capita transfer income (in yuan)	Ratio of total to transfer income (in percent)	Capita total income (in yuan)	Annual per capita transfer income (in yuan)	Ratio of total to transfer income (in percent)
1985	749	66	8.8	547	—	—
1990	1,523	250	16.4	990	—	—
1995	4,288	735	17.1	2,338	66	2.8
2000	6,317	1,212	19.2	3,146	148	4.7
2001	6,907	1,362	19.7	3,307	163	4.9

[a] At current prices.

Source: National Bureau of Statistics, *China Statistical Abstract* (2002).

infrastructure areas such as irrigation, roads, communications, and so on. The low level of rural public services not only restricts rural residents from improving their living standards, but also from developing new abilities and creating new opportunities, making them more susceptible to poverty.

The gap in farmers' income per capita among different regions is also growing. As noted earlier, the poverty population in western areas is very large and the degree of poverty is very deep. According to the data in *A Monitoring Report on China's Rural Poverty* (2000), the ratios between per capita income of farmers in the east and in the middle to that in the west are 1.27 and 1.05, respectively in 1980, increasing to 1.92 and 1.30 in 2000. Using similar data, Li Shi *et al.* (1999) also note an increasing gap in per capita net income in rural areas among different provinces, calculating a rise in the Gini coefficient from 0.19 in 1988 to 0.23 in 1995.

Furthermore, income inequality within rural regions is increasing. Prior to reforms, income inequality within China's rural areas was not large. According to an estimation made by the NBS of China (2001), the Gini coefficient of rural residents' income in 1978 was 0.21–0.22 (Table 3.13).[7] Ahmad and Wang (1991) find the income gap among rural residents to be shrinking during the period 1978–82, with the Gini coefficient going from 0.32 to 0.22. However, the income gap within China's rural areas appears to have grown since the mid-1980s. According to the estimation made by the NBS of China (2001), the Gini coefficient of per capita income of rural households increased from 0.23 in 1985 to 0.34 in 1995, and was 0.35 in 2000. Similarly, Khan and Riskin (1998) estimated that the Gini coefficient on rural income increased from 0.34 in 1988 to 0.42 in 1995. When grouping people according to their income, we find that the relative gap between the group with the highest income and the group with the lowest income has increased from 13.0 times to 14.7 times. The fiscal distribution system, with its highly

Table 3.13   China: estimates of income distribution in rural areas, 1978–2000

Year	Bureau of Statistics[a]	World Bank	Ahmad and Wang (1991)	Adelman and Sunding (1987)	Selden (1985)	Khan and Riskin (1998)	Gustafsson and Li (1999)[b]
1978	0.21	0.32		0.22	0.28		
1981	0.24	0.23	0.26		0.23		
1983	0.25	0.25		0.26	0.22		
1985	0.23	0.30					
1986	0.30	0.31	0.29				
1988	0.31					0.34	0.32
1990	0.31						
1991	0.31						
1992	0.31						
1993	0.33						
1994	0.32						
1995	0.34					0.42	0.42
1997	0.33						
2000	0.35						

[a] On the method used by the National Bureau of Statistics (NBS) for estimating the Gini coefficient, see NBS (2001, p. 29).
[b] Gustafsson and Li (1999) use the same data as Khan and Riskin (1997), but convert disposable income into equivalent income.

Sources: Selden (1985); Adelman and Sunding (1987, pp. 444–61); Ahmad and Yan (1991, pp. 231–57); World Bank (1997); Khan and Riskin (1998, pp. 221–53); Gustafsson and Li (1999); Li Shi (2000); Gustafsson and Li (2002, pp. 170–204); and Li Shi (2003, p. 390).

unequal effect not only intensifies income inequality between the urban rural populations, but also intensifies income inequality between poor people and nonpoor people in rural areas. The total amount of tax paid in rural areas by the group of people with the lowest annual income (less than Y800) was 3.4 times higher than that paid by the group of people with the highest annual income (greater than Y12,000) in 1999 (Table 3.14).

The above analysis shows that rapid economic growth alone cannot automatically solve the problem of income inequality and poverty. The fruits brought by economic growth and the opening up policy are not automatically shared by all people; on the contrary, unequal economic growth with low quality restricts people's opportunity to share the fruits. The distribution policy of the government intensifies this inequality. The fiscal expenditure and public service policies of the government are seriously preferable to cities and beneficial to urban residents. As a result, urban and rural residents have different access to education and medical care. Economic policies are also preferable to coastal areas, which is not beneficial to the development of inland areas. Tax policies are preferable to the rich, which intensifies the income gap. Only if economic growth with high quality is maintained can investment distortions be avoided and can human capital exploitation and

Table 3.14 China: average income and taxes and fees paid by income group in 1999

Income ranges	Average income[a]	Income components[b]	Taxes and fees[c]	Fees[d]
<800	522	86.5	17.5	11.5
800–1,600	1,205	82.2	10.4	6.8
1,600–2,400	1,970	73.0	6.7	4.1
2,400–3,200	2,766	60.2	5.2	2.9
3,200–4,000	3,571	46.4	4.3	2.2
4,000–6,000	4,804	41.8	3.4	1.4
6,000–8,000	6,869	30.5	3.9	1.2
8,000–12,000	9,532	22.3	2.9	0.3
>12,000	23,595	6.9	5.1	0.3

[a] Per capita net income in yuan.
[b] Share of per capita agriculture income in net income (in percent).
[c] Ratio of national taxes and local fees to average income (in percent).
[d] Ratio of local fees to average income (in percent).

Source: Lin, Ren *et al.* (2002).

utilization be fully exploited, allowing all of society to benefit from economic growth so as to prevent poverty.

3.4 New strategies for poverty reduction (2003–15)

The United Nations and the World Bank have publicly committed to reducing the world poverty population by half by 2015. China's success or failure in poverty reduction is directly related to the realization of this objective. As noted, although China has made huge strides in poverty reduction, economic growth since the middle of the 1980s has not led to corresponding poverty reduction; the pace of poverty reduction has slowed down; and some new types of poverty have arisen. Moreover, China's national poverty line is relatively low, far lower than the international poverty line prescribed by the World Bank, with the ratio of the poverty line to per capita GDP continuously declining. This means that while the gap between this part of poverty population and the social collectivity is enlarging, their relative situation is deteriorating.

Recently China's new Premier Wen Jiabao mentioned in a press conference that China's poverty line is at a low level and classified the issue of employment and poverty as one of the top three difficult tasks. However, since the "[19]87 Anti-Poverty Plan" ended in 2000, the central government has not put forward new plans on poverty reduction. The 16th National Congress of the Communist Party of China pointed out that for the first two decades of the twenty-first century, the most important goal of China is to concentrate on building a well-off society in an all-around way to the benefit of over one billion people in this period and to further develop the economy, to improve democracy, to advance science and education, to enrich culture, to foster social harmony and to upgrade the texture of life for the people. Poverty is an opposite of being well-off. Therefore, poverty reduction should be a priority in the comprehensive construction of the well-off society.

To this end, a new, larger scale antipoverty plan (2003–15) should be set down. Aimed at the current problems, the strategic direction of antipoverty efforts should be adjusted by (i) recalibrating China's poverty standard closer to the international poverty line; (ii) addressing the three types of poverty— income poverty, human poverty, and knowledge poverty; (iii) paying greater attention to increasing the chances of the vulnerable to participate in social activities and constructing the system to their express benefit; and (iv) designing comprehensive and effective antipoverty strategic framework so as to keep antipoverty policies in accordance with the relevant macroeconomic and regional development policies, and so on.

Looking at these areas in detail, we make the following suggestions. First, we see a need to adjust the national poverty line, to identify rural poverty population over again, and to establish antipoverty strategic framework according to the new poverty line. Box 3.1 lists the three schemes to estimate the rural poverty population. Scheme A is the current national poverty line; Scheme B sets the poverty line at per capita income of Y1000; and Scheme C sets it at per capita income of Y1500. Under Scheme B, the estimated rural poverty population is 100 million—between the World Bank's international poverty line. When Scheme C is adopted, the estimated rural poverty population is 240 million—very close to the estimation made by the World Bank. We suggest that Scheme B first be adopted, and then transit to Scheme C gradually. Effective measures should be taken to decrease the 100 million persons identified as below the poverty line under Scheme B in ten years, namely by 2015. Scheme C should then be taken into consideration, and new plans should be carried out to reduce poverty under the framework of Scheme C.

Second, macroeconomic and regional development policies should be adopted that benefit poverty reduction. The antipoverty experience of East Asia and China in the early 1980s shows that when policies are implemented that both effectively promote growth and fight poverty, the number of poverty population will be greatly decreased and the burden on poverty population will be lightened. These policies include:

- Macroeconomic policies aimed at increasing domestic demand connected to poverty reduction. Such policies should benefit the rural poverty population, especially peasants, with a view to reducing the gap between urban and rural areas, raising living standards of poverty population, promoting the adjustment of the rural production structure and increasing the ability of peasants to develop self-help mechanisms.

• Demand-side policies should be directed at upgrading basic facilities used by rural poverty population through realizing the "seven provisions," namely (i) water provision (tap water, clean drinking water, and other water needed for living and producing); (ii) electricity and electric grid provision; (iii) road provision (country roads or simple roads); (iv) cable provision (radio and television broadcasting); (v) telephone provision (especially public telephones); (vi) post provision; and (vii) network provision (especially public internet in rural counties and villages).

• In addition, policies are needed to help farmers to (i) adapt quicker to new agricultural structure, including the provision of support in terms of technology, financing, and extension services; (ii) develop an agricultural commodity base with high quality products and encourage the export of green (i.e., environmentally safe) food with high value-added and development of agro-processing; (iii) promote large-scale agricultural enterprises that establish contractual relationships with poor farmers and provide technical assistance and planting information to them; (iv) help farmers and communities to establish agricultural product markets and transportation and distribution systems; (v) increase farmers' employment opportunities and promote regional labor flows and migration; and improve rural basic education and public health, and so on.

• Fiscal policies should be implemented that benefit the poverty population and increase the government's contribution to the antipoverty fund. Additional revenue can be raised by increasing the individual income tax, imposing an inheritance tax, and adopting a social security tax—each of which can also increase the progressive nature of taxation. This revenue could be used to supplement the antipoverty fund, raising its proportion of GDP to 1.5 percent from the current 0.3 percent. The government should also cease giving allowances to enterprises that suffer from losses (including state-owned food supply enterprises), and instead direct these funds to the poverty population. The antipoverty fund should also be targeted at poverty-stricken villages or poor farm families instead of rural areas as a whole (in which these two groups represent at least 60 percent of the total rural population). In addition, a much larger investment should be made in poverty population's human capital, increasing it to more than 20 percent of the current antipoverty fund from the present 2–3 percent.

• Monetary policies should also benefit the broad masses of poverty population. The maintenance of macroeconomic stability, especially the general level of prices of agricultural products, has direct bearing on farmers' income; on the contrary, if the overall economy is not prosperous and agricultural prices are continuously falling, the agricultural income of the rural poverty population will be directly influenced. The government should help the poor to obtain cheap credit, and also provide interest subsidies.

The credit should be directly used to assist poverty-stricken women or families to provide necessary subsidies to them.

• Steps should be taken to help farm families adjust to trade policies adopted since entering the World Trade Organization (WTO) and produce more labor-intensive agricultural products. This includes fruits and vegetables, tea, horticultural goods, medicinal materials, and forestry and livestock products. Assistance should also be given to farm families to help enhance the quality of agricultural products and raise the productivity of agricultural inputs. Likewise, the input of the government in agricultural research and development should be increased by a large margin.

• Regional policies should be geared to reducing the regional development gap. This includes establishing a fair and normative system of fiscal transfer payments, realizing the objective of basically equalizing per capita regional resources, enhancing the ability of poverty-stricken counties and villages to provide basic public service, including the establishment of basic national standards for poverty-related spending by the government; reducing the burden of taxes and fees on poor farm families; adjusting the pivot of the government's investment in poverty-stricken areas and increasing investment in human capital. The anti-poverty office of the State Council should notify the standing committee of the National Peoples Congress (NPC) at least once a year of the distribution scheme of investment for aiding the poor population, as well as the overall effectiveness of investment, as gauged by such measurements as per capita net income of poor farmers, per capita living costs and expenditure, illiteracy rates of adults, enrollment rates of children, infant and maternal mortality rates, and so on. The office should also announce the above information and the evaluation advice given by the standing committee of NPC to the whole country. The National Auditing Office should routinely audit various expenditures made from the antipoverty fund by the central government and publicize the audit results showing irregularities. Evaluations should be made by groups of experts from China and abroad as a third party; and regular monitoring reports of regional poverty indictors should be announced by the NBS.

Third, strategies should be developed that improve employment opportunities for poor people. First, various levels of governments should make employment creation a primary development objective. Creating employment is a conscious activity; that is, the increasing employment will not be realized automatically without the government making it a top priority. This will require employment-oriented strategies and active development of labor-intensive industries. Compared with other groups, the main source of income of the urban and rural poverty population and rest of the low-income population is derived from their labor ability. To increase their employment opportunities means to increase their income-generating opportunities. Therefore, the gist of practicing employment-oriented polices is to give them priority in obtaining employment, including temporary, short-term, and flexible informal work. Second, the mobility of agricultural labor force should be actively promoted. The most pressing development problem in China is that almost one half of the labor force is concentrated in agricultural departments, where labor productivity is very low. Large-scale movement of surplus agricultural labor is both the core content of China's economic development strategy and an important measure of China's antipoverty strategies. Looking into the future, with the supply of agricultural output exceeding demand and given China's entry into WTO, farmers face less and less ability to increase their per capita income. Therefore, farmers' labor services income and nonagricultural income should be increased, with a view to reducing the rural–urban gap in income per capita. In the long term, the fundamental method for solving China's rural problems is to create opportunities to facilitate the movement of farmers into more productive activities and ultimately to decrease the number of farmers. As a result, every region should actively encourage and allow farmers to do manual work in cities and towns and improve regulations to ensure this takes place. The central government should issue documents proclaiming limitations on strict actions aimed at discriminating against the rural labor force, setting down employment policies allowing farm workers to compete justly and encouraging the orderly flow and transference of the rural labor force.

Fourth, opportunities should be created for democratic participation and opinion expression by the poor population. One of the fundamental reasons for the gap between urban and rural areas and in rural poverty among regions is that the broad masses of peasants in China have neither their own representatives advocating their views nor system for expressing their opinions. According to data on political participation, workers and farmers accounted for only 18.5 percent of total delegates of the 10th NPC. This proportion is obviously too low because the rural population makes up 64 percent of total national population. If the most fundamental and largest group of peasants is neglected in terms of representative structure, the immediate interests of peasants cannot be protected. As a result, reforms to the selection system for NPC delegates should be undertaken to ensure more peasant representatives in the range of delegates. Furthermore, the poverty population should take part in the events that can influence their lives through various channels— for example, allow them to participate in the design of poverty reduction projects and publicize the supervision and evaluation of these projects. The government should transform its role from exclusive management and control of projects to social governance and public management by encouraging and supporting the active participation of privately run departments, social groups, nongovernmental organizations, and international organizations in assisting China's poor.

Finally, the ultimate way to bring poverty reduction is to invest in people and to raise the ability of the poverty population.

• First, the educational investment in the poverty population should be increased by a large margin; the development of various rural education programs should be accelerated and nine years of compulsory education should be made a priority objective for realization. National educational funds should be directly used to assist the poverty population, such as providing for the tuition fees of children, the cost of books, a living subsidy for rural-based teachers, and an input fund for constructing schoolhouses and buying equipment. The government should also assist poverty-stricken areas in setting up semi-lodging schools, classes for young girls, and classes for minorities in primary and secondary schools. A project for educating migrants will be vigorously carried out in poverty-stricken areas in the twenty-first century. The government is already providing funds to subsidize the children of poor families who are willing to study in other places (for nine years of compulsory education or twelve years of total education). The project enables them to permanently emigrate from poverty-stricken areas and gives them the opportunity to obtain an education of the same high quality as those children in cities as "educational migrants" and with a view to eliminating poverty completely. The governments of those major cities in the east should provide funds to local primary and secondary schools to allow them to accept "educational migrants" from poverty-stricken areas.

• Second, funds should also be provided directly for basic public health services for the poverty population, in order to invest in people's health and to diminish health poverty as an important antipoverty objective. To facilitate this change, the government should reestablish the Cooperative Medical System in poverty-stricken rural areas. It should also set up a medical aid fund, which would be used to assist sick people and the poverty population by providing subsidies to cover costs related to clinical services, family planning, and childbearing. Assistance programs should also be adopted that promote low costs, high social benefits, and wide coverage. Furthermore, the government should widely disseminate information on public health care, including meals and nutrition; enhance the ability of poverty population to gain wellness and prevent diseases; and advocate that urban doctors go regularly to poverty-stricken areas for short stays to provide medical services to poor people.[8] Only when the government invests in people's health and education, reduces the birth rate of population, and enhances developmental abilities of poverty population to support themselves can knowledge poverty and human poverty be alleviated and income poverty be eliminated fundamentally.

Notes

1. Hu Angang, Professor, Director of Center for China Study, Chinese Academy of Science and Tsinghua University; Hu Linlin, PhD student, School of Public Policy

and Management, Tsinghua University; Chang Zhixiao, Associate Professor, School of Government, Peking University.
2. Sen (2003, pp. 257–8).
3. Sen (1999).
4. Khan (1999).
5. UNDP (2000).
6. The HPI is a new index adopted by the UNDP in 1997 to measure the degree of poverty. The HPI comprises three main elements of the human condition: life expectancy, knowledge access, and living standard. Life expectancy is reflected by the share of the population that does not live to age 40; knowledge access is measured by the adult (over age 15) illiteracy rate; and living standard comprises the share of the population without access to safe drinking water, without access to basic medical care, and, among those under age 5, designated as underweighted children.
7. The Gini coefficient is estimated by Adelman and Sunding (1987) to be 0.22 and by Selden (1985) to be 0.28—both in 1978.
8. The government provides small funding to undergraduates and postgraduates of medical colleges who are willing to go to poor rural areas to establish medical practices and provide medical services.

References

Adelmen, Irma and David Sunding, 1987, "Economic Policy and Income Distribution in China," *Journal of Comparative Economics*, Vol. 11, pp. 444–61.

Ahmad, Ehtisham and Yan Wang, 1991, "Inequality and Poverty in China: Institutional Change and Public Policy, 1978 to 1988," *The World Bank Economic Review*, Vol. 5, pp. 231–57.

Bourguignom, Francois and Christian Morrison, 2002, "Inequality Among World Citizens: 1820–1992," *American Economic Review* (September), pp. 727–44.

Gustafsson, B. and Li Shi, 2002, "Income Inequality Within and Across Counties in Rural China, 1988 and 1995," *Journal of Development Economics*, Vol. 69, pp. 170–204.

——, 1999, "Is China Become More Unequal?," in *Further Research of China's Residents' Income Distribution*, ed. by Zhao Renwei, Li Shi, and Li Siqin (Beijing: Chinese Fiscal and Economic Press).

Hu Angang, ed., 2002, *Globalization Challenging China* (Beijing: Peking University Press).

Jiang, Yonghua and Gao Hongbin, eds, 1998, *The Financial Aid to the Poor by the Central Government* (Beijing: China's Financial Press).

Khan, Azizur R., 1999, *Poverty in China in the Period Globalization* (Geneva: International Labor Organization).

—— and Carl Riskin, 1998, "Income and Inequality in China: Composition, Distribution and Growth of Household Income, 1988 to 1995," *China Quarterly*, Vol. 154, pp. 221–53.

Li Chunbo, 2001, "The Research on the Gap of Human Capital and Economic Development Among Regions in China" (Master's thesis; Beijing: School of Public Policy and Management, Tsinghua University).

Li Shi, 2003, "Retrospections and Expectation on Research of China's Income Distribution," *Economics Quarterly* (Beijing: China Center for Economic Research, Peking University).

Li Shi, 2000, "Economic Insecurity of Urban Households in China in 1990s," paper prepared for a workshop on *Development Toward Human Economic, Social and Environmental Security*, Beijing (October 30–November 1).

——, Zhao Renwai, and Zhang Ping, 1995, "Theoretical Illustration and Experience Analysis of China's Income Distribution Fluctuation," in *Further Research on China's Residents' Income Distribution*, ed. by Zhao Renwai, Li Shi, and Li Siqin (Beijing: Chinese Fiscal and Economic Press).

Lin Yifu, Ren Tao *et al.*, 2002, *Issue of Chinese Farmers' Tax Burden* (Beijing: China Center for Economic Research, Peking University).

National Bureau of Statistics of China, 2003, *The Statistical Communiqué of China's National Economic and Social Development in 2003* (March).

——, 2001, data on rural income distribution as reported by the Research Office on Rural Social Economy (Beijing).

——, 2000, Working Group on Rural, Social, and Economic Investigation, *A Monitoring Report on China's Rural Poverty* (Beijing: China Statistics Press).

——, 1999, *Comprehensive Statistical Data and Materials on 50 Years of New China* (Beijing: China Statistics Press).

——, 1998, *China Population Statistics Yearbook* (Beijing: China Statistics Press).

—— (various years), *China Statistical Abstract* (Beijing: China Statistics Press).

—— (various years), *China Statistical Yearbook* (Beijing: China Statistics Press).

Ren Bo, 2003, "Breakthrough of Policies Towards Rural Migrant Workers," *Journal of Finance and Economy* (China), Issues 3 and 4.

Selden, Mark, 1985, "Income Inequality and the State," in *Chinese Rural Development*, ed. by William Parish (New York: M.E. Sharpe, Inc.).

Sen, Amartya, 2003, "The Conceptual Challenge of Evaluating Inequality and Poverty," *Economics Quarterly* (Beijing: China Center for Economic Research, Peking University).

——, 1999, *Development as Freedom* (New York: Alfred A. Knopf), as republished in 2002 (Beijing: People's University of China Press).

State Statistical Bureau, 1990, *China Social Statistics* (Beijing).

——, 1986, *Rural Residents Survey Yearbook* (Beijing: Rural Research Office).

United Nations Development Programme, 2000, *Overcoming Human Poverty* (New York).

——, 1995, *Human Development Report* (New York: Oxford University Press).

World Bank, 2003, *Global Economic Prospects and the Development Countries* (Washington, DC).

——, 2000, *World Development Report 2000/2001: Attacking Poverty* (Washington, DC).

——, 1997, *Sharing Rising Incomes: Disparities in China* (Washington, DC).

—— (various years), *World Development Indicators* (Washington, DC).

4
Reform Strategies in the Indian Financial Sector

Saugata Bhattacharya and Urjit R. Patel[1]

4.1 Introduction

Financial sector reforms in India in the 1990s have undeniably advanced the objectives of significantly opening the constituent segments to competition and liberalized operations. India now has a world-class equity markets infrastructure; measures are steadily being implemented to build up liquid debt markets; and banks are moving toward, even if they remain some way off, international prudential norms.

Despite this progress, one may be forgiven for a lingering perception that, if one were to start scratching the surface, things do not seem to have changed decisively. There remains a disjunction in the reported systems and structures that have ostensibly been established for safe and efficient intermediation and the perception of its soft underbelly by various stakeholders. While the discerning reader is informed almost daily of some problem or the other, official statistics indicate that most efficiency parameters are non-threatening and even improving. Yet, even in academic and policy conclaves, there emerges a sense of widespread dissatisfaction (not to mention unease) regarding the possibility of systemic risk posed by the financial sector. While there are not many overt signs of failures, by way of defaults and payments crises, there are increasing signs of structural strains in the system. The banking system remains saddled with large amounts of bad loans. The recent years have seen a succession of distress in and failures of various intermediaries, necessitating the provision of "comfort and support" from the government. Institutions remain characterized by both political and regulatory forbearance.

Is there a fundamental problem in the financial sector in India, warranting the sense of unease? By fundamental, we mean a threat to the stability of the system. Or is this more a problem of lingering inefficiency in intermediating resources, negatively impacting investment and growth? Are the discrepancies now evident simply the outcome of more stringent information disclosure requirements? Or has there been a tangible disconnect between the "ratio-centric" reforms specified by regulators and the intrinsic operating practices of many intermediaries and the environment in which they function? Are norms sufficient in mitigating financial sector fragility in the absence of effective enforcement?

This chapter seeks to investigate the validity of the unease about a systemic fragility of the financial sector. It attempts to *inter alia* explore the apparent divergence between "facts" and perception. The conflict, between the objectives of establishing an efficient intermediation process for channeling funds to finance private investment and the need of the government to use the intermediaries for it owns to ameliorate its increasing fiscal stress, may explain to some extent the divergence between the reported statistics and the perceived distress in the sector.

The lessons of the turbulence of the Asian markets have been assimilated in various degrees by policymakers and regulators the world over. Overt and blatant abuse of depositor flows is now largely a thing of the past. The next lesson on financial sector risks was provided in the United States a couple of years later. Despite having one of the most transparent and efficient systems, the speed and complexity of financial transactions demonstrated the pressures that can potentially be exerted on regulatory mechanisms. One of the important revelations that emerged is the increasing interlinkages between the real and financial segments of the economy. Increasing efforts to involve the private sector in economic activity in India has lent urgency to devising new regulatory and enforcement structures and practices.

There is now a large literature on the reform actions in the banking, para-banking, securities and insurance segments in India[2] for a comprehensive overview. There is, however, yet little unified enunciation of the rationale and strategies underlying these changes; these are mostly available through scattered articles and speeches. An observer of the Indian financial markets may be hard-pressed to decipher a cogent message that is sought to be delivered by policymakers and regulators and will be correct in his or her conclusion that the strategy has centered on loosely interconnected strands of a "Basle regulatory framework." The main contention of the chapter is that while reforms have reduced the fragility of the sector, it has not addressed the broader environment in which the financial sector, operates. In an attempt to construct a coherent framework to assess the efficacy of reforms in the Indian financial sector, we both develop an institutional scaffolding to embed the disparate reform strategies as well as explore select weaknesses that continue to exert a debilitating influence. Ahluwalia (2002) offers a succinct review of the political economy considerations underlying the reforms, and some of the issues raised in that paper merit deeper exploration.

The prevalent official view is that India now has quite well-developed and sophisticated institutions for both financial intermediation and regulation. This is at best only partially correct. Institutions are not merely organizations and bodies of people. They are primarily the contracts and rules that govern transactions, as well as the mechanisms through which these contracts are enforced. Contracts are critically important given the speed and complexity of modern financial transactions and the huge information inadequacies and asymmetries that are consequently generated. And it is the incentive structures underlying these contracts that are quite distorted.

One of the major distortions is that involvement of the government—not just ownership of various intermediaries—in most segments of the sector remains high. Some of the associated costs are well known: the unwarranted and onerous oversight by a multitude of government audit and law enforcement agencies, high levels of deposit preemption through mandated reserves, directed lending requirements, political meddling, and so on. The systemic implications of this feature have been extensively explored, both analytically and through an empirical assessment in Patel and Bhattacharya (2003) and Bhattacharya and Patel (2002), respectively. They argue that these distortions are more severe in India than official statistics indicate, in large part because government involvement in intermediation is much more widespread than mere ownership. The system, even after a decade of reforms, retains many discrepancies that allow banks to both sidestep regulatory norms and simultaneously avoid taking "prudent risks." Intermediaries continue to exist with significant corpuses of funds that invest large amounts in "socially significant" activities and yet whose functions remain relatively opaque. The chapter argues that the sense of unease may, in part, emanate from the lack of information relating to the operations of not just these intermediaries but also pertaining to other activities and practices in the sector. Other operational and policy distortions remain entrenched: asymmetries in prudential norms for lending to the private sector and investing in government securities allow safe havens for bank deposits. This phenomenon is furthermore aggravated by a seemingly limitless supply of (perceived) risk-free government securities that finance the government's fiscal deficit, ambiguities in asset classification and income recognition of legacy "development" projects plagued by time and cost overruns, inadequacies in systems for intermediating financial savings in semi-urban and rural areas, and so on.

A singular aspect of financial sector reforms in India has been that while change has come to the "look and feel" of organizations associated with intermediation, it has primarily revolved around the introduction of stricter sector regulatory standards. Caprio (1996) argues that regulation-oriented reforms cannot deliver the desired outcome unless banks are restructured simultaneously; this includes introduction of measures that empower banks to work the new incentives into a viable and efficient business model and encourage prudent risk-taking. These mechanisms are also meant to *inter alia* mitigate the "legacy costs" that continue to burden intermediaries even after restructuring. Some of these costs, in the Indian context, apart from the consequences of public ownership, are well known: weak foreclosure systems and legal recourse for recovering bad debts, ineffective exit procedures for both banks and corporations, and so on. In addition, during difficult times, fiscal stress is sought to be relieved through regulatory forbearance; there are demands for (and occasionally actual instances of) lax enforcement (or dilution) of income recognition and asset classification norms. A multiplicity of "economic" regulators, most of them not wholly independent, deters enforcement of directives.[3]

We focus primarily on the *strategy*, as opposed to the *actions*, of reform that have been undertaken. Given the systemic distortions already enunciated, the absence of a cogent strategy that addresses the kinds of issues raised by Caprio (1996) is likely to render the actions of reform largely ineffective. Of particular concern are the institutions, processes, and intermediaries that have the potential of severely disrupting the sector. We feel that a very serious lacuna in the oversight framework is the inadequate attention that has been devoted to the role of market discipline for banks and some of the other large government-sponsored systemically important financial institutions like the Life Insurance Corporation of India (LIC) and Employees' Provident Fund Organisation (EPFO). At best, it has been seen as a supplement to supervisory discipline; at worst, the actual functioning of the system has actively militated against attempts at market discipline. Practices such as cross-holdings by institutions of common and preference shares, a flat-rated and non-risk based deposit insurance system, directed lending, investments of behemoth public sector intermediaries and retention of interest rate floors for select financial instruments are instances of these hindrances.

The crux of the arguments in this chapter is that the regulatory processes and ratios that have been gradually introduced as cornerstones of safety and efficiency in the financial sector are only a subset of the comprehensive institutional changes that are needed for "effective" reform and market discipline. We argue that there still persist deeper intrinsic shortcomings that have a high probability of negating the desired reform outcomes and that the strategy to enhance the soundness and efficiency of the sector has to be a two-step strategy, with a set of prudential and regulatory norms to infuse short-term stability and the development of market-discipline to impart long-term efficiency. Adapting a framework that had earlier been developed for a different context by Rodrik (2002), we attempt to situate the required reforms into the following categories: (i) market stabilization, (ii) market regulation, (iii) market creation, and (iv) market legitimization, with each reinforcing and complementing the processes already in place. While the reform measures have touched on aspects of each, they have been in no sense looked upon as a whole; the resulting contradictions may have weakened the effectiveness of the individual measures. As a result, intermediaries have still not graduated from being predominantly resource conduits to risk-management entities offering the cheapest possible capital to firms.

As in any paper that deals with sector-wide issues, the scope of the subject is extensive. Paucity of space does not permit us to provide a detailed description of the sector nor of all the changes that are still ongoing in different segments. The focus of this chapter is predominantly the banking sector rather than capital markets. The reasons are twofold: (i) the likelihood of problems emerging in the future appears greater among the set of deposit-taking institutions, especially given their deeper links to the public sector;[4] and (ii) the impact of inefficiencies in the banking sector is likely to be greater on future economic growth.[5] India also has many institutions—for instance, contractual savings institutions like insurance and pensions—that straddle both the banking sector (as deposit-taking institutions) and capital markets (where they deploy these deposits). While the chapter does not deal in detail with these aspects (which are likely to become increasingly important in the future), it does explore the potential systemic implications of the lending practices of the largest public sector intermediaries in nonbank segments.

The structure of the chapter is as follows. Section 4.2 recounts the reform actions and changing characteristics of the financial sector in India. Section 4.3 attempts to deconstruct the reform strategy underpinning these actions and analyzes the institutional, policy and regulatory context in which these reform actions were undertaken, including our perception of the main unfulfilled tasks for taking these reforms to their logical conclusion. In doing this, it attempts to take a view on the extent to which changes in the broader environment in which intermediaries function have been compatible with the official stance of reform. Section 4.4 then explores those structural characteristics of intermediation that need to be addressed if reforms in the financial sector are to achieve their stated objectives. These aspects, among others, include the overhang of the past (primarily the legacy of nonperforming assets), and the weaknesses relating to some large public sector financial intermediaries that have the potential of creating problems for the sector. Section 4.5 concludes.

4.2   Reform in the financial sector

After a decade of reforms and deregulation, the financial sector—including markets, institutions, and products—has changed, sometimes beyond recognition. The banking sector has undergone several watershed structural reforms, the capital markets are deeper and more liquid, and equity markets are currently booming. In September 2003, Standard and Poor's (S&P) revised upwards their outlook on the Indian banking sector from negative to stable and Fitch Ratings assessed that economic reforms have considerably "strengthened" financial sector fundamentals.

4.2.1   Genesis and drivers of reform

At the onset of reforms, the heavy hand of government had been omnipresent in the financial sector, and there was very limited market-based decision making. Bank deposit and lending rates were mostly controlled. Statutory preemptions and directed lending requirements left banks little discretionary funds for commercial lending. Term lending and intermediation of contractual savings (effectively insurance) were almost completely dominated by public sector intermediaries (with the probable exception of housing finance). There were no debt markets as such; the government's debt issues were structured in a primarily "administrative" manner by the Reserve Bank of India (RBI). A proper yield curve was nonexistent in the face of RBI interventions across the term structure of interest rates. Monetization of government deficit was automatic. The Controller of Capital Issues used to determine the pricing and magnitude of primary issues and broker-owned stock exchanges reportedly manipulated share prices.

The genesis of financial sector reform in India was the aftermath of the fiscal and external crises of the early 1990s, when many segments of economic activity were gradually freed. It was realized early on that deregulated activity required liberalized financial systems to raise resources efficiently. As domestic reforms progressed, increasing integration with global markets then became another catalyst for further reforms. Foreign entry into the banking, mutual funds and later, the insurance segments has been progressively allowed. At the same time, a series of financial crises over the years, triggered by disparate events in various countries, have alerted policy makers and regulators to the potential fragility of intermediaries in a deregulated environment and resulted in ongoing modifications and improvements in processes and disclosure requirements (see Table 4.1 for the changing profile of various segments of the sector).

4.2.2   The banking sector

Significant financial deepening has taken place over the last three decades (Table 4.2). The ratio of broad money (M3) to gross domestic product (GDP) has increased from 24 percent in 1970/71 to 63 percent in 2000/01, and the number of bank branches have increased eightfold. Commercial banks, especially public sector banks (PSBs), have an inordinately large presence in rural and semi-urban areas, which accounts for much of their expansion in recent decades. While only 34 percent of their deposits are sourced from and 23 percent of their advances are disbursed in these areas, 70 percent of their branches are located there.[6] The RBI licensing conditions for new private sector banks stipulate that, after a moratorium period of three years, one out of four new branches has to be in rural areas, thereby adding significantly to operating costs in an intensely competitive environment. This branching requirement occurs despite the prevalence of a large network of post offices that might ideally channel small savings, as well as specialized regional rural banks, cooperatives and other intermediaries working through National Bank for Agriculture and Rural Development.

Table 4.1 India: comparative profile of financial intermediaries and markets (in billions of rupees, unless otherwise specified)

	1990/91	1998/99	2002/03
Gross domestic savings	1,301	3,932	5,500
(in percent of GDP)	24.3	22.3	24.0
Bank deposits outstanding	2,078	7,140	13,043
(in percent of GDP)	38.2	40.5	50.1
Small savings deposits, public provident funds, etc.	1,071	3,333	3,810
(in percent of GDP)	20.0	19.1	15.4
Mutual funds (assets under management)	253	858	1,093
(in percent of GDP)	4.7	4.9	4.2
Public/regulated nonbank finance companies' deposits	174[a]	204	178
(in percent of GDP)	2.4	1.2	0.7
Total borrowings by development finance institutions (outstanding)	—[b]	2,108	901
(in percent of GDP)	—	12.0	3.5
Annual stock market turnover (BSE and NSE)[c]	360[d]	15,241	9,321
(in percent of GDP)	5.6	79.0	35.8
Stock market capitalization (BSE and NSE)[c]	845[d]	18,732	11,093
(in percent of GDP)	15.8	97.1	42.6
Annual turnover of stock market turnover (in percent)	—[b]	24	276
Turnover of government securities (excluding repos) through subsidiary general ledger (monthly average)	—[b]	310	2,287
(in percent of GDP)		1.8	9.0
Volume of corporate debt traded at NSE (excluding commercial paper)	—[b]	9	58

[a] Denotes figures at end-March 1993.
[b] Not comparable to later periods.
[c] Bombay Stock Exchange (BSE) and National Stock Exchange (NSE).
[d] Pertains to the BSE only.

Sources: Reserve Bank of India, *Handbook of Statistics on the Indian Economy* and *Report on Trend and Progress of Banking in India* (various years); and National Stock Exchange, *Indian Securities Market: A Review* (2003).

Table 4.2 India: decadal indicators of financial deepening

	1970/71	1980/81	1990/91	2000/01
Broad money (M3) to GDP (in percent)	24	39	47	63
Bank branches (per 1,000 persons)	0.02	0.05	0.07	0.07

Sources: Reserve Bank of India and authors' estimates.

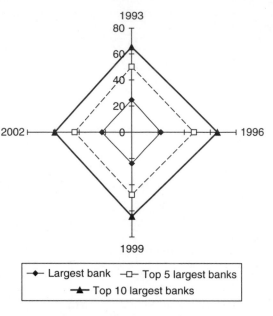

1999

| ◆ Largest bank   ◻ Top 5 largest banks |
| ▲ Top 10 largest banks |

Figure 4.1   India: concentration of banking sector (share of total banking sector assets controlled by each group, in percent)

Sources: Shirai (2001) and authors' estimates.

Banks continue to dominate financial intermediation[7] with bank deposits now accounting for half of financial savings. Much of this segment is publicly owned and accounts for an overwhelming share of financial transactions. After a hiatus of over twenty years, private banks were allowed to be established in 1993, but their share in intermediation, albeit increasing, continues to be low. Moreover, Figure 4.1 shows that there has been little change in the degree of concentration in the banking sector over the period 1993–2002, as measured by the m-bank concentration indicator.[8] While interest rates for the banking sector have been largely freed, except for savings deposits with maturities of 15 days or less, there still remains considerable stickiness arising from the fixed (although lowered) interest rates on small savings instruments and provident funds.

Banks are likely to need capital in the future, despite almost all of them having met the prescribed capital adequacy norms as of end-March 2003.[9] If the risk-weighted assets of scheduled commercial banks (SCBs) are to grow in line with the projected growth of the economy over 2003/04–2008/09, additional capital requirement of these banks may exceed Rs 500 billion, assuming a 10 percent capital adequacy requirement.[10] Although the current response to the public issue offerings of several banks may appear to rebut

Table 4.3 India: cost of bank rescues (in billion of rupees)

	1993/94	1994/95	1995/96	1996/97	1997/98	1998/99	2001/02
Capital infusion	57.0	52.9	8.5	15.1	27.0	4.0	18.0
Cumulative infusion	97.0[a]	149.9	158.4	173.5	200.5	204.5	222.5

[a] Includes Rs 40 billion injected prior to 1993.

Sources: Ministry of Finance, *Economic Survey* (various years); Reserve Bank of India, *Annual Report, Monetary Policy Statement, Report on Trend and Progress of Banking in India, Report on Currency and Finance* (various years), and *Monthly Bulletin* (various issues); Industrial Development Bank of India (IDBI), *IDBI Report on Development Banking* (various years); and National Stock Exchange, *Indian Securities Markets: A Review* (2002).

this concern, a combination of weaknesses in equity markets in a downturn and large loan portfolios accumulated in prior growth periods could constrain banks from accessing capital markets.[11] Even the stronger banks may soon be constrained by the prescribed floor of the RBI and government shareholding. Although the government has been toying with the idea of statutorily reducing its mandated 51 percent shareholding in PSBs down to 33 percent, there has not been much progress.[12] Besides fresh equity issues through the capital market, this requirement in the past has, in large measure, been met by continual infusion of capital by the government, often through indirect methods, even when there was little danger of systemic risk (see Table 4.3 for the cost of bank bailouts in the past). Banks have reportedly requested the RBI to raise the ceiling of 10 percent of their investment portfolio that is currently allowed with a view to increasing their Tier II capital.

Total gross nonperforming assets (NPAs) of banks were estimated to be 9.5 percent of outstanding advances at end-March 2003.[13] This problem might be more serious than it seems, since the accounting requirements are still less stringent than the Basle norms of income recognition and asset classification; and, there are other ambiguities—in definitions of project completion classification, financial closure, lending procedures, and so on—elaborated later. A minor digression might be worthwhile here. One of the factors that is widely deemed to have been a large contributory factor for NPAs is the policy of directed and priority sector lending. In light of the numbers on the sector-wise origins of NPAs, as of end-March 2002 (Table 4.4), the notion of directed lending being the primary culprit may need to be nuanced (even if just a little). While the share of priority sector NPAs in the total is about 40 percent, it should be noted that total loans outstanding to the priority sector (as a percentage of total loans) at end-March 2001 was about 34 percent.[14] At the same time, it is noteworthy that banks have to adhere to the statutory directed credit share of 40 percent of incremental deposits (if necessary, through mechanisms such as Rural Infrastructure Development Fund). In comparison to these percentages, therefore, the share of priority sector NPAs is disproportionate.

Table 4.4   India: segment-wise distribution of gross nonperforming assets (as of March 31, 2002)

	Amount	
	In billions of rupees	In percent of total NPAs
Public sector units	11	1.6
Large- and medium-scale industries and other nonpriority sectors	394	57.9
Total nonpriority sectors	405	59.5
Agriculture	82	12.0
Small-scale industries	121	17.8
Other priority sectors	73	10.7
Total priority sectors	276	40.5

Source: Reserve Bank of India, *Report on Trend and Progress of Banking in India 2001–02*.

4.2.3   Other intermediaries

The share of non-banking finance companies (NBFCs) as intermediaries rose in the period following the opening of capital markets. However, a combination of an economic slowdown and loss of investor confidence (following a series of scandals), together with increasingly stringent regulatory norms, has resulted in a marked and persistent decline in their business. Although the assets under the management of mutual funds (MFs) in India (including the Unit Trust of India (UTI)) accounted for just about a twelfth of total bank deposits in 2002/03, they are becoming increasingly significant. Following the string of troubles at UTI, investors made significant redemptions; the share of UTI's assets in total MFs fell from 84 percent in 1996/97 to under 38 percent in 2002/03. Resources mobilized by funds other than the UTI have increased over the last couple of years, partially due to tax incentives on dividends paid out by MFs.

Contractual savings institutions will play a critical role in developing capital markets, by *inter alia* helping to narrow the spread between long- and short-term interest rates thereby reducing the cost of capital for both equity and debt finance. The scope in this regard is considerable. Indian insurance premium payments account for a small fraction of total financial savings and lag far behind their Western (and even Chinese, on per capita terms) equivalents.[15] A number of companies have already entered the life and general insurance segments, introducing much needed competition in these fields.

4.2.4   Capital markets

The economic and financial turmoil in Asia in the late 1990s provided evidence of the relative failure of the banking sector in imparting market signals on the then current situation and future expectations. Other crises in the past, notably in Mexico, also indicate that when a financial system predominantly relies on its banks, the scope for systemic risk and vulnerability increases. The most likely reason is their proximate role in risk and liquidity management, information revelation, and corporate governance. Well-functioning money and capital markets can help to prevent localized liquidity shocks from leading to a failure of solvent banks. In addition, they facilitate government debt management and monetary policy transmission, and provide a channel for privatization. Capital markets will also have an increasingly important role in India in enabling financial institutions (FIs) and NBFCs to access funds in an environment where public deposits may not be readily forthcoming.

Fixed income markets

The functioning of debt markets in India since the inception of reforms has been undisputedly transformed. The government dominates the debt market, comprising about three-fourths of outstanding debt in 2001/02,[16] but only a small part of its total outstanding stock is traded—a mere 0.7 percent daily,[17] compared to 15.5 percent in the United States.[18] At present, PSBs, which are the biggest holders of these securities, have little incentive to enhance returns through active trading. However, a market has gradually emerged as banks become increasingly more profit oriented and the RBI risk-management requirements become more stringent. Another reason has been the gradual reduction in counter-party risk prevalent in the over-the-counter market through the establishment of the Clearing Corporation of India. Trading volumes in government securities, which had exceeded trading volumes in the equity segment during 2001/02 for the first time, increased (as a proportion of equity turnover) from 24 percent in 1998/99 to 276 percent in 2002/03.[19]

Financial institutions have also been large issuers of debt. Their issues have increased in size and complexity, especially after other cheaper government-based avenues of funds were curtailed. New financial instruments have been introduced, encompassing a whole spectrum of liquidity, risks, and returns. At one end, "money-like" instruments such as "liquid" mutual funds, bonds with call and put options and others traded on stock exchanges now compete with traditional assets like bank deposits. At the other, deep discount bonds and zero coupon bonds complement traditional contractual savings instruments. These developments have led to the emergence of a relatively more meaningful (although still distorted) yield curve.

Equity markets

Equity markets grew at a rapid rate during the 1990s. The market capitalization to GDP ratio, which was only around 6 percent in 1983, spurted to over 97 percent in 1998/99, before settling down to a more modest 43 percent in

2002/03.[20] Even this is markedly higher than the levels prevailing prior to economic reforms. Indian bourses have simultaneously made significant progress in the three critical areas of trading, depositories, and settlements; giving them a world-class trading infrastructure. Trading has by now become automated—the "pit" is extinct. The settlement cycle has been shortened to T + 2 since April 2003 from T + 5 a year earlier.

Derivatives

As India moves toward implementing the Basle II framework, risk-management techniques and products will become increasingly important. With the amendment of the Securities Contracts (Regulation) Act (SCRA) in early 2000, trading in derivatives of securities commenced in June 2000, beginning with index futures contracts based on the National Stock Exchange of India S&P–CNX–Nifty Index and Bombay Stock Exchange BSE-30 (Sensex) Index. This was followed by approval for trading in options based on these two indices and options on individual securities. As for institutional hedging, following the amended SCRA, deals with notional principals of forward rate agreements and interest rate swaps have increased dramatically since they were progressively introduced from 2000/01, but the capital markets are a long way off from exchange traded derivatives, especially in fixed income products. Table 4.5 provides indicative magnitudes of derivatives volumes in India.

The shortcomings of benchmark zero coupon yield curves in India are hindering proper pricing of derivatives. One reason is that financial market developments have affected trading horizons of securities,[21] especially for longer tenor instruments, thereby flattening the yield curve.[22] However, some derivatives markets are gradually developing.[23] In November 2002,

Table 4.5   India: volume of activity in cash and derivatives markets in 2002/03

Market Type	Cash turnover	Derivatives	Derivatives activity (in percent of cash turnover)
Foreign exchange (in billions of US dollars)[a]	276	662	239
Interest rates (in trillions of rupees)[b]	28.0	1.5	5.4
Equity (in trillions of rupees)[c]	9.3	4.4	47.2

[a] Gross turnover in the interbank spot and forward markets in 2001/02.
[b] Estimated annual turnover of Government of India securities, corporate bonds, and swaps in 2002/03.
[c] Gross turnover on the Bombay Stock Exchange and National Stock Exchange in 2002/03.

Sources: ICICI Bank, presentation on "Indian Derivatives Markets: Future Prospects" to the Federation of Indian Chambers of Commerce and Industry's Convention on Capital Markets (August 2003).

foreign institutional investors were granted permission to hedge their entire investments in Indian equity markets, up from the 15 percent ceiling allowed earlier.

4.3 Deconstructing the reform strategy

4.3.1 The framework of reforms

Increased efficiency, systemic stability and financial deepening with greater access have been the three objectives for the decade-long reforms in the financial sector. Sector liberalization, a prudential framework and increased competition, it is claimed, has admirably advanced these objectives. This officially declared stance of financial sector reform, however, does seem to be somewhat at variance with ground realities. Although many intermediaries and markets are rapidly moving toward world standards (in terms of prudential norms and systems) with increasingly sophisticated processes (including risk-management tools and extensive use of information technology (IT)), they have also concomitantly taken on a very different risk profile. In this new operating environment, there remain features of the financial sector that are incompatible with the processes and systems critical for both efficient functioning and commercial viability. This is especially true in banking, where, despite progress in terms of prudential norms, risk management, and lower NPAs, systemic weaknesses still remain obdurately entrenched.

First, it is fairly incontrovertible that the financial system still, in effect, remains predominantly configured to serve the government in its objectives of conducting, redirecting, and allocating resources for itself (ostensibly for investment and development). The concern is the extent of the adverse impact on the sector's role in intermediating resources efficiently for private investment. Second, the belief of depositors and investors that the system is insulated from systemic risk and crises because government involvement engenders a sense of confidence in the system, making deposit runs somehow unlikely, even when the system becomes insolvent. In effect, has the government "signed a social contract" with depositors that substitutes "support and comfort" to intermediaries in lieu of market discipline in attempting to mitigate systemic risk?

The reality of financial sector reform in India, as evidenced by the actual conduct of monetary and fiscal policy during the corresponding period, is complex. Financial market efficiency and stability requires more than a patchwork of rules, regulations, ratios, and directives. For instance, recent studies[24] suggest that countries with legal systems that strengthen creditor rights, contract enforcement, and accounting practices have better functioning financial intermediaries than countries that do not. We argue that a broader combination of actions, circumstances, and institutions have combined to seriously distort the incentives that are critical for the market discipline, which is now globally acknowledged to be a more effective oversight mechanism for intermediaries.[25]

With a view to organizing these distortions into a coherent whole, we adapt a framework explored in Rodrik (2002)—formulated in the context of general economic development—to the analysis of the financial sector reform strategy in India. This framework is institution-specific and is meant to buttress the economic analysis of trade-offs of market discipline and government intervention. While banking and financial reforms in India have comprised a set of actions that can be broadly grouped into enabling, strengthening, and institutional, we focus on the third plank—the framework in which financial sector reforms in India have been conducted—the crux of the argument being that weaknesses in this area are crucial for understanding the sector's travails. We group the current shortcomings and required actions related to reforms in the financial sector into the classification used by Rodrik (2002), namely (i) market stabilization; (ii) market regulation; (iii) market creation; and (iv) market legitimization. These four elements are unbundled and re-aggregated into three broad categories (see Table 4.6), which are more familiar and amenable to our analysis in terms of the information available. These categories are the profligate fiscal environment, regulatory forbearance, and public ownership of institutions. While reform measures have touched on aspects of each category, when considered as a whole; contradictions emerge that have weakened the effectiveness of the individual measures. We now explore these categories in more detail.

4.3.2   The fiscal environment

There are two sets of consequences to the increasing preemption of financial savings by the government. First is the well-known argument of crowding out private investment, either directly or through manipulating interest rates. Second, and more insidiously, is a dilution of the credit creating role of intermediaries—"lazy banking"[26]—resulting from the distortion of risk and return signals that encourage banks to divert their liabilities into the relatively more attractive government securities.

Pre-emption of financial resources

The borrowings of the public sector—center and states and other government-owned entities—have increased steadily. The discrepancy between the saving and investment of the public sector is growing larger, and in 2001/02 the public sector utilized a fourth of domestic savings, while actually dissaving 2.5 percent of GDP. The overall public sector fiscal deficit has risen from 8.3 percent of GDP in 1995/96 to currently around 11–12 percent of GDP.[27] The government is also increasingly relying on banks to finance its resource requirements—banks' holdings of central and state government securities increased from 27 percent of their deposits in 1998/99 to about 42 percent in 2002/03, as Table 4.7 indicates.

Table 4.6   India: institutional processes in the reform strategy of the financial sector

Role of institutions	Objective	Mapping to the Indian (financial) context	Addressing specific shortcomings
Market stabilization	Stable monetary and fiscal management	Profligate fiscal environment	Lower preemption of resources by government Greater efficacy of central bank functions
Market regulation	Mitigating the impact of scale economies and informational incompleteness	Regulatory forbearance Public ownership of institutions	Appropriate prudential regulation Imposition of market discipline Transparency and information disclosure
Market creation	Enabling property rights and contract enforcement	Public ownership of institutions	Enforcement of creditor rights Effective dispute resolution mechanisms
Market legitimization	Providing social protection, conflict management, and market access	Profligate fiscal environment Regulatory forbearance Public ownership of institutions	Mixing social and commercial objectives (e.g. rural branch requirements for banks) Appropriate deposit insurance Capital markets enforcement Effective redress of investor grievances

Sources: Rodrik (2002) and authors' adaptation.

Table 4.7   India: portfolio allocation of lendable resources of scheduled commercial banks (in percent of total deposits)

Period	Balances with RBI	Nonfood credit	Investments in government securities
1980s[a]	12.6	60.3	24.2
1990s[a]	12.1	52.8	29.8
2003	5.8	53.1	41.6

[a] Annual averages.

Sources: Reserve Bank of India, *Report on Currency and Finance 1998–99* and *Report on Trend and Progress of Banking in India 2001–02*.

Not only is the government appropriating an increasing share of financial savings for itself, it is increasingly influencing the process of intermediation in its favor. While restrictions on applicable interest rates (especially on the lending side) have been freed considerably, statutory preemptions (statutory liquidity ratio (SLR) and even cash reserve ratio) remain at high levels by international standards, thereby distorting banks' lending decisions. The share of priority sector loans of PSBs in their bank credit also has consistently remained above those of private and foreign banks and, since 1995/96, has also been above the statutory floor. Furthermore, banks have repeatedly been used by the government as quasi-fiscal instruments, including *de facto* sovereign borrowings for shoring up foreign exchange reserves. It is well known, moreover, that the State Bank of India (SBI) is often used by the central bank as an indirect conduit for managing exchange rates. Finally, apart from direct appropriation, the government is also facilitating lending activity through credit enhancements and guarantees. Despite awareness of the inherent dangers, government guarantees have actually increased, from 9.8 percent of GDP in 1996/97 to over 12 percent in 2000/01.

Credit creation role of banks

An ironic outcome of the new realities is that the government has managed to expand the proposed transformation of weak banks into "narrow" banks (that had been mooted earlier) to the entire banking sector! It has effectively "narrowed" the entire sector into a repository of "safe" government securities. As a result, banks in India seem to have curtailed their credit creation role. SCBs have surpassed, quite endogenously, the statutory SLR preemptions of 38.5 percent of their net demand and time liabilities (NDTLs) observed during the pre-reform days. Outstanding government and other approved securities held by the SCBs were over 45 percent of NDTLs at end-September 2003, much higher than the mandated SLR of 25 percent (Figure 4.2).[28]

In deciding on a trade-off between increasing credit flows and investing in government securities, the economic, regulatory, and fiscal environment is stacked against the former. Commercial lending is currently inhibited *inter alia* by ongoing structural changes in corporate financing patterns and multiple oversight processes for PSBs. Banks also face distortions arising from interest rate restrictions. These come mainly in the form of (i) continuing floors on short-term deposits; and (ii) various prime lending rate (PLR)-related guidelines on loans to small- and medium-scale enterprises and priority sectors, with these factors keeping banks' commercial lending rates artificially high. As a result, banks' treasury operations continue to be an important source of improved profitability.[29] On the one hand, there is arrayed against PSB disbursing officers the entire administrative oversight machinery, including India's Parliament, Central Bureau of Investigation, Central Vigilance Committee, Comptroller and Auditor General, Enforcement Directorate,

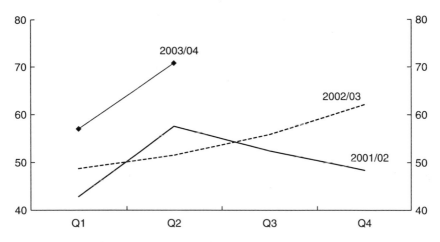

Figure 4.2 India: banks' investment in government securities[a] (ratio of government securities to total deposits at end-quarter, in percent)

[a] For SCBs, on a fiscal year basis (April–March).

Sources: Reserve Bank of India, *Handbook of Statistics on the Indian Economy* (2002 and 2003) and *Weekly Statistical Supplement* (various issues).

and so on. On the other, declining interest rates have made holding government securities more profitable. An unintended consequence of the increasingly tighter prudential norms that banks are being forced to adhere to has been a further shift in the deployment of deposits to government securities and other investments that carry comparatively lower risk weights.[30]

4.3.3 Regulatory forbearance

The increasing complexity of financial transactions points not just to the close links between the banking and securities segments (especially in increasingly sophisticated markets), but also to the extreme difficulty of exercising regulatory oversight of such transactions. As argued earlier, although a ratio-centric prudential and risk-management framework has been progressively implemented and several structures related to financial sector development (especially capital market) are in place, shortcomings in enhancing sector efficiency lie in the broader framework within which the sector functions. And while control has become increasingly sophisticated, with most intermediaries and at least some processes geared toward risk management, this change is hampered by structural weaknesses and contradictions, as the periodic eruptions of crises demonstrate.[31]

The RBI has gradually implemented the Basle framework for banks, even if it does not, as of now, require intermediaries to fully adhere to these norms. It is in the process of exploring the Basle II framework and is moving toward risk-based supervision of banks. But the government ownership of large

Table 4.8 Reserve Bank of India: prompt corrective action framework

Trigger	Trigger point	Mandatory actions	Discretionary actions by the RBI
1.1 Capital to risk-weighted assets ratio (CRAR)	Between 6 and 9 percent	Submission and implementation of capital restoration, restrictions on the expansion of risk-weighted assets, prior approval of the RBI for new branches and lines of business, pay-off of costly deposits and certificates of deposits (CDs), reduced or suspended dividends	Ordered recapitalization, reduced stake in subsidiaries, shedding of risky business, caps on deposit interest rates, restrictions on borrowings from the interbank market, revision of credit/investment strategies and controls
1.2	Between 3 and 6 percent	*Other than those in 1.1*, ordered recapitalization, reduced overseas presence and/or stake in subsidiaries, caps on deposit interest rates, revision of credit/investment strategies and controls, employment of consultants for business restructuring, establishment of new management board, reduced advances, capital expenditures, and overhead	Change in the promoters and/or owners, wage freeze and/or voluntary retirement scheme (VRS), merger or liquidation
1.3	Less than 3 percent	*Other than those in 1.2*, wage freeze and/or VRS, merger or liquidation, appointment of observers to monitor the performance of the bank	

			Prior approval of the RBI for new branches and lines of business, reduced overseas presence, reduced or suspended dividends, employment of consultants for revamping credit administration, reduced stake in subsidiaries
2.1 Gross nonperforming assets (NPAs)	Between 10 and 15 percent	Special drive to reduce NPA stock and contain fresh NPAs, review of loan policy, upgrade of credit appraisal skills and systems and loan review mechanisms for large loans, effective follow-up of suits filed, establishment of proper credit risk-management policies, reduced loan concentration, restrictions on loan portfolio growth	
2.2	Over 15 percent	Other than these in 1.2, reduced overseas presence, reduced or suspended dividends, employment of consultants for revamping credit administration, reduced stake in subsidiaries, discussion with bank's board on a corrective plan of action	
3.1 Return on assets (ROA)	Below 0.25 percent	Pay-off of costly deposits and CDs, reduced or suspended dividends, reduced administrative expenses, special drive to reduce NPA stock and contain fresh NPAs, prior approval of the RBI for new branches and lines of business, restrictions on borrowings from the interbank market, reduced capital expenditures within board-approved limits	Cap on deposit interest rates, wage freeze and/or VRS

Source: Reserve Bank of India, *Discussion Paper on Prompt Corrective Action* (2000).

segments of intermediaries will inevitably vitiate the market discipline on which the efficacy of this supervision is predicated. For instance, public ownership results almost inevitably in either a fiscal infusion to recapitalize banks and term-lending development intermediaries, or, in a tight fiscal situation which provides little elbow room for the government to clean up the banking system, a substitution of regulatory forbearance for its inability to fill the recapitalization gap. When intermediaries have not been able to access capital markets for their capitalization, they have resorted to "double gearing," by cross-purchasing each other's papers, often at the behest of the government. If even this measure is not feasible (or is deemed undesirable), weakening of Basle norms is the sole respite for banks. The whole process is likely to result in a vicious cycle: fiscal compulsions lead to the use of intermediaries (banks and FIs) as quasi-fiscal instruments by the government, the consequent asset additions increase the capital requirements of these entities, and the poor quality of these assets hampers intermediaries from raising capital through the markets, thereby necessitating a loosening of regulatory restrictions, which, in turn, provides government more elbow room to further exploit the resources of these intermediaries.

The changing process of supervision

The thrust of regulatory oversight is changing from an across-the-board imposition of prudential norms to a more sophisticated and "customized" approach. The RBI initiated a Prompt Corrective Action (PCA) scheme in December 2002 on a trial basis to direct preemptive adjustments at troubled banks in response to early signs of financial vulnerability. A risk-based supervision approach is also in the works, as a prelude to the full implementation of the Basle II structure around 2006.

The PCA scheme is intended to apply prudential regulations in a more flexible and structured manner, depending on the degree of prospective trouble of the bank, in contrast to the uniform approach of the Basle framework. It envisages a response from the regulator based on three trigger points relating to the (i) capital to risk-weighted assets ratio (CRAR), (ii) net NPAs to net advances ratio, and (iii) return on assets. In principle, the rationale of the scheme is sound, relying as it does on a linkage between the deterioration in a bank's financial performance and the consequent stipulations associated with the bank rather than a one-size-fits-all application of prudential norms. The PCA scheme can thus be considered a bridge to the market-based orientation of supervision put forward in Table 4.8, which outlines the threshold levels of the trigger points as well as the mandatory and discretionary actions that need (or should) be initiated by the respective intermediary.

The operation of this scheme, however, leaves much to be desired. In the first place, the PCA regime does not require the concerned bank and the regulator to make public the precise shortfalls under which the PCA regime is triggered, which is against the spirit of greater accountability and

Table 4.9 Reserve Bank of India norms on exposure limits for banks and financial institutions

Industry/Sector	Single Company	Group
15 percent of gross exposure	15 percent of the capital funds[a]	40 percent of the capital funds
	20 percent of the capital funds for infrastructure projects	50 percent of the capital funds for infrastructure projects

[a] Capital funds comprise share capital, Tier 1 and 2 capital, and reserves and surplus.

Source: Reserve Bank of India, *Report on Trend and Progress of Banking in India 2002–03*.

transparency that is central to the Basle framework. Fears of a public disclosure of the PCA regime causing a run on the concerned bank are likely to have been exaggerated.

Exposure ceilings are part of prudential norms imposed by the financial sector regulators worldwide. However, for rapidly growing emerging countries with large investment requirements, these norms can often become a constraint on growth. Infrastructure projects are a prominent example. Given the dilapidated state of the sectors consequent upon the low investments that have characterized these sectors in India and the urgent need for upgrading these assets, infrastructure projects may perforce have to look to foreign markets to access funds that are denied by regulatory norms in the domestic markets (Table 4.9),[32] despite abundant funding sources in India. To worsen matters, there are often restrictions on the ability of projects to access both equity and debt funds abroad as well.

The institutional framework of supervision

There remain two lacunae in the regulatory structure, however, that hamper efficacious supervision of the financial sector. The first set of weaknesses relates to the oversight structure imposed by regulations. This includes the whole gamut of processes, starting from appointments, accountability, jurisdictions, and enforcement powers. The second set of weaknesses involves the operating practices used by regulators, namely requirements for information disclosure.[33] Poor enforcement against past malfeasance remains a prime source of the mistrust of retail investors in most primary issues. A failure to address deep-seated issues—like disclosures, monitoring, and enforcement—and instead tinker with arbitrary incentives for investors (like dividend taxes and small savings returns) has led to policy responses that have been alternatively overzealous and halting.[34]

On the first set of weaknesses, the burden imposed by the oversight structure relates to the multiplicity (and often overlapping jurisdictions) of regulators, especially given the increasingly integrated nature of financial and commercial transactions. While the number and jurisdiction of regulators continues to remain a subject of academic argument and political dispute, a real danger remains of sector regulators transforming themselves into sectoral "fund managers" for their individual domains in the financial markets. An illustrative instance is the *Report of the Joint Committee on Stock Market Scam*, probing the 2001 stock market swindle, which indicts the RBI for its "weak and ineffective supervisory role" and notes that the central bank and the Registrar of Cooperative Societies were often issuing cross-directives. Simultaneously, the report faulted the Securities and Exchange Board of India (SEBI) and the Ministry of Finance's (MoF) Department of Company Affairs (DCA) (then a part of the Ministry of Law, Justice, and Company Affairs) for incessant delays in initiating action based on the SEBI's *Preliminary Investigation Report*, as a result of interminable squabbling about which regulatory or government entity was statutorily responsible for initiating action against companies "named" for market manipulation.

The feasibility or even desirability of establishing an integrated financial markets regulator on the lines of the Financial Services Authority (FSA) of the United Kingdom is also a matter of debate. From the limited information available on the functioning of the umbrella High Level Coordination Committee on Financial and Capital Markets (HLCC), this body—established in the early stages of financial reform, chaired by the RBI Governor and comprising representatives of the SEBI and MoF—might not be entirely effective in light of its composition. The HLCC, for instance, has little control over the actions of state registrars, which are often lax in implementing RBI directives. Another important set of shortcomings relates to composition of and appointments to the regulatory bodies. The perception is that appointments to the boards of independent regulatory bodies are often dilatory and discretionary.[35] For instance, despite the enabling provision for increasing the number of SEBI board members from six to nine in the SEBI Amendment Act of 2002, the Board currently has just two whole-time members, down from three in 2002/03 (surely a dearth of work cannot explain the vacancies).

On the second set of weaknesses, information disclosure norms are still inadequate given the degree of market discipline needed to supplement current financial sector regulation. The nontransparent nature of disclosure requirements of banks and FIs make a quantitative assessment of the extent of the problems difficult. Even in these information enabled times, the number of organizations that post their annual reports on websites is minimal. Regulatory decisions are often made without a discussion and consultation process, on the lines of the better utility regulators. Even the investigation reports of the regulator are confidential. Case files of securities markets enforcement have only started being available recently as training devices for financial sector regulators.

The multiple and often contradictory roles of the RBI—as a financial sector regulator, major owner of intermediaries, monetary policy authority and investment banker to the government—have arguably vitiated the central bank from fully implementing them. As lead arranger for the government's borrowing program, the RBI has to manage the issue of government paper with a view to ensure subscription at the lowest interest cost. In its role as monetary policymaker, it has to manage system liquidity, in part by using direct and indirect instruments to affect the term structure of interest rates. Interest rate formation is a monetary policy prerogative and internal debt management must be undertaken within this rate structure. Insidiously, the actions of the RBI—in discharging its roles as the government's investment banker (through influencing primary market yields on government treasury instruments, by taking on new issue devolvement and other measures designed to reduce the cost of borrowing) and debt manager (through the management of the average maturity of debt)—are interfering with the establishment of a proper yield curve. The interventions across the term structure of interest rates impinges on the RBI's ability in conducting its core function—monetary policy—which hinges on a credible market-determined benchmark yield curve as the transmission channel to interest rates.

4.3.4 Ownership of intermediaries and other rigidities

India is one of a number of countries with intermediaries used by the government to allocate and direct financial resources to both the public and the private sector. Government ownership of banks in India is, barring China, the highest among large economies (Figure 4.3).[36] There is another large segment of intermediaries that has not attracted requisite attention, specifically the FIs, which were responsible for 70 percent of total loans sanctioned in 2000/01.[37] The lending portfolios and processes of some of these entities are more opaque than banks and, given their significant exposure to government and other public sector entities, is cause for greater concern. The portfolios of some FIs are also heavily concentrated in a few sectors, which make them more vulnerable to economic downturns.

The involvement of the public sector, in particular the government, in intermediation is much wider than mere ownership numbers indicate; its ambit stretches across the mobilization of resources, direction of credit, appointment of management, regulation of intermediaries, provision of "comfort and support" to depositors and investors, and so on. In the process, the incentive structures that underlie the functioning of financial intermediaries are blunted and distorted to the extent that they override the safety systems that have nominally been put in place. There are two ways in which this dominance skews incentives and magnifies distortions. First, public ownership of intermediaries vitiates the profit maximizing incentive for requiring optimal co-financing from borrowers; intermediaries know that hard budget constraints no longer hold. Public equity issues in the primary capital markets have been falling since the middle of the post-reform period, implying decreasing levels of co-financing—at least in a transparent and,

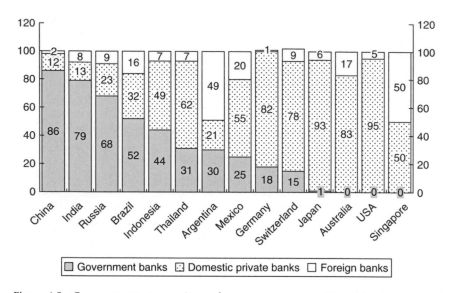

Figure 4.3   Cross-country comparison of government ownership of banks (share of total banking sector assets controlled by each ownership group, in percent)

Source: Boston Consulting Group, presentation to the Confederation of Indian Industry Banking Summit (2003).

therefore, a more desirable form. On the other hand, private placements of both debt and equity instruments have increased during this period. However, the bulk of these placements have predominantly been in fixed-income instruments, often subscribed by publicly owned intermediaries, where the due diligence may be less than exemplary. Second, the high degree of government involvement in the financial sector reinforces the belief of depositors and investors that the system is insulated from systemic risk and crises. This involvement engenders a sense of confidence in investors in the system, making deposit runs somehow unlikely, even when the system becomes insolvent.

While selective regulatory forbearance might be justified to mitigate financial panics, the government's blanket guarantee makes such forbearance difficult to calibrate and has the effect of sharply increasing system-wide moral hazard. A virtual certainty of sustained bailouts by the government has replaced a policy of "*constructive ambiguity*" with one of "*destructive unambiguity*."[38] Depositors, borrowers and lenders all know that the government is the guarantor. Since, for all intents and purposes, *all* deposits are covered by an umbrella of implicit government guarantees, there is little incentive for "due diligence" by depositors. As a result, any semblance of market discipline for lenders in deploying funds is further eroded, as witnessed most recently in the case of cooperative banks. The regularity of "sector restructuring packages" (for steel and textiles and proposed most recently for telecommunications), also diminishes incentives for borrowers for mitigating the credit risk associated with their projects.

The large fiscally funded recapitalizations of banks in the early and mid-1990s may be rationalized as having been designed to prevent a system-wide collapse at a time when the sector had been buffeted by the onset of reforms and had not yet developed risk mitigation systems. Moreover, the overall reforms were designed to enhance domestic and external competition, which adversely affected the banks' past loans and balance sheets. The nascent state of capital markets at that time also was a hindrance to accessing equity capital without a large risk premium. The impact of this support, though, has been considerably reduced, if not eliminated, by the series of ongoing bailouts, with seemingly little by way of binding reciprocating requirements imposed on intermediaries to prevent repeats of these episodes. It needs to be recognized that the only sustainable method of ensuring capital adequacy in the long run is through improved earnings, not further government recapitalization or even private capital mobilization.

Deposit insurance

The Deposit Insurance and Credit Guarantee Corporation (DICGC) came into existence in 1978 as a statutory body through an amalgamation of the erstwhile separate Deposit Insurance Corporation and Credit Guarantee Corporation. It has a relatively liberal structure for insuring deposits compared to international norms.[39] Depositors in India do not have to bear co-insurance on the insured deposit amount and the ceiling insured amount (Rs 100,000) is five times the per capita GDP. Banks are required to bear the insurance premium of Rs 0.05 per Rs 100 per annum (insurance protection is available to depositors free of cost). As of 2001/02, about 74 percent of the total deposits of commercial banks were insured.[40] The DICGC extended its guarantee support to credit granted to small-scale industries from 1981 and to priority sector advances from 1989. However, from 1995, housing loans have been excluded from the purview of guarantee cover. Some of the major recommendations of the 1999 Working Group constituted by the RBI to examine the issue of deposit insurance are withdrawing the function of credit guarantee on loans from the DICGC and instituting a risk-based pricing of the deposit insurance premium instead of the present flat-rate system. A new law, superseding the existing one, is supposedly to be passed in order to implement the recommendations.

Institutional rigidities

Apart from the government's preemption of resources, lingering institutional bottlenecks and practices in the public and private sectors are both creating and reinforcing conditions for vitiated commercial discipline. This subsection consolidates indicative and anecdotal evidence of financial fragility, which may necessitate some reevaluation of inferences drawn from published (and audited) results of the sector. The practices outlined are difficult to quantify and can only be delineated as "stylized facts." First, there has been an absence of effective bankruptcy and foreclosure procedures, which has forced intermediaries to roll over existing substandard debt, usually debt-equity swaps,[41] thereby continually building up the fragility of their asset portfolio and further diluting debt–equity norms. This has had the inevitable consequence of encouraging intermediaries—both lending and investing institutions—to approach the government for bailouts with disquieting regularity. Let alone large players, very few banks are "too small to fail," with even the humblest of cooperative banks granted support. Thankfully, the Securitization and Reconstruction of Financial Assets and Enforcement of Securities Interest (SARFAESI) Act of 2002 offers some scope for relief. Second, the holding company (pyramid) structure of many Indian corporations implies a separation of ownership from control, which creates strong incentives for diversion of funds among group companies (tunneling).

The resulting inefficiencies not only distort lending and deposit rates, but also create a major incentive for smaller and more efficient intermediaries (for example, foreign banks) to behave like "Stackelberg" followers and extract rents, in the sense that they continue to retain high lending rates (despite comparatively low operating costs), as well as to carve out large loan shares in lucrative business segments, thereby maintaining higher operating margins than the PSBs.[42] An important implication of the structural weaknesses and the distortions engendered is the proper pricing of associated premia . As a consequence, the net interest spreads of the system as a whole may be above the "optimal" levels. The outcome is that, while this has helped to keep the inefficient public sector intermediaries' heads "above the water," the efficient ones have simply been able to "ride the wave," as it were.

4.4   A good beginning, but . . . aspects of financial intermediation

Section 4.3 elaborated on elements of the institutional framework that we feel have been key obstacles to promoting the market discipline needed for enhancing the efficiency of financial intermediation. This section illustrates the lacunae in the framework by examining select processes and strategies that have been instituted to improve the overall efficiency of the system.

4.4.1   Dealing with nonperforming assets

The level of NPAs is one that has attracted the most alarmist statements about India's financial system. Before examining methods proposed to deal with the stock of NPAs, we assess the ramifications of the existing stock of NPAs, especially in relation to bank capitalization. Special emphasis is accorded to the PSBs, given their dominance in the banking sector. As on

Table 4.10 India: loan classification of scheduled commercial banks[a] (as of March 31, 2002; in billions of rupees)

	Standard assets	Substandard assets	Doubtful assets	Loss assets	Total nonperforming assets (NPAs)	Total advances
Public sector banks	4,529	158	337	71	565	5,094
Old private banks	392	18	27	4	49	441
New private banks	700	29	39	0	68	768
Foreign banks	478	9	10	9	28	506
Total SCBs	6,099	214	412	84	710	6,809

[a] Banks are required to provision for NPAs at 100 percent for loss assets; at 100 percent of the unsecured portion plus 20–50 percent of the secured portion for doubtful assets, depending on the period the loan has been in this category; and at 10 percent on the outstanding balance for substandard assets.

Source: Reserve Bank of India, *Report on Trend and Progress of Banking in India 2001–02.*

end-March 2002, gross NPAs of SCBs and FIs (excluding investment institutions) amounted to Rs 710 billion and Rs 118 billion, respectively, or totaling about 3.3 percent of GDP.[43] NPAs of NBFCs were another Rs 33 billion.

Focusing on the PSBs, which are widely considered to be the most vulnerable group, the stock of gross and net NPAs amounted to Rs 565 billion and Rs 280 billion, respectively, the difference being provisioning of Rs 286 billion (Table 4.10). As against this, total capital of the PSBs was Rs 575 billion. The cumulative provisions against loan losses of PSBs amounted to 42.5 percent of their gross NPAs at end-March 2002, which is lower than international standards, (foreign banks in India were, on average, estimated to have a provisioning rate of 75 percent).[44] This level of provisioning represented 70 percent of loss and doubtful assets as of end-March 2002. When SCBs are considered as a whole, net profits increased to Rs 142 billion in 2002/03 (1 percent of total assets), but admittedly due to higher noninterest income. This amount, at least conceptually, is two-thirds of the substandard assets of SCBs. Even if the true level of NPAs is double of that as officially reported, as is widely claimed by industry analysts, the situation is unlikely to result in a systemic crisis. In fact, the stress on the *banking* sector that is claimed to originate in their bad loans *may* be exaggerated. Unlike their counterparts elsewhere in Asia, bad loans of banks in India tend to be concentrated in heavy industries, infrastructure projects, or "priority" sectors rather than in real estate or the stock market. Total advances of SCBs to the so-called sensitive sectors, that is, capital markets, real estate and commodities, was Rs 232 billion at end-March 2002—a mere 3.6 percent of the total loans and advances portfolio.

While the data suggests that NPAs of financial intermediaries in India are not likely to precipitate a crisis, it should be noted that several independent agencies have reexamined the official figures and take a more measured view.

CRISIL estimated that the gross NPAs of SCBs were Rs 1,300 billion at end-March 2002—more than 80 percent higher than the officially reported data. Similarly, Fitch Ratings has estimated that the net NPAs of SCBs at end-March 2002 would have gone up from 51.5 percent of net advances to 11.5 percent of net advances, if a 90-day norm (as adopted in April 2004) had been in place instead of the 180-day norm now being used. However, the validity of these estimates is difficult to ascertain. The estimates of NPAs by both CRISIL and Fitch were obtained using sample techniques and extrapolating results to the entire system, which makes their validity difficult to ascertain. Nonetheless, they raise some concerns about the seriousness of the NPA problem.

The RBI issued revised guidelines on asset classification in 2002, according to which a loan is classified as an NPA at an SCB if interest or principal payments are overdue by 180 days or if interest is overdue for 180 days or principal for 365 days at an FI. Even within the confines of these relatively liberal norms, there remain glaring loopholes in the treatment of stressed assets. For instance, the Dabhol Power Company's power project, to which Indian lenders have an exposure of Rs 62 billion, is still not classified as an NPA, despite interest and principal repayments remaining overdue for more than 180 days. This arises from the definition of "financial closure of projects under implementation" adopted by the RBI. The RBI, to its credit, has expressed concern regarding large project loans that continue to be classified as standard despite loan service delays, merely by dint of the project continuing to be "under implementation." An independent group constituted in 2002 to look into such projects (and establish deemed completion dates) has estimated that intermediaries have already disbursed about Rs 360 billion to 26 such projects with a total cost of Rs 560 billion and with a debt component of about Rs 390 billion. The concept of disbursement only after "financial closure" of projects had not been followed in the past based on the erstwhile "development" approach of banks and FIs to lending.

Debt recovery tribunals

Procedures for recovery of bad assets have, in the past, been cumbersome at best and ineffective at worst. Banks used to file suits for recovery of bad loans in debt recovery tribunals (DRTs) only as a last resort.[45] Adhivarahan (2003) cites a report prepared by the RBI's Banking Supervision Department based on data from 33 banks (27 public sector and 6 private sector), which finds that 15 of these banks did file suits after exhausting other means of recovery. The amounts involved in suit filed cases accounted for 26.2, 33.9, and 46.4 percent of these banks' NPAs, in 1996, 1997, and 1998, respectively. However, recoveries were generally meager at 7.3, 4.7, and 4.3 percent, respectively. The report goes on to note that in view of such meager recovery, "the banks before filing suit weigh the likely recovery prospects out of the suit and the opportunity cost of any amounts that could be recovered immediately."

In light of the inadequacies of the DRT arbitration, the government of India and the RBI have instituted various settlement mechanisms like the Settlement Advisory Committee, Lok Adalats (Peoples' Courts), and nondiscretionary and nondiscriminatory one-time settlement (OTS) schemes for NPAs up to Rs 50 million.[46] An interinstitutional corporate debt restructuring (CDR) mechanism also has been established to provide a transparent mechanism for restructuring debts of "viable entities" facing payment problems due to internal and external factors. At least regarding infrastructure projects, our experience with the CDR mechanism does not inspire confidence.

Asset reconstruction and securitization

Given the various shortcomings of the various approaches used to tackle loan defaults, a landmark development in the reform of the financial sector in India was the enactment of the SARFAESI Act effective June 2002.[47] The Act, meant to facilitate foreclosures and enforcement of securities in cases of default and to enable banks and FIs to realize their dues, marked a major change in the balance of power between lenders and borrowers. It empowers secured creditors, without intervention of a court or tribunal, to enforce any "security interests" created. The Act has also created an enabling framework for asset reconstruction companies (ARCs) and securitization in general (see Box 4.1).

Although the SARFAESI Act is a significant step in dealing with the stock of existing NPAs of the banking sector (and, more importantly, instilling

---

Box 4.1   Salient features of the SARFAESI Act 2002

A securitization or asset reconstruction company (ARC) with own funds of not less than Rs 20 million may be established, in compliance with RBI prudential norms. This company may acquire assets of any bank or financial institution (FI) by issuing debentures or bonds. Notices of acquisition of financial assets may be sent by banks or FIs to a defaulter (an obligor), who will then make payments to the ARC. In the case of nonperforming assets, a secured creditor is entitled to serve a notice to the borrower to discharge his liabilities within 60 days. In case of failure to do this, the creditor is entitled to take possession of the secured assets. A shareholder of an ARC holding at least 75 percent of a defaulter's securities may call for a meeting of all other shareholders in the ARC, with the resolution of this meeting binding. Appeals by aggrieved borrowers to Debt Recovery Tribunals (DRTs) are allowed only after the borrower deposits 75 percent of the disputed amount and, in cases of adverse decisions, then appeals to a Debt Recovery Appellate Tribunal (DART). The same rules apply to interest earned from these assets. No civil court has jurisdiction to entertain a suit for a case that has been filed before a DRT or DART.

Sources: Securitization and Reconstruction of Financial Assets and Enforcement of Securities Interest Act 2002; Ministry of Finance, *Economic Survey 2002–03*; and Reserve Bank of India, *Annual Report 2002–03*.

discipline among borrowers), some loopholes still remain. It *inter alia* addresses only one aspect of credit risk, that is, the power of a lender to takeover collateral. However, the Act ignores the broader aspect of creditors' rights and introduces yet another disincentive to extending credit by skewing banks toward secured loans. This represents an inefficient form of credit expansion in an economy where the share of services is large and growing. Likewise, our rough estimate suggests that one-third of outstanding NPAs are beyond the purview of the Act, given exemptions on all loans to the agricultural sectors and on interest due of less than Rs 0.1 million. Expectedly, there has also been confusion over the definition of "default" under the Act, as well as the *modus operandi* of issuing notices, taking possession, and disposing of such securities.[48]

A criticism of SARFAESI Act has been that flawed lending practices of intermediaries have in the past contributed in undermining commercial viability of the project for which the loan was disbursed. For instance, a corporation claimed that delays in disbursement of working capital and substitution by high cost bridge loans had increased the project cost and rendered it unviable. To level the playing field somewhat for future lending (keeping in mind principles of "natural justice"), the RBI issued *Guidelines for Lenders Liability and a Fair Practices Code for Lenders* in May 2003, addressing issues of transparency in loan application, conduct of proper due diligence, disbursement and sanction timelines and processes, recovery procedures, and so on.

Owing to Supreme Court concerns of "serious defects" in the SARFAESI Act, it stayed the Act in August 2003 following holding up questions about the constitutional validity of the Act but with some caveats for a petition filing. The Court cited the Act as being inordinately biased towards creditors, especially the requirement to deposit 75 percent of the disputed amount before approaching a debt tribunal. A tentative judgment was issued by the Supreme Court in March 2004, which held up the constitutional validity of the Act, but with some caveats for proceeding on further asset foreclosures and sales. This judgment has effectively paved the way for full-fledged operation of the Asset Reconstruction Company of India Limited (ARCIL)—India's first ARC.[49]

4.4.2   Reforming nonbank intermediaries

As mentioned in Section 4.3, although the focus of prudential regulations has been the banking segment, the proximate source of serious problems in India's financial sector has often been other intermediaries. Although a series of piece-meal fixes have lugubriously corrected some of the maladies of FIs, there remain a few other intermediaries whose asset portfolios have the potential of imparting systemic instability in the financial sector. We briefly examine the asset portfolios of two such intermediaries, the LIC and the EPFO (see Box 4.2). A point to note is the opacity of their asset portfolios, a shortcoming which is especially serious in the case of the latter.

Box 4.2 Investment patterns of large financial institutions

This box provides an overview of the investment patterns of several large nonbank financial intermediaries. Assets of these institutions can be characterized, in part, as "socially oriented investments."

Life Insurance Corporation (LIC)

The investments of the LIC are intended to "channelize the savings mobilized for the welfare of people at large" and are defined as investments that "help to improve the quality of life of the people at large through improvements of basic amenities like potable water, drainage, housing, electrification and transport." Assets under this head include investments in central and state government securities (as well as those guaranteed by governments) and loans to various socially oriented schemes. It is noteworthy that the LIC's asset portfolio is large (equivalent to 8 1/3 percent of India's GDP in 2000/01).

Although the LIC does not publish a complete breakdown of its investments into equity and debt, a partial breakdown in the table below shows that incremental investments in equities (line II.f) and debt (line II.g) increased by 31 percent and 34 percent, respectively, in 2000/01.

Employees' Provident Fund (EPF) and Employee Pension Scheme (EPS)

The EPF is subject to investment norms prescribed by the government of India in 1998, and also tends to channel funds into asset holdings similar to the LIC. A breakdown of the EPF's investment as well as those of the EPS is shown in the figure below.

Life Insurance Corporation of India: Utilization of Funds
(as of March 31, 2001)

	Amounts outstanding (in billions of rupees at book value)		In percent of total	In percent of subtotal
	1999/ 2000	2000/ 2001	2000/ 2001	2000/ 2001
I. Loans				
a. State electricity boards/ power corporations	70.7	75.6	4.3	23.5
b. State government housing (including the Delhi Development Authority and Police Housing Corporation)	27.3	31.4	1.8	9.8

	Amounts outstanding (in billions of rupees at book value)		In percent of total	In percent of subtotal
	1999/ 2000	2000/ 2001	2000/ 2001	2000/ 2001
c. National Housing Bank	10.0	9.3	0.5	2.9
d. Housing finance societies (including the Life Insurance Corporation) (LIC)	63.7	74.9	4.3	23.3
e. Municipalities/Zila Parishads/water supply and sewerage boards	20.0	24.3	1.4	7.6
f. State road transport corporations	3.8	3.9	0.2	1.2
g. Private sector power generation companies	1.1	1.5	0.1	0.5
h. Joint stock companies (including public sector undertakings) and cooperative societies	28.3	26.6	1.5	8.3
Total loan portfolio	289.3	321.6	18.4	100.0
II. Investments in securities				
a. Government of India securities	705.3	851.4	48.6	60.8
b. State government securities	119.2	143.7	8.2	10.3
c. Other government securities (including Kisan Vikas Patras)	35.6	35.0	2.0	2.5
d. Roadways, ports, railways	0.9	3.3	0.2	0.2
e. Private sector power generation	13.7	14.6	0.8	1.0
f. Shares (including holdings in LIC Mutual Fund)	114.8	149.9	8.6	10.7
g. Debentures and bonds[a]	150.8	202.7	11.6	14.5
Total investments	1,140.3	1,401.1	80.1	100.0
III. Special deposits with the Government of India	20.4	18.6	1.1	—
IV. Other items (unidentified)	9.1	8.8	0.5	—
Total	1,459.1	1,750.1	100.0	—

[a] Including those issued by the Industrial Reconstruction Bank of India, Rural Electrification Corporation, Small Industries Development Bank of India, state finance corporations, state level development banks, and port trusts.

Source: Life Insurance Corporation of India Annual Report 2001–02.

Investment norms prescribed for the Employees' Provident Fund
Organisation's Employees' Provident Fund (in percent)

Investment category	Investment shares
1. Central government securities	25
2a. Government securities created and issued by the state government	15
2b. Any other negotiable securities whose principal and interest is fully and unconditionally guaranteed by the central or a state government	—
3a. Bonds and securities of "public financial institutions," public sector companies (including public sector banks), and Infrastructure Development Finance Company	40
3b. Certificates of deposit (CDs) issued by a public sector bank	—
4. Any of the three categories above, to be decided by the Board of Trustees	20

Source: Employees' Provident Fund Organisation (EPFO), *Annual Report 2001–02*.

Investments of the Employees' Provident Fund and Employees' Provident
Scheme corpuses in various instruments, end-March 2002[ab]

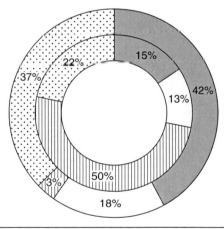

[a] Outer ring is Employees' Provident Fund; inner ring is Employees' Provident Scheme.
[b] Figures (in percent) represent share of total investments.
[c] Including government guaranteed securities.

Source: EPFO, *Annual Report 2001/02*.

The LIC had a total business of Rs 7300 billion (in terms of sums assured) as of March 2001, and a corpus in its Life Fund of Rs 1860 billion. The book value of the LIC's "socially oriented investments"—mainly comprising government securities holdings and social sector investments—amounted to Rs 1253 billion at end-March 2001 or 72 percent of the LIC's total portfolio value of Rs 1750 billion (equivalent to 8.4 percent of GDP in 2000/01).[50] A staggering 84 percent of its total portfolio comprises exposure to the public sector.

Compared to the LIC, the EPFO's accounts are considerably more opaque. Cumulative contributions to the three schemes of the EPFO, that is the Employees' Provident Fund (EPF), Employees' Pension Scheme (EPS) and Employees' Deposit Linked Insurance, amounted to Rs 1271 billion as of end-March 2002. Total cumulative investments of these three schemes were Rs 1390 billion (5.6 percent of GDP), with the EPF being the largest scheme. The EPFO does not come under the purview of an independent regulator, with oversight resting on three sources: the Income Tax Act (1961), EPF Act (1952) and Indian Trusts Act (1882). When the RBI relinquished its role as portfolio manager of the EPF funds in 1995, the SBI was appointed to the role. It is estimated that the average real annual compound rate of return over the period 1986–2000 was 2.7 percent (Asher (2003)). A rough estimate in Patel (1997a) indicates that the EPS was actuarially insolvent. The EPFO's reluctance to make public its actuarial calculations does little to assuage this concern.

4.4.3   Domestic financial fragility and external sector strength

The relatively minor impact in India of the turbulence that swept the East Asian economies in the late 1990s is widely ascribed to the closed capital account. With the increasing international financial integration in India, a closed capital account is becoming increasingly more difficult to maintain. The road map for full capital account convertibility (CAC) that was laid out in RBI (1997) specified elaborate preconditions on indicators of vulnerability. The report singled out health of the financial system as the most important precondition to moving to CAC. Since the report's release, the benchmarks that have not been met for CAC invariably relate to longstanding problems with strong undercurrents in political economy, specifically the persistence of large fiscal deficits (which have worsened since 1997) and state of India's financial system.

The main deficiency in India's external sector indicators currently pertains to its low international credit rating, which has hovered around the speculative grade for most of the last decade and is generally attributed to unhealthy fiscal indicators. A significant improvement in the country's fiscal health is unlikely even in the medium term, and indeed could be compounded by the government's seemingly *carte blanche* policy toward financial intermediary bailouts, the uncertainty regarding the magnitude of unfunded pension commitments of the central and state governments and concerns over the quantum of credit guarantees and enhancements provided by central and state governments that may have to be honored. It could be argued[51] that India will maintain large foreign exchange reserves as a signal to compensate for internal weaknesses (both fiscal and financial) and global uncertainties through the strength in its external accounts, much like the perception in the case of China.

4.5 Conclusion

We have attempted to discern and define the strategies that have underpinned financial sector reforms in India during the 1990s, and then to identify the institutional features that have, in some significant measure, mitigated the effectiveness of these reforms. Despite a significant strengthening of financial intermediaries and transactions systems in both the banking sector and the capital markets, especially the latter, there remain significant weaknesses. While India has advanced considerably along the route mapped by international organizations like the Bank for International Settlements and International Organization for Securities Commissions in developing financial markets, these measures, although useful for reducing systemic risks, may prove inadequate in the face of structural distortions, flawed practices, and insipid enforcement. Most of the recommendations of the Narasimhan Committee II that have been accepted and introduced, although significant, are in the nature of ratios, rates, and accounting norms. The same progress has not been attained with regard to structural and systemic aspects of the reform agenda. Financial sector reforms have to be more widely encompassing than supervision by central bank regulators; an integral part is the wider environment in which intermediaries function, and their operational freedom and ability to take commercial decisions. In the absence of market discipline and given the level of government intervention, the reform actions are likely to have only a limited impact on the efficiency of the intermediation process and prudential norms result in little effective change.

Some restrictions on the banking sector (that are part of the prudential requirements) may also be inconsistent with the ability of intermediaries to raise needed resources in the near future. For instance, in order to prevent connected lending (one of the original motives for bank nationalization), private banks in India cannot have corporate owners who own more than 10 percent of the bank's equity capital. Precluding this route could constrain the ability of some new private sector banks to expand networks and offer more services. Attempts to mix commercial and social objectives (for instance, rural bank branch requirements) also serve to increase the costs of intermediation.

India is unlikely to suffer a full-blown systemic crisis, witnessed in different contexts in various countries. Its financial sector inefficiencies are likely to simply simmer, with occasional payments crises, like the one at the dominant mutual fund over the last five years. However, the cumulative inefficiencies and grim fiscal outlook, with the concomitant regulatory forbearance that public involvement inevitably entails, are certain to retard India's transition to a high growth trajectory. The persistent unease with the state of the system, it can be speculated, arises from the recognition that the perceived safety of intermediaries is due more to the "social contract" between the government and depositors (that is, the Indian public) than a real robustness in the health of the sector.

The system of intermediation will not improve appreciably in the absence of any serious steps toward changing incentives, which remain blunted by public sector involvement (of which ownership is an important aspect). To sharpen these incentives, outright privatization may not be sufficient, but it *is* necessary. It is the first step to a true relinquishing of management control, which remains far beyond the scope envisaged in the Banking Companies (Acquisition and Transfer of Undertakings) Bill tabled in Parliament, designed to reduce the government holding in nationalized banks to 33 percent, but allowing it to retain the "public sector character" of these banks by maintaining effective control over their boards and restricting the voting right of nongovernment nominees. Attempts to shed the commercial risks of investors, borrowers, and depositors (through implicit bailouts and other means of accommodating fragility) will almost certainly lead to economic risks during slowdowns, creating a new kind of instability.

Given the increasing integration of financial markets, there is also a need to shift reform focus from individual intermediaries to a system level. An important component in this shift is enhancing intermediaries' ability to de-risk their asset portfolios. Undoubtedly, the SARFAESI Act of 2002 is a crucial step forward in addressing bad loans, but, on its own, is limited in scope and has been beset by various legal challenges. Establishing asset reconstruction companies, even under private management, will serve only to tackle the overhang of existing bad assets—they *per se* do little to correct the distortions in incentives that are intrinsic to large parts of the system.

The banking sector is caught in a cleft stick. On the one hand, a predatory fiscal regime has injected a large corpus of government securities into the market that offer an attractive risk-adjusted return for banks, given the increasingly stringent risk-management regulatory framework in place. On the other, government ownership of many of these institutions increases aversion for "good" commercial risk by imposing an idiosyncratic combination of blunted incentives for credit creation and disincentives from the intrusive oversight by numerous government (investigative) agencies. It is ironic that the government has (unintentionally) managed to expand the proposed transformation of weak banks into "narrow" banks, a move that had been mooted earlier, to the entire banking sector! Through an entirely endogenous evolution, we seem to have moved back to the pre-reform days, at least in this respect.

Notes

1. Hindustan Lever Limited (Unilever India) and Infrastructure Development Finance Company Limited (IDFC), respectively. The opinions presented in the paper are those of the authors and not necessarily of the institutions to which they are affiliated.
2. See Bhattacharya and Patel (2002).
3. For instance, cooperative banks have been lax in implementing RBI notifications on lending to brokers.
4. Apart from commercial banks, the largest of these other deposit-taking institutions are also government owned (including the EPFO), with many cooperative banking institutions having been singled out for their close links to the local political establishments.
5. For instance, it is periodically reported in the media that accounting and regulatory loopholes in banks are used as conduits for various irregularities in equity and debt transactions.
6. RBI, *Statistical Tables Relating to Banks in India, 2001–02*.
7. See Reddy (2002) and Patel (2000) for a detailed exposition.
8. The market share of assets of the "m" largest banks.
9. The capital to risk-weighted assets ratio (CRAR) for scheduled commercial banks is currently 9 percent.
10. This figure is calculated assuming a nominal GDP growth rate of 11 percent per annum over 2003/04–2007/08 and then using simple extrapolations based on outstanding bank deposits and credit-deposit ratios as at end-March 2003.
11. See Patel (1997b) for a conceptual underpinning.
12. The Banking Companies (Acquisition and Transfer of Undertakings) Bill and the Financial Institutions Laws (Amendment) Bill were tabled in Parliament in 2000, but have not yet been enacted.
13. RBI *Annual Report 2002–03*. The ratio of net NPAs to advances is 4.5 percent. Estimates by various ratings and other agencies put this number much higher.
14. RBI, *Statistical Tables Relating to Banks in India, 2001–02*.
15. In 2000, India ranked 78th in terms of insurance density (that is, premia per capita, equivalent to about US$10, as compared to US$15 in China) and 52nd in terms of insurance penetration (that is, premia as a percent of GDP, which was 2.3 percent). As a share of gross domestic savings, insurance premiums in India in 1999 were 9 percent compared to 52 percent in the United Kingdom and 35 percent in the United States and Europe (Insurance Regulatory Development Authority, *Annual Report 2001–02*).
16. Total outstanding marketable debt at the end of 2001/02 was approximately Rs 8500 billion (41 percent of GDP), of which central government securities was Rs 5363 billion; state government, Rs 1040 billion; and (informed estimates) of public sector undertakings and private corporate bonds, Rs 2000 billion (Tahir (2002)).
17. Calculated from figures in the RBI's *Monthly Bulletin* (October 2003) and *Handbook of Statistics on the Indian Economy 2002–03*.
18. "Treasury Debt Management" presentation by Timothy Bitsberger, United States Treasury Department, 2003.
19. RBI, *Annual Report 2002–03* and *Monthly Bulletin* (October 2003).

20. See various RBI *Annual Reports*.
21. For instance, defeasance periods (that is, holding period for assets) of debt instruments have declined to about 30 days at present from an average of 90–100 days two years earlier.
22. Given the RBI's apparent decision to increase the average maturity of government debt, with a consequent increased issuance of longer dated securities, increased trading interest in these securities and subsequently increased illiquidity premiums for shorter dated papers has flattened the yield curve.
23. For example, exchange traded derivatives for stock indexes and individual stocks at the NSE.
24. Calomiris and Powell (2000) and Feldstein (1999).
25. Demirguc-Kunt and Levine (1999), Jagtiani *et al.* (1999), and Karacadag and Shrivastava (2000). In market-oriented systems, the banking sector as a whole as well as individual banks are penalized, as choice clients desert them for stronger competitors. The cost of capital increases as credit ratings and share prices fall, and trading gets tougher as counterparties cut back on long established credit lines.
26. An expression used by a Deputy Governor of the RBI.
27. See Buiter and Patel (1997) for a formal assessment of the sustainability of India's fiscal stance.
28. RBI, *Weekly Statistical Supplement* (October 11, 2003). It is also noteworthy that 52 percent of the outstanding stock of government securities is held by just two public sector institutions: the SBI and the LIC.
29. Trading profits (in securities) of PSBs in 2001–02 jumped more than 2.5 times that of the previous year and accounted for 28 percent of operating profits (RBI, *Report on Trend and Progress of Banking in India, 2001–02*).
30. Banks were advised in April 2002 to build up an investment fluctuation reserve (IFR) to a minimum 5 percent of their investments in the categories "held for trading" and "available for sale" within five years. At end-June 2003, the total IFR of SCBs amounted to only about Rs 100 billion (that is 1.7 percent of investments under the relevant categories). While 12 banks had yet to make any provisions for an IFR, 20 had built their IFR up to 1 percent and 65 had an IFR exceeding 1 percent (RBI, *Mid-Term Credit and Monetary Policy Statement*, 2003).
31. "Individual cases of financial fraud in themselves may not constitute a scam. But persistent and pervasive misappropriation of public funds falling under the purview of statutory regulators and involving issues of governance become a scam" (Government of India, *Report of the Joint Committee on Stock Market Scam* (2002)).
32. Few countries have regulatory limits on exposures to certain sectors (see RBI, *Report on Trend and Progress of Banking in India 2001–02* (Box 2.1)). Of the ones that do, the restrictions pertain to "sensitive" sectors like property and share-related loans.
33. See Bhattacharya and Patel (2003a).
34. See Bhattacharya and Patel (2003b).
35. Compare this to the confirmation hearings for the Securities and Exchange chairman in the United States Congress or the recommended procedures of the Nolan Committee for public appointment in the United Kingdom, including those for the FSA chairman.
36. La Porta *et al.* (2001) and Hawkins and Mihaljek (2001) outline the characteristics of financial systems that are dominated by government-owned intermediaries.
37. FIs' share of total loans outstanding at end-March 2003 was about 20 percent, compared to about 50 percent at end-March 2001. The decline is partially due to the reclassification of the merged ICICI Bank as a commercial bank.
38. Mishkin (1999) and Mohanty and Patel (2000), respectively.

39. Demirguc-Kunt and Kane (2001).
40. *DICGC Annual Report 2001–02*.
41. Forms of the reportedly widespread practice of "ever-greening" assets.
42. Bhattacharya and Patel (2001).
43. This amounts to US$18 billion, compared to China's nonperforming loans, officially reported at US$307 billion, after having transferred US$170 billion to the four asset management companies.
44. RBI, *Report on Trend and Progress of Banking in India, 2001–02* (p. 25).
45. Recovery cases over Rs 1 million can be filed by banks and FIs in the DRTs. Between March 1994 and March 2002, 56,988 cases involving a sum of Rs 1087 billion were filed before the 29 DRTs and 5 Debt Recovery Appellate Tribunals. Of these, 23,393 cases, involving an amount of Rs 186 billion, had been disposed of, with banks recovering Rs 47 billion, or a recovery rate of about 26 percent (Adhivarahan (2003)).
46. The RBI issued a fresh OTS scheme in January 2003 for compromise settlement of NPAs up to Rs 100 million but not covering cases of willful default or malfeasance.
47. The Act was formally passed by parliament in November 2002, after having been promulgated as an ordinance in June 2002.
48. RBI guidelines issued in April 2003 define a willful defaulter as one who has not used bank funds for the purpose for which they were taken and who has not repaid bank loans despite having adequate liquidity.
49. The ARCIL was formally established under Section 3 of the SARFAESI Act as a securitization and reconstruction company with effect from August 29, 2003. It had an initial equity of Rs 100 million, with the ICICI Bank, Industrial Development Bank of India (IDBI), and SBI each having a 24.5 percent stake in ARCIL (with the remaining held by Housing Development Finance Corporation, IDBI Bank, and UTI Bank). Another Asset Care Enterprises (ARC), is being promoted by the Industrial Finance Corporation of India (with a 33 percent stake), Punjab National Bank (26 percent), the Tourism Finance Corporation of India (10 percent), and the rest by the LIC.
50. Social sector investments include loans to State Electricity Boards, housing, municipalities, water and sewerage boards, State Road Transport Corporations, roadways, and railways. However, these account for only about a fifth of the socially oriented investments portfolio, with the balance accounted for by government and government guaranteed securities.
51. Kapur and Patel (2003).

References

Adhivarahan, V., 2003, "Case Management and ADR for the Banking Sector," paper presented at the Law Commission of India conference on *Case Management and ADR*, New Delhi (May).

Ahluwalia, M. S., 2002, "Financial Sector Reforms in India: An Assessment," paper presented at the Harvard University conference on *Financial Reforms Across Asia*, Cambridge, MA. (December).

Asher, M. G., 2003, "Reforming India's Social Security System," mimeo (May) (Singapore: National University of Singapore).

Bhattacharya, S. and U. R. Patel, 2003a, "Markets, Regulatory Institutions, Competitiveness and Reforms," theme paper presented at the Global Development Network workshop on *Understanding Reform*, Cairo (January).

Bhattacharya, S., 2003b, "New Regulatory Institutions in India: White Knights or Trojan Horses?" paper presented at a Harvard University conference on *Public Institutions in India: Performance and Design*, Cambridge, MA.

——, 2002, "Financial Intermediation in India: A Case of Aggravated Moral Hazard?" Center for Research on Economic Development and Policy Reform Working Paper No. 145 (July) (Palo Alto, CA: Stanford University).

——, 2001, "Financial Intermediation and Aggravated Moral Hazard: Theory and an Application to India," mimeo (Mumbai: Infrastructure Development Finance Company Limited (December)).

Bitsberger, Timothy, 2003. "Treasury Debt Management," presentation (Washington, DC: United States Treasury Department).

Boston Consulting Group, 2003, presentation to Confederation of Indian Industry Banking Summit, New Delhi.

Buiter, W. H. and U. R. Patel, 1997, "Budgetary Aspects of Stabilization and Structural Adjustment in India," in *Macroeconomic Dimensions of Public Finance, Essays in Honor of Vito Tanzi*, ed. by M. Blejer and T. Ter-Minassian (London: Routledge).

Calomiris, C. W. and A. Powell, 2000, "Can Emerging Market Bank Regulators Establish Credible Discipline?" NBER Working Paper No. 7715 (Cambridge, MA: National Bureau of Economic Research).

Caprio, G., 1996, "Bank Regulation: the Case of the Missing Model," paper presented at the Brookings Institution and KPMG conference on *Sequencing of Financial Reform*, Washington, DC.

Demirguc-Kunt, A. and R. Levine, 1999, "Bank-Based and Market-Based Financial Systems: Cross-Country Comparisons," Policy Research Working Paper No. 2143 (Washington, DC: The World Bank).

Demirguc-Kunt, A. and E. J. Kane, 2001, "Deposit Insurance Around the World: Where Does it Work?" paper prepared for the World Bank conference on *Deposit Insurance*, Washington, DC. (July).

Deposit Insurance and Credit Guarantee Corporation, 2002, *Annual Report 2001–02* (Mumbai).

Employees' Provident Fund Organisation, 2002, *Annual Report 2001–02* (New Delhi).

Feldstein, M., 1999, "Self Protection for Emerging Market Economies," NBER Working Paper No. 6907 (Cambridge, MA: National Bureau of Economic Research).

Government of India, 2002, *Report of the Joint Committee on Stock Market Scam*, 2002 (New Delhi: Joint Parliamentary Committee).

Hawkins, J. and D. Mihaljek, 2001, "The Banking Industry in the Emerging Market Economies: Competition, Consolidation and Systemic Stability—an Overview," BIS Papers No. 4 (August) (Basel: Bank for International Settlements).

ICICI Bank, 2003, presentation on "Indian Derivatives Markets: Future Prospects," to the Federation of Indian Chambers of Commerce and Industry's Convention on Capital Markets, Mumbai (August).

Industrial and Development Bank of India (IDBI) (various years), *IDBI Report on Development Banking* (Mumbai).

Insurance Regulatory Development Authority (India), 2003, *Annual Report 2001–02* (Hyderabad).

Jagtiani, J., G. Kaufman, and C. Lemieux, 1999, "Do Markets Discipline Banks and Bank Holding Companies? Evidence from Debt Securities," *Emerging Issues* (June) (Federal Reserve Bank of Chicago).

Kapur, D. and U. R. Patel, 2003, "Large Foreign Currency Reserves: Insurance for Domestic Weaknesses and External Uncertainties?" *Economic and Political Weekly* (March 15–21), pp. 1047–53.

Karacadag, C. and A. Shrivastava, 2000, "The Role of Subordinated Debt in Market Discipline: The Case of Emerging Markets," IMF Working Paper No. 00/215 (Washington, DC: International Monetary Fund).

La Porta, R., F. L. de-Silanes, and A. Shleifer, 2001, "Government Ownership of Banks," mimeo (Cambridge, MA: Harvard University).

Life Insurance Corporation of India, 2002, *Annual Report 2001–02* (Mumbai).

Ministry of Finance (India), *Economic Survey* (various years).

Mishkin, F. S., 1999, "Financial Market Reform," mimeo (New York: Columbia University).

Mohanty, N. and U. R. Patel, 2000, "Moving Ahead with Financial Sector Reform," mimeo (Mumbai: Infrastructure Development Finance Company Ltd.).

National Stock Exchange of India, *Indian Securities Markets: A Review* (various years).

Patel, U. R., 2000, "Outlook for the Indian Financial Sector," *Economic and Political Weekly* (November 4–10), pp. 3933–8.

———, 1997a, "Aspects of Pension Fund Reform: Lessons for India," *Economic and Political Weekly* (September 20–26), pp. 2395–402.

———, 1997b, "Emerging Reforms in Indian Banking: International Perspectives," *Economic and Political Weekly* (October 18–24), pp. 2655–60.

Patel, U. R. and Bhattacharya, S., 2003, "The Financial Leverage Coefficient: Macroeconomic Implications of Government Involvement in Intermediaries," Center for Research on Economic Development and Policy Reform Working Paper No. 157 (Palo Alto, CA: Stanford University).

Reddy, Y. V., 2002, "Monetary and Financial Sector Reforms in India: A Practitioner's Perspective," paper presented at the Cornell University, Program on Comparative Economic Development conference on *The Indian Economy*, Ithaca, NY (April).

Reserve Bank of India, 2003, *Mid-Term Credit and Monetary Policy Statement* (November).

———, 2003, *Weekly Statistical Supplement* (various issues).

———, 2000, *Discussion Paper on Prompt Corrective Action*.

———, 1997, *Report of the Committee on Capital Account Convertibility*, S. S. Tarapore (Chairman) (Mumbai).

——— (various years), *Annual Report*.

——— (various years), *Handbook of Statistics on the Indian Economy*.

——— (various years), *Monetary Policy Statement*.

——— (various issues), *Monthly Bulletin*.

——— (various years), *Report on Currency and Finance*.

——— (various years), *Report on Trend and Progress of Banking in India*.

——— (various years), *Statistical Tables Related to Banks in India*.

Rodrik, D., 2002, "After Neo-Liberalism, What?" mimeo (June) (Cambridge, MA: Harvard University).

Shirai, S., 2001, "Assessment of India's Banking Sector Reform from the Perspective of the Governance of the Banking System," paper presented at the United Nations Economic and Social Commission for Asia and the Pacific–Asian Development Bank joint workshop on *Mobilizing Domestic Finance for Development*, Bangkok (November).

Tahir, M., 2002, "Development of Bond Market in India," paper presented at the Japan–Singapore Economic Partnership Agreement workshop on the *Development of Bond Markets in Asia*, Singapore (October).

5
Financial System Reform and Economic Development in China

Chen Yuan[1]

This chapter reviews the role of China's financial sector in its economic development, and the challenges that lie ahead. It comes at a time when the world economy is apparently in a stage of readjustment and recovery, with the current key focus now to work toward long-term sustainable economic growth. I speak cautiously regarding this assessment of recovery, because many challenges lie ahead. In the first half of 2003 alone, the global economy suffered from a number of negative economic shocks, including the Iraqi war, rapidly rising oil prices, and the SARS epidemic. Adding to the economic malaise in 2003 were the imponderables of geopolitical risks, the volatility of major currencies and stock markets, and continuous deflation in some Asian countries. Given such potential crises and risks on the economic horizon, it is prudent and even extremely important to enhance the early warning and response capabilities of the international financial systems. In particular, developing countries, China among them, must deepen their economic systems and strengthen their institutions if they are to promote long-term growth that will weather such global challenges and shocks.

Let me make a simple statement that catalyzes China's development strategy in finance: Long-term sustainable economic growth requires the development of a sound and efficient financial system that accommodates the coordinated development of three forms of finance—budgetary finance, bank finance, and securities finance. They are like the three legs of a stool—stable where they complement each another, wobbly if they are not level. Each type has its advantages and limitations and each is associated with an important set of functions and rules of the game. In a balanced economy with long-term sustained growth, all three must develop in complementarity.

Budgetary finance is relatively straightforward: it realizes the government's fiscal policy objectives and helps facilitate the development of market credit, enterprise credit, and social credit by capitalizing on the role of the government and the use of its sovereign credit standing; allocation of resources is through the budgetary revenue and expenditure approach. Budgetary finance can be considered a rudimentary form of direct financing that requires

132

no repayment. However, given the needs and size of China and India (large by any global standard), budgetary finance has very real limitations and certainly cannot be expected to achieve all desired goals.

By comparison, bank finance operates through the intermediation of banks in compliance with relevant regulations requiring asset security and capital and interest repayment. Importantly, there is a significant multiplier effect that bank finance brings to project realization. However, it is an indirect form of financing in a market economy, and its effectiveness is predicated on the premise of a well-developed credit culture and infrastructure, as there are public and market constraints within economies that are transiting toward fully developed market economies. The achievement of national economic development objectives necessitates the strategic use of bank finance as a public policy tool as well as a commercial medium. China Development Bank is a case study for just such a banking institution that effectively intermediates between budgetary finance and commercial credit.

In contrast, securities finance or capital market finance is a direct form of financing in a market economy; it envisages widespread and direct participation by the public. However, securities finance remains significantly constrained by public sentiment and its availability and costs are susceptible to wide market fluctuations. By definition, securities investors directly assume market risks, so this form of finance relies on the existence of a relatively large number of investors with the sophistication, means, and ability to shoulder such risks. Unfortunately, such a large class of citizenry with those qualities is an element generally lacking in developing countries

Case studies of various national economies show that their economic development can be analyzed through the paradigm of the evolutionary process of these three forms of finance. Witness the stark contrast between the developing countries of Asia and the developed countries of Europe and North America. The latter feature highly developed and modern market economies, where bank finance and securities finance are capable of more efficient resource allocation than budgetary finance. They boast a well-developed capital market, which has been fine-tuned over the course of many years and played a crucial role in their successful economic development. Underpinning such advanced securities finance and capital markets are populations that accept and rely on a social credit culture embracing complementary systems of legal discipline, market and regulatory discipline, and moral discipline.

Today, most Asian countries remain largely dependent on bank finance while their securities finance remains relatively underdeveloped—China certainly falls in this category. Moreover, Asian bank finance and securities finance are burdened by historical legacies, both in attitudes and actions that result from past mistakes in budgetary finance. Our banks have necessarily shouldered financial risks that would be unacceptable in developed markets. This exposes an inherent flaw in bank finance—risks are deferred to the future, where liability only compounds. Problem loans create problematic banks and troubled banking systems. This drawback has yet to be redressed by Asian banks in general and it is not merely a Chinese problem. Indeed, nonperforming loans made 20 years ago are still troubling the Japanese economy.

China is a developing economy, where, by definition, the three forms of finance are not balanced. By definition, our economy lacks the sophisticated financial institutions and educated citizens to fully appreciate their advantages. Prior to relatively recent reforms and opening our economy to world markets, China's economic development was largely the fruits of budgetary finance. In the last twenty years, China has developed a financial framework largely reliant on bank finance. The disparity between the three is striking:

- China's current annual fiscal revenue is something in excess of Y1 trillion.
- China's bank deposits amount to Y18 trillion; whilst its bank loans total Y14 trillion.
- The total capitalization of our stock market is valued at a mere Y4 trillion.

In the nonfinancial sectors, the ratios of financing through treasury bonds, bank loans, corporate bonds, and stocks to total financing are even more unbalanced, with treasury bonds and bank loans presently accounting for 15 and 80 percent, respectively, and the remaining 5 percent in corporate bonds (1 percent) and stocks (4 percent). This relative overweight in bank financing fails to exploit the synergistic efficiencies of the three forms of financing and has resulted in large amounts of nonperforming assets given the absolute size of bank finance. Due to the weak economic foundations that underpin our financial institutions, together with our outdated and erratically enforced regulatory policies, China is now facing an arduous task in its development.

The lesson is clear: China's economic progress has been achieved in spite of our backward financial institutions when it should have occurred through the assistance of those same institutions. Going forward, we must either lose our inefficient financial infrastructure or we will lose pace in our economic development. Like three engines that seriously need tuning and balancing, our economy will inevitably break down unless budgetary finance, bank finance and securities finance are in balance and acting in a complementary fashion. This balance will generate growth more than simply the aggregate sum of financing—it will entail a conceptual, methodological, and behavioral dynamic that will enhance the power, efficiency, and reputation of our financial system. We believe that budgetary finance will act as the catalyst and play a key role in transforming our economy into one driven by the market. We see bank finance and securities finance as the foundation pilings of our future socialist market economy.

Attention needs to be drawn to five issues:

- We must make effective use of the dominant role of bank finance. On the one hand, it is necessary to develop securities finance through strengthening the banking system, to keep long-term and short-term capital in proportion and to develop a prudential risk-management system aimed at mitigating long-term and short-term financial risks. On the other hand, application of the principles and methods of capital markets to the instrument of bank finance may serve to develop bank finance to a higher level of maturity, efficiency, and security.
- We must fully utilize the macroeconomic adjustment and regulatory function of fiscal and monetary policies, and transit from a heavy dependence on governmental finance toward a combination of governmental and market finance. The government should take advantage of market finance and adapt its financing accordingly.
- We must provide a fertile ground for fostering capital markets and ensuring the mutual promotion and development of the loan market, the bond market, and the stock market.
- We must establish and enhance the credit environment so as to facilitate the robust operation of the economy and its financial markets. This entails building a framework for credit culture and risk management by providing clear rules of the game for all investment and financing activities. This remains a priority and requires the concerted effort of government, the financial sector, business enterprises, and the public.
- We must cautiously address issues concerning the utilization of foreign capital, especially considering the risk of short-term capital outflows. As you know, foreign capital is assuming an increasingly significant role in economic development of every country, given rising economic and financial globalization. Both China and India must draw from the experience of the recent Asian financial crisis and the Latin American economic crises of the 1980s and learn to cope with issues inherent to the opening up of capital markets and short-term capital flows in a global economy.

As we work to achieve these five objectives, we must never forget: financial institutions are the foundation and heart of modern market-based economic institutions. Such a market system is a production and service economy integrated into a complex set of elements, including corporate governance practices, financial infrastructure, the investment and financing system (including capital markets), information disclosure transparency, sector competition, and market supervision, together with the critical roles of macroeconomic adjustment and regulation. Of all of these elements, the financial institutions are the most important; and therefore, their modernization is essential.

Modernization of financial institutions will bring clear-cut processes and procedures in response to the need for unambiguous regulations concerning legal entities, corporate governance, ownership and property rights, while the modernization of the financial infrastructure will involve accounting standards, payment systems, credit systems, performance reviews, and law enforcement. To give an analogy, financial institutions are like the cells of the market organism, while infrastructure activities parallel those of the internal regulatory organs. Both elements are interdependent, essential, and complementary, and they operate in a seamless environment.

The modernization of China's financial system and institutions envisioned here calls for the joint efforts of government, the financial sector, business enterprises, and the public to see the job done. In other words, it has to be the convergent work of the entire economy. The fundamental economic and financial institutions in developed countries are the product of scores of hundreds of years of transition and improvement. China, as a latecomer, can leap frog directly from a primitive to advanced financial stage, bypassing the glitches and errors that time has lain bare. China, with its strong economic growth and abundance of resources and capacity, has at present an excellent opportunity to tackle the mission of total financial institution modernization. We have the momentum economically, so now is the time for our government to prioritize financial institution modernization at a high tier on the national agenda. Government credit should be intensively utilized within this program.

Targeted development finance can play an important role in correcting prior market failures and institutional defects. This has proven itself on a global basis, even in developed countries. There are instances where governments can and should directly commit funds to initiate measures and create and restructure the financial institutions that will implement those measures. The United States, Germany, Japan, and the Republic of Korea all have such institutions. With sovereign assistance, targeted development finance can promote quality corporate governance, aid in restructuring the enterprise as a proper legal entity, strategize cash flow management and evolve a credit culture. In such a climate, project funding, societal improvement, and institutional modernization are developed in parallel. In practice, targeted development finance functions in the following way: (i) it integrates sovereign credit with market performance effectively; (ii) it combines quasi-treasury bonds with asset management methods; and (iii) it aligns its advantages in financing with that of government in organizing and restructuring enterprise capacity to meet policy objectives.

China and India are two great nations that are the inheritors of two great ancient civilizations. Today the issues of development and globalization confront us both and we face the same or similar opportunities as well as challenges. We can learn from one another with respect to reform and development, and it is beneficial that we do so. China Development Bank wishes to import from India advanced management education and technology. We wish to strengthen cooperation between our nations and advance the exchange of talent and trade. We see economic collaboration as a progenitor to increased trade and development for us both, and in so doing, a further contributing factor to long-term economic prosperity for Asia and the world.

I conclude this chapter by citing a famous former leader, who said, "There will be no real Asia–Pacific century until both China and India are well-developed."

Note

1. Governor, China Development Bank.

6

Bank Financing in India

Abhijit Banerjee, Shawn Cole, and Esther Duflo[1]

6.1 Introduction

The Indian banking sector has been remarkably successful in some respects. Its immense size and enormous penetration in rural areas are exemplary among developing countries, as is its solid reputation for stability among depositors. The penetration in rural areas has been associated with a reduction of poverty and a diversification out of agriculture.[2] However, in recent years, it has been widely viewed as being both expensive and inept. In particular, it has been argued that most banks are overstaffed, that a large fraction of their assets are nonperforming, and that they under lend, in the sense of not putting enough effort into their primary task of financing industry.[3] A wide range of remedies have been suggested ranging from strengthening the legal system to punish defaulters, to abolishing the targeted lending programs (so-called priority sector rules), to privatization of the entire banking system.

Many of these recommendations have been controversial, partly because there is relatively little hard evidence directly supporting the implied judgments or even confirming the main diagnoses behind them. The challenge here is twofold:

- First, the problems facing banks are mutually reinforcing, which makes it difficult to identify the primary cause (if any). For example, underlending and large nonperforming assets (NPAs) inflate banks' operating costs, which they cover by setting high interest rates. This leads to further underlending by these banks. In another example, banks with a large existing stock of NPAs naturally attract more public scrutiny. This makes their loan officers adopt a more conservative stance, also resulting in underlending.
- Second, and more importantly, most of these judgments are made without an appropriate counterfactual. Credit–deposit ratios could be low because (i) banks are not trying to lend; (ii) marginal loans are too risky;

or (iii) capital adequacy is too low. In addition, banks may face insufficient demand. It is also not clear why we should necessarily believe that privatization would alleviate the problem of underlending or NPAs.[4] A comparison of public and private banks today is not appropriate because so far the private banks in India, for the most part, have limited themselves to dealing with corporate clients.

This chapter pulls together a recent body of evidence on the question of underlending and argues that there is clear evidence that socially and even privately profitable lending opportunities remain unexploited in the current environment. It then discusses why this might be the case. The chapter concludes with a discussion of the relevant policy responses, including the possibility of foreign investment.[5]

6.2   Is there underlending?

Identifying underlending

A firm is considered to be getting too little credit if the marginal product of capital in the firm is higher than the rate of interest that firm is paying on its marginal unit of borrowing. We propose identifying credit constraints by the following observation—if a firm that is *not* credit constrained is offered some additional credit at a rate below what it is paying on the market, the best way to make use of the new loan is to pay down its current market borrowing, rather than to invest more. Since a nonconstrained firm would invest only until the marginal product of capital equaled the rate of interest, the additional investment would yield a lower return. By contrast, a constrained firm would increase investment.

In Banerjee and Duflo (2003), we test these predictions by taking advantage of a recent change in the so-called priority sector rules in India—all banks in India are required to lend at least 40 percent of their net credit to the "priority sector," (which includes small-scale industry (SSI)), at an interest rate of no more than 4 percent above their prime lending rate. In January 1998, the limit on total investment in plants and machinery for a firm to be eligible for inclusion in the SSI category was raised from Rs 6.5 million to Rs 30 million. Our empirical strategy focuses on the firms that became newly eligible for credit in this period and uses firms that were always eligible for priority sector credit as control. The results from our analysis are reported briefly in the subsections that follow.

Specification

Through much of this section, we will estimate an equation of the form

$$y_{it} - y_{it-1} = \alpha_y \, \text{BIG}_i + \beta_y \, \text{POST}_t + \gamma_y \, \text{BIG}_i * \text{POST}_t + \varepsilon_{yit} \qquad (6.1)$$

with y taking the role of the various outcomes of interest (credit, revenue, profits, etc.), the dummy BIG conveying a large firm (explained below), and the dummy POST representing the post-January 1998 period. We are in effect comparing how the outcomes change for the big firms after 1998 with how they change for the small firms. y is expressed here as a growth rate, thus, it is, in effect, a triple difference in equation (6.1). As such, we can allow small firms and big firms to have different rates of growth and for the rate of growth to vary from year to year. However, we also assume that there would have been no differential changes in the rate of growth of the various outcomes for small and large firms in 1998, in the absence of the change in priority sector regulations. Using the (log) credit limit and (log) next year's sales (or profit), respectively, in place of y in equation (6.1), we obtain the first stage and the reduced form of a regression of sales on credit, using the interaction BIG * POST as an instrument for credit.

Data

We use data from loan portfolios of a better performing Indian public sector bank (PSB). The loan folders include information on profit, sales, credit sanctions, and interest rates, as well as figures that loan officers are required to calculate (e.g. projections of the bank's future turnover and credit needs) to determine the amount to be lent. Our sample comprises 253 firms (including 93 newly eligible firms for priority lending) from 1997–99.

Results

Estimation of equation (6.1) using bank credit as the outcome shows that the change in priority lending regulations greatly affected those who got priority sector credit. In Table 6.1, panel A, column (2) of, for the sample of firms where there was a change in credit limit, the coefficient of the interaction BIG * POST is 0.24 in the credit equation, with a standard error of 0.09. However, this increase in credit was not accompanied by a change in the rate of interest (column (3)). Nor did it lead to reduction in the rate of utilization of the limits by the big firm (column (4))—the ratio of total turnover (the sum of all debts incurred during the year) to credit limit is not associated with the interaction BIG * POST. Rather, the higher credit limit resulted in an increase in bank credit utilization by the firms.

We also find that the additional credit in turn led to increased sales. The coefficient of the interaction BIG * POST in the sales equation, in the sample where the credit limit was increased, is 0.21, with a standard error of 0.09 (column (5)). By contrast, in the sample where there was no increase in credit limit, the interaction BIG * POST in the sales equation is close to zero (0.05) and insignificant (column (8)), which suggests that the result in column (4) is not driven by a failure of the identification assumption. In summary, sales increased almost as fast as loans in response to the reform. This is an indication that there was no substitution of bank credit for nonbank credit (e.g. trade credit) as a result of the reform, and that firms are credit constrained.[6]

Table 6.1 Are firms credit constrained?

Sample	Complete sample	Sample with change in limit						Sample with no change in limit	
	Any change in limit (1)	Log(loan)$_t$ − Log(loan)$_{t-1}$ (2)	Log(interest rate)$_t$ − Log(interest rate)$_{t-1}$ (3)	Log(turnover/limit)$_{t+1}$ − Log(turnover/limit)$_{,t}$ (4)	Log(sales)$_{t+1}$ − Log(sales)$_t$		Log(profit)$_{t+1}$ − Log(profit)$_t$ (7)	Log(sales)$_{t+1}$ − Log(sales)$_t$ (8)	Log(profit)$_{t+1}$ − Log(profit)$_t$ (9)
					All firms (5)	No substitution (6)			
Panel A: Ordinary least squares[a]									
Dependent variables									
POST	−0.003	−0.115	−0.008	−0.115	0.021	0.005	0.172	0.030	−0.316
	(0.049)	(0.069)	(0.014)	(0.366)	(0.093)	(0.096)	(0.201)	(0.047)	(0.153)
BIG	−0.043	−0.218	−0.002	−0.105	−0.199	−0.191	−0.645	0.077	0.058
	(0.053)	(0.079)	(0.014)	(0.147)	(0.094)	(0.101)	(0.219)	(0.053)	(0.309)
BIG•POST	−0.008	0.244	0.012	0.267	0.209	0.184	0.752	0.052	0.034
	(0.078)	(0.099)	(0.019)	(0.355)	(0.055)	(0.099)	(0.387)	(0.109)	(0.531)
Number of observations	489	155	141	39	116	105	107	255	209
Panel B: Two-stage least squares (2SLS)[b]									
Dependent variable									
Log(loan)$_t$ − Log(loan)$_{t-1}$					0.896		2.713		
					(0.463)		(1.290)		
Number of observations					116		107		

[a] Standard errors in parentheses (corrected for heteroskedasticity and clustering at the sector level).
[b] 2SLS regressions using BIG • POST as the instrumental variable. The regression controls for BIG and POST dummies.

Sources: Data from a public bank in India and authors' estimates.

In column (7), we present the effect of the reform on profit, which is even bigger than that on sales—0.75, with a standard error of 0.38. We note that the effect of the reform on profit is due to the gap between the marginal product of capital and the *bank* interest rate; in other words, it combines the subsidy effect and the credit constraint effect. Even if firms were not credit constrained, their profit would increase after the reform if more subsidized credit is made available to them, because they substitute cheaper capital for more expensive capital. Here again, we see no effect of the interaction BIG * POST in the sample without a change in limit (column (9)), which lends support to our identification assumption.[7]

The instrumental variable (IV) estimate of the effect of loans on sales and profit implied by the reduced form and first stage estimates in columns (2), (5), and (7) are presented in Table 6.1, panel B, columns (5) and (7).[8] We note that the coefficient in column (5) is a lower bound of the effect of bank credit on sales, because the reform should have led to some substitution of bank credit for market credit. The IV coefficient is 0.90, with a standard error of 0.46. It suggests that the effect of working capital on sales is very close to 1, a result which implies that there cannot be equilibrium without credit constraints. Referring to column (7), the IV estimate of the impact of bank credit on profit is 2.7. We can use this estimate to get a sense of the average increase in profit caused by every rupee in lending. The average size of the loan in the sample is Rs 96,000. Therefore, an increase of Rs 1000 in the size of the loan corresponds to a 1.04 percent increase. Using the coefficient of loans on profits, an increase of Rs 1000 in lending, therefore, causes a 2.7 percent increase in profit. At the mean profit, which is Rs 37,000 in the sample, this would correspond to an increase in profit of Rs 999. Thus, the increase in profits resulting from an increase in loans is nearly identical *net of interest*. This gap is far too large to be explained by the subsidy in the interest rate to SSI firms.

Conclusion

These results provide definite evidence of very substantial underlending; some firms clearly can absorb much more capital at high rates of return. Moreover, the firms in our sample are by Indian standards quite substantial— these are not the very small firms at the margins of the economy, where, even if the marginal product is high, the scope for expansion may be quite limited. In Section 6.3, we try to investigate the connection between these results about the pattern of lending and the way lending is carried out in India.

6.3   Lending practice in India

Official lending policies

While nominally independent, PSBs are subject to intense regulation by the Reserve Bank of India (RBI), including current rules governing the amount of bank lending. In this section, we describe these rules, examine to what extent they are followed, and determine which non-policy variables influence lending decisions.

Specification

Historically, two methods have been used to calculate the maximum permissible bank financing of a firm—the "working capital" approach and the "turnover" approach. The working capital approach is based on the presumption that firms' current assets are illiquid, and that firms should cover 25 percent of the financing gap with equity capital, and 75 percent with bank credit.[9] Thus maximum permissible bank financing is defined as:

$$0.75 * \text{Current Assets} - \text{Other Current Liabilities} \qquad (6.2)$$

The turnover approach defines firms' financing needs to be 25 percent of projected turnover, and allows firms to finance 80 percent of this need from banks—that is, up to 20 percent of turnover. Maximum permissible bank financing is thus defined as:

$$\text{Min} (0.20 * \text{Projected Turnover}, 0.25 * \text{Projected Turnover}$$
$$- \text{Available Margin}) \qquad (6.3)$$

where the Available Margin is Current Assets less Current Liabilities, as calculated from a firm's balance sheet. The margin is deducted because it is presumed that the firms' other financing will continue to be available. Note that if the turnover-based rule were followed exactly, firms' available margin would be precisely 5 percent of turnover, and the two amounts in equation (6.3) would be equal.[10]

For the bank examined here, the loan officer was supposed to calculate both equation (6.3) and the older rule represented by equation (6.2) for all loans below Rs 40 million (including all loans in our sample). The largest permissible limit on the loan was the maximum of these two numbers. No rules prohibit banks (including the PSB examined here) from lending less than the limit, and it is not clear how (or how often) the limit is actually enforced. Thus, we turn to the actual practice of lending.[11]

Data

We use the same data source (described above) to look at what bankers actually do. Since we have data on current assets and other current liabilities, it is trivial to calculate the limit according to the traditional working capital gap-based method of lending (LWC). We can also calculate the limit for turnover gap-based method (LTB). The maximum of LTB and LWC is, according to the rules, the real limit on how much the banker can lend to the firm.

Results

We show the comparison of the actual limit granted and max(LTB, LWC) in Table 6.2. In 78 percent of the cases, the limit granted is smaller than the amount permitted. Most strikingly, in 64 percent of the cases for which we know the amount granted in the previous period, the amount granted is exactly equal to the amount granted in the previous period. Given that inflation was 5 percent or higher during the sample period, the real amount of the loans, therefore, decreases between the two adjacent years in a majority of the cases. To make matters worse, in 73 percent of these cases, the firm's sales increased, implying, as we presume, a greater demand for working capital. Further, this is the case despite the fact that according to the bank's own rules, the limit could have gone up in 64 percent of the cases (note that getting a higher limit is simply an option and does not cost the firm anything unless it uses the additional financing).

We report the results of the regression of the actual limit granted on information that might be expected to play a role in its determination in Table 6.3. Not surprisingly, the amount of past lending is a very powerful predictor of today's lending. In column (1), we regress the (log) current loan amount on the (log) past loan amount and the (log) loan limit according to the rules. Even though the bank's rule never refers to past loan as a determinant of permissible sanction, the coefficient of past loan is 0.76, with a t-statistic of 18. The maximum permissible limit is also significant, with a coefficient of 0.26. This suggests that a change in the previous granted limit increases the current granted limit by three times as much as a change in the maximum permissible limit as calculated by the bank.

Table 6.2   Bank financing—granted, maximum, and previous limits of a PSB[a]

	Actual limit granted versus limit on turnover basis		Actual limited granted versus bank's official policy		Actual limit granted versus previous granted limit[b]		Bank's official policy versus previous official policy[b]	
	(1)	(2)	(1)	(2)	(1)	(2)	(1)	(2)
Smaller	255	62.2	542	78.2	22	4.4	153	34.8
Same	81	19.8	9	1.3	322	64.1	6	1.4
Larger	74	18.0	142	20.5	158	31.5	281	63.9
Same as 1997	23	25.0	2	1.3	37	5.3	0	0.0
Same as 1998	25	20.7	2	0.9	109	68.1	2	1.3
Same as 1999	27	16.2	4	1.9	156	70.3	4	2.2

[a] Column (1) is the number of loans approved or allowed in relation to the maximum permissible bank financing under the indicated limit or policy. Column (2) is the share of these loans in relation to the maximum permissible bank financing (in percent).
[b] Previous granted limit refers to the number of loans approved under the working capital approach (or old rule); previous official policy refers to the number of loans allowed under the maximum limit of the working capital approach.

Sources: Data from a public sector bank in India and authors' estimates.

Table 6.3 Determinants of the working capital limit and interest rate[a]

| | Dependent variable | | | | |
| | Log (granted limit) | | | Interest rate | |
Independent variables	(1)	(2)	(3)	(4)	(5)
Log (previous granted limit)	0.757	0.540	0.455	−0.198	−0.260
	(0.04)	(0.059)	(0.084)	(0.108)	(0.124)
Previous interest rate				0.823	0.832
				(0.038)	(0.041)
Log (maximum limit as per bank's rule)[b]	0.256 (0.042)				
Log (LTB), calculated by the bank		0.145		−0.019	
		(0.036)		(0.102)	
Log (LTB), calculated by authors			0.102		−0.025
			(0.025)		(0.090)
Log (LWC), using turnover projected by bank		0.240	0.279	0.091	0.083
		(0.046)	(0.061)	(0.083)	(0.084)
Log (profits/assets)		0.021	−0.001	−0.048	−0.036
		(0.017)	(0.021)	(0.043)	(0.044)
Dummy for negative profit		−0.037	0.053	−0.045	−0.037
		(0.115)	(0.129)	(0.272)	(0.266)
Log (total net worth/debt)		−0.104	−0.112	−0.064	−0.087
		(0.029)	(0.032)	(0.076)	(0.070)
Log (assets)		0.080	0.143	0.063	0.168
		(0.056)	(0.065)	(0.104)	(0.118)
Log (interest earned/granted limit) for previous year			0.005 (0.037)		
Constant	0.011	−0.009	−0.021	2.547	2.180
	(0.079)	(0.154)	(0.195)	(0.749)	(0.843)
R^2	0.952	0.955	0.962	0.878	0.881
Number of observations	298	241	145	198	194

[a] Standard errors in parentheses (corrected for clustering at the account level).
[b] The maximum limit as per the bank's rule is max(LTB calculated by the bank, LWC), where LTB is the limit calculated according to a working capital gap-based method of lending and LWC is the limit on a turnover gap-based method of lending.
Sources: Data from a public sector bank and authors' estimates.

We "unpack" the official limit in column (2), including separately the bank's LTB, LWC, and profits. As in the previous regression, the past loan amount is the most powerful predictor of current loan amount. Both limits enter the regression. Neither profits nor a dummy for negative profits enter the regression. Columns (4) and (5) do the same thing for interest rates—past interest rates are the only significant determinant of current interest rates.

In sum, the actual policy followed by the bank seems to be characterized by systematic deviation from what the rules permit in the direction of inertia.

To the extent that limits do change, what seems to matter is the size of the firm, as measured by its turnover and outlay, and not by its profitability or loan utilization. It could be argued that inertia is actually rational, which results from the fact that the past loan amount picks up all the information that the loan officer has accumulated about the firm that we do not observe. However, at least three reasons exist why this is probably not the case.

- First, firms' financing needs change, if only because of inflation, while loan levels are often constant in nominal dollars.
- Second, the importance of past loans is no different for younger versus older firms, about which the former bank presumably has less information.
- Finally, past loans do not predict future profits, while past profits do. This is important because negative profits predict loan default, while past loans, LTB, and LWC do not.[12]

Conclusion

This section suggests an extremely simple explanation of why many firms in India appear to be starved of credit. Banks seem remarkably reluctant to make fresh lending decisions; in two-thirds of the cases examined here, there is no change in the nominal loan amount from year to year. While lending rules are indeed rigid, this inertia goes substantially beyond what they dictate. Moreover, loan enhancement is unrelated to a firm's profits. Loan officers' indifference to profits is entirely consistent with the rules governing bank lending in India, which do not pay even lip service to the need to identify profitable borrowers. Yet, current profits predict future losses and therefore future defaults, while turnover does not. In other words, a banker who made better use of profit information would likely do a better job at avoiding defaults. Moreover, he would also better identify firms whose marginal product of capital is the highest. Lending based on turnover, by contrast, may skew the lending process toward firms that have been able to finance growth out of internal resources and therefore do not need additional loans nearly as much.

6.4   Understanding lending practices

The abiding puzzle is why the bankers choose to behave in this particular way. The rules are stringent, but rarely bind. Banks decline to lend to firms with very high marginal products of capital. The bank we studied did not lack available funds; between 1996 and 2001, total nominal deposits in our bank grew at an annual rate of 23 percent, while advances grew only 19 percent.

In this section, we report new evidence on three commonly discussed reasons for underlending, summarized as follows:

- First, many feel that because lending officers in PSBs face the wrong incentives, they may be more concerned about making bad loans (and appearing corrupt) than finding profitable opportunities.

- Second, it is suggested that bankers may prefer to make risk-free loans to the government, rather than exert the effort to screen and monitor private borrowers.
- Finally, it is possible that the marginal default rate is high enough to make it unprofitable to increase lending.

6.4.1 Inertia and the fear of prosecution

Since PSBs are owned by the government, employees of these banks are treated by law as public servants and thus subject to government anticorruption legislation. Although the Central Vigilance Commission (CVC), which is charged in India with investigating unscrupulous bank lending practices, argues that honest bankers have nothing to fear, there is an impression among bankers that it is very easy to be charged with corruption if loans go bad. Since bankers face at best weak rewards for making successful loans, they may prefer to simply approve past loan limits, rather than take a new decision.[13]

In the rest of this section, we look at whether there is any evidence for the so-called fear psychosis based on Cole (2002). The basic idea is simple—we ask whether bankers who are "close to" bankers who have been subject to CVC action slow down lending in the aftermath of that particular CVC action.

Specification

We use bank-level monthly lending data to estimate the effect of vigilance activity on lending, using the following equation:

$$y_{it} = \alpha_i + \beta_t + \sum_{k=0}^{w} \gamma_k D_{i,t-k} + \varepsilon_{it} \tag{6.4}$$

where y_{it} is the (log) credit extended by bank i in month t, α_t is a bank fixed effect, β_t is a month fixed effect, and $D_{i,t-k}$ is an indicator variable for whether vigilance activity was reported by the CVC for that bank i in month $t - k$. Standard errors are adjusted for serial correlation and heteroscedasticity. The basic idea is to compare a bank that was affected by the vigilance activity with other PSBs, before and after the vigilance event. Since it is not clear precisely which event window to use, we let the data decide, estimating models which allow effects of vigilance activity to take from one month to four years to appear.

Data

Monthly credit data by bank were provided by the RBI. Data on frauds are naturally very difficult to come by; but, in an effort to punish corruption through stigma, the CVC has published a list containing the name, position, employing bank, and punishment of the individual officer(s) charged with major frauds. The list consists of 87 officials in PSBs during 1992–2001. Approximately 72 percent of these frauds relate to illegal extension of credit. Summary statistics for credit data and the CVC fraud data are listed in Table 6.4.

Table 6.4 Summary statistics for corruption study

	Mean	Median
Panel A: Credit data[a]		
January 1992 (in 1994 rupee prices)		
Loans, cash credit, and overdrafts	156,943	74,942
	(214,331)	
Log (loans, cash credits, and overdrafts)	16.98	16.65
	(0.830)	
January 2000 (in 1994 rupee prices)		
Loans, cash credit, and overdrafts	296,060	166,431
	(382,644)	
Log (loans, cash credits, and overdrafts)	12.24	12.02
	(0.753)	
Sample size		
Number of public sector banks	27	
Number of months (January 1992–May 2001)	111	
Number of observations	2,997	

Panel B: Corruption data

Yearwise distribution of cases

	1993	1994	1995	1996	1997	1998	1999	2000
Advice	1	4	4	6	10	10	7	9
Order	1	3	2	6	6	7	9	3
Total	2	7	6	12	16	17	16	12

Distribution of content of CVC advice and orders (in percent)

	CVC advice	CVC order
Action		
Prosecution	12.2	0.0
Charge sheet filed	0.0	1.1
Information awaited	0.0	15.7
Dismissal of employee	18.9	24.7
Compulsory retirement	5.6	4.5
"Major penalty"	45.6	2.3
Pay reduction		
Unspecified reduction in pay	4.4	4.5
Reduction in pay 1 grade	2.2	22.5
Reduction in pay 2 grade	7.8	2.3
Reduction in pay 3 grade	1.1	4.5
Reduction in pay 4 grade	2.2	16.9
Reduction in pay 5 grade	0.0	1.1
Total	100.0	100.0

[a] Standard deviations in parentheses.

Sources: Reserve Bank of India (credit data) and Central Vigilance Commission (corruption data); and authors' estimates.

Results

Our estimation results are presented in Table 6.5, showing three similar specifications. Columns (1), (2), and (3) provide estimates for the windows of 1, 12, and 48 months, respectively. Vigilance activity appears to have a clear effect on lending decisions, resulting in a reduction of credit supplied by all the branches of the sample bank by about 3–5 percent. This effect is estimated precisely and is significantly different from zero at the 5 percent level for the contemporaneous effect (column (1)) and at the 1 percent level

Table 6.5 Effect of vigilance activity on credit[a]

Indicator for vigilance activity[b]	Past activity[c]			Future activity[d]	
	(1)	(2)	(3)	(4)	(5)
Indicator for fraud in					
Contemporaneous	−0.055	−0.040	−0.037	−0.042	−0.037
	(0.027)	(0.019)	(0.019)	(0.020)	(0.020)
3 months		−0.039	−0.032	−0.035	−0.031
		(0.018)	(0.016)	(0.016)	(0.016)
6 months		−0.031	−0.023	−0.029	−0.027
		(0.016)	(0.014)	(0.015)	(0.014)
12 months		−0.036	−0.018	−0.018	−0.015
		(0.016)	(0.012)	(0.014)	(0.010)
18 months			−0.028		−0.006
			(0.013)		(0.010)
24 months			−0.012		−0.001
			(0.013)		(0.011)
36 months			−0.014		0.009
			(0.015)		(0.008)
48 months			−0.022		0.022
			(0.028)		(0.015)
Month fixed effects	Y	Y	Y	Y	Y
Bank fixed effects	Y	Y	Y	Y	Y

[a] Columns (1)–(5) present panel regressions of log (credit) extended by 27 public sector banks over a period of 111 months, resulting in 2997 observations. Standard errors (robust to heteroskedasticity and serial correlation) are reported in parentheses.
[b] The independent variable is a dummy variable indicating whether the CVC had charged or punished an officer of a particular bank in a particular month.
[c] Columns (2) and (3) examine how the effect persists over time. In column (2), log (credit) is regressed on dummies to measure the effect of *past* vigilance activity in a bank on lending over the past 1–12 months. For readability, only the coefficients for the contemporaneous effect and 3, 6, and 12 months are reported. Column (3) traces the effects over the past 48 months; again, only coefficients for the contemporaneous effect and select months are reported.
[d] Columns (4) and (5) measure the effect of *future* vigilance activity on lending. For example, the "3 months" coefficient in columns (4) and (5) is a dummy for whether there is vigilance activity at time $t + 3$. Dummies are included for each future month up to 12 months ahead in column (4), and up to 48 months ahead in column (5).

Sources: Reserve Bank of India and Central Vigilance Commission; and authors' estimates.

for the joint parameters of zero to 24 months in columns (2) and (3). It is also quite persistent, appearing in the data at its original level for up to 18 months following the vigilance activity, and only becomes statistically indistinguishable from zero at two years after the CVC decision or judgment.

This economic effect seems to be sizable in terms of the money multiplier. For example, if the overall coefficient of 0.03 were accurate for a bank such as the State Bank of India (SBI)—the largest PSB, providing approximately a quarter of all bank credit in the economy—decisions on whether to pursue vigilance cases could have measurable macroeconomic effects.

Conclusion

There seems to be some evidence that the fear of being investigated is reducing lending by a significant extent—banks where someone is under investigation slow down lending relative to their own mean level of lending. This leaves open the question of whether this is a desirable reaction, since it is possible that the loans not granted are the loans that are unlikely to be repaid. However, it also raises the possibility that honest lenders are being discouraged by excessively stringent regulations.

6.4.2   Lending to the government and the easy life

The ideal way to look at the easy life hypothesis would be to estimate the elasticity of bank lending to the private sector with respect to the interest rate on government securities or the interest rate spread between private loans and government securities. The problem is that the part of the variation that comes from changes in the government yields is that it is the same for all banks and therefore is indistinguishable from any other time-varying effect on lending. In addition, while variation comes from the rates charged across banks, it cannot possibly be independent of demand conditions in a bank and other unobserved time-varying bank-specific factors. Therefore, we cannot estimate the true elasticity of lending by regressing loans on the spread.

Our strategy is to focus on a more limited question, which we hope to answer somewhat more convincingly—are banks more sensitive to interest rates on government securities in a slow-growth environment? We start by identifying the banks that are particularly likely to be heavily invested in the "easy life." For historical reasons, this set of banks has most of its branches in the states that are currently growing slower than the rest. Our hypothesis is that it is these banks that have a particularly strong reason to invest heavily in government securities, since in a slow growth environment, it is harder to identify really promising clients. They also probably have more "marginal" loans that they are willing to cut and reduce, or not increase, when the interest rates paid on government bonds increases. It is therefore these banks that should be particularly responsive to changes in the interest rate paid by the government.

Specification

We define $\text{GROWTH}_{it} = \ln(\text{SDP}_{it}) - \ln(\text{SDP}_{i,t-1})$, where SDP is a moving average of growth rates for the previous three years of state domestic product, with $\text{AVGROWTH}_{it} = \sum_{t-3}^{t-1}(\text{GROWTH}_{it})$. In addition, a bank environment growth index is constructed as the weighted average of the growth rates in the states in which a bank operates, or $\text{BKGROWTH}_{bit} = \sum_{i\in\text{states}} \omega_{bi} * \text{AVGROWTH}_{bit}$, where the weights ω_{bi} are the percentage of bank branches that bank b had in state i in 1980, or $\omega_{bi} = N_{bi}/\sum_{i\in\text{states}} N_{bs}$.[14]

Data

The outcome we focus on is the (ln) credit to deposit ratio (CD) at the end of March of each year for 25 public sector and 20 private sector banks. Two minor PSBs were excluded due to lack of data, while the new private sector banks were excluded for reasons of comparability. The data are from the RBI. For our measure of interest rate spread, we take the difference of the SBI's prime lending rate and a weighted average rate on central government securities (SPREAD).

Results

We test this hypothesis using linear regression. To measure the effect of interest rates and the growth environment faced by banks on lending, we estimate the following equation:

$$\ln(\text{CD}_{bit}) = \alpha + \beta * \text{BKGROWTH}_{bit}$$
$$+ \gamma^+(\text{SPREAD}_t * \text{BKGROWTH}_{bit}) * I_{\text{Spread}_t>0}$$
$$+ \gamma^-(\text{SPREAD}_t * \text{BKGROWTH}_{bit}) * I_{\text{Spread}_t<0}$$
$$+ \theta_i + \varphi_b + \delta_t + \varepsilon_{bit} \tag{6.5}$$

where α is a constant; $I_{\text{Spread}_t>0}$ $(I_{\text{Spread}_t<0})$ are indicator variables for whether the spread is positive (negative);[15] φ_b is a bank fixed effect; θ_i is a state fixed effect; and δ_t is a year fixed effect. Standard errors are adjusted for serial correlation.

While we see that the credit to deposit ratio is higher in states with more favorable growth rates, we are most interested in the coefficients γ^- and γ^+, which measure how banks in different growth environments differentially react to changes in the interest rate spread (Table 6.6). The negative and statistically significant coefficient on γ^+ suggests that banks in high-growth environments substitute toward government securities (and away from bank loans) *less* when the spread falls. We interpret this to mean that banks in low growth states are more sensitive to government interest rates because they

Table 6.6   Interest rate spreads, bank credit, and state growth[a]

	State growth[b]		Synthetic growth index[c]	
	1985–2000 (1)	1992–2000 (2)	1985–2000 (3)	1992–2000 (4)
Independent variables				
BKGROWTH	1.412	1.538	2.195	2.634
	(0.624)	(1.209)	(0.970)	(1.165)
SPREAD * BKGrowth, when spread > 0	−0.175	−0.137	−0.257	−0.219
(γ^+ in equations (6.5))	(0.110)	(0.119)	(0.104)	(0.103)
SPREAD * BKGrowth, when spread < 0	0.480	0.592	−0.079	0.473
(γ^- in equations (6.5))	(0.521)	(0.405)	(0.791)	(0.562)
R^2	0.46	0.43	0.71	0.63
Number of observations	415	730	402	710
Year fixed effects	Y	Y	Y	Y
State fixed effects	Y	Y	N	N
Bank fixed effects	N	N	Y	Y

[a] Standard errors (robust to heteroskedasticity and serial correlation) are in parentheses.
[b] The growth rate in the state in which the headquarters of each bank is located.
[c] The weighted average of growth rates of states in which each bank operates.

Sources: Reserve Bank of India and authors' estimates.

face less attractive projects to finance, and therefore are more likely to put funds in government securities as returns on these instruments become more attractive.

Conclusion

The evidence seems to be consistent with the view that banks are especially inclined toward the easy life in states where lending is hard because of growth conditions. This suggests that high rates on government securities tend to hurt the firms that are relatively marginal from the point of view of the banks, such as firms in slow growing states and smaller and less established firms.

6.4.3   The risk of default

We report the cumulative default rate for the firms in the sample already in the priority sector in 1997 in Table 6.7, column (1), that is for the small firms referred in Section 6.2. The default rate for these firms averages about 2.5 percent a year during the period 1998–2002—the same rate as reported in earlier studies by Banerjee and Duflo (2001 and 2003). The default rate for firms that come into priority sector in 1997 is reported in column (2), or the big firms in Section 6.2. We see that the cumulative default rate for these firms is lower than that for the small firms in 1997 and remains lower after

Table 6.7 Nonperforming assets of priority sector borrowers at a public sector bank

Year	Cumulative share of NPAs for small and big firms (in percent)	
	Small	Big
1997	0.000	0.011
1998	0.026	0.011
1999	0.052	0.023
2000	0.078	0.057
2001	0.118	0.092
2002	0.125	0.137

Sources: Data from a public sector bank in India and authors' estimates.

these firms are included in the priority sector in 1998. When most of the big firms are once again dropped from the priority sector in 2000, the default rate remains lower than small firms through 2001 but then slightly exceeds small firms in 2002 (by 0.12 percentage points). It is therefore rather implausible that the firms receiving loan enhancements after being included in the priority sector are so much more risky than other firms that their loan limits should not have been increased.

6.5 Conclusion—policy responses

Bank credit in India does not necessarily seem to flow to firms and individuals who have the greatest potential use for it. To correct this deficiency, we first suggest amending lending rules so that they are more responsive to current and future profitability, which we see as a better safeguard against potential NPAs. This is largely because firm profitability seems to be a good predictor of future default. However, choosing the right way to include profits in the lending decision is not easy. If a firm is and will continue to be unprofitable, it makes sense for a bank to cease lending to the firm. On the other hand, cutting off credit to a generally profitable firm suffering a temporary shock may push it into default. The difficulty lies in distinguishing the two. One solution may be to categorize firms into three groups: (i) profitable to highly profitable firms, wherein lending responds to profitability and more profitable firms getting more credit; (ii) marginally profitable to loss-making firms that were recently highly profitable, but have been hit by a temporary shock wherein the existing rules for lending may continue to work well; and

(iii) firms with a long track record of losses, or which have been hit by a permanent shock (e.g. the removal of tariffs for a good in which a major competing economy like China enjoys a substantial cost advantage). For this last group, lending should be discontinued, but also in a way that offers firms a mechanism for resolving NPAs. Of course, it is not always going to be easy to distinguish temporary and permanent shocks, but loan officers should use information from past performance, as well as industry experience as a whole to make this judgment.

Second, we see reason for changing the incentive structure faced by loan officers in approving bank loans, so that fear of reprisal from poor lending decisions does not make them excessively risk averse. Understandably, if loan officers are corrupt, or are afraid to act for fear of appearing corrupt, giving them the additional responsibility discussed above may not be advisable without providing better incentives. A number of small steps may go some distance toward this goal. First, to avoid a climate of fear, there should be a clear separation between investigation of individual loans and investigation of loan officers. A loan should be investigated first; that is, was the originally sanctioned amount justifiable at the time it was given, or were there obvious warning signs. Only if a *prima facie* case can be made that the failure of the loan was predictable, should the loan officer be investigated. The authorization to investigate a loan officer should be based on the most objective available measures of his performance, that is, all previous loan decisions, with weight given both to successes and failures. A loan officer with a good track record should be allowed a number of mistakes (and even suspicious looking mistakes) before he is open to investigation. Banks should also create a division staffed by personnel with strong reputations, who would have a mandate to make some high risk loans. Officers posted to this division should be explicitly protected from investigation for loans made while in this division.

Third, parts of the incentive structure that banks face as a whole should change to increase the availability of bank credit. On the one hand, lower government interest rates appear to have a strong effect on the willingness of bankers to make loans to the private sector. On the other hand, priority sector lending requirements, contrary to popular belief, are not necessarily an inefficient allocation of capital.[16] In fact, these loans appear to have very high marginal products of capital. In addition, while they are slightly more likely to default, the amount of the default is relatively small. Therefore, we see no reason to believe that abolishing priority sector lending will improve bank performance substantially. In fact, it could end up reinforcing the tendency of the banks to make only conservative loans. There is other evidence that suggests that targeted lending programs are effective in other countries, including the United States.[17] Notwithstanding this, we do think that the eligibility criteria for priority sector loans could be rationalized. For example, based on the evidence above, we favor a higher limit for value of plant and machinery in order to be eligible for priority lending. However, the increase could be combined with a time limit on eligibility—after a certain number of years, firms should establish a reputation as reliable borrowers and begin borrowing from the market. A priority sector client that has borrowed from a bank for some time without convincing the bank of his/her creditworthiness is perhaps not worth retaining. Second, the size of the gap between the marginal product of capital and the interest rate suggests the possibility of letting banks charge substantially higher interest rates to the priority sector than they are currently permitted, making it more attractive to lend to the priority sector. This increase could be gradual, making it easier for firms to endure the transition.

Fourth, bank privatization and, in particular, the sale to large multinationals is unlikely to solve the problem of underlending, though it will probably help remove some of the most egregious examples of inaction and surely reduce the degree of overstaffing. It is generally thought that the PSBs are more responsive than private banks to carrying out directives related to social banking. However, analysis of loan-level data reported in Cole (2004) suggests that this may not be a truism; controlling for size, old private sector banks did not lend significantly less to SSI than PSBs (they did lend less to agriculture). On the other hand, regulatory forbearance initially allowed new private sector banks to lend significantly less than targeted levels to priority sector. Even when obliged to meet priority lending requirements, many private banks instead chose to place an equivalent amount of money in low-return government bonds (Business India, 1997). This simply transfers the responsibility to identify and nurture new talent back to the government. Therefore, privatization without stricter enforcement of the priority sector lending requirements could probably end up hurting smaller firms. This is not to say that privatization is an unreasonable option, but rather that it should be accompanied by some efforts to reach out more effectively to the smaller and less well-established firms, not just to ensure more equitable treatment, but also to earn highest returns on capital.

A possible step in this direction would be to encourage established reputable firms in the corporate sector (including multinationals) to set up small specialized companies whose only job is to lend to small firms in a particular sector and possibly in particular locations. In other words, these institutions would be similar to the many finance companies that do extensive lending all over India, but with links to a much bigger corporate entity and therefore greater overall creditworthiness. The banks would then lend to these entities at a rate somewhat below the cost of capital—instead of doing priority sector lending—and these corporate entities, essentially as finance companies, would then on-lend to firms in their domain. By being small and connected to a particular industry, they would have a stronger capacity to acquire detailed knowledge of the firms in the industry and, in turn, would have more incentives to avoid underlending.

Notes

1. Department of Economics, Massachusetts Institute of Technology (all); Research Associate, National Bureau of Economic Research, and Research Fellow, Center for Economic and Policy Research (Duflo only). This research would not have been possible without generous assistance from several parties. We thank the Reserve Bank of India (RBI), in particular Y.V. Reddy, R.B. Barman, and Abhiman Das, for generous assistance with technical and substantive issues. We also thank Abhiman Das for performing calculations, which involved proprietary RBI data. We are grateful to the staff of the public sector bank we studied for allowing us access to their data. We gratefully acknowledge financial support from the Alfred P. Slone Foundation. Shawn Cole is also grateful for support from a National Science Foundation Fellowship. Finally, we thank Tata Consulting Services, in particular Jayant Pendharkar and M.K. Sen, for their help in understanding the Indian banking industry, and N. Sankaranarayanan for his superb organization of the data collection project.
2. Burgess and Pande (2003).
3. Narasimhan Committee, Government of India (1991).
4. Privatization of banks would almost surely eliminate the problem of overstaffing; but in all likelihood, the government would still have to pay for it through some voluntary retirement scheme, which would be made a condition of the sale.
5. There is a literature on credit constraints in the OECD—see for example Fazarri, Hubbard and Petersen (1998) or Lamont (1997). For more on the theory of credit markets in developing countries, see Banerjee (2003).
6. A similar result holds for the sample of firms which borrowed from the market both before and after the reform, and thus had not completely substituted bank borrowing for market borrowing.
7. Column 1 of Table 6.1 shows that profitablility of firms in the sample with no change in the credit limit were not affected by the reform, suggesting the use of these firms whose loan limits were not changed as a control group to test our identification assumption.
8. The regression presented in column 2 of Table 6.1 is not the actual first stage, because it uses the entire sample. The actual first stage is very similar; the coefficient of the interaction is 0.23 in the sample used in the sales equation.
9. This includes credit from all banks. Following this rule implies that the current ratio will be over 1.33, and the rule is often formulated as the requirement that the current ratio exceeds 1.33.
10. A turnover-based approach is common in the United States, where inventories serve as collateral. In India, inventories do not seem to provide adequate security, as evidenced by high default rates. Second, venture capitalists, who in the United States provide significant financing to promising firms, are largely absent in India. Thus, it may be desirable for banks in India to lend more to profitable firms (as they do not default) and to rapidly growing firms (current rules in India prohibit projecting annual turnover to grow at a rate above 15 percent).
11. Based on Banerjee and Duflo (2001).
12. Banerjee and Duflo (2001).
13. See, for example, Tannan (2001, p. 1579). The latter source quotes a working group on banking chaired by M.S. Verma as saying, "The [working group] observed that it has received representation from the managements and the unions of the banks complaining about the diffidence in taking credit decisions. . . . This is due to investigations by outside agencies on the accountability of staff in respect to some of the NPAs."

14. State domestic product data are from India's Central Statistical Organization; interest rate and branch location data are from the RBI.
15. Because a negative spread occurs only twice and therefore is a quite rare situation (in a perfectly flexible market, banks facing a negative spread should eliminate all credit from their portfolios), we allow a separate coefficient on (SPREAD$_t$ * BKGROWTH$_{bit}$) when the spread is negative.
16. Joshi and Little (1994).
17. Zinman (2002).

References

Banerjee, Abhijit, 2003, "Contracting Constraints, Credit Markets, and Economic Development," in *Advances in Economics and Econometrics: Theory and Applications, Eight World Congress of the Econometric Society*, Vol. III, pp. 1–46, ed. by M. Dewatripoint, L. Hansen, and S. Turnovsky (Cambridge: Cambridge University Press).

Banerjee, Abhijit and Esther Duflo, 2003, "Do Firms Want to Borrow More? Testing Credit Constraints Using a Directed Lending Program," BREAD Working Paper No. 2003–5 (Boston: Bureau for Research and Economic Analysis of Development).

——, 2001, "The Nature of Credit Constraints. Evidence from an Indian Bank," mimeo (Cambridge: Massachusetts Institute of Technology).

——, 2000, "Efficiency of Lending Operations and the Impact of Priority Sector Regulations," mimeo (Cambridge: Massachusetts Institute of Technology).

Burgess, Robin and Rohini Pande, 2003, "Do Rural Banks Matter? Evidence from the Indian Social Banking Experiment," mimeo (March) (New York: Columbia University).

Business India, 1997, "Banking Missing Out on Targets" (July 14).

Cole, Shawn, 2004, "Bank Ownership, Bank Lending Behavior, and Political Capture: Evidence from India," mimeo (Cambridge: Massachusetts Institute of Technology).

——, 2002, "Corruption, Vigilance, and the Supply of Credit," mimeo (Cambridge: Massachusetts Institute of Technology).

Fazzari, S., R.G. Hubbard, and Bruce Petersen, 1998, "Financing Constraints and Corporate Investment," *Brookings Papers on Economic Activity*, Vol. I, pp. 141–95.

Government of India, 2001, "Special Chapter on Vigilance Management in Public Sector Banks" (New Delhi: Central Vigilance Commission).

——, 2000, "Cases Referred to the Central Vigilance Commission by Public Sector Banks: A Critical Analysis" (New Delhi: Central Vigilance Commission).

——, 1991, *Report of the Committee on the Financial Sector*, M. Narasimhan (Chairman) (New Delhi: Ministry of Finance).

Joshi, Vijay and I.M.D. Little, 1994, *India: Macroeconomics and Political Economy, 1964–1991* (New Delhi: Oxford University Press).

Lamont, Owen, 1997, "Cash Flows and Investment: Evidence from Internal Capital Markets," *Journal of Finance*, Vol. 51, No. 2, pp. 83–109.

Tanan, M., 2001, *Banking Law and Practice in India* (New Delhi: India Law House).

Zinman, Jonathan, 2002, "Do Credit Market Interventions Work? Evidence from the Community Reinvestment Act," mimeo (September) (Federal Reserve Bank of New York).

7
Trade Liberalization and Its Role in Chinese Economic Growth

Nicholas R. Lardy[1]

7.1 Introduction

In terms of their participation in the international economy it would be difficult to envision two more contrasting cases than China and India. Whether the base line is the time of independence for India (1947) or the founding of the People's Republic of China (1949), the beginning of Chinese economic reforms in the late 1970s or the initiation of Indian economic reforms in 1991, China's trade performance has been distinctly superior. Even after a decade of economic reform, India's share of global trade in 2000 was only 0.7 percent, two-thirds less than in 1948.[2] By contrast, as shown in Table 7.1, China's share of global trade by 2002 more than tripled in the past half century and is currently six times that of India.[3] Most of the increase in China's share of global trade has occurred in the 25 years since reform and opening began in 1978.

The contrast is also evident in the trade rankings of the two countries. Consistent with its declining share of global trade, India's rank as a global trader has fallen steadily over the past half century. By 2002 there were 25 countries with total trade exceeding that of India.[4] In contrast China's rank has risen steadily from the thirtieth largest trading country in 1977, on the eve of economic reform, to the seventh largest trader in 2000.[5] Since that time China's trade performance has become even more robust, even as global trade expansion has slowed markedly. In 2001 and 2002 China's trade first surpassed that of Canada and then that of the United Kingdom to become the sixth and then the fifth largest trading country. In 2003, China's trade growth was so rapid that it easily surpassed that of France and consequently ranked fourth in global trade in 2002. China's import growth of 40 percent in 2003 was sufficiently high so that its total imports substantially exceeded those of Japan for the first time. Indeed China's total trade in 2003 of US$851.21 billion barely surpassed Japan's trade turnover of US$851.17 billion, making China the world's third largest trading economy.[6]

Table 7.1   China's and India's shares of global trade[a]

	ca 1950	2002
China	1.5	4.8
India	2.2	0.8

[a] The base year for data on China is 1953, and for India is 1948.

Source: World Trade Organization, *World Trade Report 2003* (Appendix Table 1A.1).

Comparing India and China, it is also telling that China's trade turnover *increased* by US$230 billion in 2003, roughly twice the *level* of India's trade turnover in the same year.[7]

This chapter consists of two parts. The first (Section 7.2) provides a brief summary of the unilateral trade liberalization that China undertook during the reform period, even prior to its accession to the World Trade Organization (WTO). By a number of measures, China transformed its economy from one of the most protected to perhaps the most open among all developing economies. The second part of the chapter (Section 7.3) analyzes the implications of increased openness for economic growth. The central theme is that increased openness dramatically increased competition in the domestic market and that competition has contributed to a substantial transformation of the economy, particularly in the state-owned sector.

7.2   Trade liberalization in China

Prior to the late 1970s, China's commodity trade was determined almost entirely by economic planning. The State Planning Commission's import plan covered more than 90 percent of all imports. The Commission designed the import plan to increase the supplies of machinery and equipment, industrial raw materials, and intermediate goods that were in short supply and needed to meet physical production targets for high priority final goods. The export plan was similarly comprehensive, specifying the physical quantities of more than 3000 individual commodities. A handful of foreign trade corporations owned and controlled by the Ministry of Foreign Trade was responsible for carrying out the trade plan prior to 1978. Each of these corporations typically dealt in a narrow range of commodities for which it was the sole authorized trading company. Since the planning process was carried out in physical terms, the exchange rate and relative prices played little role in determining the magnitude and commodity composition of China's foreign trade.

The consequences of these policies for both the volume and the commodity composition of foreign trade were quite adverse for the efficiency of domestic resource allocation and rate of economic growth. A significant share of China's exports consisted of goods for which China did not enjoy a comparative advantage in production. And producers of export goods had no economic incentive to expand their international sales owing to plan production targets. That, in turn, impaired China's ability to finance imports embodying advanced technology that could have contributed to productivity growth and economic expansion.

There were several manifestations of these inefficiencies. Most obviously, the volume of China's trade grew relatively slowly. China's share of world trade dropped markedly, from 1.5 percent in 1953 to only 0.6 percent in 1977.[8] Not only did this system depress the overall volume of trade, it distorted the commodity composition of foreign trade, particularly on the export side. Rather than concentrating on labor-intensive goods, China exported significant quantities of capital-intensive goods.[9]

The system of physical planning of foreign trade, which was responsible for a relatively irrational pattern of exports, was gradually dismantled in the 1980s and by the end of the 1990s was largely abandoned. While the government, through its foreign trade companies, continued to maintain direct control of imports and exports of a handful of important commodities, most trade was decentralized and increasingly market determined. This was made possible by a dramatic expansion in the number and type of firms authorized to engage in foreign trade, reforms to the pricing of traded goods so that international prices of traded goods were increasingly transmitted to the domestic market, and the adoption of exchange rate policies that did not discriminate against exports. As direct trade controls were phased out, the regime developed a foreign trade system relying much more on indirect instruments, such as tariffs and nontariff barriers, to regulate the flow of imports and exports.

On the import side, in the early years of the reform era China maintained an extraordinarily complex and highly restrictive system of controls, including not only the usual policy instruments, such as tariffs, quotas, and licensing requirements, but also an array of other tools. These tools included limiting the number of companies authorized to carry out trade transactions and restricting the range of goods that each of these companies was allowed to trade, import substitution lists, a system of registration for select imports, and commodity inspection requirements.

By the time China entered the WTO in 2001, the import regime had been almost entirely transformed. As reflected in Figure 7.1, the average statutory tariff, which stood at the relatively high level of 56 percent in 1982, was reduced to 15 percent by 2001. The share of all imports subject to licensing requirements fell from a peak of 46 percent in the late 1980s to fewer than 4 percent of all commodities by the time China entered the WTO.[10] The state abolished import substitution lists and authorized tens of thousands of companies to engage in foreign trade transactions, undermining the monopoly

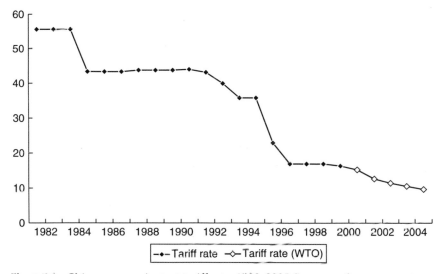

Figure 7.1   China: average import tariff rate, 1982–2005 (in percent)

Sources: Lardy (2002, Table 2.1); World Bank, *World Bank Development Indicators 1999* (Table 6.6) for 1992–94 and 1996–98; and She (2003) for 2002–2005 (expected).

powers of state trading companies for all but a handful of commodities. The transformation was similarly far reaching on the export side. At their peak in 1991, for example, two-thirds of all exports were subject to export licensing and quotas. But by 1999, only 8 percent of all exports were so encumbered.

Three other policies were critical to the rapid expansion of China's foreign trade over the past 25 years. The first is the reform of the pricing and allocation of foreign exchange. In the pre-reform era the state fixed the exchange rate at an overvalued level to implicitly subsidize the import of high priority capital goods that could not be produced domestically. Overvaluation of the domestic currency, naturally, led to excess demand for foreign exchange relative to supply, necessitating a rigid system of exchange control. The key elements of this control system were the requirement that exporters surrender 100 percent of their foreign exchange earnings to the government, rigid limitations on the rights of individuals to hold foreign currency, and strict controls on the outflow of capital.

Beginning in the early 1980s, the state gradually modified these features of the foreign exchange system. Exporters were allowed to retain a share of their foreign exchange earnings. That gave them the ability to finance imports without the need to seek permission to purchase foreign exchange, which was a substantial incentive to sell into the international market. And, perhaps most importantly in the long run, over time the government substantially devalued the domestic currency from a nominal exchange rate of

Y1.5 to the US dollar at the outset of reform to Y8.7 in 1994 when the prevailing dual exchange rate system was ended by fixing the official exchange rate at the rate then prevailing in the parallel foreign exchange market.[11] In real terms China's currency lost just over 70 percent of its value between 1980 and 1995. But the adoption of the market-clearing rate in 1994, however, suggests that the cumulative change in the official exchange rate up to that time was necessary to eliminate the historic overvaluation of the currency. Two years later the Chinese authorities announced that the currency was convertible on current account transactions, meaning that importers could purchase foreign exchange without restriction.

A second policy supporting the rapid growth of China's foreign trade was the decision of the State Council in 1984 to rebate the indirect taxes that reduced the profitability of exporting. This reform is sanctioned under WTO rules, and it allowed China, which relies heavily on indirect taxes such as the value-added tax, to compete fairly with countries that rely primarily on direct taxes such as the corporate and individual income tax.

A third policy that helps to explain the rapid expansion of China's exports over the past two decades is the duty drawback system that supports China's export processing program. This system, which was formalized in the second half of the 1980s, rebates import duties on raw materials, parts and components, and so forth when these goods are used for export processing. That allows export processing to take place at world prices, free from tariff or domestic pricing distortions. The rapidly increasing share of total exports contributed by processing suggests the importance of this initiative. By 2003, processed exports reached US$242 billion and accounted for 55 percent of China's total exports.[12]

The dramatic effect of these reforms on the volume of China's foreign trade is reflected in the summary data presented at the outset of this chapter. Equally important have been the changes in the commodity composition of China's trade, particularly on the export side. As the reforms took hold, export growth became increasingly concentrated in labor-intensive products in which China has a relatively strong comparative advantage. In the early years of reform, China exported primarily agricultural products and petroleum and its byproducts. Later, China shifted increasingly into manufactured goods, particularly light manufactures. Thus, the share of primary products in total exports fell by almost four-fifths, from an average of 45 percent in the first half of the 1980s to only 10 percent by 1999.[13]

China's fastest growing exports have been labor-intensive manufactures—textiles, apparel, footwear, and toys. Between 1980 and 1998, exports of these items rose more than tenfold from US$4.3 billion to US$53.5 billion. The share of China's total exports accounted for by these four product categories soared from 6.9 percent in 1980 to 29.1 percent by 1998. For each of these products China's share of total world exports rose rapidly. In textiles, its share almost doubled, from 4.6 percent in 1980 to 8.5 percent in 1998.

The increase was even faster for apparel, where China's share of global exports more than quadrupled, from 4.0 percent to 16.7 percent over the same period. Even more dramatic was the expansion in the world market share for toys—from 2.3 percent in 1980 to 17.9 percent in 1998. China's share of the world market for footwear rose the fastest of all, soaring from 1.9 percent in 1980 to 20.7 percent in 1998.[14]

More recently, China has become an important location for the assembly of consumer electronics, computers and other information technology products. While some of these goods have a high tech appearance, the high value parts and components are still mostly sourced offshore. For example, import content accounts for 84 percent of the value of exports of high tech products such as electronics and information industry products.[15] While these goods are high tech compared to footwear and toys, China's comparative advantage in the assembly of these products stems from the same factor as its comparative advantage in apparel, footwear, and toys—relatively abundant labor. The growing importance of these goods is reflected in the US market, where imports from China rose by more than a third, from US$26 billion in 2000 to US$35 billion in 2002. In that two-year span China displaced the European Union, Mexico, and Japan to become the largest supplier of high tech goods to the United States.[16]

7.3 Effects of competitiveness on openness

China's substantial trade growth has introduced substantial new competition into its domestic market. One measure of the potential competitive effect of trade for any country is the ratio of its imports to gross domestic product (GDP), sometimes called the import ratio. As reflected in Figure 7.2, China's import ratio increased from under 15 percent in 1990 to 30 percent in 2003. Thirty percent is more than three times Japan's import ratio of 9 percent in 2003, almost two-and-a-half times India's import ratio of 13 percent and more than twice the 14 percent import ratio for the United States.[17]

In addition to imports, competition is enhanced through the domestic sale of goods produced by foreign affiliates located in China. This is particularly important in China since by the end of 2003 cumulative inward foreign direct investment (FDI) was about US$500 billion, by far the largest of any emerging market economy. Over half of inward FDI has gone into the manufacturing sector, where there are very few restrictions on foreign ownership. The economic importance of foreign affiliates in China is reflected in their contribution to manufactured goods output, which in 2002 stood at almost 30 percent.[18] Contrary to the impression that foreign affiliates have invested in China mostly as a manufacturing platform for sales into the global market, about 60 percent of the output of joint ventures and wholly foreign-owned firms is sold on the domestic market.[19] From the point of view of local firms without foreign ownership, the competitive effects of imported

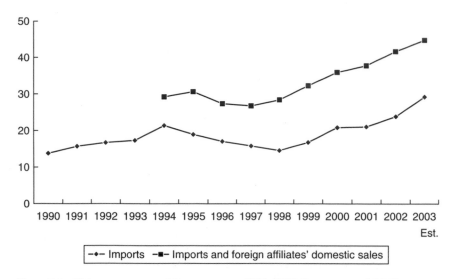

Figure 7.2   China: openness of the economy, 1990–2003 (in percent of GDP)

Sources: Lardy (1995, p. 1066); *China Statistical Yearbook (CSY) 1995* (pp. 375 and 381) for 1990–94; *CSY 1997* (pp. 411 and 417) for 1992–96; *CSY 1998* (pp. 620 and 636) for 1997; *CSY 2000* (p. 407 and 603) for 1998–99; *CSY 2003* (pp. 462–3, 670) for 2000–02; and Ministry of Commerce website (www.mofcom.gov.cn) and China Economic News (February 16, 2004, p. 7) for 2003.

goods and of goods produced by foreign affiliates but sold on the domestic market are similar. In both cases the goods will reflect whatever advantages of foreign technology, finance, management, and marketing can be brought to bear. The sum of imports plus the domestic sales of foreign affiliates relative to GDP, shown in the top line of Figure 7.2, grew from just under 30 percent in 1994 to 45 percent in 2003.

Three indicators suggest that increased competition is having a transforming influence on China's domestic economy. The three are the decline in employment in the state sector, the dramatic shrinkage in the rate of inventory accumulation, and the upturn in profitability of China's state-owned manufacturing firms.

Even as China's economic transformation was gathering speed in the 1980s and early 1990s, the number of staff and workers employed in the state sector continued to expand. As is reflected in the top line of Figure 7.3, by 1995 the total number of staff and workers employed in the state sector exceeded 109 million, representing an increase of 35 million or by more than 50 percent since reforms got under way in 1978.[20] That situation has dramatically reversed since the mid-1990s. Between 1995 and the end of 2002, the number of staff and workers employed in the state sector declined by 40 million or more than a third, falling significantly below the level of

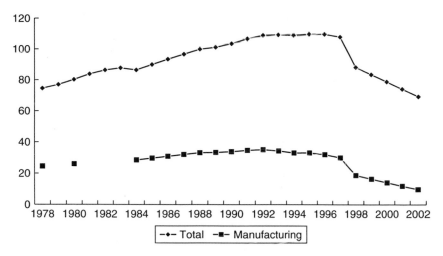

Figure 7.3   China: state employment, 1978–2002[a] (in millions of persons)

[a] Annual data from 1990 onwards.

Sources: China Statistical Yearbook (CSY) 1989 (p. 103); *CSY 1990* (p. 115); *CSY 1991* (p. 109); *CSY 1992* (p. 111); *CSY 1993* (p. 111); *CSY 1995* (pp. 90 and 92); *CSY 1996* (p. 96); *CSY 1997* (p. 102); *CSY 1998* (p. 136); *CSY 1999* (pp. 142 and 144); *CSY 2000* (pp. 118–19 and 124); *CSY 2001* (pp. 110–111 and 116); *CSY 2002* (pp. 120–1 and 126); and *CSY 2003* (pp. 126 and 134).

1978 for the first time. The shrinkage of employment in the state sector has been very large and very compressed time wise.

In manufacturing the story is similar through the early 1990s. But, as is reflected in the steep slope of the bottom line in Figure 7.3, the decline since then has been even more abrupt. In the 1980s and early 1990s the share of manufactured goods output produced in the state sector was shrinking, as the output share of the private sector and foreign affiliates grew. Nonetheless, after 1978, employment in state-owned manufacturing establishments increased by more than 10 million, reaching a peak of more than 35 million in 1992. But by the end of 2002, state-owned manufacturing establishments employed fewer than 10 million people. Through a combination of management and worker buyouts that converted firms from public to private, some company bankruptcies, and substantial workforce downsizing in firms that remained state-owned, manufacturing jobs in the state sector have declined by almost three-quarters from their peak.

Declining inventory accumulation is a second indicator of how competition is transforming China's economy. Inventory accumulation, shown in Figure 7.4, averaged a breathtakingly high 6 percent of GDP in the run up to the Asian financial crisis in 1997. Economic growth in this period averaged 11 percent in real terms, but 6 percent of output every year went into inventories, a large portion of which was never sold. In the period 1998–2002,

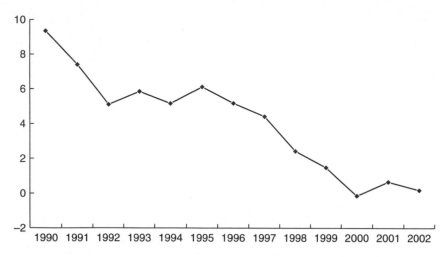

Figure 7.4   China: inventory accumulation, 1990–2002 (in percent of GDP)

Sources: *China Statistical Yearbook (CSY) 1999* (pp. 67–8); *CSY 2001* (pp. 61–2); *CSY 2002* (pp. 62–4); and *CSY 2003* (p. 68).

inventory accumulation has come down to an average of only 0.9 percent of GDP. The improvement reflects the combined effect of two changes. First, the main objective of state enterprises is no longer to provide employment. Profitability has become the main indicator for evaluating firm performance. Enterprise managers in recent years have had the authority to reduce the number of workers, so production for inventory has gone down. Second, state-owned banks, under pressure to increase the return on the funds that they lend, are apparently less willing to provide state-owned companies with seemingly unlimited lines of working capital credit. Thus firms are both less willing and also less able to finance the build up of inventories.

As a consequence of the ability of state-owned manufacturing firms to lay off excess workers and given a reduction of the rate at which they accumulate unsold inventories, profitability in China's state-owned sector has improved significantly in recent years. Figure 7.5 shows that the return on assets of state-owned manufacturing companies, which had declined continuously for 20 years, has risen significantly since hitting a low in 1998. The return on assets (defined here as the ratio of pretax profits to the sum of the depreciated value of fixed assets plus working capital) was 9.1 percent in 2002, compared to only 5.0 percent in 1998.[21]

7.4   Conclusion

China is perhaps the best example of the positive connection between openness and economic growth. Reforms transformed China from a highly

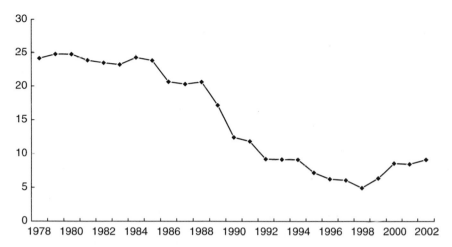

Figure 7.5 China: profitability of state-owned manufacturers, 1978–2002 (in percent)
Sources: China Statistical Yearbook (CSY) 1995 (pp. 392–5 and 403); *CSY 1996* (pp. 419 and 429); *CSY 1997* (pp. 428–31 and 439); *CSY 1999* (pp. 433 and 435); *CSY 2000* (pp. 441–2); *CSY 2001* (pp. 411 and 413); *CSY 2002* (pp. 433 and 435); and *CSY 2003* (pp. 469 and 471).

protected market to perhaps the most open developing economy by the time it came into the WTO at the end of 2001. The focus of this chapter has been on manufacturing, but China's WTO commitments are leading to a very significant opening in services as well. For example, the chief US negotiator on China's WTO accession characterized China's commitment to liberalize its distribution system as "broader actually than any WTO member has made."[22] Thus, the positive stimulus that international competition provides for technical change and managerial efficiencies will not be limited to manufacturing but also will extend increasingly to the services sector, where China's commitments to increased openness go beyond those made by all other members of the WTO.

Notes

1. Senior Fellow, Institute for International Economics, Washington, DC.
2. Srinivasan and Tendulkar (2003, p. 11).
3. The comparison is even more striking if one uses, as do Srinivasan and Tendulkar (2003), Chinese data from the late 1940s. At that time China's trade, only 0.9 percent of global trade, was acutely depressed by the civil war between the Nationalist and Communist Parties.
4. World Trade Organization (2003, Appendix Table 1A.1).
5. Lardy (2002, p. 4).
6. National Bureau of Statistics of China (NBSC) (2004) and Japan External Trade Organization (JETRO) (2003).
7. NBSC (2004) and Reserve Bank of India (2004).

8. Lardy (1994, p. 1).
9. Lardy (1992, pp. 695–700).
10. Lardy (2002, pp. 33 and 39).
11. Just prior to the unification of the two rates at the market rate, 80 percent of all foreign exchange trading was in the parallel, unrestricted market.
12. NBSC (2004).
13. NBSC, *China Statistical Yearbook (CSY) 2002* (p. 613).
14. Lardy (2002, p. 56).
15. Jia Hepeng (2004) and Fu Jing (2004).
16. American Electronics Association (2003, p. 5).
17. The import ratio for Japan calculated from trade data reported by the JETRO (2003); GDP data are from the Japan Statistics Bureau, and exchange rate data are from the Bank of Japan (2004). India's import ratio is calculated from Ministry of Statistics (2004) and Reserve Bank of India (2004) data. The United States' import ratio is calculated from Bureau of Economic Analysis (2004) data.
18. Measured on a gross value basis. See NBSC, *CSY 2002* (p. 459).
19. For the period 1994–2002, the annual share of output of foreign manufacturing affiliates sold on the domestic market has ranged between 55.0 percent and 63.5 percent. See Lardy (1995, p. 1066); *CSY 1995* (pp. 375 and 381) for 1994; *CSY 1997* (pp. 411 and 417) for 1995–96; *CSY 1998* (pp. 620 and 636) for 1997; *CSY 2000* (pp. 407 and 603) for 1998–99; *CSY 2003* (pp. 462–3 and 670) for 2000–02; and Ministry of Commerce website (www.mofcom.gov.cn) and *China Economic News* (February 16, 2004, p. 7) for 2003.
20. This analysis is based on the number of staff and workers rather than the number of employed persons because a breakdown of the latter by sector is not provided in the *China Statistical Yearbook*. The difference in the scope of the two definitions of employment is minor. For example, retired workers who are rehired are counted in the number of people employed but not in the number of workers and staff. In 2002, the number of employed persons in state-owned units was 3.5 percent greater than the number of staff and workers in state-owned units. See NBSC, *China Statistical Yearbook 2003* (pp. 126, 134, and 179–82).
21. For state-owned companies and state-controlled shareholding companies. See *CSY 1999* (pp. 432–5) and *CSY 2003* (pp. 468–71).
22. U.S. Ambassador Charlene Barshefsky (1999).

References

American Electronic Association, 2003, *Tech Trade Update 2003* (Washington, DC).

Bank of Japan, 2004, *Foreign Exchange Rates* (monthly data).

Barshefsky, Charlene, 1999, "U.S. Trade Policy in China," prepared testimony before the United-States Senate Finance Committee (April 13).

Bureau of Economic Analysis, 2004, *International Economic Account* and *National Economic Accounts* (Washington, DC: United States Department of Commerce).

China Economic News (various issues) (Hong Kong: Economic and Information Agency).

Fu Jing, 2004, "Nation Biggest Producer of TV, Cell Phone, Monitor," *China Daily* (Beijing) (February 5).

Japan External Trade Organization, 2003, "Japan International Trade in Goods," *Statistics and Surveys*.

Japan Statistics Bureau (various issues), *Monthly Statistics of Japan*.

Jia Hepeng, 2004, "Foreign Trade Growth a Double-Edged Sword," *China Daily Business Weekly* (January 20).

Lardy, Nicholas R., 2002, *Integrating China into the Global Economy* (Washington, DC: Brookings Institution Press).

——, 1995, "The Role of Foreign Trade and Investment in China's Economic Transformation," *The China Quarterly*, No. 144 (December).

——, 1994, *China in the World Economy* (Washington, DC: Institute for International Economics).

——, 1992, "Chinese Foreign Trade," *The China Quarterly*, No. 131 (September).

Ministry of Commerce (China) website (www.mofcom.gov.cn).

Ministry of Statistics and Programme Implementation (India), 2004, *National Accounts* (New Delhi: Central Statistical Organization).

National Bureau of Statistics of China, 2004, "Statistical Communiqué of the People's Republic of China on National Economic and Social Development in 2003" (February 26).

—— (various years), *China Statistical Yearbook* (various years) (Beijing: China Statistics Press).

Reserve Bank of India, 2004, *Monthly Bulletin* (April) (Mumbai).

She, Zhongguo Xinwen, 2003, "Reduced Customs Tariffs Adding to the Challenge," *Foreign Broadcast Information Service* (China) (January 2).

State Statistical Bureau (various years), *China Statistical Yearbook* (Beijing: China Statistics Press).

T.N. Srinivasan and Suresh D. Tendulkar, 2003, *Reintegrating India with the World Economy* (Washington, DC: Institute for International Economics).

World Bank, 2004, *India at a Glance* (February 9) (Washington, DC).

——, 1999, *World Development Indicators 1999* (Washington, DC).

World Trade Organization, 2003, *World Trade Report 2003* (Geneva).

8
India in the 1980s and the 1990s: A Triumph of Reforms

Arvind Panagariya[1]

8.1 Introduction

While public opinion in India continues to move toward the view that liberalization has been good, that more of it is needed, and that its pace must be accelerated, the view in some scholarly and policy circles has turned skeptical. It is being argued that the average annual growth rate of gross domestic product (GDP) hit the 5.6 percent mark in the 1980s, well before the launch of the July 1991 reforms. Moreover, the growth rate in the 1990s was not much higher. Therefore, liberalization cannot be credited with having made a significant difference to growth in India.[2]

The main proponents of this skepticism are DeLong (2001) and Rodrik (2002). DeLong writes

> What are the sources of India's recent acceleration in economic growth? Conventional wisdom traces them to policy reforms at the start of the 1990s. Yet the aggregate growth data tells us that the acceleration of economic growth began earlier, in the early or mid-1980s, long before the exchange crisis of 1991 and the shift of the government of Narasimha Rao and Manmohan Singh toward neo-liberal economic reforms. (2001, pp. 5–6)

He further adds

> Thus apparently the policy changes in the mid- and late-1980s under the last governments of the Nehru dynasty were sufficient to start the acceleration of growth, small as those policy reforms appear in retrospect. Would they have just produced a short-lived flash in the pan—a decade or so of fast growth followed by a slowdown—in the absence of the further reforms of the 1990s? My hunch is that the answer is "yes." In the absence of the second wave of reforms in the 1990s it is unlikely that the rapid growth of the second half of the 1980s could be sustained. *But*

hard evidence to support such a strong counterfactual judgment is lacking. [Emphasis added]

Rodrik (2002) picks up on DeLong's view, who speculates that: "the change in official attitudes in the 1980s, toward encouraging rather than discouraging entrepreneurial activities and integration into the world economy, and a belief that the rules of the economic game had changed for good may have had a bigger impact on growth than any specific policy reforms." It is not entirely clear as to what *policy* message is to be gleaned from this skepticism. Neither DeLong nor Rodrik suggests that the reforms of the 1990s were detrimental to the growth process. DeLong explicitly states that in the absence of the second wave of reforms in the 1990s, it is unlikely that the rapid growth of the second half of the 1980s could have been sustained. Rodrik is more tentative, emphasizing the change in official *attitudes* over the change in actual *policies*, possibly implying that if attitudes had changed for good, growth would have been sustained even without the reforms of the 1990s.

This interpretation itself raises two immediate questions: Is there evidence demonstrating that official attitudes changed significantly during the 1980s and, if so, how was this change conveyed to the public? Most observers of India are likely to question the view that there had been a significant shift in official attitudes in the 1980s. Indirect evidence of the general dominance of the old attitudes can be found in the care the then Finance Minister and now Prime Minister Manmohan Singh took in packaging the bold reforms of 1991, describing them as a continuation of the old policies. A careful reader of Singh's historic 1991 budget speech is bound to be struck by the effort he made to draw a close connection between his proposals and the policies initiated by India's first Prime Minister Jawaharlal Nehru and carried forward by his grandson Rajiv Gandhi. As noted in Panagariya (1994), Singh continuously reiterated the usefulness of the past policies in the speech and repeatedly referred to the contributions of Nehru to development, while also recalling the just-assassinated former Prime Minister Rajiv Gandhi's dream of taking India into the twenty-first century.

More direct evidence that old attitudes persisted can be found in comments made by N.K. Singh on an earlier draft of this chapter. Singh, who was directly involved in policymaking in India during the 1980s and 1990s and is currently Member, Planning Commission, noted the following:

I am somewhat intrigued by the statement of Delong and Rodrik stressing change in official attitude over change in policies implying that if attitude changed for good, growth would have been sustained even without reforms in the 1990s. Even today, more than change in policies we are struggling with change in attitude. The first reflex of any observer of Indian economy or potential foreign investor would be that while policies may not be so bad it is the attitude particularly of official ones which becomes the Achilles['] heel. In fact the 1980s and even the 1990s have seen far-reaching change in policies which have not translated them-selves fully into changes in attitudes. This attitudinal change indeed constitutes a major challenge in our reform agenda.

It is also worth noting that the view that liberal economic policies did not make a significant contribution to the shift in growth during the 1980s extends well beyond reform skeptics and includes some of the ardent reform advocates. Joshi and Little (1994, chapter 13), who have been champions of reforms and have extensively studied Indian macroeconomic policies in the 1980s, recognize the role of reforms but regard fiscal expansion financed by external and internal borrowing as the key to the acceleration of growth during the 1980s.[3] This is also the view expressed indirectly by Ahluwalia (2002a, p. 67), who states that while growth record in the 1990s was only slightly better than in the 1980s, the 1980s growth was unsustainable, "fuelled by a build up of external debt that culminated in the crisis of 1991." Srinivasan and Tendulkar (2003) attribute some role to the reforms, but they too underplay them in stating

India's exports increased over this period [1980s] of piecemeal reforms, but this was more due to a real exchange rate depreciation *mostly as a result of exogenous forces than due to an active policy* of nominal devaluation or due to *explicit policy reforms* aimed at reducing trade barriers. Growth performance was also distinctly better in the 1980s than in the earlier period. This surge in growth, however, was supported on the demand side by unsustainable fiscal policies, and it ended with an economic crisis in 1991. [Emphasis added]

Finally, Das (2000) gives the strongest impression of all writers that reforms originated with the July 1991 package announced by Manmohan Singh:

[I]n July 1991 . . . with the announcement of sweeping liberalization by the minority government of P.V. Narasimha Rao . . . [that] opened the economy . . . dismantled import controls, lowered customs duties, and devalued the currency . . . virtually abolished licensing controls on private investment, dropped tax rates, and broke public sector monopolies . . . [w]e felt as though our second independence had arrived: we were going to be free from a rapacious and domineering state.

Among those who have ventured to attribute the acceleration in growth in the 1980s to liberalization are Desai (1999), Pursell (1992), and Virmani (1997). Desai focuses on industry deregulation and growth and Pursell on trade liberalization in the 1980s. I draw on their work later, particularly the latter. The discussion in Virmani (1997) is brief, but he attributes the shift in the growth rate in the 1980s virtually *entirely* to liberalization. Moreover, he views the liberalization measures during the 1980s and the 1990s as "sub-phases" of an overall phase.

Even if one concedes that a change in attitude on the part of officials had taken place, the question remains how officials could have conveyed this change to entrepreneurs without a change in the policy or its implementation? It is only through policy changes such as the expansion of the Open General Licensing (OGL) list at the expense of the banned and restricted import licensing lists and change in the implementation strategy, as for instance, by issuing import licenses more liberally, that officials could convey the change in their attitudes to entrepreneurs. By extension, the absence of further reforms would have surely signaled to entrepreneurs a reversion back to the old attitudes.

At the same time, reforms played a significant role in spurring growth in the 1980s. The difference between the reforms in the 1980s and those in the 1990s is that the former were limited in scope and without a clear roadmap whereas the latter were systematic and systemic.[4] The 1990s reforms were also qualitatively different from those in the 1980s in that they represented a broad acceptance of the idea that entrepreneurs and markets were to be given priority over government in the conduct of economic activity and that government interventions required proper justification rather than be accepted by default.

This said, the reforms in the 1980s must be viewed as precursor to those in the 1990s rather than a part of the isolated and sporadic liberalizing actions experienced in the 1960s and 1970s, but often reversed within a short period. While liberalization was *ad hoc* and implemented quietly ("reforms by stealth" is the term often used to describe it), inroads were made into virtually all areas of industry and the foundation was laid for more extensive reforms in July 1991 and beyond. The 1980s reforms also proved particularly crucial to building the confidence of politicians regarding the ability of policy changes such as currency devaluation, trade liberalization, and investment de-licensing to spur growth without disruption. It is questionable, for example, whether the July 1991 reform package would have been politically acceptable in the absence of the experience and confidence in liberal policies acquired during the 1980s.

The policy versus attitude change issue aside, the key question is whether minor changes in either policy or attitudes in the 1980s produced the same outcome as the major reforms in the 1990s. In this chapter, I demonstrate that the skeptical view offered by Rodrik and DeLong overstates the growth and understates the reforms during the 1980s. The main conclusions of this chapter are that

- Growth during the 1980s, while higher than in previous decades, was still fragile, highly variable across years, and unsustainable.

- Central to the high growth rate in the 1980s was the extraordinarily high growth of 7.6 percent during 1988–91. Absent this growth, the average growth in the 1980s would be significantly lower than in the 1990s.
- Ultimately, this growth culminated in a crisis in June 1991, having been propelled in part by fiscal expansion financed by borrowing abroad and at home.
- Last, in contrast to the 1980s, once the 1991 reforms took root, growth became less variable and actually sustainable, with a slight upward shift in the mean growth rate.

Despite more than two decades of relatively good growth, India continues to lag behind China, with the economy of the former expanding at 5–6 percent a year compared to the 8 percent for the latter. The key reason for the difference is that industry has failed to grow rapidly in India and still accounts for only a quarter of the GDP compared with half in the case of China. If India is to catch up with China, some key reforms aimed at helping industry grow faster are essential: revised labor laws that give firms the right to reassign and layoff workers under reasonable conditions; an end to the small-scale industry (SSI) reservation, which still reserves most of the labor-intensive products for small firms; streamlined bankruptcy laws; and tariff levels comparable to or lower than those in the East Asian economies.

The remainder of this chapter is organized as follows. In Section 8.2, I contrast the experience during the 1980s with that in the 1990s, arguing that growth in the former period was fragile and unsustainable. In Section 8.3, I link the shift in the growth rate in the 1980s to the conventional economic reforms both in terms of policy changes and outcomes. In Section 8.4, I discuss the role played by expansionary fiscal policies supported by both internal and external borrowing that made the growth process unsustainable. In Section 8.5, I describe briefly the main reforms undertaken since 1991 and their impact. In Section 8.6, I offer remarks on why growth in the 1990s has continued to fall behind that of China and what India could do to catch up. Finally, in Section 8.7, I summarize the chapter and offer concluding remarks.

8.2 The fragility of growth in the 1980s

In comparing India's growth performance prior to the July 1991 reforms and that following them, the conventional practice is to draw the line at fiscal year 1990/91 (April–March) and thus divide the time period into the decades of the 1980s and the 1990s. But this division does not accurately reflect the division into periods prior to and following the July 1991 reforms. Indeed, because 1991/92 was the crisis year and the 1991 reforms were a response to rather than the cause of the crisis, the conventional practice creates a serious distortion by including the year 1991/92 into the post-1991 reform period.

The July 1991 reforms and the subsequent changes could not have begun to bear fruit prior to 1992/93.

Therefore, for the purpose of this chapter, I take 1991/92 as the dividing line between the two periods. The post-1991 reform period is defined to start in 1992/93 and last until the latest year for which data are available, 2002/03. The pre-1991 reform period precedes this period with the starting date left vague at this point. Though it may be argued that the June 1991 crisis was the result of the policies of the pre-1991 reform period and therefore the year 1991/92 legitimately belongs in it, where appropriate, I present the analysis with and without this year included in the pre-1991 reform period. *Throughout the chapter, unless otherwise stated, the terms "1980s" and "1990s" refer to the pre- and post-1991 reform periods as per these definitions.*

The difficulty in pinpointing the date of shift in the growth rate does not allow us to precisely define the starting point of the "1980s" growth period. Fortunately, however, two important related facts remain valid regardless of which starting date we choose. First, the years 1988–91, when the economy grew at the extraordinarily high average annual rate of 7.6 percent, are critical to obtaining an average growth rate for the 1980s (again defined here as 1981/82 to 1991/92) that is comparable to the growth rate for the 1990s (1992/93 to 2002/03), or 5.3 percent versus 5.9 percent (Table 8.1).[5] If one excludes the crisis year, 1991/92, from the pre-reform period, the average growth rates in the 1980s rises to 5.7 percent, virtually identical to the 1990s (Table 8.2). Second, the variance of growth rates during the 1980s is statistically significantly higher than that in the 1990s. In this sense, growth during the first period was fragile relative to that in the second and, indeed, culminated in the June 1991 crisis.

To get the most accurate picture on growth performance in the 1980s versus the 1990s, it is necessary for a moment to consider average annual growth rates until 1987/88. If we take the ten-year period from 1978/79 to 1987/88, the average growth rate is an unimpressive 4.1 percent. In 1988, anyone looking back at the ten-year experience would have concluded that India was still on the Hindu growth path. Indeed, even limiting ourselves to 1981/82 to 1987/88, we get an average growth rate of only 4.8 percent, which is strictly below the growth rate of 4.9 percent achieved during the Fifth Five-Year Plan (1974–79). Thus, had it not been for the unusually high average growth rate of 7.6 percent during 1988–91, we would not have reason to debate whether the reforms of the 1990s made a significant contribution to growth. The implication is that any explanation of growth in the 1980s must explain the exceptionally high growth during 1988–91.[6]

As noted, growth was subject to higher variance in the 1980s compared to the 1990s (Figure 8.1). More importantly, we can test the hypothesis formally that growth was more volatile in the 1980s by applying the standard F-test. Variances of growth rates during the 1980s and the 1990s are reported in Table 8.3, taking various cutoff dates for the former period. Irrespective of

Table 8.1   India: real GDP growth, 1951/52–2002/03

Year	Growth rate	Year	Growth rate
1951/52	2.3	1977/78	7.5
1952/53	2.8	1978/79	5.5
1953/54	6.1	1979/80	−5.2
1954/55	4.2	1980/81	7.2
1955/56	2.6	1981/82	6.0
1956/57	5.7	1982/83	3.1
1957/58	−1.2	1983/84	7.7
1958/59	7.6	1984/85	4.3
1959/60	2.2	1985/86	4.5
1960/61	7.1	1986/87	4.3
1961/62	3.1	1987/88	3.8
1962/63	2.1	1988/89	10.5
1963/64	5.1	1989/90	6.7
1964/65	7.6	1990/91	5.6
1965/66	−3.7	1991/92	1.3
1966/67	1.0	1992/93	5.1
1967/68	8.1	1993/94	5.9
1968/69	2.6	1994/95	7.3
1969/70	6.5	1995/96	7.3
1970/71	5.0	1996/97	7.8
1971/72	1.0	1997/98	4.8
1972/73	−0.3	1998/99	6.5
1973/74	4.6	1999/00	6.1
1974/75	1.2	2000/01 (P)[a]	4.4
1975/76	9.0	2001/02 (Q)[b]	5.6
1976/77	1.2	2002/03 (Q)	4.4

[a] P = Provisional estimate.
[b] Q = Quick estimate.

Sources: Ministry of Finance, *Economic Survey 2002–03* (Table 1.1) and author's estimates.

which cutoff dates we choose for the 1980s, we uniformly reject the null hypothesis of no higher variance in the 1980s than in the 1990s in favor of the alternative that variance was higher in the 1980s. The conclusion that growth in the 1980s was more fragile than in the 1990s thus receives unequivocal support in the data.[7]

The critical question to which I turn next concerns the sources of the shift in the growth rate in the 1980s, especially the subperiod 1988–91. In the Sections 8.3 and 8.4, I argue that two broad factors account for much of the spurt. First, liberalization played a significant role. On the external front, policy measures such as import liberalization, export incentives, and a more realistic real exchange rate contributed to productive efficiency. On the internal front, the freeing up of several sectors from investment licensing

Table 8.2 India: average real GDP growth in select periods

Period	Growth rate
Prior to the shift in growth rate	
1951/52–1973/74	3.6
Pre-1991 reform period	
1981/82–1990/91	5.7
1981/82–1991/92	5.3
1977/78–1990/91	5.1
Memorandum items: Pre-1991 reform period	
1974/75–1978/79	4.9
1978/79–1987/88	4.1
1981/82–1987/88	4.8
1988/89–1990/91	7.6
Post-1991 reform period	
1992/93–2001/02	6.1
1992/93–2002/03	5.9

Sources: Ministry of Finance, *Economic Survey 2002–03* (Table 1.1) and author's estimates.

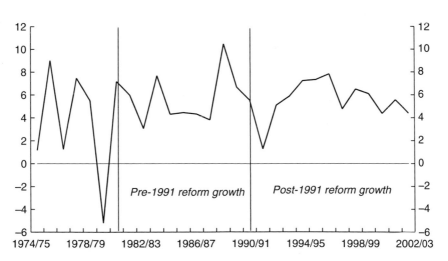

Figure 8.1 India: real GDP, pre- and post-reform (annual percentage change)
Sources: Ministry of Finance, *Economic Survey 2002–03* (Table 1.1) and author's estimates.

Table 8.3   India: variance of GDP growth rates, 1980s and 1990s

Period	Variance	Ratio to variance in 1990s[a]
1981/82–1991/92	6.1	4.1[b]
1980/81–1990/91	4.6	3.1[c]
1981/82–1990/91	4.8	3.3[c]
1977/78–1990/91	12.5	8.5[d]
1992/93–2002/03	1.5	—

[a] Defined as 1992/93–2002/03.
[b] Significant at 2.5 percent level; *F-test* in brackets [*F*0.025 (10, 10) = 3.72].
[c] Significant at 5 percent level [*F*0.05 (10, 10) = 2.98; *F*0.05 (9, 10) = 3.0].
[d] Significant at 1 percent level [*F*0.01 (12, 10) = 4.71].

Sources: Ministry of Finance, *Economic Survey 2002–03* (Table 1.1) and author's estimates.

reinforced import liberalization and allowed faster industrial growth. Second, both external and internal borrowing allowed the government to maintain high levels of public expenditures and thus boost growth through demand. Unfortunately, these factors carried with them the seeds of the June 1991 macroeconomic crisis that brought the economy to a grinding halt.[8]

8.3   Connection to liberalization

To appreciate the role of liberalization in stimulating growth in the 1980s, it is useful to begin with a brief historical background on import controls in India. In their pioneering study, Bhagwati and Desai (1970) provide the most comprehensive and systematic documentation of the wide sweep of the interventionist policies that had come to exist by the late 1960s. As they note, general controls on all imports and exports had been present since 1940. After Independence in 1947, import controls were relaxed through the expansion of the OGL list in a stop-go fashion, with the First Five-Year Plan (1951–56) representing a period of "progressive liberalization" (Bhagwati and Desai, 1970, p. 282). But a foreign exchange crisis in 1956/57 put an end to this phase of liberalization, and comprehensive import controls were restored and maintained until 1966. In June that year, under pressure from the World Bank, India devalued the rupee from 4.7 rupees to 7.5 rupees per dollar. The 57.5 percent devaluation was accompanied by some liberalization of import licensing and cuts in import tariffs and export subsidies for approximately a year. But by 1968, intense domestic reaction to the devaluation led India to turn inward with a vengeance.[9] Almost all liberalizing initiatives were reversed and import controls tightened. This regime was consolidated and strengthened in the subsequent years and remained more or less intact until the beginning of a period of phased liberalization in the late 1970s.

According to Pursell (1992), the severity of the controls was reflected in a decline in the proportion of non-oil and non-cereals imports in GDP from the low level of 7 percent in 1957/58 to the even lower level of 3 percent in 1975/76. Since consumer goods imports had been essentially banned, the incidence of this decline was principally borne by machinery, raw material, and components. The impact on the pattern of industrialization and level of efficiency was visible. In discussing the economic toll of these policies, Pursell (1992) notes that

> During this period, import-substitution policies were followed with little or no regard to costs. They resulted in an extremely diverse industrial structure and high degree of self-sufficiency, but many industries had high production costs. In addition, there was a general problem of poor quality and technological backwardness, which beset even low-cost sectors with comparative advantage such as the textiles, garment, leather goods, many light industries, and primary industries such as cotton. (pp. 433–4)

Pursell (1992) goes on to say that

> Although import substitution reduced imports of substitute products, this was replaced by increased demand for imported capital equipment and technology and for raw materials not domestically produced or in insufficient quantities. During the 1960s and the first half of the 1970s, the former demand was suppressed by extensive import substitution in the capital goods industries and attempts to indigenize research and development. By about 1976, however, the resulting obsolescence of the capital stock and technology of many industries was becoming apparent, and a steady liberalization of imports of capital equipment and of technology started soon after.[10] (p. 434)

Two factors facilitated the emergence of the liberalization phase. First, as already hinted above by Pursell (1992), by the mid-1970s, industrialists themselves were beginning to find the strict regime counterproductive and started pressing the government for the relaxation of controls. A domestic lobby in favor of liberalization of imports of raw materials and machinery had come to exist. At the same time, given these imports had no domestic substitutes, there was no counter lobby. Second, improved export performance and overseas workers remittances from the Middle East had led to the accumulation of a comfortable level of foreign exchange reserves. These reserves lent confidence to policymakers and bureaucrats who had lived in perpetual fear of a balance of payments crisis. Against this background, the following subsection considers successively the reforms undertaken starting in the late 1970s and their impact on the economy.

8.3.1   Reforms during the 1980s

In view of the continuing dominance of the leftist ideology in India, pre-1991 reforms were introduced quietly and without fanfare. Therefore, the term "liberalization by stealth," often used to describe them, is fully justified. Yet, this description gives the misleading impression that the reforms were marginal or inconsequential to the growth performance. As I will argue below, the reforms in the 1980s were deeper than is generally appreciated and had a distinct impact on growth rates.

Though the process of relaxing the regulation of industry began in the early 1970s and of trade in the late 1970s, the pace of reform picked up significantly only in 1985. Major changes were announced between 1985 and 1988 with the process continuing to move forward thereafter. Indeed, during this latter period, liberalization had begun to take a somewhat activist form. In turn, GDP growth and the external sector registered a dramatic improvement in performance. As already noted, GDP growth averaged 7.6 percent from 1988/89 to 1990/91. Annual export growth, which was a paltry 1.2 percent rate during 1980–85, rose to a hefty 14.4 percent during 1985–90 (Table 8.4). Broadly, the reforms of the 1980s, which were largely in place by early 1988, can be divided into five categories.

Open general licensing

The OGL list was steadily expanded in the 1980s, after having disappeared earlier. The list was reintroduced in 1976 with 79 capital goods items on it. The number of capital goods items included in the OGL list expanded steadily, reaching 1007 in April 1987, 1170 in April 1988 and 1329 in April 1990. In parallel, intermediate inputs were also placed on the OGL list and

Table 8.4   India: average growth rates of non-oil merchandise trade in select periods[a]

Year	Exports	Imports
1970/71–1974/75	16.2	17.8
1975/76–1979/80	13.7	12.3
1980/81–1984/85	1.2	7.1
1985/86–1989/90	14.4	12.3

[a] Based on trade in current US dollars.

Sources: Reserve Bank of India, *Handbook of Statistics on Indian Economy 2001* (Table 115) and author's estimates.

their number, too, expanded steadily over the years, reaching 620 by April 1987 and 949 in April 1988 (based on the best available information). According to Pursell (1992, p. 441), imports that were neither canalized nor subject to licensing (mainly OGL imports) increased from about 5 percent in 1980/81 to 30 percent in 1987/88. The inclusion of an item into the OGL list was usually accompanied by an "exemption," which amounted to a tariff reduction on that item. In almost all cases, the items on the list were machinery or raw materials for which no substitutes were produced at home. As such, their contribution to increased productivity was likely to be significant.

Canalized imports

The decline in the share of canalized imports was another major source of liberalization. Canalization refers to monopoly rights of the government for the imports of certain items. Between 1980/81 and 1986/87, the share of these imports in total imports declined from 67 percent to 27 percent. Over the same period, canalized non-petroleum, oil and lubricants (POL) imports declined from 44 percent to 11 percent of the total non-POL imports. This change significantly expanded the room for imports of machinery and raw materials.[11]

Export incentives

Several export incentives were introduced or expanded, especially after 1985, which helped expand imports directly through ties to exports and indirectly by a relaxation of the foreign exchange constraint. Replenishment (REP) licenses were given to exporters, allowing them to import items on the restricted list (i.e. items not on OGL or canalized list and allowed to be imported under highly restrictive conditions), even if they had domestic import-competing counterparts. Exporters were given REP licenses in amounts that were approximately twice their import needs and were freely tradable on the market. Thus, the REP licenses also provided a source of input imports for goods sold in the domestic market. Even though there were limits to the import competition provided through these licenses, as the volume of exports expanded, the volume of these imports expanded as well. This factor is particularly important during 1985–90 in explaining rapid export growth.

In addition to a substantial widening of the coverage of products available to exporters against REP licenses, other export incentives were introduced between 1985/86 and 1989/90, which Joshi and Little (1994, p. 184) refer to as the "quasi-Southeast Asian style" reforms. These incentives included (i) an income tax deduction of up to 50 percent of business profits attributable to exports (in 1985/86 budget) and up to 100 percent of export profits (in 1988/89 budget); (ii) a reduction in the interest rate on export credit from 12 percent to 9 percent; and (iii) an allowance from October 1986 of duty-free imports of capital goods in select "thrust" export industries. In addition, in April 1988, exporters' access to imported capital goods was increased by widening the OGL list and by making some capital goods available selectively to exporters without going through "indigenous clearance." Exporters were also given assurances that incentives announced in the export–import policy would not be reduced for a period of three years.

Industry decontrol

Another major source of liberalization was a significant relaxation of industrial controls and related reforms. First, industrial delicensing received a major boost in 1985 when 25 industries were delicensed.[12] By 1990, this number reached 31. The investment limit below which no industrial license would be required was raised to Rs 500 million in backward areas and Rs 150 million elsewhere, provided the investments were located in both cases at stipulated minimum distances from urban areas of certain sizes. Traditionally, the industrial licensing system had applied to all firms with fixed capital in excess of 3.5 million rupees. There remained 27 major industries subject to licensing regardless of the size and location of investment, including a number of major industries like coal, large textile units using power, motor vehicles, sugar, steel, and a large number of chemicals. Products subject to SSI reservation were also off-limits, though the asset ceiling of firms designated as SSI units was raised from Rs 2.0 million to Rs 3.5 million. Second, broad banding, which allowed firms to switch production between similar product lines such as trucks and cars, was introduced in January 1986 in 28 industry groups. This provision was significantly expanded in the subsequent years and led to increased flexibility in many industries. In some industries, the impact was marginal, however, since a large number of separate product categories remained due to continued industrial licensing in those products. Third, starting in 1986, firms that reached 80 percent capacity utilization in any of the five years preceding 1985 were assured authorization to expand capacity up to 133 percent of the maximum capacity utilization reached in those years.

However, firms that came under the purview of the Monopolies and Restrictive Trade Practices (MRTP) Act were subject to different rules and could not take advantage of the above policy changes. To relax the hold of the licensing and capacity constraints on these larger firms, the asset limit above which firms were subject to MRTP regulations was raised from Rs 200 million to Rs 1000 million in 1985/86. As a result, as many as 90 out of 180 large business houses registered under the MRTP Act were freed from restrictions on growth in established product lines. The requirement of MRTP clearances for 27 industries was also waived altogether. In addition, firms subject to MRTP in a number of industries were made exempt from industrial licensing provided they were located at least 100 kilometers away from large cities. MRTP firms were allowed to avail themselves of the general de-licensing measures in sectors in which they were not considered dominant undertakings. These measures significantly enhanced the freedom of large firms (with assets exceeding Rs 1000 million) to enter new products.

Other industrial reforms came through the abolishment of price and distribution controls on cement and aluminum. Decontrol in cement eliminated black market, led to expanded production, and brought prices down to the previously controlled levels within a short time. New entrants intensified competition, which led to improvements in quality along with the decline in the price. In addition, there was a major reform of the tax system. The multipoint excise duties were converted into a modified value-added tax (MODVAT), which enabled manufacturers to deduct excise paid on domestically produced inputs and countervailing duties paid on imported inputs from their excise obligations on output. By 1990, MODVAT came to cover all subsectors of manufacturing except petroleum products, textiles, and tobacco. This change significantly reduced the taxation of inputs and the associated distortion. In parallel, a more smoothly graduated schedule of excise tax concessions for SSI firms was introduced, which reduced incentives for them to stay small.

The relaxation of industrial controls reinforced the ongoing import liberalization. In the presence of these controls, firms had to have an investment license before they could approach the import-licensing authority for machinery and raw material imports. For products freed of industrial licensing, this layer of restrictions was removed. More importantly, under industrial licensing, even for products on the OGL list, machinery imports were limited by the approved investment capacity and raw material imports by the requirements implied by the production capacity. With the removal of licensing, this constraint was also removed.

Exchange rate realignment

The final and perhaps the most important source of external liberalization came through exchange rate realignment in the mid-1970s and again starting in the mid-1980s. The real depreciation of the rupee stimulated rapid export growth and led to foreign reserves accumulation, which subsequently paved the way for import liberalization. Both the import-weighted and export-weighted real exchange rates depreciated steadily from 1974/75 to 1978/79, with Pursell (1992) computing the approximate change in the former at 30 percent and in the latter at 27 percent. Following this period, the real exchange rate appreciated marginally for a few years, and then stayed more or less unchanged until the mid-1980s, when it once again began to depreciate steadily thereafter. Based on calculations made by Joshi and Little (1994, chapter 7), the real exchange rate depreciation totaled about 30 percent from 1985/86 to 1989/90. They note that the exchange rate realignment in the second half of the 1980s, at least, reflected a considerable change in the official attitude toward exchange rate depreciation.[13]

8.3.2   Impact of reforms

Low and/or declining barriers to trade constitute a necessary condition for sustained rapid growth (Panagariya, 2003) and India's experience during the 1980s is no exception to this proposition. We may squabble about the magnitude of trade and industrial liberalization during these years. But it is difficult to overlook the impact of the reduction in many direct and indirect barriers to trade on non-oil exports and imports, without which growth would have been scuttled. In this context, it is worth noting that during the 1980s, India was also helped by the discovery of oil and the spread of the Green Revolution, which helped reduce the need for oil and food imports and, thus, free up foreign exchange for other imports. That these developments helped cannot be denied. At the same time, had India not responded by opening up trade and investment rules, the opportunity offered by these developments would have been lost.

The impact of reforms in the 1980s can be seen most clearly on India's trade flows. Besides compositional changes brought about through expansion of the OGL list and a reduction in canalized imports, there was considerable expansion in the level of imports during the 1970s and the second half of the 1980s. Increased growth in exports due to the steady depreciation of the real exchange rate and in remittances from the overseas workers in the Middle East had begun to relax the balance of payments constraint during the first half of the 1970s, leading to the expansion of non-oil imports at the annual rate of 17.8 percent. This rapid expansion continued during the second half of the 1970s with non-oil imports registering an impressive 15 percent annual growth rate over the ten-year period spanning 1970–79. In contrast, in the subsequent five years when the real exchange rate appreciated slightly and the income growth slowed, non-oil imports expanded only 7.1 percent per annum. Again, during 1985–90, they grew to 12.3 percent. Thus, liberalized licensing rules flexibly accommodated the increased demand for imports during the fast-growth periods.

The impact of liberalization is also evident in higher import penetration, as measured by the imports-to-GDP ratio (Table 8.5). For non-oil imports, this ratio bottomed out in 1976/77 at 4.1 percent. Starting in 1977/78, fortuitously the year in which the real exchange rate depreciated substantially, this ratio began to rise, reaching 5.1 percent in 1980/81. In the subsequent years, it showed a moderate downward trend reaching 4.8 percent in 1984/85. In 1985/86, when the Rajiv Gandhi-era reforms were kicked off, the ratio began to climb up steadily again until it reached 6.0 percent by 1989/90. This rise is especially important since GDP itself grew at a relatively high rate during these years.

The impact of reforms can also be seen in industrial growth, which accelerated from 4.5 percent in 1985/86 to a peak of 10.5 percent in 1989/90 (and averaged 9.2 percent per annum during 1988–91). This growth was aided by

Table 8.5 India: non-oil merchandise exports and imports, 1970/71–1989/90 (in percent of GDP)

Year	Non-oil exports	Non-oil imports
1970/71	3.3	3.3
1971/72	3.3	3.3
1972/73	3.6	3.1
1973/74	3.8	3.7
1974/75	4.3	4.3
1975/76	4.8	4.9
1976/77	5.7	4.1
1977/78	5.3	4.4
1978/79	5.2	4.7
1979/80	5.3	4.9
1980/81	4.7	5.1
1981/82	4.5	5.0
1982/83	4.0	4.6
1983/84	3.7	5.0
1984/85	4.0	4.8
1985/86	3.7	5.3
1986/87	3.9	5.6
1987/88	4.2	5.1
1988/89	4.7	5.7
1989/90	5.5	6.0

Sources: Reserve Bank of India, *Handbook of Statistics on Indian Economy 2001* (Table 115) and author's estimates.

a rise in the import penetration ratio in the capital goods sector, which went from 11 percent in 1976/77 to 18 percent in 1985/86 (Goldar and Renganathan (1990)). The trend appears to have continued subsequently. Malhotra (1992) notes that the incremental capital–output ratio, which had reached as high as 6 at times, fell to approximately 4.5 during the 1980s. These observations are consistent with the finding by Joshi and Little (1994) that the productivity of investment increased during the 1980s, especially in private manufacturing. More recently, Chand and Sen (2002) take a systematic look at the relationship between trade liberalization and manufacturing productivity using three-digit industry data spanning 1973–88, with their major results presented in Table 8.6.[14] They find that protection declines over the sample period in intermediate and capital goods sectors but not consumer goods sector. Moreover, there is a significant improvement in total factor productivity growth (TFPG) in all three sectors (consumer, intermediate, and capital goods) in 1984–88 compared with the two earlier periods. Thus, the jump in TFPG coincides with the liberalization in capital and intermediate goods.[15]

Table 8.6 India: changes in protection and growth in productivity by industry classification (unweighted average)

Industry classification	Consumer goods	Intermediate goods	Capital goods
Protection (in percentage points)[a]			
1974–78	4.5	0.4	−1.8
1979–83	−1.1	1.4	1.7
1984–88	−0.4	−5.4	−4.3
Total factor productivity growth (in percent)			
1974–78	−0.5	−1.2	−1.6
1979–83	−1.2	−3.1	−1.5
1984–88	5.1	4.8	3.7

[a] Average annual change (in percentage points) of unweighted import tariffs.

Source: Chand and Sen (2002).

Joshi and Little (1994, chapter 13) also address the issue of the shift in the growth rate during the 1980s. They analyze the years 1960/61 to 1989/90 dividing them into a low-growth period from 1960/61 to 1975/76 and a high-growth period from 1976/77 to 1989/90. Average annual growth rates during these periods were 3.4 and 4.7 percent, respectively, and statistically significantly different from each other at 5 percent level of significance.[16] A key finding of Joshi and Little is that increased investment cannot be credited with the increase in the growth rate during 1976–90 over that during 1960–76. Rather, they find that increased demand through fiscal expansion, more efficient use of the existing resources (due to liberalization) and the rise in the real yield on investment in private manufacturing were the principal sources of the shift in the growth rate.[17]

Neither Joshi and Little nor Chand and Sen separately analyze the period 1988–91, which is crucial to obtaining comparable growth rates between the 1980s and the 1990s. Prima facie it would seem that the results of Chand and Sen would hold even more strongly for this period. The reason is that average annual industrial growth of 9.2 percent during 1988–91 was significantly higher than 6.2 percent growth achieved during 1984–88. In view of the fact that private investment as a proportion of GDP did not rise, the substantially higher growth in industrial output is likely to be the result of increased productivity and therefore related to the 1980s reforms.

8.4   Unsustainable public expenditure and external borrowing

While the importance of liberalization of industry and trade for the shift in the GDP growth rate during the 1980s can hardly be denied, rising government expenditures at home accompanied by increased borrowing abroad also played a role. The borrowing fueled public investment, which contributed directly and indirectly to raising private output. External borrowing also helped bridge the gap between exports and imports. Based on the trade data presented by the RBI in India's balance of payments, the merchandise trade deficit ran between 2.5 and 3.0 percent of GDP throughout the 1980s, considerably higher than earlier decades.[18]

Foreign debt increased from US$20.6 billion in 1980/81 to US$64.4 billion in 1989/90 (Joshi and Little, 1994, p. 186). The accumulation was especially rapid during the second half of the decade with long-term borrowing rising from the annual average of US$1.9 billion during 1980/81 to 1984/85 to US$3.5 billion from 1985/86 to 1989/90. Moreover, "other" capital flows and errors and omissions went from being a large negative in the first half of the decade to a positive in the second half, likely indicating an increase in the short-term borrowing. As a result, the external-debt-to-GDP ratio rose from 17.7 percent in 1984/85 to 24.5 percent in 1989/90. Over the same period, the debt service to exports ratio rose from 18 to 27 percent.

The growth in debt was also accompanied by a rapid deterioration in the "quality" of debt between 1984/85 and 1989/90. The share of total long-term debt accounted for by private borrowers increased from 28 to 41 percent, while the share of non-concessional debt in total debt rose from 42 to 54 percent. The average maturity of debt declined from 27 to 20 years. Thus, while external debt was helping the economy grow, it was also steadily moving it toward crisis.

A similar story was also evolving on the internal front. While external borrowing helped relieve some supply-side constraints, rising current domestic public expenditures stimulated domestic demand, particularly in the services sector. Srinivasan and Tendulkar (2003) assign much of the credit for the growth during the 1980s to this demand-side factor. Government outlay for defense, interest payments, subsidies and wages (especially following the implementation of the Fourth Pay Commission recommendations) fueled current expenditures, especially in the second half of the 1980s at both the center and state levels (Table 8.7). Current expenditure averaged 18.6 percent of GDP a year in the first half of the 1980s compared to 23.0 percent of GDP a year in the second half, with defense spending, interest payments, and subsidies, rising from a yearly average of 7.9 percent of the GDP to 11.2 percent of the GDP over the same two periods.

The situation ultimately proved unsustainable as fiscal deficits mounted. The combined fiscal deficits at the central and state levels, which averaged 8.0 percent of GDP in the first half of the 1980s, went up to 10.1 percent of GDP in the second half. Continued large deficits led to a build up of a very substantial public debt with interest payments accounting for a large proportion of the government revenues. They also invariably fed into the current account deficits, which kept rising steadily until it reached 3.5 percent of the GDP and 43.8 percent of exports in 1990/91. The situation proved

Table 8.7   India: fiscal indicators, 1980/81–1989/90 (in percent of GDP)

	Average 1980/81–1984/85	1985/86	1986/87	1987/88	1988/89	1989/90	1990/91	Average 1985/86–1989/90
Revenue	18.1	19.5	20.0	20.1	19.6	20.9	19.5	20.0
Current expenditure	18.6	21.4	22.6	23.1	22.7	24.8	23.9	23.0
Of which: Defense	2.7	3.3	3.8	4.0	3.8	3.6	—	3.7
Interest	2.6	3.3	3.6	4.0	4.2	4.6	4.8	3.9
Subsidies	2.6	3.3	3.4	3.5	3.6	4.2	—	3.6
Capital expenditure	7.5	7.4	8.3	7.0	6.3	6.5	6.0	7.1
Total expenditure	26.1	28.8	30.9	30.1	29.0	31.3	29.9	30.1
Fiscal deficit	8.0	9.3	10.9	10.0	9.4	10.4	10.4	10.1

Sources: Ministry of Finance, *Indian Public Finance Statistics* (various years); Central Statistical Organization, *National Accounts Statistics* (various years, subsidies only); and Joshi and Little (1994, Table 5).

untenable in the face of external shocks emanating from the Gulf War and finally led to the June 1991 crisis. All was not lost, however, since the crisis would trigger even deeper reforms in the 1990s, which I discuss in Section 8.5.

8.5   A brief look at the 1990s

The substantial yet half-hearted reforms of the 1980s gave way to more systematic and deeper reforms of the 1990s and beyond. This time around, there was a fundamental change in approach. Until 1991, restrictions were the rule and reforms constituted their selective removal according to a "positive list" approach. But starting with the July 1991 reform package, the absence of restrictions became the rule, with a "negative list" approach used for their retention. As discussed in considerable detail in Panagariya (2004a), while the move toward this new regime has been decidedly gradual, with the process still far from complete, the shift in the philosophy is beyond doubt. To appreciate the wider sweep of reforms in the post-1991 crisis period, I again focus on reforms in two key areas: industry and external trade.

8.5.1   Deregulation of industry and investment

In a single stroke, the "Statement of Industrial Policy" dated July 24, 1991 and frequently called the New Industrial Policy, did away with most industrial licensing and myriad entry restrictions on MRTP firms. It also ended public sector monopoly in many sectors and initiated a policy of automatic approval for foreign direct investment (FDI) up to 51 percent. The new policy explicitly stated that industrial licensing would "henceforth be abolished for all industries, except those specified, irrespective of levels of investment." An exception to this rule was granted to 18 industries included in Annex II of the policy statement. True to the commitment in the policy that "Government's policy will be continuity with change," this list was trimmed subsequently until it came to include only five sectors, with all of them having justification on health, safety, or environmental grounds.[19] Alongside, the 1991 policy statement also limited the public sector monopoly to eight sectors selected on security and strategic grounds and listed in Annex I. All other sectors were opened to the private sector. In the subsequent years, Annex I has been trimmed and today, only railway transportation and atomic energy remain on it.

For MRTP firms, the New Industrial Policy did away with entry restrictions. Again, the policy was notable for its unequivocal renunciation of the past approach, specifying that:

The pre-entry scrutiny of investment decisions by so called MRTP companies will no longer be required. Instead, emphasis will be on controlling and regulating monopolistic, restrictive, and unfair trade practices rather than making it necessary for the monopoly house to obtain prior approval of Central Government for expansion, establishment of new undertakings, merger, amalgamation and takeover, and appointment of certain directors. The MRTP Act will be restructured. The provisions relating to merger, amalgamation, and takeover will also be repealed. Similarly, the provisions regarding restrictions on acquisition of and transfer of shares will be appropriately incorporated in the Companies Act.

These changes are now in place.

In the area of foreign investment, the policy statement abolished the threshold of 40 percent on foreign equity investment. The concept of automatic approval was introduced whereby the Reserve Bank of India (RBI) was empowered to approve equity investment up to 51 percent in 34 industries, listed in Annex 3. In subsequent years, this policy was considerably liberalized with automatic approval made available to almost all industries except those subject to public sector monopoly and industrial licensing. In 48 industries that account for the bulk of India's manufacturing output, the ceiling for approval under the automatic route is now 51 percent. In eight categories including mining services, electricity generation and transmission, and the construction of roads, bridges, ports, harbors, and runways, the automatic approval route is available for equity investments of up to 74 percent. The automatic approval of FDI up to 100 percent is given in all manufacturing activities in Special Economic Zones (SEZs) except those subject to licensing or public sector monopoly. Subject to licensing, defense is now open to private sector for 100 percent investment with FDI (also subject to licensing) up to 26 percent permitted.

8.5.2   External trade liberalization

The July 1991 package also made a decided break from the 1980s approach of selective liberalization on the external trade front by replacing the positive list approach of listing license-free items on the OGL list to a negative list approach. In addition, it addressed tariff reform in a more systematic manner rather than relying on selective exemptions on statutory tariffs. In subsequent years, liberalization has been extended to trade in services as well.

Merchandise trade

The July 1991 reforms did away with import licensing on virtually all intermediate inputs and capital goods. But consumer goods, accounting for approximately 30 percent of the tariff lines, remained under licensing. It was only after a successful challenge by India's trading partners in the Dispute Settlement Body of the World Trade Organization (WTO) that these goods were freed of licensing a decade later, starting April 1, 2001. Today, except for a handful of goods disallowed on environmental, health, and safety grounds and a few others that are canalized such as fertilizer, cereals, edible oils, and petroleum products, all goods can be imported without a license or other restrictions.

Tariff rates in India had been raised substantially during the 1980s to turn quota rents into tariff revenue for the government. For example, according to the Government of India (1993), tariff revenue as a proportion of imports went up from 20 percent in 1980/81 to 44 percent in 1989/90. Likewise, according to the WTO (1998), in 1990/91, the highest tariff rate stood at 355 percent, simple average of all tariff rates at 113 percent and the import-weighted average of tariff rates at 87 percent. With the removal of licensing, these tariff rates became effective restrictions on imports. Therefore, a major task of the reforms in the 1990s and beyond has been to lower tariffs. This has been done in a gradual fashion by compressing the top tariff rate while rationalizing the tariff structure through a reduction in the number of tariff bands. The top rate fell to 85 percent in 1993/94 and 50 percent in 1995/96. Though there were some reversals along the way in the form of new special duties and unification of a low and a high tariff rate to the latter, the long-run movement has been toward liberalization with the top rate coming down to 20 percent in 2004/05.

The 1990s reforms were also accompanied by the lifting of exchange controls that had served as an extra layer of restrictions on imports. As a part of the 1991 reform, the government also devalued the rupee by 22 percent against the dollar from Rs 21.2 to Rs 25.8 per dollar. In February 1992, a dual exchange rate system was introduced, which allowed exporters to sell 60 percent of their foreign exchange in the free market and 40 percent to the government at the lower official price. Importers were authorized to purchase foreign exchange in the open market at the higher price, effectively ending the exchange control. Within a year of establishing this market exchange rate, the official exchange rate was unified with it. Starting in February 1994, many current account transactions, including all current business transactions as well as those for foreign education, medical, and travel expenses were permitted at the market exchange rate. These steps culminated in India accepting the Article VIII obligations under the IMF's Articles of Agreement, which made the rupee officially convertible on the current account. The exchange rate has been kept flexible throughout the period and allowed to depreciate as necessary to maintain competitiveness. It currently stands at approximately 45 rupees per dollar.

Trade in services

Since 1991, India has also carried out a substantial liberalization of trade in services. Traditionally, the services sectors have been subject to heavy government intervention. A public sector presence has been conspicuous in the key sectors of insurance, banking, and telecommunications. Nevertheless, considerable progress has been made toward opening the door wider to private sector participation, including foreign investors.

With regard to financial sector, insurance was a state monopoly until recently. On December 7, 1999, India's Parliament passed the Insurance Regulatory and Development Authority Bill, which established an Insurance Regulatory and Development Authority (IRDA) and opened the door to private entry, including foreign investors. Now, up to 26 percent foreign investment is permitted, subject to obtaining a license from the IRDA. In banking, public sector banks still dominate, but private banks are now allowed to operate in it. Foreign investment (the combined direct and equity) up to 74 percent in the private banks is permitted under the automatic route. In addition, foreign banks are allowed to open a specified number of new branches every year or maintain wholly owned subsidiaries. More than 25 foreign banks with full banking licenses and approximately 150 foreign bank branches are in operation presently. Under the 1997 WTO Financial Services Agreement, India committed to permitting 12 foreign bank branches annually.

The telecommunications sector has also experienced much opening to private sector, including foreign investors. Until the early 1990s, the sector was a state monopoly. The 1994 National Telecommunications Policy provided for opening cellular as well as basic and value-added telephone services to the private sector with foreign investors also granted entry. Rapid changes in technology led to the adoption of the New Telecom Policy in 1999, which provides the current policy framework. Accordingly, in basic, cellular mobile, paging and value-added services, and global mobile personnel communications by satellite, FDI up to 49 percent is allowed subject to grant of license from the Department of Telecommunications. In addition, FDI up to 100 percent is permitted under certain conditions for (i) Internet service providers not offering gateways (both for satellite and submarine cables); and (ii) infrastructure providers supplying dark fiber, electronic mail, and voice mail. Finally, subject to licensing and security requirements, up to 74 percent foreign investment is allowed for Internet services providers for gateways, radio paging and end-to-end bandwidth, although government approval is necessary for FDI in the sector beyond 49 percent.

In e-commerce, FDI is allowed up to 100 percent. Automatic approval is available for foreign equity in software and almost all areas of electronics. Foreign investment up to 100 percent is also allowed in information technology units set up exclusively for exports. These units can be set up under several schemes including Export Oriented Units, Export Processing Zones, SEZs, Software Technology Parks, and Electronics Hardware Technology Parks. The infrastructure sector has now also been opened to foreign investment. FDI up to 100 percent under automatic route is permitted in projects involving the construction and maintenance of roads, ports, and harbors. For operating and maintaining ports and harbors, automatic approval for foreign equity up to 100 percent is available. In projects providing supporting services to water transport, such as operation and maintenance of piers and loading and discharging of vehicles, no approval is required for foreign equity up to 51 percent. FDI up to 100 percent is permitted in airports, with up to 74 percent through the automatic route. Foreign equity up to 40 percent and investment by non-resident Indians up to 100 percent is permitted in domestic air-transport services. Only railways remain off limits to private entry.

In the power sector, several attempts have been made since 1991 to allow private sector participation, including FDI, but without perceptible success. The most recent attempt is the Electricity Bill of 2003, which replaces the three existing power legislations dated 1910, 1948, and 1998. The bill offers a comprehensive framework for restructuring the power sector and builds on the experience in the telecommunications sector. It attempts to introduce competition through private sector entry side-by-side with public sector entities in generation, transmission, and distribution, with FDI permitted in all three activities. The bill fully de-licenses generation and freely permits captive generation. Only hydroelectric projects would henceforth require clearance from the Central Electricity Authority. Distribution licensees are free to undertake generation and generating companies can take up distribution activities. Trading has been recognized as a distinct activity, with the State Regulatory Commissions authorized to fix ceilings on trading margins, if necessary.

8.5.3   Impact of liberalization

Trade liberalization had a much more visible effect on external trade in the 1990s than in the 1980s. The ratio of total exports of goods and services to GDP in India approximately doubled from 7.3 percent in 1990 to 14.0 percent in 2000. The rise was less dramatic on the import side due to the fact that increased external borrowing was used to finance a large proportion of imports in 1990, which was not true in 2000. But the rise was still significant from 9.9 percent in 1990 to 16.6 percent in 2000. Over the same period, the ratio of total goods and services trade to GDP rose from 17.2 percent to 30.6 percent.

Liberalization also had a significant effect on growth in some of the key services sectors. Overall, the average annual growth rate in the services sector rose from 6.9 percent during the 1980s to 8.1 percent during the 1980s. As Gordon and Gupta (2003) document systematically, this growth was mostly fueled by communication, business and financial, and community services. Given substantial deregulation and opening up to private participation in at least first three of these areas, the link of this acceleration to reforms can hardly be denied.

The most disappointing aspect of the 1990s experience, however, has been a lack of acceleration of growth in the industrial sector. The lackluster performance of industry is the principal cause for at most a marginal acceleration of the growth rate in the post-1991 reform era. Average annual rate of growth in this sector was 6.8 percent during 1981–91 and 6.4 percent during 1991–2001. Given that many of the reforms were particularly aimed at this sector, this outcome is somewhat disappointing. There are at least three complementary reasons. First, due to draconian labor laws, industry in India is increasingly outsourcing its support activities so that growth in industry is actually being counted in growth in services. Second, due to some key binding constraints in areas of labor laws, SSI reservation, and power, large-scale firms are still unwilling to enter the market. Finally, large fiscal deficits continue to crowd out private investment.

8.6   Looking ahead: why India lags behind China

In this section, I look at India and China and argue that the only way India can push its growth rate to the levels experienced by China in the past two decades is by freeing the conventional industry of several continuing restraints. Evidence has already been provided in this chapter refuting the basic claim of the skeptics that the 1991 reforms have failed in India. Nevertheless, it must be acknowledged that the response of the economy to liberalization has been in an order of magnitude weaker in India than in China. Exports of goods and services grew at annual rates of 12.9 and 15.2 percent during the 1980s and the 1990s, respectively, in China. Imports exhibited a similar performance. Consequently, China's total trade to GDP ratio rose from 18.9 percent in 1980 to 34.0 percent in 1990 and to 49.3 percent in 2000.

On the foreign investment front, differences are even starker. FDI into China has risen from US$0.06 billion in 1980 to US$3.49 billion in 1990 and then to a whopping US$42.10 billion in 2000. China was slower to open its market to portfolio investment, but once it did, inflows quickly surpassed those into India, reaching US$7.8 billion in 2000. Even if we allow for an upward bias in the figures as suggested by some China specialists and downward bias in the figures for India, there is little doubt that foreign investment flows into China are several times those into India.

While some differences between the performances of India and China can be attributed to the Chinese entrepreneurs in Hong Kong and Taiwan, who have been eager to escape rising wages in their respective home economies by moving to China, a more central explanation lies in the differences between the compositions of output in the two countries. Among developing countries, India is unique in having a very large share of its GDP in the mostly informal part of the services sector. Whereas in other countries, a decline in the share of agriculture in GDP has been accompanied by a substantial expansion of the industry in the early stages of development, in India this has not happened. For example, in 1980, the proportion of GDP originating in the industry was already 48.5 percent in China, in India it was only 24.2 (Table 8.8). Services, on the other hand, contributed only 21.4 percent to GDP in China but as much as 37.2 percent in India. In the following 20 years, despite considerable growth, the share of industry did not rise in India. Instead, the entire decline in the share of agriculture was absorbed by services. Though a similar process was observed in China, the share of industry in GDP was already quite high there. As a result, even in 2000, the share of services in GDP was 33.2 percent in China compared with 48.2 percent in India.

Why does this matter? Because typically, under liberal trade policies, developing countries are much more likely to be able to expand exports and imports if a large proportion of their output originates in industry. A larger industrial sector would also require more imported inputs thereby offering

Table 8.8   India: composition of GDP (in percent)

	1980	1990	2000
China			
Agriculture	30.1	27.0	15.9
Industry	48.5	41.6	50.9
Manufacturing	40.5	32.9	34.5
Services	21.4	31.3	33.2
India			
Agriculture	38.6	31.3	24.9
Industry	24.2	27.6	26.9
Manufacturing	16.3	17.2	15.8
Services	37.2	41.1	48.2

Source: World Bank, *World Development Indicators 2002*.

greater scope for expanding trade. This same factor is at work in explaining the relatively modest response of FDI to liberal policies. Investment into industry, whether domestic or foreign, has been sluggish. Foreign investors have been hesitant to invest in the industry for much the same reasons as the domestic investors. At the same time, the capacity of the formal services sector to absorb foreign investment is limited. The information technology sector has shown promise but its base is still small. Moreover, this sector is more intensive in skilled labor than physical capital. Therefore, the solution to both trade and FDI expansion in India lies in stimulating growth in industry. The necessary steps are now common knowledge: bring all tariffs down to 10 percent or less, abolish the SSI reservation, institute an exit policy for labor, streamline bankruptcy laws, and privatize all public sector undertakings.

8.7   Conclusion

I have argued that the growth spurt in India prior to 1991 was fragile and volatile. There was a jump in the growth rate during 1977–79, a massive decline in 1979/80, a jump again in 1980–82, a return to the Hindu rate during 1982–88 (except 1983/84), a climb up again in 1988–91, and finally a crisis in 1991/92. This volatility in the growth pattern itself raises doubts about the sustainability of a 5 percent plus growth rate over the long haul. The 1991 crisis only confirmed the fundamental weakness of the underlying forces *ex post*.

In contrast, growth during the 1990s has been more robust and exhibited far less volatility. Whereas in the late 1980s, many observers of India were betting on a crisis at any time, there are few takers of such a bet today. Despite well-known vulnerabilities resulting from fiscal deficits that are as large today as in the late 1980s and the slow pace of banking reforms, few pundits are predicting an external crisis today. The external-debt-to-GDP ratio has been declining and foreign-exchange reserves at more than US$100 billion exceed the currency in circulation. Indeed, in a recent careful examination of India's vulnerability to external crises, Ahluwalia (2002b) and Panagariya (2004b) point to several key weaknesses in fiscal and banking areas and emphasize the urgency of tackling them. But both stop well short of predicting a crisis.

The acceleration of growth during the 1980s *relative* to that in the preceding decades was not achieved without important policy changes. In contrast to the generally isolated and *ad hoc* policy measures taken prior to 1980—largely aimed at reducing immediate pressures—the measures in the last half of the 1980s, taken as a whole, constituted a significant policy shift and characterized an activist reform program. For example, by 1990, approximately 20 percent of the tariff lines and 30 percent of the imports were coming in under OGL with significant exemptions on tariffs accruing to the OGL products. Import licensing on many other products was also considerably eased up. By 1988, industrial licensing had been freed up in 31 out of 58 sectors. In addition, large-sized firms were benefiting from a fivefold increase in the asset limit defining the MRTP firms and the opening of a number of avenues for the license-free entry of MRTP firms in many sectors. The increase in the asset limit freed 90 out of 180 large firms from the MRTP restrictions altogether. The 1980s reforms and their success provided crucial first-hand evidence to policymakers that gradual liberalization could deliver faster growth without causing disruption. In turn, this evidence gave policymakers confidence in undertaking the bolder and more far-reaching reforms in the 1990s.

While the changes in the 1980s were undoubtedly small in relation to those in the 1990s, they were quite significant when compared with the regime prevailing until the 1970s. In part, this fact explains why the economy, particularly industry, exhibited such a strong response. A key message of the theory of distortions is that the larger the initial distortion, the greater the benefit from its relaxation at the margin. Therefore, the large response to limited reforms is quite consistent with at least the static theory of distortions. One suspects that under plausible assumptions, this result would translate into larger growth responses to larger initial distortions in the endogenous growth models. In this respect, DeLong's observation that the elasticity of growth to reforms was higher in the 1980s than in the 1990s is not altogether inconsistent with theory, though it must be acknowledged that the response would have been short-lived in the absence of more concerted reforms later on.

DeLong's contention that we lack hard evidence to support the view that rapid growth of the second half of the 1980s could not be sustained without the second wave of reforms in the 1990s is untenable. I have argued that pre-1991 growth was itself fragile and sporadic. And even then, it ended in a balance of payments crisis. The scenario of the second half of the 1980s involving large amounts of external borrowing could not have been sustained. Absent that, more substantial reforms that improved efficiency, brought foreign investment to the country and allowed sectors such as information technology to grow constituted the only way to avoid the return to the Hindu rate of growth of the first 30 years of independence.

The key to explaining why India nevertheless continues to lag behind China is the slow growth of the conventional industry. The policy implication is that India must free the industry of continuing restraints if it is to maximize the benefits of what has been done to date. Given a virtual ban on exit and retrenchment and reassignment of workers, continuing reservation of most of the labor-intensive industries for small-scale firms, the absence of effective bankruptcy laws, and continuing high protection, Indian industry cannot match the performance of its Chinese counterpart. In some ways, given the advantage India enjoys in the information technology sector over China, its overall prospects for growth are even better than those of China but only if the conventional industry is given a fair chance.

Notes

1. Bhagwati Professor of Indian Political Economy and Professor of Economics, Columbia University. I am grateful to Jagdish Bhagwati and Kalpana Kochhar for numerous helpful comments and to T. N. Srinivasan for extended e-mail exchanges that led to many improvements in the chapter. I also thank Rajesh Chadha, Satish Chand, Douglas Irwin, Raghav Jha, Vijay Joshi, Vijay Kelkar, Ashok Mody, Sam Ouliaris, Jairam Ramesh, Jayanta Roy, Ratna Sahay, Kunal Sen, N. K. Singh, and Roberto Zagha for helpful suggestions on an earlier draft of the chapter. The chapter was completed while I was a Resident Scholar at the International Monetary Fund and has benefited from comments made at the IMF–NCAER Conference, *A Tale of Two Giants: India's and China's Experience with Reform and Growth*, November 14–16, 2003, New Delhi.

2. While the documentation to follow is limited to scholarly writings, many opponents of reforms in the political arena, including some in India's Congress Party, share this view.

3. Specifically, Joshi and Little (1994, p. 190) note: "It appears that 'Keynesian' expansion, reflected in large fiscal deficits, was a major cause of fast growth." In personal correspondence, however, Vijay Joshi has recently changed his mind. Commenting on an earlier draft of this chapter, he writes, "Joshi and Little did point to the importance of the mildly liberalizing reforms in the 1980s but in retrospect we should have put greater stress on them exactly as you have done."

4. This is not unlike the stop-go reforms in China though the latter did go much farther during the 1980s, especially in the Special Economic Zones and Open Cities.

5. We could include 1980/81 in the 1980s, but the 7.2 percent growth during this year was preceded by a 5.2 percent decline in GDP in 1979/80 and was, thus, artificially high.

6. These findings are consistent with Wallack (2003), who attempts to pinpoint structural breaks in the growth series with some success. She initially finds that with a 90 percent probability the shift in the growth rate of GDP took place between 1973 and 1987. The associated point estimate of the shift, statistically significant at 10 percent level, is 1980. When Wallack replaces GDP with gross national product (GNP), however, the cutoff point with 90 percent probability shifts to between 1980 and 1994. The associated point estimate, statistically significant at 10 percent level, now turns out to be 1987.

7. We may ask which sector among agriculture, industry, and services predominantly accounts for the higher variance in the 1980s. For each sector, the null hypothesis of equal variances across the 1980s and the 1990s fails to be rejected even at 10 percent level of significance. Differences in the variances of *total* GDP growth between the 1980s and the 1990s arise largely from movements in covariance terms between growth rates of individual sectors.

8. The role of excellent agricultural performance in yielding the high overall growth rates during 1988–91 should also be acknowledged. Whereas the years 1986/87 and 1987/88 were a disaster for agriculture due to bad weather, the subsequent three years, especially 1988/89, proved unusually good. Referring to the *Economic Survey* 2002–03 (Tables 13 and 16), agriculture and allied activities (forestry and logging, fishing, mining, and quarrying), which accounted for a little more than a third of GDP, grew at an annual average rate of 7.3 percent during 1988–91.

9. Bhagwati and Srinivasan (1975, chapter 10) highlight an important lesson in the political economy of reforms in their analysis of the 1966 devaluation. They note

that: "The political lesson seems particularly pointed with regard to the use of aid as a means of influencing recipient policy, even if, in some objective sense, the pressure is in the 'right' direction. The Indian experience is also instructive for the political timing of devaluation: foreign pressure to change policies, if brought to bear when a government is weak (both because of internal-structural reasons and an impending election, which invariably prompts cautious behavior) can be fatal." (p. 153)

10. Jagdish Bhagwati, who, upon his return from study abroad in the early 1960s, initially shared in the intellectual attitudes that helped India turn inward but quickly changed his mind in light of the realities on the ground. He tells an anecdote that aptly captures the deleterious impact protectionist policies had on the quality of Indian products. In one of the letters to Harry Johnson written during his tenure at the Indian Statistical Institute in the early 1960s, Bhagwati happened to complain about the craze he observed in India for everything foreign. Johnson promptly responded in his reply that if the quality of the paper on which Bhagwati wrote his letter was any indication of the quality of homemade products, the craze for the foreign seemed perfectly rational to him!

11. Besides the removal of monopoly trading rights, the decline in the share of canalized imports was also due to increased domestic production of non-canalized imports such as cotton, food grains, and crude oil and reduced world prices of canalized imports such as fertilizers, edible oils, nonferrous metals, and iron and steel.

12. Of these, 16 industries had been out of the licensing net since November 1975, while some were reserved for the small-scale sector.

13. Observing that starting in 1986/87, Indian exports grew considerably faster than world trade and as fast as the exports of comparable developing countries, Joshi and Little (1994) note that

> From 1985 onward exchange rate policy became more active though the fiction of a fixed basket-peg was still maintained. From a presentational point of view, the sharp devaluation of the US dollar, which began in 1985, helped a great deal. A devaluation of the real effective exchange rate could be secured by keeping the exchange rate or the rupee against the dollar constant, and in fact there was a mild depreciation in terms of the dollar as well. Cabinet approval was sought and obtained to achieve the real effective exchange rate prevailing in 1979 (thus offsetting the competitive disadvantage that had been suffered since then). When that objective had been reached, cabinet approval was again obtained to devalue the rupee further to maintain the competitive relationship vis-à-vis a narrower range of developing-country "competitor countries," many of whom depreciated in real terms along with the US dollar in 1986. This was a sensible exchange rate policy. Policymakers recognized that a real exchange rate devaluation was necessary though the terms of trade were modestly improving, because the debt-service burden had increased and a faster growth of imports was to be expected in the wake of industrial and import liberalization. (p. 183)

14. Specifically, Chand and Sen (2002) look at 30 industries, which accounted for 53 percent of gross value added and 45 percent of employment in manufacturing during 1973–88. These industries are divided approximately equally among consumer, intermediate, and capital goods. They measure protection by the proportionate wedge between the Indian and US price and estimate that TFPG in the three industry groups averaged over three non-overlapping periods: 1974–78, 1979–83, and 1984–88. This productivity growth is then related to liberalization.

15. Chand and Sen (2002) do some further tests by pooling their sample and employing a fixed-effects estimator to allow for intrinsic differences across industries with respect to the rate of technological progress. Their estimates show that on average a one percentage point reduction in the price wedge leads to a 0.1 percent rise in total factor productivity. For the intermediate goods sector, the effect is twice as large. In fact, the impact of the liberalization of the intermediate goods sector on productivity turns out to be statistically significant in all of their regressions.

16. In the data used by Joshi and Little, real GDP is measured at 1980/81 prices. As such their growth rates differ from those computed from real GDP measured at 1993/94 prices, as in this chapter. Growth rates for the two periods when 1993/94 is the base year are 3.7 percent and 4.8 percent, respectively.

17. See also Bhargava and Joshi (1990).

18. In India, balance of payments data on trade reported by the RBI differ significantly from the customs data gathered by the Ministry of Commerce and Industry's Directorate General of Commercial Intelligence and Statistics. For example, imports such as offshore oilrigs and defense expenditures would be picked up in the balance of payments data, but presumably not the customs data, therefore accounting for some of the difference.

19. The five sectors were (i) arms and ammunition, explosives and allied items of defense equipment, and defense aircraft and warships; (ii) atomic substances; (iii) narcotics and psychotropic substances and hazardous chemicals; (iv) distillation and brewing of alcoholic drinks; and (v) cigarettes/cigars and manufactured tobacco substitutes.

References

Ahluwalia, Montek, 2002a, "Economic Reforms in India since 1991: Has Gradualism Worked?" *Journal of Economic Perspectives*, Vol. 16, No. 3, pp. 67–88.

——, 2002b, "India's Vulnerability to External Crises," in *Macroeconomics and Monetary Policy: Issues for a Reforming Economy*, ed. by M. Ahluwalia, Y. V. Reddy, and S. S. Tarapore (New Delhi: Oxford University Press).

Bhagwati, Jagdish and Padma Desai, 1970, *India: Planning for Industrialization* (London: Oxford University Press).

Bhagwati, Jagdish and T. N. Srinivasan, 1975, *Foreign Trade Regimes and Economic Development: India* (New York: Columbia University Press).

Bhargava, Sandeep and Vijay Joshi, 1990, "Faster Growth in India: Facts and a Tentative Explanation." *Economic and Political Weekly*, Vol. 25, Nos. 48 and 49, pp. 2657–62.

Chand, Satish and Kunal Sen, 2002, "Trade Liberalization and Productivity Growth: Evidence from Indian Manufacturing," *Review of Development Economics*, Vol. 6, No. 1, pp. 120–32.

Das, Gurchuran, 2000, *India Unbound: A Personal Account of a Social and Economic Revolution* (New Delhi: Viking, Penguin Books India).

DeLong, J. Bradford, 2001, "India Since Independence: An Analytic Growth Narrative," available via the Internet: http://ksghome.harvard.edu/~drodrik/growth volume/DeLong-India.pdf.

Desai, Ashok, 1999, "The Economics and Politics of Transition to an Open Market Economy: India," OECD Working Paper, Vol. VII, No. 100 (Paris: OECD).

Goldar, B. and V. S. Renganathan, 1990, "Liberalization of Capital Goods Imports in India," Working Paper No. 8 (New Delhi: National Institute of Public Finance and Policy).

Gordon, Jim and Poonam Gupta, 2003, "Understanding India's Services Revolution," paper presented at the International Monetary Fund and National Council for Applied Economic Research conference on *A Tale of Two Giants: India's and China's Experience with Reform and Growth*, New Delhi (November 14–16).

Government of India, 1993, *Tax Reforms Committee: Final Report*, Part II (New Delhi: Ministry of Finance).

Joshi, Vijay and I. M. D. Little, 1994, *India: Macroeconomics and Political Economy, 1964–1991* (New Delhi: Oxford University Press).

Malhotra, R. N., 1992, "Economic Reforms: Retrospect and Prospects," ASCI Foundation Day Lecture (Hyderabad: Administrative Staff College of India).

Ministry of Finance, 2003, *Economic Survey 2002–2003* (New Delhi).

—— (various years), *Indian Public Finance Statistics* (New Delhi).

Ministry of Statistics and Programme Implementation (various years) *National Accounts Statistics* (New Delhi: Central Statistical Organization).

Panagariya, Arvind, 2004a, "India's Trade Reform: Progress, Impact and Future Strategy," available via the Internet: http://econwpa.wustl.edu/eps/it/papers/0403/0403004.pdf.

——, 2004b, "Is a Crisis Around the Corner?," comments on "A Balance Sheet Crisis in India," by Nouriel Roubini and Richard Hemming, presented at the International Monetary Fund and National Institute of Public Finance and Policy conference on *Fiscal Policy in India*, New Delhi (January 16–17), available via the Internet: http://www.imf.org/external/np/seminars/eng/2004/fiscal/pdf/panag.pdf.

——, 2003, "Miracles and Debacles: Do Free Trade Skeptics Have a Case?" available via Internet: http://www.bsos.umd.edu/econ/panagariya/apecon/polpaper.htm.

——, 1994, "India: A New Tiger on the Block?," *Journal of International Affairs*, Vol. 48, No. 1, pp. 193–221.

——, 1990, "Indicative Planning in India: Discussion," *Journal of Comparative Economics*, Vol. 14, pp. 736–42.

Pursell, Garry, 1992, "Trade Policy in India," *National Trade Policies*, ed. by Dominick Salvatore (New York: Greenwood Press), pp. 423–58.

Reserve Bank of India, 2002, *Handbook of Statistics on Indian Economy 2001* (Mumbai).

Rodrik, Dani, 2002, "Institutions, Integration, and Geography: In Search of the Deep Determinants of Economic Growth," available via the Internet: http://ksghome.harvard.edu/~drodrik/growthintro.pdf.

Srinivasan, T. N. and Suresh D. Tendulkar, 2003, *Reintegrating India with the World Economy* (Washington, DC: Institute for International Economics).

Virmani, Arvind, 1997, "Economic Development and Transition in India," paper presented at the *Tokyo Dialogue on Alternatives to the World Bank-IMF Approach to Reforms and Growth* (November 7).

Wallack, Jessica, 2003, "Structural Breaks in Indian Macroeconomic Data," *Economic and Political Weekly*, Vol. 38, No. 41, pp. 4312–15.

World Bank, 2002, *World Development Indicators 2002* (Washington).

World Trade Organization, 1998, *Trade Policy Review: India* (Geneva: WTO Secretariat).

9
Effects of Financial Globalization on Developing Countries: Some Empirical Evidence

Eswar Prasad, Kenneth Rogoff, Shang-Jin Wei, and M. Ayhan Kose[1]

9.1 Overview

The recent wave of financial globalization since the mid-1980s has been marked by a surge in capital flows among industrial countries and, more notably, between industrial and developing countries. While these capital flows have been associated with high growth rates in some developing countries, a number of countries have experienced periodic collapse in growth rates and significant financial crises over the same period, crises that have exacted a serious toll in terms of macroeconomic and social costs. As a result, an intense debate has emerged in both academic and policy circles on the effects of financial integration for developing economies. But much of the debate has been based on only casual and limited empirical evidence.

The main purpose of this chapter is to provide an assessment of empirical evidence on the effects of financial globalization for developing economies. The chapter will focus on three related questions: (i) does financial globalization promote economic growth in developing countries? (ii) what is its impact on macroeconomic volatility in these countries? (iii) what are the factors that appear to help harness the benefits of financial globalization?

The principal conclusions that emerge from the analysis are sobering, but in many ways informative from a policy perspective. It is true that many developing economies with a high degree of financial integration have also experienced higher growth rates. It is also true that, in theory, there are many channels by which financial openness could enhance growth. However, a systematic examination of the evidence suggests that it is difficult to establish a robust causal relationship between the degree of financial integration and output growth performance. From the perspective of macroeconomic stability, consumption is regarded as a better measure of well-being than output; fluctuations in consumption are therefore regarded as having a negative impact on economic welfare. There is little evidence that financial integration has helped developing countries to better stabilize fluctuations in consumption growth, notwithstanding the theoretically large benefits that could accrue to developing countries in this respect. In fact, new evidence presented in this chapter suggests that low to moderate levels of financial integration may have made some countries subject to even greater volatility of consumption relative to that of output. Thus, while there is no proof in the data that financial globalization has benefited growth, there is evidence that some countries may have experienced greater consumption volatility as a result.

This chapter offers mainly empirical evidence, rather than definitive policy implications. Nevertheless, some general principles emerge from the analysis about how countries can increase the benefits from, and control the risks of, globalization. In particular, the quality of domestic institutions appears to play a role in this respect. A growing body of evidence suggests that it has a quantitatively important impact on a country's ability to attract foreign direct investment (FDI), and on its vulnerability to crises. While different measures of institutional quality are no doubt correlated, there is accumulating evidence of the benefits of robust legal and supervisory frameworks, low levels of corruption, high degree of transparency, and good corporate governance.

The review of the available evidence does not, however, provide a clear road map for countries that have started on or desire to start on the path to financial integration. For instance, there is an unresolved tension between having good institutions in place before capital market liberalization and the notion that such liberalization in itself can help import best practices and provide an impetus to improve domestic institutions. Furthermore, neither theory nor empirical evidence has provided clear-cut general answers to related issues such as the desirability and efficacy of selective capital controls. Ultimately, these questions can be addressed only in the context of country-specific circumstances and institutional features.

This paper does not tackle the appropriate choice of an exchange rate regime or of monetary and fiscal policies. It is worth noting, however, that fixed or *de facto* fixed exchange rate regimes and excessive government borrowing appear to be major factors that have compounded the problems that some developing countries have had in managing capital flows. We leave a systematic examination of these issues for future research.

9.2   Basic stylized facts

9.2.1   Measuring financial integration

Capital account liberalization is typically considered an important precursor to financial integration. Most formal empirical work analyzing the effects of capital account liberalization has used a measure based on the official restrictions on capital flows as reported to the International Monetary Fund (IMF) by national authorities. However, this binary indicator directly measures capital controls but does not capture differences in the intensity of these controls.[2] A more direct measure of financial openness is based on the estimated gross stocks of foreign assets and liabilities as a share of gross domestic product (GDP).[3] The stock data constitutes a better indication of integration, for our purposes, than the underlying flows since they are less volatile from year to year and are less prone to measurement error (assuming that such errors are not correlated over time).[4]

While these two measures of financial integration are related, they denote two distinct aspects. The capital account restrictions measure reflects the existence of *de jure* restrictions on capital flows while the financial openness measure captures *de facto* financial integration in terms of realized capital flows. This distinction is of considerable importance for the analysis in this chapter and implies a 2 × 2 set of combinations of these two aspects of integration. Many industrial countries have attained a high degree of financial integration in terms of both measures. Some developing countries with capital account restrictions have found these restrictions ineffective in controlling actual capital flows. Episodes of capital flight from some Latin American countries in the 1970s and the 1980s are examples of such involuntary *de facto* financial integration in economies that are *de jure* closed to financial flows (i.e. integration without capital account liberalization). On the other hand, some countries in Africa have few capital account restrictions but have experienced only minimal levels of capital flows (i.e. liberalization without integration). And, of course, it is not difficult to find examples of countries with closed capital accounts that are also effectively closed in terms of capital flows.

How has financial integration evolved over time for different groups of countries based on alternative measures?[5] By either measure, the difference in financial openness between industrial and developing countries is quite stark. Industrial economies have had an enormous increase in financial openness, particularly in the 1990s. While this measure also increased for developing economies in that decade, the level remains far below that of industrial economies.

For industrial countries, unweighted cross-country averages of the two measures are mirror images and jointly confirm that these countries have undergone rapid financial integration since the mid-1980s (Figure 9.1). For developing countries, the average restriction measure indicates that, after a period of liberalization in the 1970s, the trend toward openness reversed in the 1980s. Liberalization resumed in the early 1990s but at a slow pace. On the other hand, the average financial openness measure for these countries, based on actual flows, shows a modest increase in the 1980s, followed by a sharp rise in the 1990s. The increase in the financial openness measure for developing economies reflects a more rapid *de facto* integration than is captured by the relatively crude measure of capital account restrictions.

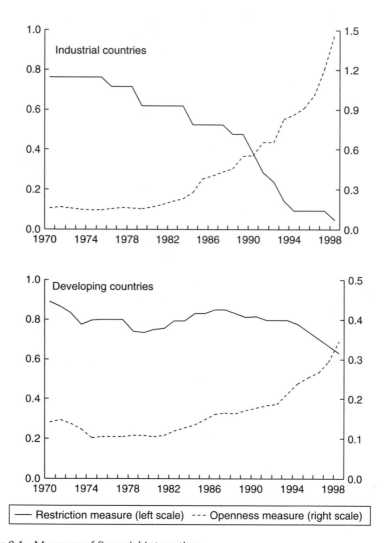

Figure 9.1   Measures of financial integration

Sources: International Monetary Fund, *World Economic Outlook* (various issues) and Lane and Milesi-Ferreti (2001).

However, the effects of financial integration in terms of increased capital flows have been spread very unevenly across developing countries. For examining the extent of these disparities, it is useful to begin with a very coarse classification of the developing countries in the sample into two groups based on a ranking according to the average of the financial openness measure over the last four decades (as well as an assessment of other indicators of financial integration).

The first group, which comprises 22 countries, is henceforth labeled as the set of More Financially Integrated (MFI) countries and the latter, which includes 33 countries, as the Less Financially Integrated (LFI) countries.[6] This distinction must be interpreted with some care at this stage. In particular, it is worth repeating that the criterion is a measure of *de facto* integration based on actual capital flows rather than a measure of the strength of policies designed to promote financial integration. Indeed, a few of the countries in the MFI group do have relatively closed capital accounts in a *de jure* sense. In general, as argued below, policy choices do determine the degree and nature of financial integration. Nevertheless, for the analysis in this paper, the degree of financial openness based on actual capital flows is a more relevant measure.

It should be noted that the main conclusions of this paper are not crucially dependent on the particulars of the classification of developing countries into the MFI and LFI groups. This classification is obviously a static one and does not account for differences across countries in the timing and degree of financial integration. It is used for some of the descriptive analysis presented below but only in order to illustrate the conclusions from the more detailed econometric studies that are surveyed in the paper. The areas where this classification yields results different from those obtained from more formal econometric analysis will be clearly highlighted in the paper. The regression results reported in this paper are based on the gross capital flows measure described earlier, which does capture differences across countries and changes over time in the degree of financial integration.

The vast majority of international private gross capital flows of developing countries, especially in the 1990s, are accounted for by the relatively small group of MFI economies. By contrast, private capital flows to and from the LFI economies have remained very small over the last decade and, for certain types of flows, have even fallen relative to the late 1970s.

9.2.2 North–South capital flows

One of the key features of global financial integration over the last decade has been the dramatic increase in net private capital flows from industrial countries (the "North") to developing countries (the "South"). The main increase has been in terms of FDI and portfolio flows, while the relative importance of bank lending has declined somewhat. In fact, net bank lending turned negative for a few years during the time of the Asian crisis.

The bulk of the surge in net FDI flows from the advanced economies has gone to MFI economies, with only a small fraction going to LFI economies. Net portfolio flows show a similar pattern, although both types of flows to MFI economies fell sharply following the Asian crisis and have remained relatively flat since then. LFI economies have been much more dependent on bank lending (and, although not shown here, on official flows including loans and grants). There were surges in bank lending to this group of countries in the late 1970s and the early 1990s.

Another important feature of these flows is that they differ substantially in terms of volatility (Wei, 2001). FDI flows are the least volatile of the different categories of private capital flows to developing economies, which is not surprising given their long-term and relatively fixed nature. Portfolio flows tend to be far more volatile and prone to abrupt reversals than FDI. These patterns hold when the MFI and LFI economies are examined separately. Even in the case of LFIs, the volatility of FDI flows is much lower than that of other types of flows. This difference in the relative volatility of different categories has important implications that will be examined in more detail later.

9.2.3 Factors underlying the rise in North–South capital flows

The surge in net private capital flows to MFIs, as well as the shifts in the composition of these flows, can be broken down into "pull" and "push" factors. These are related to, respectively, (i) policies and other developments in the MFIs and (ii) changes in global financial markets. The first category includes factors such as stock market liberalizations and privatization of state-owned companies that have stimulated foreign inflows. The second category includes the growing importance of depositary receipts and cross-listings and the emergence of institutional investors as key players driving international capital flows to emerging markets.

The investment opportunities afforded by stock market liberalizations, which have typically included the provision of access to foreign investors, have enhanced capital flows to MFIs. Since the late 1980s, stock market liberalizations in MFI economies in different regions have proceeded rapidly, in terms of both intensity and speed.

Mergers and acquisitions, especially those resulting from the privatization of state-owned companies, were an important factor underlying the increase in FDI flows to MFIs during the 1990s. The easing of restrictions on foreign participation in the financial sector in MFIs has also provided a strong impetus to this factor.

Institutional investors in the industrial countries—including mutual funds, pension funds, hedge funds, and insurance companies—have assumed an important role in channeling capital flows from industrial to developing economies. They have helped individual investors overcome the information and transaction cost barriers that previously limited portfolio allocations to emerging markets. Mutual funds, in particular, have served as an important instrument for individuals to diversify their portfolios into developing country holdings. Although international institutional investors devote only a small fraction of their portfolios to holdings in MFIs, they have an important presence in these economies, given the relatively small size of their capital markets. Funds dedicated to emerging markets alone hold on average 5–15 percent of the Asian, Latin American, and transition economies' market capitalization.

Notwithstanding the moderation of North–South capital flows following recent emerging market crises, certain structural forces are likely to lead to a revival of these flows over the medium and long term. Demographic shifts, in particular, constitute an important driving force for these flows. Projected increases in old-age dependency ratios reflect the major changes in demographic profiles that are underway in industrial countries. This trend is likely to intensify further in the coming decades, fueled both by advances in medical technology that have increased average life spans and the decline in fertility rates. Financing the post-retirement consumption needs of a rapidly aging population will require increases in current saving rates, both national and private, in these economies. However, if such increases in saving rates do materialize, they are likely to result in a declining rate of return on capital in advanced economies, especially relative to that in the capital-poor countries of the South. This will lead to natural tendencies for capital to flow to countries where it has a potentially higher return.

All of these forces imply that, despite the recent sharp reversals in North–South capital flows, developing countries will eventually once again face the delicate balance of opportunities and risks afforded by financial globalization. Are the benefits derived from financial integration sufficient to offset the costs of increased exposure to the vagaries of international capital flows? The chapter now turns to an examination of the evidence on this question.

9.3 Financial integration and economic growth

9.3.1 Potential benefits of financial globalization

In theory, there are a number of direct and indirect channels through which embracing financial globalization can help enhance growth in developing countries. Figure 9.2 provides a schematic summary of these possible channels. These channels are interrelated in some ways, but this delineation is useful for reviewing the empirical evidence on the quantitative importance of each channel.

Direct channels

North–South capital flows in principle benefit both groups. They allow for increased investment in capital-poor countries by augmenting domestic savings and, at the same time, provide a higher return on capital than is available in capital-rich countries. This effectively reduces the risk-free rate in the developing countries.

The second direct channel comes from the reduction in the cost of capital through better global allocation of risk. International asset pricing models predict that stock market liberalization improves the allocation of risk. First,

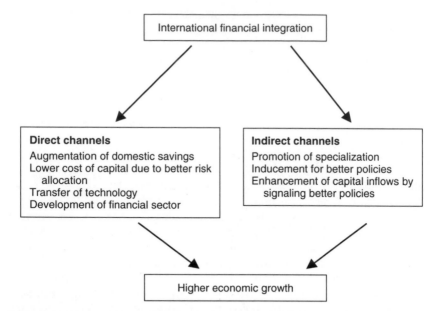

Figure 9.2   Channels through which financial integration can raise economic growth

increased risk sharing opportunities between foreign and domestic investors might help to diversify risks. This ability to diversify in turn encourages firms to take on more total investment, thereby enhancing growth. Third, as capital flows increase, the domestic stock market becomes more liquid, which could further reduce the equity risk premium, thereby lowering the cost of raising capital for investment.

Transfer of technological and managerial know-how is another direct channel. Financially integrated economies seem to attract a disproportionately large share of FDI inflows, which have the potential to generate technology spillovers and to serve as a conduit for passing on better management practices. These spillovers can raise aggregate productivity and, in turn, boost economic growth.

Stimulation of domestic financial sector development is also promoted by financial integration. It has already been noted that international portfolio flows can increase the liquidity of domestic stock markets. Increased foreign ownership of domestic banks can also generate a variety of other benefits. First, foreign bank participation can facilitate access to international financial markets. Second, it can help improve the regulatory and supervisory framework of the domestic banking industry. Third, foreign banks often introduce a variety of new financial instruments and techniques and also foster technological improvements in domestic markets. The entry of foreign banks tends to increase competition which, in turn, can improve the quality of domestic financial services as well as allocative efficiency.

Indirect channels

The notion that specialization in production may increase productivity and growth is intuitive. However, without any mechanism for risk management, a highly specialized production structure will produce high output volatility and, hence, high consumption volatility. Concerns about exposure to such increases in volatility may discourage countries from taking up growth-enhancing specialization activities; the higher volatility will also generally imply lower overall savings and investment rates. In principle, financial globalization could play a useful role by helping countries to engage in international risk sharing and thereby reduce consumption volatility. This point will be taken up again in Section 9.4. Here, it should just be noted that risk sharing would indirectly encourage specialization, which in turn would raise the growth rate.

International financial integration could also increase productivity in an economy through its impact on the government's ability to credibly commit to a future course of policies. More specifically, the disciplining role of financial integration could change the dynamics of domestic investment in an economy to the extent that it leads to a reallocation of capital toward more productive activities in response to changes in macroeconomic policies. National governments are occasionally tempted to institute predatory tax policies on physical capital. The prospect of such policies tends to discourage investment and to reduce growth. Financial opening can be self-sustaining and constrains the government from engaging in such predatory policies in the future since the negative consequences of such actions are far more severe under financial integration.

A country's willingness to undertake financial integration could also be interpreted as a signal that it is going to practice more friendly policies toward foreign investment in the future. The removal of restrictions on capital outflows can, through its signaling role, lead to an increase in capital inflows. Many countries, including Colombia, Egypt, Italy, New Zealand, Mexico, Spain, Uruguay, and the United Kingdom have received significant capital inflows after removing restrictions on capital outflows.

9.3.2 Empirical evidence

On the surface, there seems to be a positive association between embracing financial globalization and the level of economic development. Industrial countries in general are more financially integrated with the global economy than developing countries. So embracing globalization is apparently part of being economically advanced.

Within the developing world, it is also the case that MFI economies grew faster than LFI economies over the last three decades. From 1970 to 1999, average output per capita rose almost threefold in the group of MFI developing economies, almost six times greater than the corresponding increase for LFI economies. This pattern of higher growth for the former group applies over each of the three decades and also to consumption and investment growth.

However, there are two problems with concluding a positive effect of financial integration on growth from this data pattern. First, this pattern may be fragile upon closer scrutiny. Second, these observations only reflect an association between international financial integration and economic performance rather than necessarily a causal relationship. In other words, these observations do not rule out the possibility that there is reverse causation: countries that manage to enjoy a robust growth may also choose to engage in financial integration even if financial globalization does not directly contribute to faster growth in a quantitatively significant way.

To obtain an intuitive impression of the relationship between financial openness and growth, Table 9.1 presents a list of the fastest growing developing economies during 1980–2000 and a list of the slowest growing (or fastest declining) economies during the same period. Some countries have undergone financial integration during this period, especially in the latter half of the 1990s.[7] Therefore, any result based on total changes over this long period should be interpreted with caution. Nonetheless, several features of the table are noteworthy.

An obvious observation that can be made from the table is that financial integration is *not a necessary condition* for achieving a high growth rate.

Table 9.1 Fastest and slowest growing economies during 1980–2000 and financial openness[a]

Fast growing economies 1980–2000	Total percentage change (in percent of GDP)	More financially integrated?	Slowest growing economies 1980–2000	Total percentage change (in percent of GDP)	More financially integrated?
China	391.6	Yes/No	Haiti	−39.5	No
Korea	234.0	Yes	Niger	−37.8	No
Singapore	155.5	Yes	Nicaragua	−30.6	No
Thailand	151.1	Yes	Togo	−30.0	No
Mauritius	145.8	No	Cote d'Ivoire	−29.0	No
Botswana	135.4	No	Burundi	−20.2	No
Hong Kong SAR	114.5	Yes	Venezuela	−17.3	Yes/No
Malaysia	108.8	Yes	South Africa	−13.7	Yes
India	103.2	Yes/No	Jordan	−10.9	Yes
Chile	100.9	Yes	Paraguay	−9.5	No
Indonesia	97.6	Yes	Ecuador	−7.9	No
Sri Lanka	90.8	No	Peru	−7.8	Yes

[a] Growth rate of real per capita GDP, in constant local currency units.

Sources: World Bank, *World Development Indicators* (various years) and authors' calculations.

China and India have achieved high growth rates despite somewhat limited and selective capital account liberalization. For example, while China became substantially more open to FDI, it was not particularly open to most other types of cross-border capital flows. Mauritius and Botswana have managed to achieve very strong growth rates during the period, although they are relatively closed to financial flows.

The second observation that can be made is that financial integration is *not a sufficient condition* for a fast economic growth rate either. For example, Jordan and Peru had become relatively open to foreign capital flows during the period; yet, their economies suffered a decline rather than enjoying positive growth during the period. On the other hand, Table 9.1 also suggests that declining economies are more likely to be financially closed, though the direction of causality is not clear as explained before.

This way of looking at country cases with extreme growth performance is only informative up to a point; it needs to be supplemented by a comprehensive examination of the experience of a broader set of countries using a more systematic approach to measuring financial openness. To illustrate this relationship more broadly, Figure 9.3 presents a scatter plot of the growth

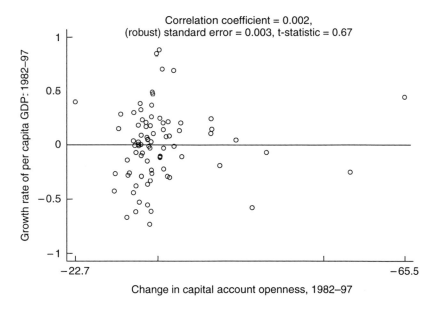

Figure 9.3 Correlation between financial openness and real per capita GDP growth 1982–97[a]

[a] Capital account openness is measured as the ratio of gross private capital inflows plus gross private capital outflows to GDP.

Source: Authors' calculation based on the data documented in Wei and Wu (2002).

rate of real per capita GDP against the increase in financial integration over 1982–97. There is essentially no association between these variables. This picture remains unchanged if one controls for the effects of a country's initial income, initial schooling, average investment-to-GDP ratio, political instability, and regional location. In fact, this finding is not unique to the particular choice of the time period or the country coverage as reflected in a broad survey of other research papers on the subject.

A number of empirical studies have tried to systematically examine whether financial integration contributes to growth using various approaches to dealing with the difficult problem of proving causation. We surveyed the 14 most recent studies on this subject. Three out of the 14 papers report a positive effect of financial integration on growth. However, the majority of the papers tend to find no effect or a mixed effect for developing countries. This suggests that, if financial integration has a positive effect on growth, it is probably not strong or robust.

Of the papers we surveyed, the one by Edison, Levine, Ricci, and Sløk (2002) is perhaps the most thorough and comprehensive in terms of measures of financial integration and in terms of empirical specifications. These authors measure a country's degree of financial integration both by the government's restrictions on capital account transactions as recorded by the IMF and by the observed size of capital flows crossing the border, normalized by the size of the economy. The data set in that paper goes through 2000, the latest year analyzed in any existing study on this subject. Furthermore, the authors also employ a statistical methodology that allows them to deal with possible reverse causality—that is, any observed association between financial integration and economic growth could result from the mechanism that faster growing economies are also more likely to choose to liberalize their capital accounts. After a battery of statistical analyses, that paper concludes that, overall, there is no robustly significant effect of financial integration on economic growth.

9.3.3 Synthesis

Why is it so difficult to find a strong and robust effect of financial integration on economic growth for developing countries, when the theoretical basis for this result is apparently so strong? Perhaps there is some logic to this outcome after all. A number of researchers have now concluded that most of the differences in income per capita across countries stem not from differences in capital–labor ratios, but from differences in total factor productivity (TFP), which, in turn, could be explained by "soft" factors or "social infrastructure" like governance, rule of law, and respect for property rights. In this case, while financial integration may open the door for additional capital to come in from abroad, it is unlikely to offer a major boost to growth by itself. In fact, if domestic governance is sufficiently weak, financial integration could cause an exodus of domestic capital and, hence, lower the growth rate of an economy.

This logic can be illustrated using the results reported in Senhadji (2000). Over the period 1960 to 1994, the average growth rate of per capita output for the group of countries in sub-Saharan Africa was the lowest among regional groupings of developing countries. The difference in physical and human capital accumulation is only part of the story for why growth rates differ across countries. The gap in TFP is the major element in explaining the difference in the growth rates.

Another possible explanation for why it is difficult to detect a causal effect of financial integration on growth is the costly banking crises that some developing countries have experienced in the process of financial integration. The results in Kaminsky and Reinhart (1999) suggest that a flawed sequencing of domestic financial liberalization, when accompanied by capital account liberalization, increases the chance of domestic banking crises and/or exchange rate crises. These crises are often accompanied by output collapses.

As a result, the benefits from financial integration may not be evident in the data. It is interesting to contrast the empirical literature on the effects of financial integration with that on the effects of trade integration. Although there are some skeptics, an overwhelming majority of empirical papers reach the conclusion that trade openness helps to promote economic growth. These studies employ a variety of techniques, including country case studies as well as cross-country regressions. In a recent paper that surveys all the prominent empirical research on the subject, Berg and Krueger (2002) conclude that "[v]aried evidence supports the view that trade openness contributes greatly to growth." Furthermore, "[c]ross-country regressions of the level of income on various determinants generally show that openness is the most important policy variable." The contrast between financial and trade openness may have important lessons for policies. While there appear to be relatively few prerequisites for deriving benefits from trade openness, obtaining benefits from financial integration requires several conditions to be in place. This is discussed in more detail later.

It is useful to note that there may be a complementary relationship between trade and financial openness. For example, if a country has severe trade barriers protecting some inefficient domestic industries, then capital inflows may end up being directed to those industries, thereby exacerbating the existing misallocation of resources. Thus, there is a concrete channel through which financial openness without trade openness could *lower* a country's level of efficiency.

Of course, the lack of a strong and robust effect of financial integration on economic growth does not necessarily imply that theories that make this connection are wrong. One could argue that the theories are about the long-run effects, and most theories abstract from the nitty-gritty of institutional building, governance improvement, and other "soft" factors that are necessary ingredients for the hypothesized channels to take effect. Indeed, developing countries may have little choice but to strengthen their financial linkages eventually in order to improve their growth potential in the long run. The problem is how to manage the short-run risks apparently associated with financial globalization. Financial integration without a proper set of preconditions might lead to few growth benefits and more output and consumption volatility in the short run, a subject that is taken up in the Section 9.4.

9.4   Financial globalization and macroeconomic volatility

9.4.1   Macroeconomic volatility

One of the potential benefits of globalization is that it should provide better opportunities for reducing volatility by diversifying risks. Indeed, these benefits are presumably even greater for developing countries that are intrinsically subject to higher volatility on account of their being less diversified than industrial economies in terms of their production structures. However, recent crises in some MFIs suggest that financial integration may in fact have increased volatility.

What is the overall evidence of the effect of globalization on macroeconomic volatility? In addressing this question, it is important to make a distinction between output and consumption volatility. In theoretical models, the direct effects of global integration on output volatility are ambiguous. Financial integration provides access to capital that can help capital-poor developing countries to diversify their production base. On the other hand, rising financial integration could also lead to increasing specialization of production based on comparative advantage considerations, thereby making economies more vulnerable to shocks that are specific to industries.

Irrespective of the effects on output volatility, theory suggests that financial integration should reduce consumption volatility. The ability to reduce fluctuations in consumption is regarded as an important determinant of economic welfare. Access to international financial markets provides better opportunities for countries to share macroeconomic risk and, thereby, smooth consumption. The basic idea here is that, since output fluctuations are not perfectly correlated across countries, trade in financial assets can be used to delink national consumption levels from the country-specific components of these output fluctuations (see Obstfeld and Rogoff (1998), chapter 5).

Notwithstanding the importance of this issue, the empirical evidence on the effects of globalization on macroeconomic volatility is rather sparse and, in particular, the evidence concerning the effects of financial integration on volatility is limited and inconclusive. In addition, the existing literature has largely been devoted to analyzing the effects of financial integration on output volatility, with little attention paid to consumption volatility. Hence, this paper now provides some new evidence on this topic.

Table 9.2 examines changes in volatility for different macroeconomic aggregates over the last four decades. Consistent with evidence presented in the IMF's September 2002 World Economic Outlook, MFI economies on

Table 9.2 Volatility of annual growth rates of select variables (percentage standard deviations, medians for each group)[a]

	Full sample 1960–99	Decade			
		1960s	1970s	1980s	1990s
Income					
Industrial countries	2.73	2.18	2.99	2.54	1.91
	(0.34)	(0.33)	(0.40)	(0.29)	(0.30)
More financially integrated	5.44	3.60	5.43	5.45	4.78
economies (MFI)	(0.50)	(0.47)	(0.45)	(0.65)	(0.72)
Less financially integrated	7.25	4.42	9.64	7.56	4.59
economies (LFI)	(0.84)	(0.53)	(1.24)	(1.23)	(0.54)
Total consumption					
Industrial countries	1.86	1.38	1.84	1.58	1.38
	(0.23)	(0.28)	(0.18)	(0.19)	(0.20)
MFI economies	4.34	3.95	4.19	3.43	4.10
	(0.47)	(0.51)	(0.54)	(0.84)	(0.53)
LFI economies	6.40	4.85	6.50	6.34	4.79
	(0.56)	(0.55)	(0.93)	(0.91)	(0.82)
Ratio of total consumption volatility to income volatility[b]					
Industrial countries	0.67	0.75	0.56	0.61	0.58
	(0.02)	(0.09)	(0.03)	(0.06)	(0.06)
MFI economies	0.81	0.92	0.74	0.76	0.92
	(0.07)	(0.13)	(0.12)	(0.11)	(0.04)
LFI economies	0.80	0.95	0.68	0.82	0.84
	(0.08)	(0.06)	(0.10)	(0.51)	(0.14)

[a] Standard errors are reported in parentheses.
[b] For the bottom panel, the ratio of total consumption growth volatility to that of income growth volatility is first computed separately for each country. The reported numbers are the within-group medians of these ratios.

Source: Authors' estimates.

average have lower income volatility than LFI economies. Interestingly, there is a significant decline in average income volatility in the 1990s for both industrial and LFI economies but a far more modest decline for MFI economies.

The third panel of this table shows that average consumption volatility in the 1990s has declined in line with output volatility for both industrial economies and LFI economies. By contrast, for MFI economies, the volatility of consumption has in fact risen in the 1990s relative to the 1980s for MFI economies. Could this simply be a consequence of higher income volatility for MFI economies?

Strikingly, for the group of MFI countries, the volatility of total consumption relative to that of income has actually increased in the 1990s relative to earlier periods. The bottom panel of Table 9.2 shows the median ratio of the volatility of total consumption growth to that of income growth for each group of countries. For MFI economies, this ratio increases from 0.76 in the 1980s to 0.92 in the 1990s, while it remains essentially unchanged for the other two groups of countries. Thus, the increase in the 1990s of the volatility of consumption relative to that of income for the MFI economies suggests that financial integration has not provided better consumption smoothing opportunities for these economies.[8]

More formal econometric evidence is presented by Kose *et al.* (2003), who use measures of capital account restrictions as well as gross financial flows to capture different aspects of financial integration, as well as differences in the degree of integration across countries and over time. This analysis confirms the increase in the relative volatility of consumption for countries that have larger financial flows, even after controlling for macroeconomic variables as well as country characteristics such as trade openness and industrial structure. However, these authors also identify an important threshold effect— beyond a particular level, financial integration significantly reduces volatility. Most developing economies, including MFI economies, are unfortunately well below this threshold.[9]

Why has the relative volatility of consumption increased precisely in those developing countries that are more open to financial flows? One explanation is that positive productivity and output growth shocks during the late 1980s and early 1990s in these countries led to consumption booms that were willingly financed by international investors. These consumption booms were accentuated by the fact that many of these countries undertook domestic financial liberalization at the same time that they opened up to international financial flows, thereby loosening liquidity constraints at both the individual and national levels. When negative shocks hit these economies, however, they rapidly lost access to international capital markets.

Consistent with this explanation, a growing literature suggests that the procyclical nature of capital flows appears to have had an adverse impact on consumption volatility in developing economies.[10] One manifestation of this procyclicality is the phenomenon of "sudden stops" of capital inflows (see Calvo and Reinhart (2000)). More generally, access to international capital markets has a procyclical element, which tends to generate higher output volatility as well as excess consumption volatility (relative to that of income). Reinhart (2002), for instance, finds that sovereign bond ratings are procyclical. Since the spreads on bonds of developing economies are strongly influenced by these ratings, this implies that costs of borrowing on international markets are procyclical as well. Kaminsky and Reinhart (2002) present more direct evidence on the procyclical behavior of capital inflows.

9.4.2   Crises as special cases of volatility

Crises can be regarded as particularly dramatic episodes of volatility. In fact, the proliferation of financial crises is often viewed as one of the defining aspects of the intensification of financial globalization over the last two decades. Furthermore, the fact that recent crises have affected mainly MFI economies has led to these phenomena being regarded as hallmarks of the unequal distribution of globalization's benefits and risks. This raises a challenging set of questions about whether the nature of crises has changed over time, what factors increase vulnerability to crises, and whether such crises are an inevitable concomitant of globalization.

Some aspects of financial crises have indeed changed over time while, in other respects, it is often déjà vu all over again. Calvo (1998) has referred to such episodes in the latter half of the 1980s and 1990s as capital account crises, while earlier ones are referred to as current account crises. Although this suggests differences in the mechanics of crises, it does not necessarily imply differences in some of their fundamental causes. Kaminsky and Reinhart (1999) discuss the phenomenon of "twin crises," which involve balance of payments and banking crises. These authors also make the important point that, in the episodes that they analyze, banking sector problems typically precede a currency crisis and that the currency crisis then deepens the banking crisis, activating a vicious spiral. In this vein, Krueger and Yoo (2002) conclude that imprudent lending by the Korean banks in the early and mid-1990s, especially to the Chaebols, played a significant role in the 1997 Korean currency crisis. Opening up to capital markets can thus exacerbate such existing domestic distortions and lead to catastrophic consequences.

One key difference in the evolution of crises is that, while the 1970s and the 1980s featured crises that affected both industrial and developing economies, these have become almost exclusively the preserve of developing economies since the mid-1990s.[11] This suggests either that advanced economies have been able to better protect themselves through improved policies or that the fundamental causes of crises have changed over time, thereby increasing the relative vulnerability of developing economies. In this context, it should be noted that, while capital flows from advanced economies to MFI economies have increased sharply, these flows among industrial economies have jumped even more sharply in recent years, as noted earlier. Thus, at least in terms of volume of capital flows, it is not obvious that changes in financial integration can by themselves be blamed for crises in MFI economies.

Is it reasonable to accept crises as a natural feature of globalization, much as business cycles are viewed as a natural occurrence in market economies? One key difference between these phenomena is that the overall macroeconomic costs of financial crises are typically very large and far more persistent. Calvo and Reinhart (2000) document those emerging market currency crises typically accompanied by sudden stops or reversals of external capital inflows are associated with significant negative output effects. Such recessions following devaluations (or large depreciations) are also found to be much deeper in emerging markets than in developed economies. In addition, the absence of well-functioning safety nets can greatly exacerbate the social costs of crises, which typically have large distributional consequences.

9.4.3   Financial globalization and volatility transmission

What factors have led to the rising vulnerability of developing economies to financial crises? The risk of sudden stops or reversals of global capital flows to developing countries has increased in importance as many developing countries now rely heavily on borrowing from foreign banks or on portfolio investment by foreign investors. These capital flows are sensitive not just to domestic conditions in the recipient countries but also to macroeconomic conditions in industrial countries. For instance, Mody and Taylor (2002), using an explicit disequilibrium econometric framework, detect instances of "international capital crunch"—where capital flows to developing countries are curtailed by supply-side rationing that reflects industrial country conditions. These North–South financial linkages, in addition to the real linkages described in earlier sections, represent an additional channel through which business cycles and other shocks that hit industrial countries can affect developing countries.

The effects of industrial country macroeconomic conditions, including the stage of the business cycle and interest rates, have different effects on various types of capital flows to emerging markets. Reinhart and Reinhart (2001) document that net FDI flows to emerging market economies are strongly positively correlated with US business cycles. On the other hand, bank lending to these economies is negatively correlated with US cycles. Edison and Warnock (2001) find that portfolio equity flows from the United States to major emerging market countries are negatively correlated with both US interest rates and US output growth. This result is particularly strong for flows to Latin America and less so for flows to Asia. Thus, the sources of capital inflows for a particular MFI can greatly affect the nature of its vulnerability to the volatility of capital flows arising from industrial country disturbances.

The increase in cross-country financial market correlations also indicates a risk of emerging markets being caught up in financial market bubbles. The rise in co-movement across emerging and industrial country stock markets, especially during the stock market bubble period of the late 1990s, points to the relevance of this concern. This is a particular risk for relatively shallow and undiversified stock markets of some emerging economies. For instance, as noted earlier, the strong correlations between emerging and industrial stock markets during the bubble period reflects the preponderance of technology and telecommunication sector stocks in the former set of markets. It is, of course, difficult to say conclusively whether this phenomenon would have occurred even in the absence of financial globalization, since stock market liberalizations in these countries often went hand in hand with their opening up to capital flows.

The increasing depth of stock markets in emerging economies could alleviate some of these risks but, at the same time, could heighten the real effects of such financial shocks. In this vein, some authors have found that a higher degree of financial development makes emerging stock markets more susceptible to external influences (both financial and macroeconomic) and that this effect remains important after controlling for capital controls and trade linkages. Consequently, the effects of external shocks could be transmitted to domestic real activity through the stock market channel.

Even the effects of real shocks are often transmitted faster and amplified through financial channels. There is a large literature showing how productivity, terms of trade, fiscal and other real shocks are transmitted through trade channels. Cross-country investment flows, in particular, have traditionally responded quite strongly to country-specific shocks. Financial channels constitute an additional avenue through which the effects of such real shocks can be transmitted. Furthermore, since transmission through financial channels is much quicker than through real channels, both the speed and magnitude of international spillovers of real shocks are considerably heightened by financial linkages.

Rising financial linkages have also resulted in contagion effects. Potential contagion effects are likely to become more important over time as financial linkages increase and investors in search of higher returns and better diversification opportunities increase their share of international holdings and, due to declines in information and transaction costs, have access to a broader array of cross-country investment opportunities.

There are two broad types of contagion identified in the literature—fundamentals-based contagion and "pure" contagion. The former refers to the transmission of shocks across national borders through real or financial linkages. In other words, while an economy may have weak fundamentals, it could get tipped over into a financial crisis as a consequence of investors reassessing the riskiness of investments in that country or attempting to rebalance their portfolios following a crisis in another country. Similarly, bank lending can lead to such contagion effects when a crisis in one country to which a bank has significant exposure forces it to rebalance its portfolio by readjusting its lending to other countries. This bank transmission channel can be particularly potent since a large fraction of bank lending to emerging markets is in the form of short-maturity loans. While fundamentals-based contagion was once prevalent mainly at the regional level, the Russian crisis demonstrated its much broader international reach.

Pure contagion, on the other hand, represents a different kind of risk since it cannot easily be influenced by domestic policies at least in the short run. There is a good deal of evidence of sharp swings in international capital flows that are not obviously related to changes in fundamentals. Investor behavior during these episodes, which is sometimes categorized as herding or momentum trading, is difficult to explain in the context of optimizing models with full and common information. Informational asymmetries, which are particularly rife in the context of emerging markets, appear to play an important role in this phenomenon. Thus, in addition to "pure contagion," financial integration exposes developing economies to the risks associated with destabilizing investor behavior that is not related to fundamentals.

9.4.4   Factors increasing vulnerability to globalization risks

Empirical research indicates that the composition of capital inflows and the maturity structure of external debt appear to be associated with higher vulnerability to the risks of financial globalization. The relative importance of different sources of financing for domestic investment, as proxied by the following three variables, has been shown to be positively associated with the incidence and the severity of currency and financial crises: the ratio of bank borrowing or other debt relative to FDI; the shortness of the term structure of external debt; and the share of external debt denominated in foreign currencies. Detragiache and Spilimbergo (2001) find strong evidence that debt crises are more likely to occur in countries where external debt has a short maturity. However, the maturity structure may not entirely be a matter of choice since, as argued by these authors, countries with weaker macroeconomic fundamentals are often forced to borrow at shorter maturities since they do not have access to longer-maturity loans. The currency composition of external debt also matters. During the Asian crisis, countries with more yen-denominated debt fared significantly worse. This could be attributed to the misalignment between the countries' *de facto* currency pegs and the denomination of their debt.

In addition to basic macroeconomic policies, other policy choices of a systemic nature can also affect the vulnerability of MFIs. Recent currency crises have highlighted one of the main risks in this context. Developing countries that attempt to maintain a relatively inflexible exchange rate system often face the risk of attacks on their currencies. While various forms of fully or partially fixed exchange rate regimes can have some advantages, the absence of supportive domestic policies can often result in an abrupt unraveling of these regimes when adverse shocks hit the economy.

Financial integration can also aggravate the risks associated with imprudent fiscal policies. Access to world capital markets could lead to excessive borrowing that is channeled into unproductive government spending. The existence of large amounts of short-term debt denominated in hard currencies then makes countries vulnerable to external shocks or changes in investor sentiment. The experience of a number of MFI countries that have suffered the consequences of such external debt accumulation points to the heightened risks of undisciplined fiscal policies when the capital account is open.

Premature opening of the capital account also poses serious risks when financial regulation and supervision are inadequate. In the presence of weakly regulated banking systems and other distortions in domestic capital markets, inflows of foreign capital could exacerbate the existing inefficiencies in these economies. For example, if domestic financial institutions tend to channel capital to firms with excessive risks or weak fundamentals, financial integration could simply lead to an intensification of such flows.[12] In turn, the effects of premature capital inflows on the balance sheets of the government and corporate sectors could have negative repercussions on the health of financial institutions in the event of adverse macroeconomic shocks.

9.5 Select factors in the benefits and risks of globalization

9.5.1 Threshold effects and absorptive capacity

While it is difficult to find a strong and robust effect of financial integration on economic growth, there is some evidence in the literature of various kinds of "threshold effects." For example, there is some evidence that the effect of FDI on growth depends on the level of human capital in a developing country. For countries with relatively low human capital, there is at best a small positive effect that can be detected in the data. On the other hand, for countries whose human capital has exceeded a certain threshold, there is some evidence that FDI promotes economic growth.

More generally, one might think of a country's absorptive capacity in terms of human capital, depth of domestic financial market, quality of governance and macroeconomic policies. There is some preliminary evidence that foreign capital flows do not seem to generate positive productivity spillovers to domestic firms for countries with a relatively low absorptive capacity, but positive spillovers are more likely to be detected for countries with a relatively high level of absorptive capacity. This evidence is consistent with the view that countries need to build up a certain amount of absorptive capacity in order to effectively take advantage of financial globalization.

The next subsection specifically discusses the role of domestic governance as a crucial element of this absorptive capacity. The importance of governance has been asserted repeatedly, particularly since the Asian crisis, but until recently there has been relatively little systematical evidence documented on its relationship with financial globalization.

9.5.2 Governance as an important element of absorptive capacity

The term governance encompasses a broad array of institutions and norms. While many of these are interrelated and complementary, it is nevertheless useful to try and narrow down a core set of governance dimensions most relevant for the discussion on financial integration. These are: transparency, control of corruption, rule of law, and financial sector supervision.

Recent evidence suggests that the quality of governance affects a country's ability to benefit from international capital flows. As discussed in Section 9.3, of the various types of capital flows, FDI might be among the most helpful in terms of boosting recipient countries' economic growth.[13] There is an intimate connection between a country's quality of domestic governance and its ability to attract FDI. Recent evidence suggests that FDI tends to go to countries with good governance, if one holds constant the size of the country, labor cost, tax rate, laws, and incentives specifically related to foreign-invested firms and other factors. Moreover, the quantitative effect of bad governance on FDI is quite large.

To reach this conclusion, corruption in the FDI recipient countries can be measured in a variety of ways. These include: a rating by Transparency International, which is a global nongovernmental organization devoted to fight corruption; a measure derived from a survey of firms worldwide as published jointly by Harvard University and the World Economic Forum in the Global Competitiveness Report; and a measure from a survey of firms worldwide conducted by the World Bank. The results from these different measures are quite consistent; all show a negative effect of corruption on the volume of inward FDI.[14] The quantitative effect of corruption is significant as well when compared with the negative effect of corporate tax rate on FDI. For example, a one standard deviation increase in host country corruption might be equivalent to an increase of about 30 percentage points in the tax rate in terms of its negative effect on FDI (Wei (1997, 2000a, and 2000b)).[15]

Many developing countries' governments are now eager to attract FDI by offering generous tax concessions or exemptions. The previous evidence suggests that an improvement of domestic governance, especially reducing corruption, would be more effective in attracting FDI without having to take measures that could reduce tax revenues, in addition to promoting more domestic investment.

Similarly, transparency of government operations is another dimension of good governance. More portfolio investment from international mutual funds tends to go to countries with a higher level of transparency (Gelos and Wei, 2002). This is true even after one takes into account the liquidity of the market, exchange rate regime, other economic risks, and a host of other factors.

9.5.3   Domestic governance and the volatility of capital flows

Previous sections documented the fact that international capital flows can be very volatile. However, different countries experience different degrees of volatility, and this may be systematically related to the quality of macroeconomic policies and domestic governance. In other words, with regard to the "sudden stops" or "sudden reversals" of international capital flows, developing countries are not purely passive recipients with no influence on the nature of capital inflows. For example, research has demonstrated that an overvalued exchange rate and an overextended domestic lending boom often precede a capital account crisis. In this subsection, attention is focused on the evidence related to the role of local governance in mitigating the volatility of capital inflows that a developing country might experience.

There is plenty of evidence suggesting that weak domestic capacity in financial regulation and supervision is likely to be associated with a high propensity of experiencing banking and currency crisis. Without an adequate financial supervision institution in place, a premature opening of the capital account could increase the risk of a financial crisis as domestic financial institutions may build up excessive risk. On the liability side, they might borrow excessively from international capital markets. On the asset side, they might expand lending to overly risky economic activities, especially where there is an explicit or implicit government guarantee. These factors could result in various types of balance sheet weaknesses, such as mismatch in maturity or currency. Furthermore, due to intersectoral linkages, balance sheet weaknesses of the government and corporate sectors could affect the health of financial institutions as well. The view that supervisory and regulatory capacity need to be sufficiently strengthened before a country engages in full-fledged liberalization of the capital account is now widely accepted.

Transparency of a government's economic policies is another dimension of domestic governance. Recent evidence suggests that the degree of transparency might affect the degree of volatility of capital inflows that a country experiences. For example, herding behavior by international investors, which is alleged to have contributed to instability in the developing countries' financial markets, tends to be more severe in countries with a lower degree of transparency.

The literature on currency crises (e.g. Frankel and Rose (1996)) points out that a country's structure of capital inflows is related to the likelihood of a crisis. More specifically, a country that relies relatively more on foreign bank credits and less on FDI may be more vulnerable to the "sudden stops" of international capital flows and have a higher chance of running into a capital account crisis.

Recent research suggests that macroeconomic policies are an important determinant of the composition of capital inflows. Recent research also presents some evidence that domestic governance as measured by the corruption indexes tilts the composition of capital flows. Specifically, countries with a weaker governance as reflected by a higher perceived level of corruption are more likely to have a structure of capital inflows that is relatively light in FDI and relatively heavy in foreign bank credits, holding other factors constant.

Governance is not the only element of domestic absorptive capacity, but is an important one. Its importance has been emphasized by the IMF Executive Board and in the international policy circles at least since the Asian financial crisis. Recent systematic research documented in this chapter has provided empirical foundation for this view. Of course, the importance of domestic governance goes beyond its role in financial globalization. The quality of governance also affects economic growth and other social objectives through a variety of other channels (documented in Mauro (1997), and Abed and Gupta (2002)).

9.6   Conclusion

The objective of the paper was not so much to derive new policy propositions as it is to inform the debate on the potential and actual benefit-risk tradeoffs associated with financial globalization by reviewing the available empirical evidence and country experiences. The main conclusions are that, so far, it has proven difficult to find robust evidence in support of the proposition that financial integration helps developing countries to improve growth and to reduce macroeconomic volatility.

Of course, the absence of robust evidence on these dimensions does not necessarily mean that financial globalization has no benefits and carries only great risks. Indeed, most countries that have initiated financial integration have continued along this path, despite temporary setbacks. This observation is consistent with the notion that the indirect benefits of financial integration, which may be difficult to pick up in regression analysis, could be quite important. Also, the long run gains, in some cases yet unrealized, may far offset the short-term costs. For instance, the European Monetary Union experienced severe and costly crises in the early 1990s as part of the transition to a single currency throughout much of Europe today.

While, it is difficult to find a simple relationship between financial globalization and growth or consumption volatility, there is some evidence of nonlinearities or threshold effects in the relationship. That is, financial globalization, in combination with good macroeconomic policies and good domestic governance, appears to be conducive to growth. For example, countries with good human capital and governance tend to do better at attracting FDI, which is especially conducive to growth. More specifically, recent research shows that corruption has a strongly negative effect on FDI inflows. Similarly, transparency of government operations, which is another dimension of good governance, has a strong positive effect on investment inflows from international mutual funds.

The vulnerability of a developing country to the "risk factors" associated with financial globalization is also not independent from the quality of macroeconomic policies and domestic governance. For example, research has demonstrated that an overvalued exchange rate and an overextended domestic lending boom often precede a currency crisis. In addition, lack of transparency has been shown to be associated with more herding behavior by international investors that can destabilize a developing country's financial markets. Finally, evidence shows that a high degree of corruption may affect the composition of a country's capital inflows in a manner that makes it more vulnerable to the risks of speculative attacks and contagion effects. Thus, the ability of a developing country to derive benefits from financial globalization and its relative vulnerability to the volatility of international capital flows can be significantly affected by the quality of both its macroeconomic framework and institutions.

In summary, while it is difficult to distill new and innovative policy messages from the review of the evidence, there appears to be empirical support for some general propositions. Empirically, good institutions and quality of governance are important not only in their own right, but in helping developing countries derive the benefits of globalization. Similarly, macroeconomic stability appears to be an important prerequisite for ensuring that financial integration is beneficial for developing countries. In this regard, the IMF's work in promulgating codes and standards for best practices on transparency and financial supervision, as well as sound macroeconomic frameworks is crucial. In addition, the analysis suggests that financial globalization should be approached cautiously and with good institutions and macroeconomic frameworks viewed as preconditions.

Notes

1. Eswar Prasad is currently chief of the Financial Studies Division in the IMF's Research Department; previously, he was chief of the China Division in the IMF's Asia and Pacific Department. Kenneth Rogoff is a professor at Harvard University and was the director of the IMF's Research Department and Economic Counselor when this chapter was written. Shang-Jin Wei is head of the Trade Unit and M. Ayhan Kose is an economist in the Economic Modeling Division—both in the IMF's Research Department. The authors are grateful to numerous colleagues at the IMF for helpful comments and discussions, and for providing data and other input into this chapter. It is an abridged version of a study with the same title (available in full-text format at www.imf.org/research) that was published as IMF Occasional Paper No. 220 in 2003. Please see that study for a description of the dataset, more detailed results, and an extensive list of references. The views expressed in this chapter are those of the authors and should not be interpreted as those of the International Monetary Fund.
2. The restriction measure is available until 1995, when a new and more refined measure—not backward compatible—was introduced. The earlier data were extended through 1998 by Mody and Murshid (2002).
3. These stock data were constructed by Lane and Milesi-Ferretti (2001). Operationally, this measure involves calculating the gross levels of FDI and portfolio assets and liabilities via the accumulation of the corresponding inflows and outflows, and making relevant valuation adjustments.
4. Other measures of capital market integration include saving–investment correlations and various interest parity conditions. These measures are difficult to operationalize for the extended time period and large number of countries in the data sample for this paper.
5. The dataset used in this paper consists of 76 industrial and developing countries (except where otherwise indicated) and covers the period 1960–99. Given the long sample period, several countries currently defined as industrial (e.g. Korea and Singapore) are included in the developing country group. The following were excluded from the dataset: most of the highly indebted poor countries (which mostly receive official flows), the transition economies of Eastern Europe and the Former Soviet Union (due to lack of data), very small economies (population less than 1.5 million), and oil-exporting countries in the Middle East.

6. Not surprisingly, this classification results in a set of MFI economies that roughly correspond to those included in the Morgan Stanley Capital International Inc. (MSCI) emerging markets stock index. The main differences are that we drop the transition economies because of limited data availability and add Hong Kong Special Administrative Region (SAR) and Singapore.
7. Table 9.1 reports the growth rates of real per capita GDP in constant local currency units. The exact growth rates and country rankings may change if different measures such as per capita GDP in dollar terms or on a PPP basis are used.
8. It should be noted that, despite the increase in the 1990s, the volatility of both private and total consumption for the MFI economies is, on average, still lower than for LFI economies.
9. For the financial integration measure used in this paper, the threshold occurs at a ratio of about 50 percent of GDP. The countries in the sample that have a degree of financial integration above this threshold are all industrial countries.
10. The notion of procyclicality here is that capital inflows are positively correlated with domestic business cycle conditions in these countries.
11. In fact, in the 1990s, the Exchange Rate Mechanism (ERM) crisis is the only significant one among industrial countries. The prolonged Japanese recession is in some sense a crisis although the protracted nature of Japan's decline, which has not featured any sudden falls in output, would not fit into a standard definition of a crisis.
12. Krueger and Yoo (2002) discuss the interactions of crony capitalism and capital account liberalization in setting the stage for the currency–financial crisis in Korea.
13. Of course, FDI could have its own problems which one might discover in the future. Moreover, the distinction between FDI and other types of capital flows is not always straightforward.
14. The term corruption should be regarded here as a shorthand for weak public sector governance. Existing empirical measures of different dimensions of public sector governance tend to be highly correlated with each other, making it difficult to identify their individual effects.
15. Of the 45 host countries studied in Wei (2000a), corruption is rated by the Business International in a range from 1 to 10. The average rating is 3.7, and the standard deviation is 2.5. The (highest marginal) corporate tax rate in the sample ranges from 10 percent to 59 percent with a mean of 34 percent and a standard deviation of 11 percent.

References

Abed, George and Sanjeev Gupta, 2002, *Governance, Corruption, and Economic Performances* (Washington, DC: International Monetary Fund).

Berg, Andrew and Anne O. Krueger, 2002, "Trade, Growth, and Poverty: A Selective Survey," paper presented at the World Bank's annual conference on *Development Economics*, Washington, DC (April).

Calvo, Guillermo, 1998, "Varieties of Capital-Market Crises," in *The Debt Burden and Its Monetary Consequences for Monetary Policy: Proceedings of a Conference Held by the International Economic Association at the Deutsche Bundesbank*, IEA Conference Volume No. 118, ed. by Guillermo Calvo and Mervyn King (New York: St. Martin's Press).

—— and Carmen Reinhart, 2000, "When Capital Inflows Come to a Sudden Stop: Consequences and Policy Options," in *Reforming the International Monetary and*

Financial System, ed. by P. Kenen and A. Swoboda, pp. 175–201 (Washington, DC: International Monetary Fund).

Detragiache, Enrica and Antonio Spilimbergo, 2001, "Crisis and Liquidity—Evidence and Interpretation," IMF Working Paper 01/2 (Washington, DC: International Monetary Fund).

Edison, Hali and Frank Warnock, 2001, "A Simple Measure of the Intensity of Capital Controls," International Finance Discussion Paper No. 705 (August) (Washington, DC: Board of Governors of the Federal Reserve).

Edison, Hali, Ross Levine, Luca Ricci, and Torsten Sløk, 2002, "International Financial Integration and Economic Growth," *Journal of International Monetary and Finance*, Vol. 21, pp. 749–76.

Frankel, Jeffery A. and Andrew K. Rose, 1996, "Currency Crashes in Emerging Markets: An Empirical Treatment," *Journal of International Economics*, Vol. 41 (3–4) (November), pp. 351–66.

Gelos, Gaston and Shang-Jin Wei, 2002, "Transparency and International Investor Behavior," NBER Working Paper No. 9260 (Cambridge, MA: National Bureau of Economic Research).

International Monetary Fund (various issue), *World Economic Outlook* (Washington, DC).

Kaminsky, Graciela and Carmen M. Reinhart, 2002, "Financial Markets in Times of Stress," *Journal of Development Economics*, Vol. 69, No. 2 (December), pp. 451–70.

——, 1999, "The Twin Crises: The Causes of Banking and Balance-of-Payments Problems," *American Economic Review*, Vol. 89, No. 3 (June), pp. 473–500.

Kose, M. Ayhan, Eswar S. Prasad, and Marco E. Terrones, 2003, "Financial Integration and Macroeconomic Volatility," *IMF Staff Papers*, Vol. 50, Special Issue, pp. 119–42.

Krueger, Anne O. and Jungho Yoo, 2002, "Chaebol Capitalism and the Currency-Financial Crisis in Korea," in *Preventing Currency Crises in Emerging Markets*, ed. by Sebastian Edwards and Jeffrey Frankel (Chicago: University of Chicago Press).

Lane, Philip R. and Gian Maria Milesi-Ferretti, 2001, "The External Wealth of Nations: Measures of Foreign Assets and Liabilities for Industrial and Developing Nations," *Journal of International Economics*, Vol. 55, pp. 263–94.

Mauro, Paolo, 1997, "The Effects of Corruption on Growth, Investment, and Government Expenditure: A Cross-Country Analysis," in *Corruption and the Global Economy*, ed. by Kimberly Ann Elliott (Washington, DC: Institute for International Economics).

Mody, Ashoka and Antu Panini Murshid, 2002, "Growing Up With Capital Flows," IMF Working Paper 02/75 (Washington, DC: International Monetary Fund).

Mody, Ashoka and Mark P. Taylor, 2002, "International Capital Crunches: The Time Varying Role of Informational Asymmetries," IMF Working Paper 02/34 (Washington, DC: International Monetary Fund).

Obstfeld, Maurice and Kenneth Rogoff, 1998, "Foundations of International Macroeconomics" (Cambridge, MA and London: MIT Press).

Reinhart, Carmen M., 2002, "Default, Financial Crises, and Sovereign Credit Ratings: Evidence from Emerging Markets," *World Bank Economic Review*, Vol. 16, No. 2, pp. 151–70.

—— and Vincent R. Reinhart, 2001, "What Hurts Most? G–3 Exchange Rate or Interest Rate Volatility," NBER Working Paper No. 8535 (Cambridge, MA: National Bureau of Economic Research).

Rogoff, Kenneth, 2002, "Rethinking Capital Controls: When Should We Keep an Open Mind?" *Finance and Development*, Vol. 39, No. 4 (December), pp. 55–56.

Senhadji, Abdelhak, 2000, "Sources of Economic Growth: An Extensive Growth Accounting Exercise," *IMF Staff Papers*, Vol. 47, No. 1, pp. 129–57.

Wei, Shang-Jin, 2001, "Domestic Crony Capitalism and International Fickle Capital: Is There a Connection?" *International Finance*, Vol. 4 (Spring), pp. 15–46.

——, 2000a, "How Taxing is Corruption on International Investors?" *Review of Economics and Statistics*, Vol. 82, No. 1 (February), pp. 1–11.

——, 2000b, "Local Corruption and Global Capital Flows," *Brookings Papers on Economic Activity*, Vol. 2.

——, 1997, "Why is Corruption Much More Taxing Than Taxes? Arbitrariness Kills," NBER Working Paper No. 6255 (Cambridge, MA: National Bureau of Economic Research).

—— and Yi Wu, 2002, "The Life-and-Death Implications of Globalization," paper presented at the National Bureau of Economic Research *Inter-American Seminar in Economics*, Monterrey, Mexico (November).

World Bank (various years), *World Development Indicators* (Washington).

10
Understanding India's Services Revolution

James Gordon and Poonam Gupta[1]

10.1 Introduction

A striking feature of India's growth performance over the past decade has been the strength of the services sector. Table 10.1 shows that on average services grew more slowly than industry between 1951 and 1990.[2] Growth of services picked up in the 1980s and further accelerated in the 1990s, when it averaged 7.5 percent per annum, thus providing a valuable prop to industry and agriculture, which grew on average by 5.8 percent and 3.1 percent, respectively.[3] Most forecasters expect that services will grow at similar if not higher rates over the next few years. Growth in the services sector has also been less cyclical and more stable than the growth of industry and agriculture (in the sense of having the smallest coefficient of variation).

The emergence of services as the most dynamic sector in the Indian economy has in many ways been a revolution. The most visible and well-known dimension of the takeoff in services has been in software and information technology (IT) enabled services (including call centers, software design, and business process outsourcing). However, growth in services in India has been much more broad-based than IT. In fact, although IT exports have had a profound impact on the balance of payments, the sector remains a small component of gross domestic product (GDP). As of 2003, business services (which include IT) were only about 1.8 percent of GDP, or accounting for 3.0 percent of total services output.

The chapter shows that almost all services subsectors in India have grown faster than GDP over time, but the pickup in growth in the 1990s was the strongest in business services, communications, and banking services,[4] followed by hotels and restaurants and community services. These activities together account for the entire acceleration in services growth in the 1990s. The growth in public administration and defense, real estate, storage, transport, and personal services in the 1990s was broadly similar to that in the previous decades.

Rapid growth of the services sector is not unique to India. The existing literature shows that as an economy matures the share of services in output

Table 10.1   India: sectoral growth rates (average growth, in percent per annum)

	1951–1980	1981–1990	1991–2000
Agriculture	2.1	4.4	3.1
Industry	5.3	6.8	5.8
Services	4.5	6.6	7.5
Real GDP	3.5	5.8	5.8

Sources: Central Statistical Organization, *National Accounts Statistics* (various years) and authors' estimates.

increases consistently. To begin with, the increase occurs along with an increase in the share of industry. Thereafter, the services share grows more rapidly, accompanied by a stagnant or declining share of the industrial sector. Consistent with this trend, India's growth experience has been characterized by a decline in the share of agriculture in GDP and an increase in the shares of industry and services. Between 1951 and 2000, the share of agriculture in GDP fell from 58 percent to 25 percent, while the share of industry increased from 15 percent to 27 percent, and the share of services rose from 27 percent to 48 percent. Of particular note are the changes during the 1990s, when the share of services in India's GDP climbed by about 8 percentage points, as compared to a cumulative increase of 13 percentage points during 1951–90. The share of industry, by contrast, remained constant during the 1990s.

This chapter explores the factors behind the dynamism of the services sector in India. One explanation suggested in the literature for the fast growth in services is that the income elasticity of demand for services is greater than one. Hence, the final demand for services grows faster than the demand for goods and commodities as income rises. Another explanation is that technical and structural changes in an economy make it more efficient to contract out business operations that were done internally by individual firms. This type of outsourcing has been called the "splintering" of industrial activity. Splintering results in an increase in net input demand for services from the industrial sector, and the services sector growing proportionately faster than other sectors.

The empirical evidence presented in the chapter shows that while splintering and high income elasticity of demand for services have served to stimulate services growth in India, it is necessary to look beyond these factors to fully explain the growth acceleration in the 1990s. In particular, important roles also seem to have been played by economic reforms and growing demand for services exports.[5]

Looking forward, our analysis suggests that the Indian services sector may experience an extra impetus to growth in coming years from exports and from liberalization. New markets for Indian services exports are just beginning to be tapped, and there is substantial scope for further high growth rates in tradable services. There is also scope for considerable growth from liberalization and the associated productivity gains in some of the services subsectors where growth has lagged behind in the 1990s. The distribution sector seems to be a prime candidate in this regard.

One caveat to our analysis is that the quality of the Indian national accounts data on services does not appear to be strong. Acharya (2003) shows that actual estimation of certain services is rather indirect and based on imprecise assumptions and lagged information. He also raises the issue that the change of base year to 1993/94 in the Central Statistical Organization (CSO) data may have affected the continuity of data and inflated the output of services sector in the 1990s. While there is merit in these arguments, there is, unfortunately, no easy way to verify the data quality. However, the comparability of data can be assessed over time by looking for a distinct break in the time series. In this context, we could not find evidence of any significant breaks, including in 1993/94. On the contrary, what we see is the growth acceleration in different services activities starting in different years, and also to be spread over a number of years rather than being confined to just one year.

The rest of the chapter is organized as follows. In Section 10.2, we place India's growth experience in perspective by reviewing the existing literature and cross-country evidence on sectoral transformation during growth. In Section 10.3, we identify the services activities where growth was particularly high in the 1990s. In Section 10.4, we analyze the various possible factors behind the recent dynamism of the services sector. Section 10.5 provides econometric analysis of the importance of each competing hypothesis to explain growth, and Section 10.6 concludes.

10.2 Growth and sectoral shares: cross-country experiences

The evolution of the sectoral shares in output, consumption, and employment as economies grow has been studied for well over fifty years. During the 1950s and 1960s, research by Kuznets and Chenery suggested that economic development would be associated with a sharp decline in the proportion of GDP generated by the primary sector, counterbalanced by a significant increase in industry and by a more modest increase in services.[6] Sectoral shares in employment were predicted to follow a similar pattern.

With the benefit of more data than was available to Kuznets and Chenery, recent literature has tended to emphasize the growing importance of services sector activity. For example, Kongsamut *et al.* (2001) analyze a sample of 123 countries for 1970–89 and show that rising per capita GDP is associated with an increase in services and a decline in agriculture both in terms of share in GDP and employment. In other words, the sectoral share given up by agriculture as the economy matures goes more to the services sector and less to industry than the Kuznets–Chenery work had suggested. The modern view is that as an economy matures, the share of services (in output, consumption, and employment) grows along with a decline in agriculture. By contrast, the share of industry first increases modestly, and then stabilizes or declines.

10.2.1   Share of services in output

Such a pattern of growth is visible in the cross-country data on shares in GDP presented in Table 10.2. These data suggest two stages of development. In the first, both industry and services shares increase as countries move from low income to lower middle income status, while in the second, the share of industry declines and that of services increases as the economy moves to upper middle and higher income levels.

How does the Indian experience fit in with this pattern? Through the 1980s at least, the fit is quite close. Figure 10.1 shows that in the period 1950–90, agriculture's share in GDP declined by about 25 percentage points, while industry and services gained equally. The share of industry has stabilized since 1990, and the entire subsequent decline in the share of agriculture has been picked up by the services sector. On the other hand, the share of services has risen by 8 percentage points in the 1990s, following a 5 percentage point gain during 1950–90. Consequently, at current levels, India's services share of GDP is higher than the average for other low income countries. A comparison of Tables 10.2 and 10.3 shows that the size of India's services sector, relative to GDP, is closer to the average of lower middle income countries.

Is India an outlier? The evidence suggests that though the Indian services sector is somewhat higher than the average, India is not that unusual. Figure 10.2 relates the share of services in GDP to the per capita income

Table 10.2   Global averages of sectoral shares of GDP in 2001[a] (in percent of GDP)

Income level	Agriculture	Industry	Services
Low income	24	32	45 Stage I
Lower middle income	12	40	48
Upper middle income	7	33	60 Stage II
High income	2	29	70

[a] Per capita GDP levels defined as follows: Low income < US$745; lower middle US$746–2975; upper middle US$2976–9205; and high > US$9206.

Source: World Bank, *World Development Indicators 2003* (Table 4.2).

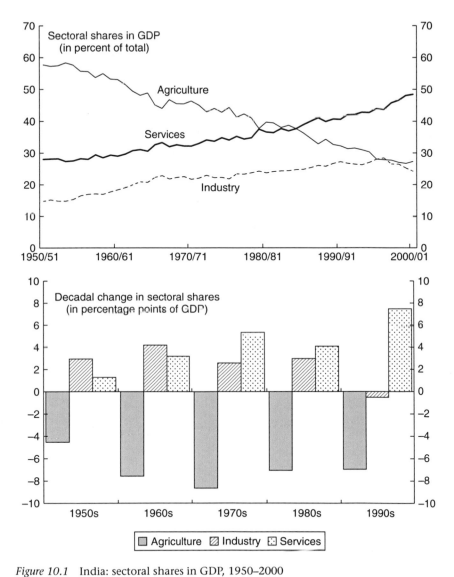

Figure 10.1   India: sectoral shares in GDP, 1950–2000

Sources: Central Statistical Organization, *National Accounts Statistics* (various years) and authors' estimates.

234

Table 10.3 India: sectoral shares of GDP, 1950–2003 (in percent of GDP)

Year	Agriculture	Industry	Services
1950	58	15	28
1980	38	24	38 Stage I
1990	33	27	41
2000	24	27	49 Stage II
2003	22	27	51

Sources: Central Statistical Organization, *National Accounts Statistics* (various years) and authors' estimates.

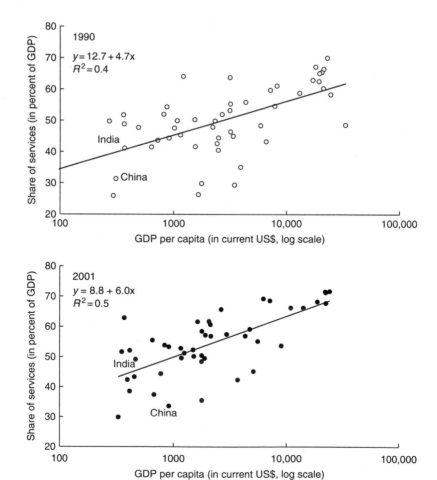

Figure 10.2 Cross-country comparison of per capita income and services share in GDP
Sources: World Bank, *World Development Indicators* (various years) and authors' estimates.

in 1990 and 2001 using data for various countries from the World Bank's *World Development Indicators* (WDI).[7] As is shown by the fitted line, the share of services in GDP is associated positively with per capita income; that is, the countries with higher per capita income also have a larger share of services in their GDP.

In 1990, the share of India's services sector in GDP was very close to the average share predicted by this linear relationship. As a result of rapid services growth in the 1990s, however, India's share in services had moved above the average share predicted by the cross-country experience by as much as 5 percentage points of GDP by 2001. Even so, in terms of having a large share of services in GDP, India is by no means an outlier. By contrast, the share of China's services sector in GDP is considerably below the cross-country average, as industry has been the driver of growth (Box 10.1).[8] In India's case, if different sectors were to grow at the same average growth rates experienced in 1996–2000, then by 2010, the share of services would increase to 58 percent. As a result, the size of India's services sector, relative to GDP, would be closer to that of an upper middle income country, even though India would still belong to the low income group.

Box 10.1   Services sector in China

India and China had quite similar sectoral shares of output in 1950. Over the next five decades, both countries experienced a sharp decline in the weight of agriculture in GDP. This process paused in China in the 1970s, but in the period since the early 1980s, when economic reforms commenced, agriculture's share has fallen by over half.

China. Sectoral shares in GDP

Year	Agriculture	Industry	Services
1951/52	50.5	20.9	28.6
1981/82	33.3	45.0	21.7
1991/92	21.8	43.9	34.3
2000/01	15.2	51.1	33.6

Sources: CEIC and authors' calculations.

Services was the fastest growing sector in India in the 1990s, but not in China. However, a notable feature of the comparison between India and China is that growth has been uniformly higher across sectors in the latter. There has, of course, been considerable debate about whether growth rates for China are overstated. Growth would still be higher in all sectors in China if the overstatement was limited to 1–2 percentage points—a common perception (for example, see IMF (1999)). Measurement issues aside, the higher growth in agriculture in China, particularly in the 1980s, is striking. Srinivasan (2002) attributes this to China having liberalized agriculture at an early stage, whereas this task still lies largely ahead in India.

Growth of services is least volatile in both India and China
For both countries, the coefficient of variations of sectoral growth rates show the services sector to be less volatile than industry, and much less volatile than agriculture. Even so, the volatility of growth is lower in China than in India if agriculture and industry are combined.

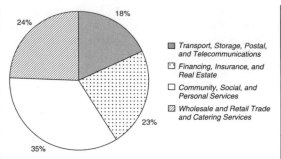

China: share of various activities in services sector in 2000 (in percent)

Sources: CEIC and authors' calculations.

Composition of the services sector is similar in India and China.
Although China's services sector is smaller as a share of GDP, the composition is much the same in both countries. The only significant difference is that community, social, and personal services are relatively larger in China. Since this sector includes government, this may reflect China's greater socialist orientation. The share of trade, hotels, and restaurants is correspondingly larger in India.

10.2.2 Share of services in employment

Even though India has experienced profound changes in output shares, the same is not true for employment shares (Table 10.4). A striking feature of India's development is that in contrast to the substantial decline in the share of agriculture in GDP, there has been rather little change in the share of employment in agriculture (Bhattacharya and Mitra, 1990). Similarly, although services rose from 42 to 48 percent of GDP during the 1990s, the employment share of services actually declined by about one percentage point during the decade. Thus, while output generation has shifted to services, employment creation in services has lagged far behind.[9] India's relatively jobless services sector growth is unlike the experience of other countries, where the services sector has also tended to gain a larger share of employment over time. India, in fact, has an exceptionally low share of services employment when compared with other countries (Figure 10.3).[10]

An interesting feature of Figure 10.3 is that the slope of the fitted line is greater than one. The normal pattern is thus for the share of services employment to rise faster than the share of output. This implies that labor productivity in services tends to fall as the services output increases.[11] In sharp contrast, since the labor share in services employment has been flat, labor productivity in Indian services has been increasing over time. In addition, the increase in labor productivity in Indian services has not been due to an increase in the relative capital intensity. This suggests that other factors have been at work in raising labor productivity, which could include the

Table 10.4   India: share of services sector in employment
and capital formation (in percent of total)

Year	Employment	Gross capital formation
1965/66	18.1	46.1
1970/71	20.0	43.7
1980/81	18.9	44.0
1990/91	24.4	41.2
1999/2000	23.5	39.6

Source: Hansda (2002b).

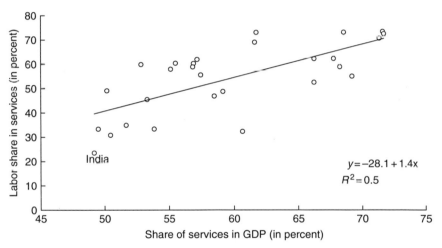

Figure 10.3   Cross-country comparison of services output and employment share
in 2001

Sources: World Bank, *World Development Indicators* (various years) and authors' estimates.

growth of services being concentrated in subsectors that are more dependent
on skilled labor than on unskilled labor or capital. This trend has no doubt
been reinforced by technological improvements, as well as by efficiency
gains resulting from liberalization (RBI, 2002). We return to these points in
Section 10.4.

10.3   Which services have grown rapidly?

In this section we identify the drivers of the acceleration in the growth in
services. The data on annual growth rate over the past 50 years (Figure 10.4)
suggest a structural break in growth in services starting in 1980. Through the

Table 10.5 India: services growth rates and sectoral shares

Sector	Activities included	Average growth in 1950s–70s and share of GDP in 1980[a]	Average growth in 1980s and share of GDP in 1990[a]	Average growth in 1990s and share of GDP in 2000[a]
Trade, hotels, and restaurants				
Trade (distribution services)	Wholesale and retail trade in commodities both produced at home (including exports) and imported, purchase and selling agents, brokers, and auctioneers	4.8	5.9	7.3
Hotels and restaurants	Services rendered by hotels and other lodging places, restaurants, cafes, and other eating and drinking places	4.8 (0.7)	6.5 (0.7)	9.3 (1.0)
Transport, storage, and communications				
Railways		4.2 (1.5)	4.5 (1.4)	3.6 (1.1)
Transport by other means	Road, water, and air transport, and other services incidental to transport	6.3 (3.6)	6.3 (3.8)	6.9 (4.3)
Storage		5.5 (0.1)	2.7 (0.1)	2.0 (0.1)
Communications	Postal, money orders, telegrams, telephones, overseas communication services, and miscellaneous communications	6.7 (1.0)	6.1 (1.0)	13.6 (2.0)

Financing, insurance, real estate, and business services Banking	Banks, Reserve Bank of India's Banking Department, post office savings bank, nonbank financial institutions, cooperative credit societies, and employees' provident funds	7.2 (1.9)	11.9 (3.4)	12.7 (6.3)
Insurance	Life, postal life, and nonlife	7.1 (0.5)	10.9 (0.8)	6.7 (0.7)
Dwellings, real estate		2.6 (4.0)	7.7 (4.8)	5.0 (4.5)
Business services		4.2 (0.2)	13.5 (0.3)	19.8 (1.1)
Legal services		2.6 0.0	8.6 0.0	5.8 0.0
Community, social, and personal services				
Public administration, defense		6.1 (5.3)	7.0 (6.0)	6.0 (6.1)
Personal services	Housekeeping, laundry, barber and beauty shops, tailoring, and other personal services	1.7 (1.6)	2.4 (1.1)	5.0 (1.1)
Community services	Education, research, scientific, medical, health, religious, and other community services	4.8 (4.0)	6.5 (4.3)	8.4 (5.5)
Other services	Recreation, entertainment, radio, TV broadcast, and sanitary services	3.4 (1.1)	5.3 (1.0)	7.1 (0.7)

[a] Share of GDP in parentheses.

Sources: Central Statistical Organization, *National Accounts Statistics* (various years) and authors' estimates.

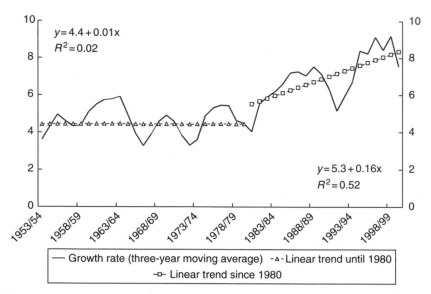

Figure 10.4   India: growth of services sector, 1953/54–2000/01 (annual percentage change)

Sources: Central Statistical Organization, *National Accounts Statistics* (various years) and authors' estimates.

1970s, the growth path was more or less flat, but the trend shifted upwards in the 1980s and then perhaps again in the 1990s. By contrast, the growth path for industry, which exhibited a declining trend during the period 1954–80, has been flat over the past two decades.

The acceleration in services growth in the 1980s and 1990s was not uniform across different activities. Some subsectors grew at a much faster rate than in the past, while other subsectors grew similar to the past trends (Table 10.5). To identify the growth drivers within the services sector, we compare the growth rates of various activities in the 1990s with their previous trend growth rates (Figure 10.5). The trend growth rates are estimated using the three-year moving average of the growth rate, with the period 1954–90 used in estimating the trend (except for banking, for which the trend is estimated using the data to 1980).

A comparison of the actual and the trend growth rates shows that growth in several services subsectors accelerated sharply in the 1990s (and for banking in the 1980s); indicating some sort of a structural break in their growth series. We call these activities fast growers. The remaining activities grew more or less at a trend rate; these we call trend growers.

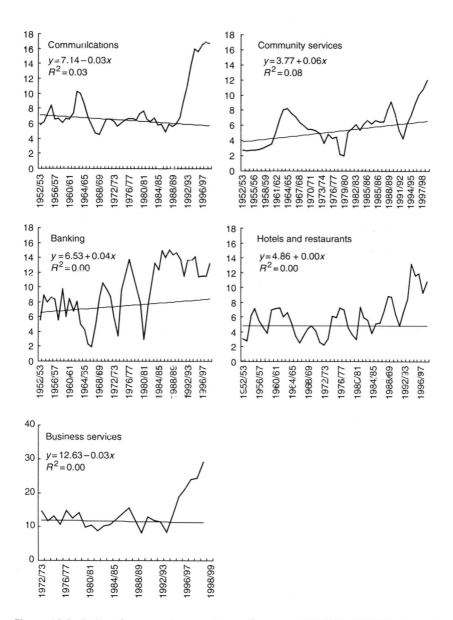

Figure 10.5 India: fast growing services subsectors, 1952/53–1998/99[a] (annual percentage change; three-year moving average)

[a] Except business services, which is 1972/73–1998/99.

Sources: Central Statistical Organization, *National Accounts Statistics* (various years) and authors' estimates.

10.3.1   Fast growers

Based on the above criterion, fast growers were as follows:

* Business services (including IT) was the fastest growing sector in the 1990s, with growth averaging nearly 20 percent a year. Though disaggregated data for this category are not available, export and software industry data indicate that the growth was mainly on account of the IT sector. Despite being the fastest growing sector, business services, particularly IT activity, was growing off a low base and its contribution to the services sector and GDP growth was quite modest in the 1990s. As we discuss later, this segment is expected to continue growing at a very high rate and is likely to contribute more significantly to services growth in the future.
* Communication services, which registered growth of 14 percent a year during the 1990s, made a significant contribution to services growth. The growth in communication was mostly due to telecommunications, which accounts for 80 percent of output.
* In the banking sector, growth jumped from about 7 percent over the period 1950–80 to 12 percent in the 1980s and 13 percent in the 1990s. Growth was most rapid in the nonbank financial institutions (which grew by 24 percent in the 1980s and 19 percent in the 1990s), followed by growth in the banks (by 10 and 9 percent, respectively, in the 1980s and 1990s). Overall, the contribution of banking to services sector growth was larger than that of the communications sector.
* Community services and hotels and restaurants increased at the trend growth rate through the early 1990s, but experienced a pick up in growth in the latter part of the decade. In community services, this was due to both education and health services (70 percent and 23 percent of value added, respectively) growing at an average rate of 8 percent in the 1990s.

10.3.2   Trend growers

Among the trend growers, the growth rate of distribution services (the largest services subsector in India) averaged about 6 percent in the 1980s, higher than in previous decades, and rose to about 7 percent in the 1990s. The rate of growth of public administration and defense averaged 6 percent in the 1990s, which was similar to the growth experienced in previous decades. Growth spiked in response to the Fifth Pay Commission awards to government employees in the late 1990s, but this did not substantially increase average sector growth for the decade as a whole.[12] The growth rate of personal services jumped to 5 percent in the 1990s, but remained below the growth in most other services activities. The other subsectors such as transport, dwellings, and storage grew more or less at the same rate in the 1980s and the 1990s as in previous decades.

10.3.3   Contribution of fast and trend growers to services growth

The fast growing activities accounted for about one-quarter of services output in the 1980s, but because of their relatively fast growth, these activities represented one-third of services output by 2000. We show the estimation of the average contribution of the fast growers and trend growers to services growth in the 1950s–1970s, the 1980s, and the 1990s in Figure 10.6. Based on our estimates, the high services growth in the 1980s was primarily due to the trend growing subsectors. These activities added about 1 percentage point of additional services growth in the 1980s, while fast growing activities made only about half the contribution. In the 1990s, by contrast, fast growing sectors made about the same contribution to services growth as the trend growing sectors. In fact, since the growth of trend growing sectors was about the same in the 1980s and the 1990s, the fast growers collectively accounted for almost all of the higher services growth in the 1990s. This is consistent with new activities and industries having sprung up in the fast growth subsectors, but not in the trend growth ones.

10.4   Explaining services sector growth

A number of studies have attempted to explain the fast growth in the share of services activity observed in cross-country data. The literature draws a distinction between demand and supply factors.[13] On the supply side, the output share of services can be boosted by a switch to a more services-input intensive method of organizing production. Such a change in production methods can arise as a result of increasing specialization as the economy matures. For example, over time, industrial firms may make greater use of specialist subcontractors to provide services that were previously provided by the firms themselves. Legal, accounting, and security services are obvious candidates to be contracted out. Bhagwati (1984) calls this process of specialization "splintering." Kravis (1985) points out that splintering can lead to growth in the share of services in GDP, even when GDP itself is not growing. On the demand side, an increase in the output share of services can arise from rapid growth in the final demand for services. This could be from domestic consumers with a high-income elasticity of demand for services, or from foreign consumers with a growing demand for the country's services exports. Demand-led growth of this type is likely to result, at least initially, in a rise in the prices of services, as well as a shift of resources into the production of services.

Services activity can also be stimulated by technological advances, whereby new activities or products emerge as a result of technological breakthrough; such advances are likely to be particularly relevant in the case of the IT and telecommunications sectors and to some extent in financial

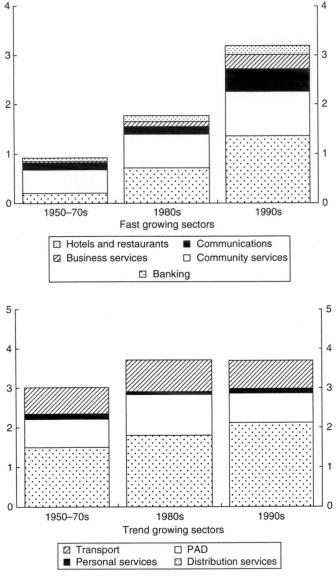

Figure 10.6 India: contribution of fast growers to services growth[a] (in percentage points of real GDP growth)

[a] Does not include the contribution of railways, legal services, storage, real estate, and other services. Hence, the total contribution shown here does not add up to the total growth rate of the services sector.

Sources: Central Statistical Organization, *National Accounts Statistics* (various years) and authors' estimates.

services (credit cards, ATMs, etc.). Liberalization can also provide a boost to services. In India, important policy reforms were made in the 1990s which were conducive to the growth of the services sector, such as deregulation, privatization and opening up to foreign direct investment (FDI). If the growth of services was previously inhibited by government controls, then policy changes may provide a positive shock that unleashes new activity and growth.

10.4.1 Splintering

As noted, changes in production technique can cause a firm to splinter and, as a result, the proportion of output originating in the services sector to increase. Such splintering would be reflected in an increase in the use of services as intermediate inputs but not as final demand. One way to estimate the importance of splintering to services growth in India is to measure the increase in input usage of services in other sectors through changes in the input–output coefficients. The matrices for different years show that the use of services sector inputs in industry increased by about 40 percent between 1979/80 and 1993/94; that is, the input–output coefficient increased from 0.15 to 0.21 (Table 10.6). In addition, the use of services inputs in agriculture almost doubled during this period, but still remained low (only 5 percent of the gross output).

Another way to show how important splintering has been in India is to look at the change in the input–output coefficients for services input in agriculture and industry, which increased by 0.03 and 0.04, respectively, during the 1980s. These coefficient changes would have increased demand

Table 10.6   India: evolution of input–output coefficients[a]

	Agriculture	Industry	Services
1979/80			
Agriculture	0.06	0.13	0.04
Industry	0.07	0.35	0.11
Services	0.02	0.15	0.10
1989/90			
Agriculture	0.17	0.04	0.04
Industry	0.14	0.37	0.17
Services	0.05	0.19	0.19
1993/94			
Agriculture	0.15	0.04	0.03
Industry	0.14	0.37	0.15
Services	0.05	0.21	0.20

[a] Units of input from a sector (in rows) required to produce one unit of output in a sector (in columns).

Source: Sastry *et al.* (2003).

for services (as a first round effect) by:

$$\Delta Y_S = 0.03 \, Y_A + 0.04Y_I \tag{10.1}$$

where Y_A, Y_I, and Y_S are output in agriculture, industry, and services, respectively. Dividing equation (10.1) through by total output Y and evaluating at the average sectoral shares during the 1980s (0.35, 0.25, and 0.40 for agriculture, industry, and services, respectively) yields:

$$\frac{\Delta Y_S}{Y_S} = \frac{((0.03 * 0.35) + (0.04 * 0.25))}{0.4} = 0.051 \tag{10.2}$$

or 5.1 percent over the decade. This would suggest that splintering may have added about 0.50 percentage point to annual services growth during the 1980s.

Since the latest input–output matrix for India is available only for 1993/94, data for the 1990s are only partial. However, a similar calculation for the period 1989/90–1993/94 yields a splintering effect on annual services growth of about 0.25 percentage point. Thus the increase in the use of services inputs is much less during the early 1990s than in the 1980s. We do not yet know whether this trend continued for the rest of the decade. However, it has already been seen that some of the fastest growing services activities in the 1990s were oriented toward final consumption (e.g. community services, communication services, and hotels and restaurants), and this would be consistent with splintering having played a less important role in boosting growth in the 1990s. Overall, thus, increases in the use of services input in other sectors over time may be partly responsible for the increase in services share in GDP. However, the changes in input usage do not appear to have accelerated in the 1990s and thus cannot explain the recent pickup in services growth.

10.4.2   Role of elastic final demand

How important a role has increasing final demand played in boosting services growth? First, the share of services in private final consumption expenditure has almost tripled since 1951 (Table 10.7). The available data do not permit a precise split of private final consumption expenditure into a goods and a services component. Nonetheless, a rough estimate can be made, which indicates a sharp rise in the growth of final demand for services in the 1990s. That is, final consumption of services grew at a rate broadly similar to services output in the 1990s (Table 10.8), whereas in the 1980s, final consumption of services grew at a slower rate (this is consistent with the observation that there may have been more splintering during the 1980s).

Another way of trying to understand how large a role could have been played by final demand is to examine the behavior of services output as a share of GDP. Figure 10.7 shows that the share in GDP of most services

Table 10.7 India: private final consumption of services

Year	Private final consumption (in percent of total)
1950/51	10.2
1970/71	13.4
1980/81	15.5
1990/91	20.4
1999/00	27.6

Source: Hansda (2002a).

Table 10.8 India: growth of services value added and final consumption and GDP (average annual percentage change)

Period	Service sector value added	Private final consumption of services	GDP
1970s	4.5	4.6	2.9
1980s	6.6	5.4	5.8
1990s	7.5	7.9	5.8

Sources: Central Statistical Organization, *National Accounts Statistics* (various years) and authors' estimates.

activities, fast as well as trend growers, has been increasing over time, which can best be described by a positive linear trend and consistent with the income elasticity of final demand for services being greater than one. However, the fast growers also exhibit a sharp increase in the ratio of output to GDP from the early 1990s. For increases in final demand to explain this rapid growth would imply huge increases in the elasticities of final demand for these activities, but there is no prior reason to expect this kind of behavioral change.

Thus, there seem to be other factors at play besides splintering and income elasticity. In addition, if the growth in services output was largely a demand side phenomenon, we should not see a decline in the relative price of the services, as we do in the data. Figure 10.8 shows that the fast growing subsectors were characterized by declining prices, which suggests that the growth in supply outpaced demand, or that productivity in these services increased. By contrast, prices in the trend growing subsectors rose faster than the GDP deflator (not shown here), which supports the theory that a different mix of supply and demand factors were at work here than in the case of the fast growers.

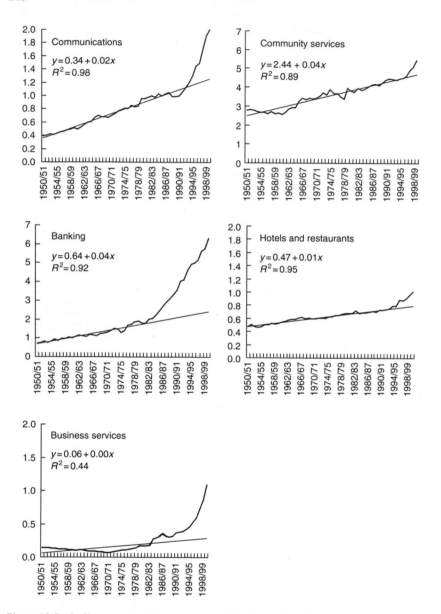

Figure 10.7 India: output of fast growers, 1950/51–1999/2000 (in percent of GDP)

Sources: Central Statistical Organization, *National Accounts Statistics* (various years) and authors' estimates.

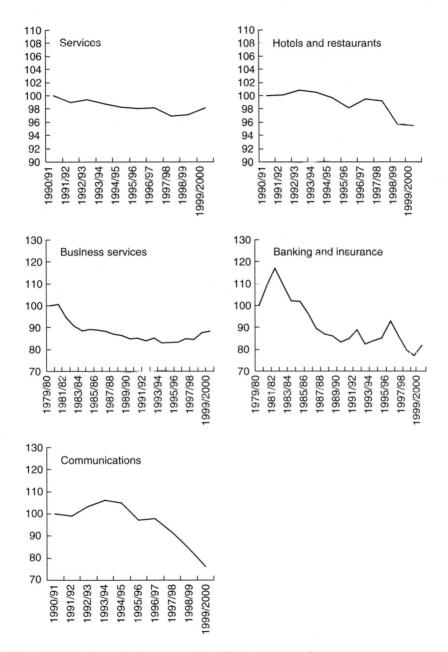

Figure 10.8 India: ratio of services price deflator to GDP deflator, 1990/91–1999/2000[a] (1991 = 100, in percent)

[a] Except business services and banking and insurance, which are 1979/80–1999/2000.

Sources: Central Statistical Organization, *National Accounts Statistics* (various years) and authors' estimates.

10.4.3   Role of foreign demand

With the advent of the IT revolution, it has become possible to deliver services over long distances at a reasonable cost, thus trade in services has increased worldwide. India has been a particular beneficiary of this trend. In India, exports of services (in US dollars) grew by an average of 15 percent a year in the 1990s, compared with 9 percent in the 1980s. Cumulatively, services exports increased fourfold in the 1990s and reached US$25 billion in 2002 (about US$7.5 billion of which was software exports). Services exports from India now exceed 1 percent of the global exports in services (Figure 10.9).[14]

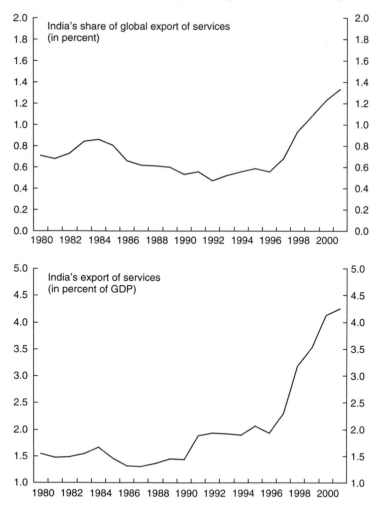

Figure 10.9   India: export of services, 1980–2001

Source: Salgado (2003).

The increase in services exports has been most dramatic in software and other business services (included in the miscellaneous services), but there has also been growth in the export of transport and travel services. As a result, the composition of services has changed dramatically in favor of miscellaneous services, which includes software exports (Figure 10.10).

In order to make a rough estimate of the contribution of services exports to growth, we need to first estimate the value added component of exports.

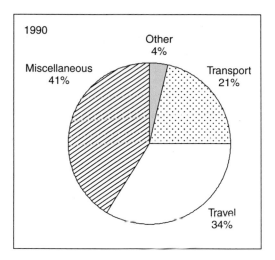

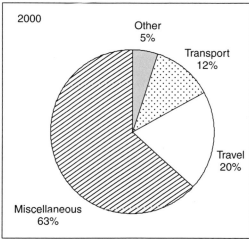

Figure 10.10   India: composition of export of services, 1990 and 2000 (in percent of total)

Source: Reserve Bank of India.

For this, we assume that input usage is same for services exports as for other services. From the input–output matrix, the input usage in services is roughly about 40 percent of gross output. Thus, about 60 percent of services exports would be value added. Assuming that this percentage remained broadly similar over time, we calculate the value added by services exports and its contribution to growth of the sector for each year in the 1980s and the 1990s. The contribution of exports to annual average services growth is calculated to be about 0.2 percentage points and 0.6 percentage points in the 1980s and the 1990s, respectively. Even though this contribution is fairly small, services exports have continued to grow rapidly in the current decade, with the growth of software exports averaging 39 percent per annum during 2000–03. With the IT sector expected to continue to flourish in the future, its contribution to growth will become increasingly significant over time.

10.4.4　Liberalization

Policy changes are also likely to be a factor behind the growth in services sector activity in India, especially changes relating to deregulation, the liberalization of FDI, and the privatization of government-owned services.[15] An example would be the telecommunications industry where inefficient provision of services by the government led to a situation of effective rationing of services until the early 1990s. As seen earlier, communications as a whole has been one of the fastest growing services subsectors in the 1990s, and liberalization undoubtedly played a major role.

In order to empirically test the relationships between services growth and liberalization measures, an index of liberalization is needed. Such an index is difficult to create using the available information. Nonetheless, preliminary evidence of the effect of reform-related measures on services growth is provided by analyzing the correlation between the flow of FDI and the increase in private sector participation in services to sector growth. The relationship between the cumulative flow of FDI and services growth in the 1990s' performance is found to be quite strong (even though this information is available only at a highly aggregated level, and the direction of causation is not clear *a priori*). The positive and significant association, as shown in Figure 10.11, holds even if we exclude the fastest growing communications sector. Similarly, the participation of the private sector in services activities also increased in the 1990s (for some activities, the share started increasing in the 1980s), as shown in Figure 10.12.[16] The relationship is likely to be stronger if we include business services, for which the data on private and public shares are not available, but most of which originate in the private sector.

10.4.5　Contribution of different factors in services growth

As the discussion above shows, many different factors played a role in explaining the growth of services in the 1990s, which we now attempt to estimate. We first estimate the trend part of the growth rates (which could be

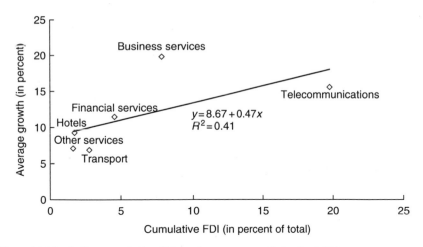

Figure 10.11 India: cumulative FDI and average growth in the 1990s

Sources: Central Statistical Organization, *National Accounts Statistics* (various years) and authors' estimates.

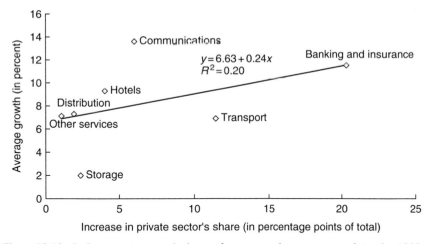

Figure 10.12 India: private sector's share of output and average growth in the 1990s

Sources: Central Statistical Organization, *National Accounts Statistics* (various years) and authors' estimates.

attributed to income elasticity and splintering effects). For this, we estimate the trend rate at which various services activities as a share of GDP increased up until 1990. We use this estimate to predict the size of the services sector during the 1990s. High income elasticity and splintering effects (unless the elasticities or the input–output coefficients change dramatically) would

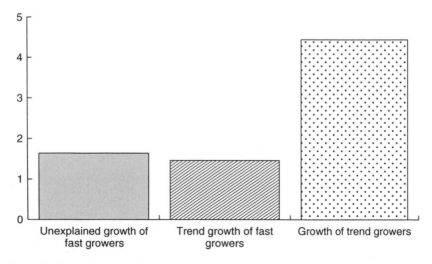

Figure 10.13   India: contributing factors to services growth in the 1990s

Sources: Central Statistical Organization, *National Accounts Statistics* (various years) and authors' estimates.

imply an increase in the share of services in GDP at a predetermined rate, but at one which is not likely to change much over time. We compare the actual share of services in GDP with our predicted share and calculate the difference. This residual (or excess) growth, which is positive for the fast growing sectors, cannot be attributed solely to elasticity and splintering effects, and therefore reflects other factors such as increased exports, policy reforms, and technological progress.[17]

As illustrated by Figure 10.13, the residual component of growth in fast growers on average accounted for 1.75 percentage points of growth of the services sector in the 1990s. The next step is to net out from the residual growth the amount of growth attributed to increased exports of services in the 1990s. This we estimate at about 0.50 percentage point. The remaining growth, or about 1.25 percentage points, can thus be attributed to factors such as reforms.

10.5   Empirical tests of competing hypotheses

Taking a different approach from Section 10.4, we empirically test for the significance of different factors in explaining growth. We estimate regression equations separately using time series data for each activity, and then pooled data for various activities. The right hand side variables in the regressions include measures of income, variations in input coefficients, trade in goods and services, and a measure of policy changes. Reasonable proxies are available for most of these variables, but constructing a satisfactory measure of policy changes in each subsector did not prove feasible.[18] We use two alternatives involving dummy variables in order to circumvent this limitation.[19]

First, we estimate separate regression equations using time series data to explain growth in each services activity. To capture the influence of reforms, we use a dummy variable for the 1990s. The justification for such a dummy is that reforms in the services sector were mostly carried out in the 1990s. After controlling for other effects, a significant coefficient for this dummy would indicate that there is an unexplained part of growth which could possibly be attributed to reforms.

The other approach we take is to use panel data for different services activities, where the observations are averaged over five-year periods. Instead of a general dummy for the 1990s, we construct a dummy variable which assigns a value 1 to activities that were liberalized in the second half of the 1980s (1980: 2), first half of the 1990s (1990: 1), and second half of the 1990s (1990: 2). However, this is only a marginal improvement over the previous approach, even so, the results are interesting as described.

10.5.1   Decade-specific dummies

For decade-specific dummies, we use a time series regression to estimate the following equation:

$$GSER_t^i = C^i + \alpha^i GCDTY_t + \beta^i GTRD_t + \gamma^i GEXS_t + \delta^i D80 + \lambda^i D90 + \varepsilon_t^i,$$

$$t = 1952 \ldots 2000, \quad \varepsilon^i \approx N(0, \sigma^{2i}) \tag{10.3}$$

The dependent variable in equation (10.3) is the annual growth rate in the ith services activity in year t. The right hand side variables include the growth rates of (i) the commodity producing sectors (GCDTY), (ii) the volume of the external trade of goods (GTRD), and (iii) the value of exports in services (GEXS). To smooth out the noise in the annual data, all growth rates are measured as three-year moving averages.[20] GCDTY is intended to capture the effect of income growth on final demand, as well as the effect of growth in other sectors on the demand for services inputs. GTRD is included to see whether increased openness of the economy to external trade has also resulted in higher growth for services. This link is expected to be important *a priori* for distribution services, transport, and hotels and restaurants. Finally, since certain sectors (especially business services and hotels and restaurants) are highly dependent on foreign demand, we include GEXS in the regressions. In order to account for any residual in growth, we also have separate dummies for the 1980s (D80) and the 1990s (D90).

The equations are estimated using ordinary least squares. Regression results reported in Table 10.9 show that for each fast growing subsector, the

Table 10.9 India: explaining services growth using time series data, 1952–2000[a]

	Fast growing activities						Trend growing activities		
	Business services	Communications	Financial services	Community services	Hotels and restaurants	Distribution	Transport	Public administration and defense	Personal services
Constant	2.010	5.800***	5.130***	4.900***	1.990***	2.520***	5.200***	7.140***	1.810***
	(0.86)	(8.10)	(3.95)	(6.60)	(3.50)	(4.80)	(10.70)	(8.40)	(4.25)
GCOMM	−0.006	0.120	0.820***	−0.030	0.720***	0.620***	0.120	−0.190	0.180*
	(−0.01)	(0.72)	(2.78)	(−0.18)	(5.56)	(5.24)	(1.11)	(−0.98)	(1.86)
GTRADE	−0.220	0.020	0.030	−0.020	0.070*	0.080**	0.100***	−0.110*	−0.050*
	(−1.45)	(0.40)	(0.36)	(−0.49)	(1.96)	(2.31)	(3.27)	(−1.88)	(−1.87)
GSEREX	0.440***	0.040	−0.090	0.010	0.005	−0.020	0.000	0.060	−0.030
	(3.70)	(1.20)	(−1.33)	(0.32)	(0.19)	(−0.76)	(−0.09)	(1.41)	(−1.43)
D80	9.300***	−0.710	2.920**	2.000***	−0.140	−0.450	−0.310	0.880	0.370
	(4.02)	(−1.01)	(2.29)	(2.78)	(−0.25)	(−0.88)	(−0.66)	(1.06)	(0.88)
D90	22.400***	5.900***	7.380***	5.400***	3.300***	1.160	0.070	0.610	3.530***
	(5.78)	(4.99)	(3.45)	(4.40)	(3.50)	(1.34)	(0.08)	(0.43)	(4.99)
R^2	0.620	0.740	0.420	0.370	0.700	0.550	0.360	0.110	0.660

[a] ***, **, * indicate significance at the 1, 5, and 10 percent levels, respectively. Regressions estimated using data for 1951–2000; the number of observations is 48 in each regression. T-value of each coefficient estimate in parentheses.

Source: Authors' estimates.

dummy for the 1990s is positive and highly significant. The demand side factors seem relatively less important in explaining growth in these activities, as their coefficients are mostly insignificant. The one exception is GEXS, which, unsurprisingly, has a positive and significant coefficient in the equation for business services (that is, IT). By contrast, in the equations for trend growing activities, at least one of the demand side variables has a significant coefficient. Another contrast is that the dummy for the 1990s is not significant in explaining the growth in most of the activities that grew at trend rates in the 1990s. The results also show that the dummy for the 1980s is significant for business, banking, and community services. For banking services, this could be due to the deregulation that began in the 1980s. For business services, the IT sector was almost nonexistent in the 1980s, so the growth is perhaps due to other activities included here. As expected, growth in commodity producing sectors and in the volume of external trade in goods are both important in explaining the growth in distribution services.

We considered two modifications in the regressions above. First, in order to capture the income effect on the growth of services demand, we include the growth rate of GDP (GGDP), rather than that of the commodity producing sectors. Second, we include separate dummies for the first and second half of the 1990s. The rationale for doing this is that some of the major reforms in the services sector were not carried out until the mid-1990s and may have affected growth more in the second half of the decade than in the first half. The results for the equation using GGDP are stronger, with its estimated coefficient larger and more significant for most activities, which is not surprising. Even with this variable, the significance of the dummy for the 1990s is retained. As expected, the results are also found to be stronger for the dummy for the second half of the 1990s than for the first half.

10.5.2 Sector-specific liberalization dummies

Using panel data regressions, we estimate the following equation controlling for fixed effects (which allows for intercepts to vary over different units).

$$\text{GSER}_{it} = C_i + \alpha \, \text{GIND}_{it} + \beta \, \text{GAGR}_{it}$$
$$+ \eta \, \text{GTG}_{it} + \gamma \, \text{GTS}_{it} + \delta \, \text{DSER}_{it} + \varepsilon_{it} \tag{10.4}$$

The regressions are estimated for the following services activities: trade, hotels, rail transport, transport by other means, storage, communications, insurance, as well as dwellings, business, community, banking, legal, and personal services. The time period used is 1970–2000, and the observations are averaged over the 1970s, 1981–85, 1986–90, 1991–95, and 1996–2000. The dependent variable is average annual growth rate in services activity i in period t. The right hand side variables are average growth rates in (i) industry (GIND) and agriculture (GAGR); (ii) the volume of external trade in goods

Table 10.10 India: explaining services growth using panel data, 1970–2000[a]

	I	II
GAGR	0.99	0.07
	(1.10)	(0.20)
GIND	1.33**	0.82*
	(2.12)	(1.88)
GTG	0.45	. . .
	(1.10)	. . .
GTS	0.15*	0.13
	(1.70)	(1.50)
DSER	5.70***	5.70***
	(3.60)	(3.60)
D90s		−1.10
		(−1.00)
R^2	0.65	0.65
Adjusted R^2	0.53	0.53
F-test for equality of	2.80 (F-statistic)	2.80 (F-statistic)
intercept across units	0.00 (p-value)	0.00 (p-value)

[a] ***, **, * indicate significance at the 1, 5 and 10 percent levels, respectively. T-value of each coefficient estimate in parentheses. The number of observations is 65 in each regression.

Source: Authors' estimates.

(GTG); and (iii) the value of exports of services (GTS) in period *t*. A dummy variable (DSER) measures whether reforms were carried out in each services subsector.

The variable which is found to be the most significant is the dummy variable for reform measures in each activity. Thus, the sectors that were opened up for FDI, external trade, or private ownership, and so on, were the ones which experienced faster growth. Among other variables, we find services growth to be significantly correlated with the growth in the industrial sector. As a robustness test, we check whether the dummy for the 1990s (D90s) yields a significant coefficient after controlling for the reform-specific dummy. Results in Column II of Table 10.10 show that the coefficient for D90s is no longer significant. Thus, we argue that the acceleration of the 1990s is likely due to reforms and that this variable is an important determinant of the higher growth during that decade.

10.6   Summary and conclusion

This chapter studies the growth of the services sector in India. It shows that in common with the experience of many other countries, the services sector in India has grown faster than agriculture and industry. As a result, the share of services in GDP has increased over time. In the 1990s, services growth was particularly strong, and this has led to the services share in output being relatively large in India compared to other countries at similar levels of development. What is also striking about India's growth experience is that the services sector does not appear to have created many jobs. Admittedly the employment data suffer from limitations. Nonetheless, unlike the experience of many countries where productivity growth in the services economy has tended to lag behind that of other sectors, it appears that the Indian services sector has been characterized as experiencing increasing labor productivity.

The acceleration in growth of the services sector in India in the 1990s was due to fast growth in the communications, banking services, business services (IT), and community services (education and health). The remaining sectors grew at a constant or trend growth rate. We show that factors such as high income elasticity of demand and increased input usage of services by other sectors have played an important part in elevating services growth. Also important, at least in the 1990s, have been factors such as economic reforms and the growth in foreign demand for services exports. Significant productivity gains appear to have occurred in the faster growing sectors, leading to a decline in their relative prices.

Our findings suggest that there is considerable scope for further rapid growth in India's service economy. That Indian services exports have strong future growth prospects is well known, but we also find that there is considerable scope for further rapid growth in other segments provided that deregulation of the services sector continues. Nevertheless, it is imperative that the industrial and agricultural sectors also grow rapidly. The relatively jobless nature of growth in India's services sector further underscores this need.

Notes

1. We are grateful to Shankar Acharya, Martin Cerisola, Deepak Mishra, Ashoka Mody, Sudip Mohapatra, Uma Ramakrishnan, Michael Wattleworth, and Sanjay Hansda for helpful comments on this chapter. We would also like to thank Mr. Kolli from India's Central Statistical Organization for his assistance with the data. Errors remain our own.
2. On a fiscal year basis ending March 31 of the stated year.
3. In this chapter, we focus on decadal performance, although there are other ways of subdividing the data, such as plan periods. Indeed, Acharya (2003) observes that services growth in India was close to the trajectory of industrial growth from 1950 to 1996/97, but that a marked divergence emerged during the Ninth Plan period (1997–2002), when services grew at 8.0 percent and industry at only 4.5 percent. In comparison to Table 10.1, a focus on plan performance tends to make the services revolution look both more dramatic and more recent in origin.
4. In this chapter, banking services include activities of commercial, post office, and savings banks, as well as nonbank financial institutions, cooperative credit societies, and employee provident funds. It excludes the insurance sector.

5. There have also been industrial sector reforms in India, which beg the question why industry has not grown as fast as services. A number of explanations suggest themselves: (i) poor infrastructure has acted as a bottleneck to industrial growth (on the other hand, some services subsectors such as transport, storage, and communications would have been equally affected); (ii) labor restrictions and small-scale reservations have disadvantaged industry more than services; (iii) the services sector has received more generous tax incentives; and (iv) faster growing services activities seem to be more intensive in skilled labor, with which India is well endowed.

6. Using pooled cross-section and time-series data, Chenery and Taylor (1968) found the industry share in GDP to be positively associated with income and population and negatively associated with primary exports. This implied a tendency for industry to gain as income rose, but that the gain would be less pronounced in small countries with substantial natural resource endowments.

7. The sample includes countries with annual GDP of more than US$10 billion for which the data are available in the World Bank's *World Development Indicators* (WDI) (55 countries).

8. One view is that this is a legacy of a centrally planned economy, where the primary focus was on agriculture and industry. Under this system, many services (such as transportation, finance, and education and health for workers) were provided by the state-owned enterprises themselves and thus would have been classified as industrial activity. Another view is that the data on China's services sector is underestimated by about 5–10 percentage points of GDP due to underreporting of the informal sector. Salient features of China's services sector are summarized in Box 10.1.

9. Some observers have stressed that Indian employment data are not of high quality. Even so, anecdotal evidence suggests that employment growth in some of the fast growing services subsectors has been quite modest. For example, the NASSCOM/McKinsey outlook for the Indian IT sector predicts that exports will rise to US$50–60 billion over the next few years, but that only a few million jobs will be created in the process.

10. Employment data in 2001 are available for fewer countries, thus Figure 10.3 includes only 28 of the 46 countries covered in Figure 10.2.

11. Earlier evidence showed that the primary cause of the higher employment share of services in the United States was the slow growth of services productivity (Inman, 1985). However, more recent work by Slifman and Corrado (1996) indicates that some of the apparent slow growth in labor productivity in the United States may be due to errors in measuring output and prices.

12. Acharya (2002) estimates that improper deflation of the effects of the Fifth Pay Commission in the National Accounts led to an overstatement of the growth of government services (i.e. public administration and defense) in the late 1990s. Hansda (2002a) recognizes that there may have been some upward distortion in the estimates for a few years as a result of the Pay Commission, but note that this was not of sufficient magnitude to affect the trend in services growth, which increased in the 1990s, even if public administration and defense is excluded altogether.

13. Kravis (1985) and Francois and Reinhart (1996).

14. Salgado (2003).

15. Technically, it is the relative speed of liberalization that counts—service activity can be stimulated by rapid deregulation of services or by slow liberalization of other sectors, such as industry.

16. Joshi (2002) examines the relationship between overall growth and the private and public shares of investment and GDP since the 1960s. He notes that there has been a significant increase in the share of investment by the private sector during the 1990s, and this has been matched by a faster growth of the services output originating in the private sector.
17. By definition, we find that trend growers do not exhibit any residual growth. The entire growth in these activities is attributed to elasticity and splintering effects.
18. A more precise way to account for the effect of reforms on services would have been to create separate indices for liberalization in the industry, external, and the services sectors. However, usually more than one type of reforms was carried out in a particular year, so it is not possible to create separate dummies for liberalization in different sectors.
19. Using simple dummy variables is a very crude way to proxy reforms. They have the limitations that the dummies cannot be used to isolate the effects on growth of reforms or other events that might have been happening in the 1990s. In addition, these dummies neither precisely capture the timing of the reforms nor measure the extent or intensity of reforms.
20. See Table 10.11 for a complete description of the data.

Table 10.11   Sources of data and construction of variables

Variable name	Construction of variable[a]	Source
Variables used in regression equation (10.3)		
$GROW_i$	Average growth rate of output in activity i during the 1990s	Own calculations using Central Statistical Organization (CSO) data
GCDTY	Three year moving average of growth rate in the commodity producing sectors	Own calculations using CSO data
GTRADE	Three-year moving average of growth rate of the volume of external trade (exports and imports) of goods	Own calculations using data from *Reserve Bank of India (RBI) Bulletins*
GSEREX	Three-year moving average of growth rate of services exports	Own calculations using data from *RBI Bulletins*
D80	Dummy variable which takes the value one for the years 1981–90, and 0 otherwise	
D90	Dummy variable which takes the value one for the years 1991–2000, and 0 otherwise	
Variables used in regression equation (10.4)		
$GROW_{it}$	Average growth rate of activity i in period t	Own calculations using CSO data
GIND	Average growth rate of industrial sector	Own calculations using CSO data

Continued

Table 10.11   Continued

Variable name	Construction of variable[a]	Source
GAGR	Average growth rate of agriculture	Own calculations using CSO data
GTMERC	Average growth rate of external trade (exports and imports) of merchandise	Own calculations using data from *RBI Bulletins*
GTSER	Average growth rate of exports of services	Own calculations using data from *RBI Bulletins*
DSER	Dummy variable, which takes a value 1 if a particular services activity was liberalized significantly in period *t*, and 0 otherwise. The following observations were assigned a value of 1: hotels (1990: 1 and 1990: 2), transport by other means (1990: 2), community services (1990: 2). All other observations were accorded a value 0. 1990:1 signifies first half of the 1990s	Created using information from many different sources

[a] All growth rates are calculated using data in constant prices; external trade data are in US dollars.

Source: Authors' descriptions.

References

Acharya, Shankar, 2003, "What's Happening in Services," *Business Standard* (Mumbai) (December 23).

——, 2002, "India's Medium-Term Growth Prospects," *Economic and Political Weekly* (July 13), pp. 2897–906.

Bhagwati, Jagdish, 1984, "Splintering and Disembodiment of Services and Developing Nations," *World Economy*, Vol. 7, No. 2, pp. 133–43.

Bhattacharya, B.B. and Arup Mitra, 1990, "Excess Growth of Tertiary Sector in Indian Economy, Issues and Implications," *Economic and Political Weekly* (November 3), pp. 2445–50.

CEIC Economic Database (India), CEIC Data Company Ltd. (Hong Kong).

Chenery, Hollis B. and L.J. Taylor, 1968, "Development Patterns: Among Countries and Over Time," *Review of Economics and Statistics*, Vol. 50, pp. 391–416.

Francois, Joseph, F. and Kenneth A. Reinhart, 1996, "The Role of Services in the Structure of Production and Trade: Some Stylized Facts from a Cross-Country Analysis," *Asia-Pacific Economic Review*, Vol. 1, No. 2 (May).

Hansda, Sanjay Kumar, 2002a, "Services Sector in the Indian Economy: A Status Report," *RBI Staff Studies* (Mumbai: Reserve Bank of India, Department of Economic Analysis and Policy).

——, 2002b, *Sustainability of Services and Services-Led Growth: An Input Output Exploration of the Indian Economy* (Mumbai: Reserve Bank of India).

Inman, Robert, P. (ed.) 1985, "Introduction and Overview," in *Managing the Service Economy: Prospects and Problems* (Cambridge: Cambridge University Press).

International Monetary Fund, 1999, *World Economic Outlook* (Washington, DC).

Joshi, Dharmakirti, 2002, "The Public Private Balance: A Macro View," Discussion Paper Series (Mumbai: CRISIL Center for Economic Research).

Kongsamut, Piyabha, Sergio Rebelo, and Danyang Xie, 2001, "Beyond Balanced Growth," IMF Working Paper 01/85 (Washington, DC: International Monetary Fund).

Kravis, Irving, B., 1985, "Services in World Transactions," in *Managing the Service Economy: Prospects and Problems*, ed. by Robert P. Inman (Cambridge: Cambridge University Press).

Ministry of Statistics and Programme Implementation (various years) *National Accounts Statistics* (New Delhi: Central Statistical Organization).

Reserve Bank of India, 2002, *Report on Currency and Finance 2000–01* (Mumbai).

Salgado, Ranil, 2003, "India's Global Integration and The Role of the IT Sector," in *India: Selected Issues and Statistical Appendix*, IMF Staff Country Report No. 03/261 (Washington, DC: International Monetary Fund).

Sastry, D.V.S., Balwant Singh, Kaushik Bhattacharya, and N.K. Unnikrishnan, 2003, "Sectoral Linkages and Growth Prospects: Some Reflections on the Indian Economy," in *Economic and Political Weekly*, Vol. 38, No. 24, pp. 2390–97.

Slifman, L. and C. Corrado, 1996, "Decomposition of Productivity and Unit Costs," mimeo (Washington, DC: Board of Governors of the Federal Reserve System).

Srinivasan, T.N., 2002, "China and India: Growth and Poverty, 1980–2000," mimeo (New Haven, CT: Yale University).

World Bank (various years), *World Development Indicators* (Washington, DC).

11
Capital Account Controls and Liberalization: Lessons for India and China

Jonathan Anderson[1]

11.1   Capital controls in emerging markets

The extensive literature on capital controls and capital account liberalization in emerging market economies generally identifies two types of capital controls: first, targeted measures aimed at slowing the pace of short-term portfolio inflows and outflows; and second, pervasive restrictions on a broader range of external capital transactions.[2]

In the first category, a country which may already be fairly open to portfolio capital flows experiences a period of "overheated" portfolio inflows, or sharp outflows in a crisis environment, and as a result adopts measures to moderate the resulting pressures on the economy. Brazil, Chile, Colombia, Malaysia, and Thailand are commonly cited examples. The tool kit for managing capital flows includes unremunerated reserve requirements, limits on open currency positions, taxes on cross-border flows, quantitative limits on portfolio transactions, and regulated interest rates for nonresident accounts.

The most important characteristics of these measures are (i) they are generally short-term in nature, aimed at specific episodes of excessive volatility; (ii) policymakers' main concern is the domestic impact on interest rates and money growth; and (iii) they are almost always associated with fixed exchange rates.

By contrast, the second category of capital controls applies to more closed economies, usually in a state-led planning context, such as the developing economies in Latin America and Asia before the mid-1980s, or transition economies such as the former Soviet Union and China. Here, the purpose is to allow full policy control of domestic resources without worrying about external influence and volatility; in many cases, the authorities are interested in sheltering the domestic banking system from external competition, and, more generally, protecting the economy from the effects of resource misallocation. As a result, the tools for the second category are also different: outright prohibitions on inflows and outflows, mandatory approvals for capital transactions, multiple exchange rate regimes, selective granting of licenses for cross-border investment, and often current account restrictions as well.

Which countries control capital flows? Quantitatively, this turns out to be a very difficult question to answer. The IMF's Annual Report on Exchange Arrangements and Exchange Restrictions (AREAER) does provide a fairly exhaustive list of external capital account restrictions according to standardized categories, but it is far from straightforward to gauge the actual "tightness" of restrictions simply by looking at the legal provisions. IMF staff calculations for the year 1997 show that most emerging markets maintain at least some effective restrictions on capital flows; as Figure 11.1 shows, the average restrictiveness score for 15 major emerging markets was 5 out of 10 (10 being the most restrictive).

For Asian countries, we create an index of capital account restrictiveness based on the following three measures: (i) the number of capital account categories in which countries maintain restrictions, according to the IMF's AREAER; (ii) a subjective assessment of the "tightness" of restrictions—that is, how easy it is in practice to move portfolio capital in and out of regional economies (based on investors' trading experience); and (iii) the historical volatility of non-foreign direct investment (FDI) capital flows (defined later), measured as the difference between peak inflows and peak outflows (as a share of gross domestic product (GDP)).

The results are shown in Figure 11.2. As expected, China and India appear as the most restrictive Asian countries, followed by the mid-size Asian export economies (Indonesia, Korea, Philippines, Malaysia, Taiwan, and Thailand). It also comes as no surprise that the higher income Asian group of Japan, Singapore, and Hong Kong maintain much more open capital account regimes.

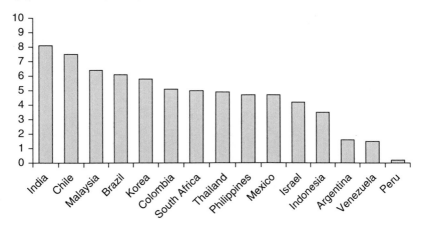

Figure 11.1 Capital account restrictiveness index in emerging market economies[a]

[a] An index of "10" signifies complete restrictiveness.

Source: Ariyoshi *et al.* (2000).

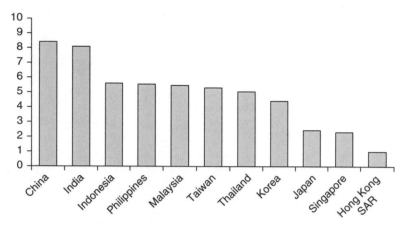

Figure 11.2 Capital account restrictiveness index in Asian economies[a]
[a] An index of "10" signifies complete restrictiveness
Source: Ariyoshi *et al.* (2000).

11.2 Do capital controls "work"?

Before discussing the liberalization experience, we need to address the basic question of whether capital controls have proven effective in the first place. And, in fact, the evidence is profoundly mixed. Most episodes of targeted restrictions slowed inflows or outflows, but generally did not relieve underlying pressures or fully insulate the economy (e.g. Chile in the 1990s, Venezuela in the mid-1990s and recent years, Thailand in the mid- to late-1990s, and Malaysia since 1997). Economies with more extensive capital restrictions have had more success in avoiding external imbalances and pressures, such as China during the Asian financial crisis. However, even a restrictive regime is no guarantee of immunity (India's balance of payments crisis of 1991–92 is a good example).

The broad correlation between capital account restrictiveness and the capital flow volatility is shown in Figure 11.3, providing some general results for Asian economies. The measure of volatility focuses on portfolio capital flows (defined as identified non-FDI flows in the balance of payments plus so-called errors and omissions—which we assume to be predominantly capital account-related).The left bar of the chart shows the largest absolute inflow/outflow as a share of GDP (from 1980 onward) and the right bar the maximum "swing," that is, the difference between the historical peak inflow and the historical peak outflow. As expected, China and India show up as relatively stable, while very open economies such as Hong Kong and Singapore recorded much larger portfolio movements. Despite its relatively

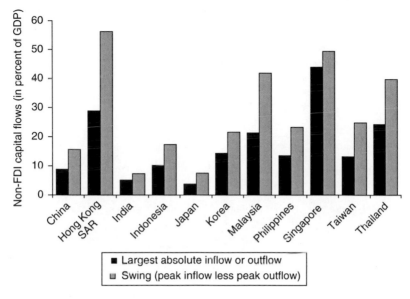

Figure 11.3 Capital volatility in Asia
Sources: CEIC Data Company Ltd and UBS estimates.

open capital account profile, Japan recorded the smallest portfolio swings in the region—but this can also be explained by the large absolute size of the Japanese economy.

Looking at Figures 11.4 through 11.7, however, we find that the experience of individual Asian economies is not so straightforward. Figures 11.4, 11.5, and 11.6 portray historical balance of payments flows for China, India, and Japan respectively over the past 15 years, and Figure 11.7 shows the same trends for the remaining Asian economies as a group.

As before, India and Japan have both seen very limited capital volatility when calculated as a share of GDP (despite their very different stances on capital account restrictions). On the other hand, the data for China are very surprising; despite having the most restrictive capital account regime on paper, the actual volatility of capital flows was substantial—in fact, the swing in flows was just as large as for the rest of Asia as a region, with a peak-to-trough range of more than 15 percent of GDP. In short, it is difficult to conclude that capital controls have been uniformly effective in the Asian region.

Finally, there is another, broader sense in which capital controls have proved ineffective. Remember that the stated purpose of capital account restrictions is to promote macroeconomic stability and protect economies from undue volatility; however, regional experience suggests that by giving domestic policymakers more leeway to "misbehave" at home, restrictive

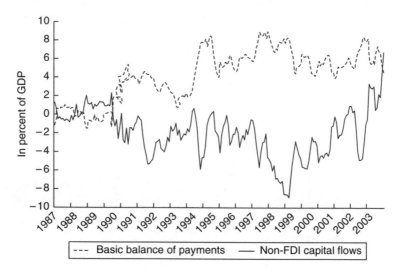

Figure 11.4　China: balance of payments flows, 1987–2003
Sources: CEIC Data Company Ltd and UBS estimates.

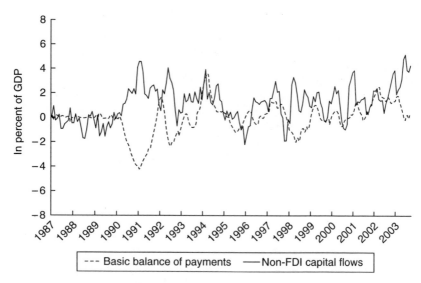

Figure 11.5　India: balance of payments flows, 1987–2003
Sources: CEIC Data Company Ltd and UBS estimates.

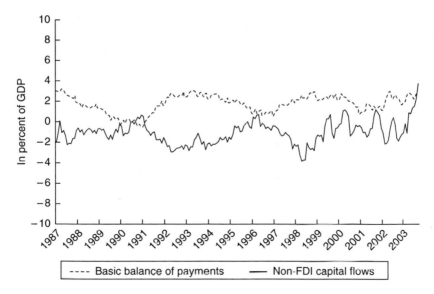

Figure 11.6 Japan: balance of payments flows, 1987–2003
Sources: CEIC Data Company Ltd and UBS estimates.

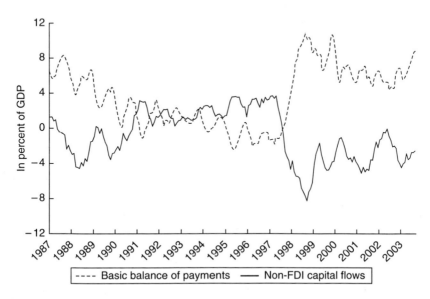

Figure 11.7 Balance of payments flows for Asia ex-Japan, 1987–2003
Sources: CEIC Data Company Ltd and UBS estimates.

external controls can actually worsen the situation by misallocating resources at home. For example, if we look at the (pre-1997) history of Asian "bubbles," we find that most tended to occur in an environment of insulated capital flows without external market discipline (most notably Japan, Korea, Taiwan, and Thailand in the 1980s, and China in the 1990s).

11.3 The lessons of liberalization

To begin with, a word on the theoretical effects of capital account opening. There is a diverse body of academic literature on the topic, but most authors tend to agree on the following points:

- *Volatility*: Nearly everyone agrees that capital account liberalization can lead to significant external and domestic volatility, particularly if countries are unprepared. The large "sequencing" literature stresses the role of financial sector development, macroeconomic policy capacity, and exchange rate management in managing the volatility.
- *Direction*: In theory, liberalization can lead to net inflows just as often as to net outflows, depending on macroeconomic management and the relative level of domestic returns.
- *Desirability*: Needless to say, there have been sharp divisions and debates over the desirability of liberalization following the financial crises of the 1990s; however, the mainstream answer is still a guarded "yes."

In practice, the liberalization experience has brought both "good" and "bad" examples, which provide interesting lessons in each case.

On the positive side, developed economies generally had an easier time liberalizing capital transactions. This reflects in part the strength of market institutions and the depth of domestic financial and macroeconomic policy capacity—and in part "good timing," as the richer countries generally opened at a time when global capital flows were much smaller as a share of output. Among emerging markets, we have seen far fewer unambiguous success stories with portfolio capital liberalization during the past 15 years; Chile, Hungary, Malaysia, Peru, and Taiwan are among the commonly cited examples. These cases are connected by three common factors: (i) gradual opening, (ii) supporting macroeconomic policies; and (iii) good luck in the timing of liberalization.

On the negative side, the 1997–98 Asian crisis is a textbook example of how relatively rapid liberalization combined with weak macroeconomic policy capacity led to disaster. Two factors in particular stand out: (i) Asian countries kept fixed exchange rates too long; and (ii) most economies had very poor banking supervision and regulation. The "budget trap" has been another common pitfall, as a number of rapid liberalization cases (such as Russia, Romania, and Argentina) foundered on their inability to resolve chronic underlying fiscal problems—and once again, fixed exchange rates are a key culprit in the process.

11.4 The experiences of China and India

In terms of the timing and process of capital account liberalization, India and China have been remarkably similar. Both started with a more or less completely closed capital account in the 1970s and the 1980s, in the context of a heavily state-influenced, planned economy. And in both countries, the first wave of liberalization came in the early 1990s in the context of wider reforms—in India as part of the restructuring package after the 1991 balance of payments crisis, and in China during the external opening championed by Deng Xiaoping.

India's liberalization initially focused on FDI and equity portfolio inflows, and subsequently widened to include investment in some debt instruments as well as equity outflows. Cross-border credit and other portfolio transactions are more heavily regulated, and as we saw above, have been relatively limited (to date, most portfolio flows relate to nonresident Indian accounts). Since the mid-1990s, the stated aim has been to move toward full convertibility, and in 1997 the so-called Tarapore Committee issued a detailed framework and time plan. However, the outbreak of the Asian crisis slowed momentum through the early part of the current decade, and as of this writing the capital account remains relatively closed (as shown by the historical lack of stock market or interest rate correlation vis-à-vis overseas counterparts). In terms of supporting measures, India's banking system is considered to be among the better regulated in Asia; the main area of concern is the government budget, as the fiscal deficit remains large and outstanding debt is substantial.

In China, the initial liberalization was limited to FDI inflows, and this remained the case for the rest of the decade. The original intent was to take advantage of strong investment interest on the part of Hong Kong and Taiwanese companies, but the subsequent bubble economy led to a veritable explosion of FDI inflows from all sources. Since 2000, we have seen a very cautious opening of equity inflows as well as FDI outflows, but most remaining portfolio transactions remain strictly controlled. As in India, Chinese equity and debt markets have almost no historical correlation to outside markets (and unlike India, the lack of correlation persists through to the present day). However, as noted earlier, China recorded very substantial informal capital outflows during the 1990s, mostly in the form of unrecorded "errors and omissions," and is now receiving significant informal capital inflows. Therefore, what appear to be onerous capital regulations on paper are often successfully surmounted by Chinese firms and financial institutions.

As in India, the Chinese government announced its intention to pursue full capital account convertibility in the mid-1990s—and also as in India, plans were broadly put on hold following the onset of the Asian crisis, where they remain today. On the other hand, China's fiscal position compares favorably to that in India, with a smaller consolidated deficit, relatively low debt and rapidly growing tax revenues. However, the Chinese state banking system is in considerably worse shape than Indian financial institutions. Indeed, the condition of banks is one of the biggest obstacles to further aggressive capital account liberalization in China.

11.5   China versus India—who wins?

In comparing the capital liberalization experiences of India and China, there is a common perception that the "Chinese model" has been more successful and should be emulated by other emerging market economies. This conclusion is based on (i) the very high FDI inflows into the mainland economy; (ii) the absence of external crises or volatility; and (iii) the high and stable official domestic growth performance.

We agree that China's experience has been positive and highlights the need to move gradually and methodically. However, we also find that the common perceptions stated earlier are somewhat misguided. First of all, while China's FDI inflows have been high as a share of GDP, peak FDI inflows into other economies have been higher—and there is actually a positive correlation between portfolio capital openness and FDI (Figure 11.8). Second, as we saw above, China's non-FDI capital flows have been quite volatile, with higher average volume as a share of GDP compared to India. Finally, when measured correctly, China's domestic growth pattern has been anything but stable, with three distinct boom–bust cycles over the past

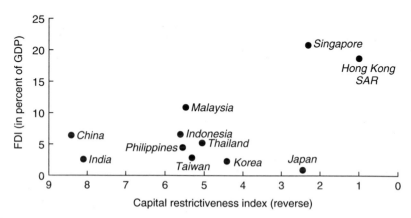

Figure 11.8   Capital openness versus peak FDI inflows for Asia

Sources: CEIC Data Company Ltd and UBS estimates.

20 years. In other words, when put in proper perspective, the relative experiences of China and India have actually been quite similar—that is, China does not represent a more successful "third path."

11.6 Summary lessons for China and India

Looking at the relevant experience of other emerging markets, as well as the history of China's and India's own liberalization experience, we see four broad lessons for the two economies. As it turns out, these are very much in line with the general academic consensus, but we feel they bear repeating here in any case.

First, go forward—but at a rational pace. China and India themselves are an eloquent testament to the long-term benefits of external opening; however, throwing open the doors to unfettered portfolio capital flows can very easily lead to excessive volatility and macroeconomic risks, particularly in economies with such a long history of closed markets and state-led growth models.

Second, resolve banking system problems before liberalizing credit and portfolio movements. This applies not only to banks' balance sheets *per se*, but also to broader corporate restructuring, privatization, and the establishment of effective prudential supervision.

Third, ensure that the economy has adequate macroeconomic and financial policy capacity. In China, the main areas for improvement (aside from the banking system) are the liberalization of interest rates and the development of market-based monetary policy instruments. In India, by far the main obstacle is the control of fiscal deficits.

Finally, move to a flexible exchange rate regime. Nearly every emerging financial crisis has involved a "one-way" bet on the currency—and countries are particularly vulnerable during initial portfolio liberalization. Here, India has already made significant strides, while China is still exploring the issue at home.

Notes

1. Chief Economist, Asia, UBS Investment Bank.
2. See, for example, Edwards (1998), Eichengreen and Mussa (1998), Ariyoshi *et al.* (2000), and De Gregorio *et al.* (2000).

References

Ariyoshi, Akira, Karl Habermeier, Bernard Laurens, Inci Ötker-Robe, Jorge Iván Canales-Kriljenko, and Andrei Kirilenko, 2000, *Capital Controls: Country Experiences with Their Use and Liberalization*, IMF Occasional Paper No. 190 (Washington, DC: International Monetary Fund).
CEIC Economic Database, CEIC Data Company Ltd. (Hong Kong).

De Gregorio, José, Sebastian Edwards, and Rodrigo O. Valdés, 2000, "Controls on Capital Inflows: Do They Work?," NBER Working Paper No. 7645 (Cambridge, MA: National Bureau of Economic Research).

Edwards, Sebastian, 1998, "Capital Flows, Real Exchange Rates, and Capital Controls: Some Latin American Experiences," NBER Working Paper No. 6800 (Cambridge, MA: National Bureau of Economic Research).

Eichengreen, Barry, and Michael Mussa,1998, *Capital Account Liberalization: Theoretical and Practical Aspects*, IMF Occasional Paper No. 172 (Washington, DC: International Monetary Fund).

Union Bank of Switzerland (UBS), Zurich.

12
Capital Account Liberalization: The Indian Experience

Narendra Jadhav[1]

12.1 Introduction

When India and China successfully withstood the contagion from the East Asian crisis in 1997, the relatively restrictive capital account regime of these two countries was generally highlighted as the savior. Unlike the pre-crisis period when capital controls were generally viewed as a taboo, policy thinking in the post-crisis period has changed dramatically, with several emerging market economies slowing down the pace and content of liberalization of capital controls with a view to limiting their vulnerability to crisis. The benefits and costs of an open capital account appear more ambiguous today than what many researchers and policymakers had believed in the pre-crisis period. In this context, the approach to capital account liberalization as adopted by India and China has become an important subject of international policy discussions.

"When knowledge is limited, the rule for policymakers should be—first do no harm."[2] Forms of liberalization that may not solve any problem but can potentially become a source of instability and must be avoided. Following this dictum, India has followed a gradual and calibrated approach toward capital account liberalization. In particular, the Indian policy toward capital flows has laid emphasis on encouraging larger non-debt and longer-maturity debt flows, since the benefits associated with such flows may clearly outweigh the costs. On the other hand, the policy has retained controls on short-term debt inflows and also on capital outflows involving residents.

Today, the policy challenges for India arising from capital account liberalization broadly fall under two categories:

- Management of the surge in capital flows, and
- Achieving preconditions that could create room for further liberalization of the capital account.

On the management of flows, in the face of weak domestic absorption of foreign capital and with a managed float exchange rate regime in India, the

275

large reserves accretion in recent years has given rise to a challenge on the monetary management front. Even though effective sterilization has helped in regaining control over the money supply, the costs associated with sterilization have been an issue, which is still being widely debated. Some have even argued that the reserves accumulation policy has adverse growth implications and must be abandoned in favor of a regime characterized by a flexible exchange rate and full market absorption of foreign capital. Others view the recent surge in capital flows as a response to positive interest rate differentials in the face of a stable/appreciating exchange rate. Therefore, the conditions that cause such surge in inflows must change. On the preconditions for the further liberalization of flows, some argue that the overemphasis on such, in particular fiscal consolidation and a strong financial system, has also been viewed as the factor that has slowed progress on liberalization of capital account. All these views clearly indicate the trade-offs that may be involved in current policy choices in the context of capital account liberalization. This chapter is aimed to clarifying some of these issues based on an assessment of the costs and benefits of capital account liberalization against the background of India's specific circumstances and needs.

Section 12.2 reviews the received wisdom on capital account liberalization by drawing upon theoretical literature as well as country experiences. The preconditions that emerge are also briefly discussed before dealing with issues involved in the sequencing of capital account liberalization. A cross-country perspective on the policy preference for the broad framework of capital account liberalization is provided in Section 12.3 by assessing the impact of capital account liberalization on improving allocative efficiency, disciplining macroeconomic policy, and spurring economic growth. Also discussed are the effectiveness of capital controls; and the appropriateness of the international financial architecture to deal with challenges arising from capital mobility. Section 12.4 details India's approach, which has been diagnosed against the above benchmarks.

12.2   Costs and benefits, preconditions and sequencing

Capital controls have conventionally been used the world over to deal with situations of weak balance of payments. Over time, they have also been increasingly viewed as an instrument of monetary and exchange rate autonomy. In a number of countries, application of capital controls allowed the authorities to manipulate interest rates and exchange rates so as to attain the objectives of internal and external balance. The "Impossible Trinity" (i.e. the incompatibility between monetary policy independence, an open capital account, and a fixed or managed exchange rate regime) also validated a role for capital controls in countries operating a fixed or managed exchange rate regime. Subsequent analyses based on asymmetric information and herd behavior in financial markets suggested that capital controls may help in dealing with market failures more effectively, particularly those arising from volatility in short-term capital flows and exchange rates. As pointed out by Johnston and Tamirisa (1998), capital controls are more likely to exist in countries with a fixed or managed exchange rate regime, lower per capita incomes, larger government consumption (as a share to gross domestic product (GDP)) less independent central banks, larger current account deficits, low levels of economic development, high tariff barriers, and large black market premia.

Over the years, however, open capital accounts have been advocated quite strongly for developing economies, even when the perceived benefits of capital account liberalization were deemed to be limited. For example, Gilbert *et al.* (2000) argued that "if the benefits of capital market liberalization are smaller for the poorest countries than for the middle income countries, the same is probably also true of the costs."

12.2.1 The case for an open capital account

In assessing the case for and against capital account liberalization, the benefits of an open capital account are typically expected to be the following:

- Brings greater financial efficiency, specialization and innovation by exposing the financial sector to global competition;
- Attracts foreign capital, to developing countries needed to sustain an excess of investment over domestic saving;
- Provides residents the opportunity to base their investment and consumption decisions on world interest rates and tradables prices, which could enhance their welfare;
- Enables aggregate saving and investment to be optimized, by setting prices right, leading to both allocative efficiency and competitive discipline;
- Permits both savers and investors to protect the real value of their assets through risk reduction, by offering the opportunity to use global markets to diversify portfolios;
- Avoids capital controls so as to discourage hidden capital flight and/or financial saving diversion into real assets, gold, and so on, which might otherwise be brought on during periods of macroeconomic stability and lead to a suboptimal use of internal resources.

It should be noted that capital controls are not very effective, particularly when current account is convertible, as current account transactions create channels for disguised capital flows. Capital controls must also be intended to insulate domestic financial conditions from external financial developments, but here too, they are increasingly becoming ineffective. The influence of external financial developments has been increasing over the years even in countries with extensive capital controls, as the costs of evading these controls have declined and the attractiveness of holding assets in offshore markets have increased. Finally, there is the "squeezing on a balloon argument," with capital being fungible. Therefore, restrictions on one form of capital and not on others would quickly lead to displacement of flows to the uncontrolled segment.[3]

12.2.2   The case against an open capital account

The cost of an open capital account can be summarized as follows:

- Leads to the export of domestic savings, which for capital scarce developing countries would cripple the financing of domestic investment.
- Weakens the ability of the authorities to tax domestic financial activities, income, and wealth.
- Exposes the economy to greater macroeconomic instability arising from the volatility of short-term capital movements and the risk of large capital outflows and associated negative externalities.
- Premature liberalization—that is, if the speed and sequencing of reforms are not appropriate—could initially stimulate capital inflows that would cause the real exchange rate to appreciate and thereby destabilize an economy undergoing the fragile process of transition adjustment and structural reform. Once a stabilization program lacks credibility, currency substitution and capital flight could trigger a balance of payments crisis, exchange rate depreciation, and spiraling inflation.
- Commodity convertibility rather than financial convertibility is of greater welfare significance.
- Diverts resources from tradable to nontradable sectors as a result of the real effective exchange rate (REER) appreciation arising from larger capital inflows following capital account liberalization. This could happen in the face of rising external liabilities and, as a result, there could be a risk of the "Dutch disease effect."
- Leads to financial bubbles, especially through irrational exuberance of investment in real estate and equity markets financed by unbridled foreign borrowing.
- Exposes the distortions in the price of borrowing from abroad vis-à-vis the domestic market and, under such circumstances, creates conditions where private firms borrow more than what is socially optimal. This generally increases the cost of foreign borrowing for all borrowers.

12.2.3   Preconditions for capital account liberalization

The ever growing literature on capital account liberalization has called for the following preconditions to be met:

- Substantially narrow the differences between domestic and external financial market conditions and establish a flexible interest rate structure.
- Reduce the fiscal deficit and undertake deficit financing in a noninflationary way (i.e. a complete avoidance of use of inflation tax), and limit and/or reduce taxes on income, wealth, and transactions to international levels.

- Implement an appropriate exchange rate policy, with greater flexibility as the degree of openness increases.
- Restructure and recapitalize domestic financial institutions (FIs), and strengthen their prudential supervision.
- Enhance domestic competition by fostering greater allocative and operational efficiency within the financial sector.
- Reduce restrictions inhibiting wage price flexibility.
- Introduce second generation reforms—the promotion of domestic competition, increased transparency and accountability, good governance, labor reforms, and measures to ensure more equitable growth.

12.2.4 Sequencing of capital account liberalization

In the neoclassical framework, capital inflows contribute to economic growth primarily by supplementing domestic saving. In contrast, in the endogenous growth framework, the economic growth attributed to capital flows comprise the spillover effects associated with foreign capital in the form of new technology, skills, and products, as well as the positive externalities arising from more efficient domestic financial markets and the resultant improved resource allocation. Since the spillovers and externalities associated with different forms of foreign capital could vary, a pecking order approach to the composition of capital flows is often advocated, which could help in prioritizing capital inflows based on perceived growth enhancing role of each form of capital. Symmetrically, prioritization of outflows has also been emphasized in the literature.

McKinnon (1973) underscored that restrictions on trade in goods and services should be liberalized prior to capital transactions. He argued that large capital flows might come in response to opening up of the capital account and could give rise to real exchange rate appreciation, which in turn could erode trade competitiveness and thereby constrain trade liberalization. McKinnon and Pill (1996) viewed that liberalization of the capital account should wait till the reform process in the banking sector is completed and yields the desired result. Gilbert *et al.* (2000) sounded a serious precautionary note, "even with the best possible sequencing, mistakes will be made and crises will occur." It is widely contended that costs outweigh the benefits when the sequencing of liberalization becomes faulty and therefore, it is the attainment of preconditions that should determine the sequencing of liberalization.

12.3 Cross-country perspective

A country's policy approach to its capital account essentially involves a search for answers to some broad questions:

- Can free mobility of capital ensure an efficient allocation of global savings?
- Does capital account liberalization promote higher growth?

- Can financial openness discipline domestic macroeconomic policies?
- Can capital controls be effective?
- Is the design of the international financial architecture appropriate to deal with the challenges arising from free capital mobility?

The growing global macroeconomic imbalances—as evidenced by the large and sustained current account deficit of the United States—suggests that markets may, at times, allocate global saving differently from what may be perceived by policymakers as appropriate and sustainable in the long run. The distribution of the private capital flows to emerging markets also reveals the high degree of concentration in a few countries. Despite the available empirical research on the determinants of capital flows, the behavior of capital flows at times cannot be explained by any fundamentals, as the market often gets dominated by herd behavior driven by noise rather than news. For instance, the Southeast Asian countries received US$94 billion in 1996 and another US$70 billion in the first half of 1997. In the second half of 1997, however, there was an outflow of US$102 billion. Such order of reversal in a single year can hardly be explained by fundamentals alone.

The beneficial effects of capital account liberalization on growth are also ambiguous. An empirical assessment conducted by Rodrik (1998) found that, "there is no evidence that countries without capital controls have grown faster, invested more, or experienced lower inflation." Indeed, highlighting the possible presence of reverse causality—that is, countries with better overall economic performance favoring removal of capital controls—the study concluded that empirical relationships between open capital account and economic performance are more likely to hide the negative relationship than explaining any positive relationship. "Capital controls are essentially uncorrelated with long-term economic performance once other determinants are controlled for." A caveat is in order here. In empirical analyses, statistical measure of the degree of capital control has all along been a major irritant. As noted by Cooper (2001), "results (of empirical analyses) cannot be considered decisive until we have better measures of the intensity, as opposed to the mere existence, of capital controls."

There is, however, some unanimity on the point that open capital account exerts pressures to discipline the domestic macroeconomic and financial environment. Gruben and McLeod (2001) studied the potential link between two important developments in the 1990s—greater financial openness across a large number of countries and the significant decline in global inflation. The link between the two could arise from the penalties for excess money creation under an open capital account regime. They concluded that by giving rise to disinflation, open capital account could contribute to higher growth. Another study by Kim (2003) that analyzed the disciplinary effects of an open capital account on the fiscal deficit suggests that complete freedom for outward capital mobility could be associated with a reduction in budget deficit by 2.3 percent of GDP. Gourinchas and Jeanne (2002) emphasized that many emerging countries may actually benefit from the discipline effect rather than the conventional resource allocation effect. They concluded, "capital account openness is not always and everywhere a necessary condition for an economic take-off."

On the effectiveness of capital controls, country experiences are varied, depending, at times, on the form of control used (Box 12.1), the specific areas that are picked for liberalization (Table 12.1), and the motive behind the use of controls (Table 12.2). The broad lesson from country experiences suggests that to be effective, controls may have to be comprehensive and strongly enforced and must be accompanied by fundamental economic reforms so that controls are not seen as a substitute for reforms. Most importantly, capital controls need not work in the face of persistent presence of incentive for circumvention, particularly in cases of attractive return differentials in the offshore market and growing expectations of currency depreciation.

Box 12.1   Types of capital controls

Capital controls have in general taken two main forms: (i) direct or administrative controls and (ii) indirect or market-based controls.

- Direct or administrative capital controls restrict capital transactions and/or the associated payments and transfer of funds through outright prohibitions, explicit quantitative limits, or approval procedures (which may be rule-based or discretionary). Administrative controls typically seek to directly affect the volume of the relevant cross-border financial transactions. A common characteristic of such controls is that they impose administrative obligations on the banking system to control flows.
- Indirect or market-based controls discourage capital movements and the associated transactions by making them more costly to undertake. Such controls may take various forms, including dual or multiple exchange rate systems, explicit or implicit taxation of cross-border financial flows (e.g. a Tobin tax), and other predominantly price-based measures. Depending on their specific type, market-based controls may affect the price and/or volume of a given transaction.
  - In dual (two-tier) or multiple exchange rate systems, different exchange rates apply to different types of transactions. Two-tier foreign exchange markets have typically been established in situations in which the authorities regard high short-term interest rates as imposing an unacceptable burden on domestic residents and attempt to split the market for the domestic currency by either requesting or instructing domestic financial institutions not to lend to those borrowers engaged in speculative activity. Foreign exchange transactions associated with trade flows, foreign direct investment (FDI), and usually foreign portfolio investment (FPI) are excluded from the restrictions. In essence, the two-tier market attempts to raise the cost to speculators

of the domestic credit needed to establish a net short domestic currency position, while allowing nonspeculative domestic credit demand to be satisfied at normal market rates. Two-tier systems can also accommodate excessive inflows and thus prevent an overshooting exchange rate for current account transactions. Such systems attempt to influence both the price and quantity of capital transactions. Like administrative controls, they need to be enforced by compliance rules and thus imply the administration of resident foreign exchange transactions and nonresident domestic currency transactions in order to separate current and capital transactions.

○ Explicit taxation of cross-border flows involves the imposition of taxes or levies on external financial transactions, thus limiting their attractiveness, or on income resulting from holdings by residents of foreign financial assets or holdings by nonresidents of domestic financial assets, thereby discouraging such investments by reducing their overall rate of return. Tax rates can be differentiated to discourage certain types of transactions or maturities. Such taxation could be considered a restriction on cross-border activities if it discriminates between foreign and domestic assets or between nonresidents and residents.

○ Indirect taxation of cross-border flows, in the form of noninterest bearing compulsory reserves/deposit requirements (URR hereafter) has been one of the most frequently used market-based controls. Under such schemes, banks and nonbanks dealing on their own account are required to make zero-interest deposits with the central bank of the domestic or foreign currency equivalent to a certain proportion of the inflows or of the net positions in foreign currency. URRs may seek to limit capital outflows by making them more sensitive to domestic interest rates. For example, when there is downward pressure on the domestic currency, a 100 percent URR imposed on banks would double the interest income forgone by switching from domestic to foreign currency. URRs may also be used to limit capital inflows by reducing their effective rates of return; these returns may also be differentiated to discourage particular types of transactions.

○ Other indirect regulatory controls have the characteristics of both price- and quantity-based measures and involve discrimination between different types of transactions or investors. Though they may influence the volume and nature of capital flows, such regulations may at times be motivated by concerns arising from domestic monetary control or prudential regulation. Such controls include (i) the provisions for the net external position of commercial banks, (ii) asymmetric open position limits that discriminate between long and short currency positions or between residents and nonresidents, and (iii) certain credit rating requirements to borrow abroad. While not a regulatory control in the strict sense, reporting requirements for specific transactions have also been used to monitor and control capital movements (e.g. derivative transactions and non-trade related transactions with nonresidents).

Sources: International Monetary Fund, *World Economic Outlook* (1997, 1998, and 2001) and Ariyoshi *et al.* (2000).

Table 12.1 Type of capital transactions that could be subject to controls

Type of transaction	Inflows	Outflows
I. Capital and money markets		
Shares or other securities of a participating nature	Purchase locally by nonresidents	Sale or issue locally by nonresidents
Bonds or other debt securities		
Money market instruments		Purchase abroad by residents
Collective investment securities		
II. Derivatives and other instruments	Purchase locally by nonresidents	Sale or issue locally by nonresidents
	Sale or issue abroad by residents	Purchase abroad by residents
III. Credit operations		
Commercial and financial credits	To residents from nonresidents	By residents to nonresidents
IV. Guarantees, sureties, and financial backup facilities	To residents from nonresidents	By residents to nonresidents
V. Direct investment		
Inward direct investment		Outward direct investment
		Controls on liquidation of direct investment
Real estate transactions nonresidents	Purchase locally by Sale locally by nonresidents	Purchase abroad by residents
Provisions specific to commercial banks	Nonresident deposits Borrowing abroad	Deposits overseas Foreign loans
Personal capital movements[a] nonresidents	To residents from nonresidents	By residents to
VI. Settlements of debts abroad by immigrants	Transfer into the country by immigrants	Transfer abroad by emigrants
Provisions specific to institutional investors		Limits (maximum) on securities issued by nonresidents and on portfolio invested abroad
		Limits (maximum) on portfolio invested locally

[a] Deposits, loans, fits, endowments, inheritances, and legacies.

Sources: International Monetary Fund, *World Economic Outlook* (1997, 1998, and 2001) and Ariyoshi *et al.* (2000).

Controls on outflows can be broadly classified into preventive controls and curative controls. While the former intend to prevent the emergence of a balance of payments crisis, the latter could be applied as a means to manage a crisis (as in the case of Malaysia). Yoshitomi and Shirai (2000) present a review of the empirical studies on the effectiveness of both variants of control, which suggests that, "in almost 70 percent of the cases where the controls on outflows were used as a preventive measure, a large increase in

Table 12.2 India: purpose of capital controls

Purpose of control	Method	Direction of control	Example
General revenue finance war effort	Controls on capital outflows permit a country to run higher inflation with a given fixed-exchange rate and also hold down domestic interest rates.	Outflows	Most belligerent use during World War I and World War II
Financial repression/credit allocation	Governments that use the financial system to reward favored industries or to raise revenue may use capital controls to prevent capital from going abroad to seek higher returns.	Outflows	Common in developing countries
Correct a balance of payments deficit	Controls on outflows reduce demand for foreign assets without contractionary monetary policy or devaluation. This allows a higher rate of inflation than otherwise would be possible.	Outflows	US interest equalization tax, 1963–74
Correct a balance of payments surplus	Control on inflows reduce foreign demand for domestic assets without expansionary monetary policy or revaluation. This allows a lower rate of inflation than would otherwise be possible.	Inflows	German Bardepot scheme, 1972–74
Prevent potentially volatile inflows	Restricting inflows enhances macroeconomic stability by reducing the pool of capital that can leave a country during crisis.	Inflows	Chilean encaje, 1991–98

Prevent financial destabilization	Capital controls can restrict or change the composition of international capital flows that can exacerbate distorted incentives in the domestic financial system	Inflows	Chilean encaje, 1991–98
Prevent real appreciation	Restricting inflows prevents the necessity of monetary expansion and greater domestic inflation that would cause a real appreciation of the currency.	Inflows	Chilean encaje, 1991–98
Restrict foreign ownership of domestic assets	Foreign ownership of certain domestic assets—especially natural resources—can generate resentment.	Inflows	Article 27 of Mexico's constitution
Preserve savings for domestic use	The benefit of investing in the domestic economy may not fully accrue to savers to that economy, who as a whole, can be made better off by restricting the outflow of capital.	Outflows	
Protect domestic financial firms	Controls that temporarily segregate domestic financial sectors from the rest of the world may permit domestic firms to attain economies of scale to compete in world markets.	Inflows and outflows	

Source: Neely (1999).

capital flight was observed after their imposition." The support for using curative control came from Krugman (1998), who suggested temporary use of controls amidst a crisis to avoid the adverse effects of the alternative—that is, a sharp rise in interest rates to defend the exchange rate.[4]

The Malaysian case offers several interesting lessons. The Malaysian ringgit fell sharply from RM 2.5 per US dollar in the second quarter of 1997 to RM 4.2 per US dollar in the second quarter of 1998. Initially, the authorities tried to defend the depreciation through tight monetary policy.[5] In the face of a large difference in the onshore and offshore interest rates, controls were implemented in September 1998 to prevent speculative activities. The controls banned transfers between domestic and foreign accounts and between foreign accounts, prohibited the extension of ringgit credit to nonresident banks and brokerage firms, prevented repatriation of investment for one year (amounting to a compulsory one year holding period requirement), and fixed the exchange rate at RM 3.8 per US dollar. In February 1999, price-based controls replaced prudential/quantitative controls, with levies on repayment of debt and repatriation of profits.[6] These measures allowed nonresidents to withdraw funds, but also penalized them for early withdrawals. From September 1999 onward, the measures were further simplified and partially lifted. The major advantage of these controls, besides stemming speculation, was in terms of giving policy discretion to the authorities for restoring market confidence.[7] On the other hand, as noted by Yoshitomi and Shirai (2000), the success of controls in Malaysia should not be overemphasized because controls were imposed almost 14 months after the crisis started, by which time large part of the speculative outflows had already occurred. The controls were also introduced against the backdrop of an undervalued exchange rate, which enhanced the probability of success.

Unlike the controls on outflows, in discussions relating to the effectiveness of controls on inflows, one generally refers to the Chilean experience. During 1978–82, when Chile experienced surge in capital flows, external loans up to 24 months maturity were forbidden, and those with maturities from 24–36 months were subjected to noninterest-yielding reserve requirement ranging from 10–25 percent. Prudential regulations also helped in limiting the foreign liabilities of commercial banks, which were linked directly to the banks' equity. Chile, however, could not avoid a crisis despite such restrictions in 1982. Chilean capital controls, thus, may have given a false sense of security.[8]

In the early 1990s, Chile again used similar instruments. In June 1991, all external loans were subjected to 20 percent noninterest-yielding reserve requirement.[9] In May 1992, the reserve requirement was raised to 30 percent and also extended to most other forms of foreign capital including trade credits, American Depository Receipt (ADR) issues by Chilean companies, and other portfolio inflows, and FDI. In June 1998, when Chile experienced capital outflows, the reserve requirement was reduced to 10 percent, and subsequently to zero percent in September 1998 (alternative forms of such taxes and their equivalents and the motive behind their use are set out in Table 12.3).[10] In assessing the effectiveness of these controls, Edwards (1999) emphasized the need (i) to slowdown the volume of capital inflows and to tilt the composition in favor of longer maturities; (ii) to avoid real exchange rate appreciation that stemmed from surges in capital flows; and (iii) to maintain a domestic interest rate different from foreign rates so that domestic rates could be used as part of independent monetary policy to attain monetary policy goals. Overall, the experience of Chile suggests that none of these objectives could be eventually met, which validates the argument that controls on inflows may not be effective.[11]

Finally, the inappropriateness of the international financial architecture to deal with the crises arising from open capital account has been recognized in the post-East Asian crisis period. As underscored by Gilbert *et al.* (2000), "within a cost-benefit framework, the benefits are seen as more modest than had previously been supposed, while the crisis has increased our estimates of the potential costs of liberalization." The change in international thinking on the issue appears quite stark in the context of the decision of the Interim Committee in April 1997 favoring an amendment of the International Monetary Fund's (IMF) Articles of Agreement to make liberalization of the capital account as part of its mandate (Eichengreen, 1999). Despite the recent international initiatives on crisis prevention and resolution, the international architecture falls short of the requirement of enhancing confidence in emerging economies while designing country-specific strategies for capital account liberalization. Unlike in the pre-crises period, the need for entrenching preconditions has come to the forefront of policy thinking in deciding on the pace, timing, content, and sequencing of liberalization.

12.4 The Indian approach

In India, capital account liberalization received policy attention in the aftermath of the 1991 external payments crisis. As part of the overall restructuring package of the external sector, it aimed at reducing reliance on debt creating flows—particularly short term—while encouraging foreign investment, especially FDI. While the focus was primarily on attracting adequate private capital of the desired composition, during surges in capital flows, policy measures were also directed at regulating inflows. Under a gradual liberalization of both FDI and FPI, the Indian rupee for all purposes has been made convertible for foreign investors. However, restrictions on capital outflows involving residents continue. Such controls have indeed served the needs of the external sector and the overall economy well, and many of them can be removed depending on lasting progress on the aforementioned preconditions.

Table 12.3 Three proposals for "sand in the wheels" capital controls, and how they differ

	Chile's deposit requirement on inflows	Eichengreen–Wyplosz deposit requirement proposal	Total tax proposal
Motive	Prevents over-indebtedness	Protects the balance of payments	Reduces volatility in the exchange rate (and raises revenue)
Tax applied to	Capital inflows	Capital outflows (and inflows)	All foreign exchange transactions, including trade
Paid immediately by	Foreign investors	Banks	All traders (mostly banks)
Paid immediately to	Central bank (foreign currency earnings)	Central bank (seignorage only)	Tax authority (domestic revenue)
Relationship of tax amount to interest rate	Rises with foreign interest rate	Rises with domestic interest rate	Invariant to interest rate
Relationship to maturity	Fixed amount (falling with maturity in percent per annum terms) when maturity less than one year	Falls with maturity, but does not apply to intra-day trading	Fixed amount. In percent per annum terms, falls continuously with maturity
Where imposed	One country (facing inflows)	One country (facing outflows)	Must be worldwide
Probable level of tax rate	Moderate (30 percent of the interest rate)	High (to discourage speculative attacks)	Low (to avoid distortions and substitution)

Source: Frankel (1999).

12.4.1 Linkage between current and capital account

The Indian experience of capital account liberalization, like many other developing countries was preceded by trade liberalization, most notably the virtual elimination of import licensing and a progressive shift of restricted items of imports to Open General Licenses (OGL). At the same time, a reduction of tariff rates was initiated in the early 1990s, with the average tariff rate more than halved between early and late 1990s. The long-term objective of India's tariff reduction is to bring such rates in line with those prevailing in the member economies of Asia-Pacific Economic Cooperation. Tariff reduction was followed by removal of nontariff barriers. Between 1999 and 2001, India eliminated all quantitative restrictions on imports, which were earlier imposed for balance of payments consideration.

Initial reform measures were directed at current account convertibility leading to acceptance of Article VIII of the IMF's Articles of Agreement in August 1994. Foreign exchange regulations, however, built in certain safeguards related to current account transactions. The precautionary safeguards stemmed from the recognition of possible linkages between capital account and current account transactions, like capital outflows in the guise of current transactions. Such safeguard measures, which strengthened the effectiveness of the management of the capital account included:

- Requiring the repatriation and surrender of export proceeds, while allowing a portion of it to be retained in foreign currency accounts in India, which could be used for approved purposes;
- Allowing authorized dealers to sell foreign exchange for underlying transactions based on documentary evidence; and
- Placing indicative limits on the purchase of foreign exchange to meet different kinds of current account transactions, which were reasonable in relation to the purpose.

12.4.2 Preconditions for capital account liberalization

Even before the onset of the East Asian crisis of 1997, India had worked on an appropriate road map for capital account liberalization through its Committee on Capital Account Convertibility (also referred to as the Tarapore Committee).[12] A report prepared by the committee recommended detailed measures for achieving capital account convertibility, including specification of the preconditions, sequence and time frame for undertaking such measures, and suggestion of the necessary domestic policy measures and institutional framework changes. The findings and recommendations of the report appear particularly path-breaking, when assessed in the context of similar recommendations that started flowing from almost every quarter, albeit, only after the East Asian financial crisis. The unique aspect of the committee's report was its emphasis on the importance of preconditions and

Table 12.4 India: current position and preconditions suggested for capital account convertibility

Preconditions in report on capital account convertibility	Current status
I. Fiscal consolidation	
Reduction in the gross fiscal deficit as a percentage of GDP from 4.5 percent in 1997/98 to 4.0 percent in 1998/99 and further to 3.5 percent in 1999/2000.	Gross fiscal deficit as a percentage of GDP stood at 5.9 percent during 2002/03 and is budgeted at 5.6 percent for 2003/04.
II. Mandated inflation rate	
The mandated rate of inflation for three years should average 3–5 percent.	The realized (not mandated) inflation rate in 2002/03 was 3.4 percent.
Reserve Bank of India should be given freedom to attain mandate of inflation approved by Parliament.	Although inflation is an important objective of monetary policy, there is no targeted/mandated inflation approved by the Parliament.
III. Strengthening of the financial system	
Interest rates to be fully deregulated in 1997/98 and any formal or informal interest rate controls must be abolished.	All interest rates (except savings bank interest rate) have been deregulated.
Cash reserve requirement (CRR) to be reduced in phases to 8 percent in 1997/98, 6 percent in 1998/99, and to 3 percent in 1999/2000.	CRR reduced to 4.5 percent by 2003/04.
Nonperforming assets (NPAs) as share of total advances to be brought down in phases to 12 percent in 1997/98, 9 percent in 1998/99, and to 5 percent in 1999/2000.	NPAs of the public sector banks as a share of total advances have come down from 16.0 percent at end-March 1998 to 11.1 percent at end-March 2002.

100 percent marked-to-market valuation of investments for banks.	The original concept of 100 percent marked-to-market valuation has been replaced by the revised concept of banks classifying their entire portfolio into three categories: "Held to Maturity," "Available for Sale," and "Held for Trading." Investments in the first category should not exceed 25 percent of total holdings; in the other two categories, banks have the freedom to decide the proportion of assets, as these investments will be marked-to-market.
Best practices on risk management and accounting/disclosure norms be implemented.	Risk management guidelines have been issued (broadly covering credit risk and market risk), and the regulatory and supervisory system has been strengthened to ensure effective monitoring, transparency, and compliance with prudential standards.
IV. Important macroeconomic indicators	
A monitoring band of +/–5 percent around the neutral real effective exchange rate (REER) to be introduced and attained through intervention whenever the REER goes outside the band.	The exchange rate policy has no explicit/implicit target (whether point or band). The market has generally ensured an exchange rate path that avoids major misalignment in terms of REER.
Debt service ratio to be reduced to 20 percent from 25 percent of total exports.	Debt service ratio has steadily declined from 19.5 percent in 1997/98 to 14.6 percent in 2002/03.
The foreign exchange reserves should not be less than six months of imports.	As at end-March 2003, foreign exchange reserve cover was for more than a year's import.

Source: Reserve Bank of India, *Report on Currency and Finance 2001–02* (2003).

sequencing, despite the strong wave in favor of capital account convertibility that prevailed prior to the East Asian crisis. The recognized preconditions in the report included fiscal consolidation, low inflation, comfortable foreign exchange reserves, and a strong and resilient financial system, which have hence received wider support. Only on an appropriate exchange rate regime that could be consistent with capital account convertibility was the report's recommendation somewhat inconsistent with the now popular "Impossible Trinity." Capital account convertibility may require a more flexible exchange rate, and any fixed or managed regime may become vulnerable to attack once the capital account is opened up. Real exchange rate targeting and the associated loss of a nominal anchor also have implications for monetary policy independence. Recognizing these limitations, the Indian authorities rightly did not accept the recommendation of the committee to confining the movement of the REER to within a band of +/−5 percent, but still practice a managed float regime. The exchange rate that evolved under this regime (since March 1993) has successfully avoided both large volatility and major misalignment in terms of a REER appreciation.

Subsequent to the report, substantial liberalization of the capital account has been made, particularly with respect to inward foreign investment. This has been possible due to significant progress toward achieving the preconditions for liberalization, as noted in Table 12.4. Specifically, India has managed to achieve the following preconditions:

- A mandatory annual average inflation rate of 3–5 percent (as against the realized rate of 3.4 percent in 2002–03);
- A deregulated interest rate environment (except rates on bank savings deposits and small savings schemes);
- A reduction of the cash reserve requirement (CRR) to the statutory minimum of 3 percent (as against the current requirement of 4.5 percent);
- An external debt service ratio of 20–25 percent of total exports (as against 14.6 percent in 2002/03);
- Foreign exchange reserves providing an import cover of more than six months (as against 17 months at end-October 2003); and
- The adoption of best practices for risk management, accounting standards, and disclosure norms by banks and FIs.

On the other hand, India has yet to make considerable progress on other preconditions such as:

- Fiscal consolidation with a stipulation of reducing the gross fiscal deficit to 3.5 percent of GDP by 1999/2000 (as against 5.9 percent in 2002/03 and budgeted estimate of 5.6 percent in 2003/04);[13] and
- Further strengthening of the financial system with the indicative gross nonperforming assets (NPAs) in total outstanding loans to be brought

down to 5 percent by 1999/2000 (as against reduction in gross NPAs of public sector banks from 16 to 11 percent in 2001/02).[14]

12.4.3 Operationalizing capital account convertibility

It needs no emphasis that mere attainment of the preconditions for capital account convertibility may not be enough to go for full liberalization. The approach toward capital account convertibility must be consistent with the overall policy framework that is assigned to the objective of growth and stability. Incremental higher growth that comes at the expense of greater instability should be avoided. Indeed, avoiding instability itself has emerged as a major precondition to achieving higher growth. Needless to say, liberalization measures have already been undertaken in areas that are clearly beneficial and need priority attention in India. As underscored by Panagariya (1998), "most of the benefits of capital mobility can be reaped via partial mobility, principally equity and direct foreign investment." Within India, however, some have preferred more extreme forms of capital account convertibility. Virmani (1999), for example, had advocated that every resident individual should be allowed to use up to US$50,000 per annum to purchase goods and services abroad and to open a bank account abroad. It was also recommended that corporations and businesses be allowed to make financial capital transfers abroad (including opening bank accounts with a check facility) up to a limit of US$50,000 per annum. Indeed, most of these suggestions for liberal overseas investment have been recently implemented with a robust external sector and burgeoning foreign exchange reserves.

India considers capital account liberalization as a process and not a single event. As highlighted by Reddy (2000), in its gradual and cautious approach for operationalizing capital account convertibility in India, a clear distinction is made between inflows and outflows, with asymmetrical treatment from the control angle for inflows (less restricted), outflows associated with inflows (free) and other outflows (more restricted). Differential restrictions are also applied to residents versus nonresidents, to individuals (highly restrictive) versus corporate entities (restrictive), and financial intermediaries like commercial banks (more restrictive) and institutional investors (less restrictive). A combination of direct administrative controls (i.e. interest rate ceilings) and market-based instruments of control (i.e. tax rates or reserve requirements) is used to ensure a prudent approach to managing the capital account.

The policy of ensuring a well-diversified capital account with a rising share of nondebt liabilities and low percentage of short-term debt in total debt liabilities, is amply reflected in India's policies on FDI, FPI, and external commercial borrowing (ECB). Quantitative annual ceilings on ECB along with maturity and end-use restrictions broadly shape the ECB policy. Nonresident Indian (NRI) deposits have also been liberalized, while the policy framework has imparted stability to such flows. FDI is encouraged through a liberal but dual route: a progressively expanding automatic route and a case-by-case route. FPI, which also has been progressively liberalized, is restricted to select players, particularly approved institutional investors and NRIs. Indian companies are also permitted to access international markets through ADRs/GDRs, subject to approval. Foreign investment in the form of Indian joint ventures abroad is also permitted through both automatic and case-by-case routes. Restrictions on outflows involving Indian corporations, banks, and other foreign exchange earners (e.g. exporters) have also been liberalized over time, subject to certain prudential guidelines.

12.4.4   Management of debt-creating inflows

The major plank of external debt management has been (i) maintaining a strict control on short-term debt; (ii) encouraging long-term debt; (iii) avoiding the bunching of repayments, gradual liberalizing debt inflows by prioritizing them with regard to their utilization for productive investments; and (iv) providing necessary flexibility to borrowers for risk management of their debt portfolio. As a result of this prudent external debt management, there has been a significant turnaround in debt indicators for India. While the debt-to-GDP ratio declined from a peak of 38.7 percent in 1991/92 to 20.0 percent in 2002/03, debt service ratio was more than halved from a high of 35.3 percent in 1990/91 to 14.7 percent in 2002/03. Reflecting the consolidation in external debt, India is now classified as a "less" indebted country by the World Bank, in sharp contrast to being nearly classified as a "severe" indebted country in the early 1990s. Another crucial feature in India's external debt management is a history of strong commitment toward making no compromise on honoring debt service obligations, as it has never defaulted on any external obligations.

External commercial borrowing

External commercial borrowing (ECB) has been guided by the overall consideration of prudent external debt management. Access to ECB has been generally restricted to resident Indian corporations and development financial institutions, thereby keeping out banks from such borrowings. At the same time, ECB have been subjected to overall annual ceilings, maturity norms and end-use restrictions. Effective February 2004, companies can borrow up to US$500 million under the 'automatic route', and above this limit with the Reserve Bank of India's (RBI) approval.[15] End-use and maturity prescriptions have also been substantially liberalized in recent years, besides permitting ECB for rupee expenditures. Indian corporations can now access ECB from any recognized lender with a minimum maturity of three years subject to a ceiling on spreads over London Inter-Bank Offered Rate (LIBOR). End-use restrictions for financing real estate and equity market investment are still in force (except for developing integrated townships and financing public enterprise disinvestment).

A distinguishing feature of the liberalized regime is to provide greater flexibility to companies in managing their exposure on ECB. This is being done by allowing prepayment under the automatic route (without any ceiling) and also permitting hedging through rupee forward covers (up to one year as is currently available) and rupee options (introduced in June 2003). Furthermore, in order to enable corporations to hedge exchange rate risks and raise rupee resources domestically, they are permitted to enhance rupee-denominated structural obligations with credit from abroad extended by banks, FIs, and joint venture partners. While these measures will encourage companies to hedge their exposure and thereby limit risks on their balance sheets, given their long-term exposure to currency risks, there is an urgent need to develop the nascent rupee derivatives market expeditiously. Following the policy imperatives, gross disbursement of ECB (excluding India Development Bonds (IDBs), Resurgent India Bonds (RIBs) and India Millennium Deposits (IMDs)) declined from a peak of US$7.4 billion in 1997/98 to US$1.9 billion in 2002/03, reflecting reduced reliance on debt financing. Net flows (excluding IDBs, RIBs and IMDs), in fact, turned negative in 1998/99, reflecting the reduced recourse to ECB as well as prepayment undertaken by corporations in recent years to take advantage of soft interest rates prevailing in the overseas market.[16]

Nonresident deposits

Significant changes have been made in the policy framework for NRI deposits held by the Indian banking system, which constitute a major portion of external debt for India. The balance of payments crisis of 1990/91 demonstrated the volatility of NRI deposits due to large interest differentials and explicit exchange rate guarantee provided by the Government of India at the time. Since then, the policy has been aimed at attracting stable deposits. This has been achieved through:

- The withdrawal of exchange rate guarantees on various deposits;
- A policy induced shift in favor of local currency-denominated deposits;
- The rationalization of interest rates on rupee-denominated NRI deposits;
- Linking interest rates on foreign currency-denominated deposits to LIBOR for,
  - Deemphasizing short-term deposits (up to 12 months) in case of foreign currency-denominated deposits, and
  - Making NRI deposits fully repatriable.[17]

The reserve requirement on these deposits has also been varied as an instrument to influence monetary and exchange rate management and to regulate the size of the inflows depending on the country's requirements.

Outstanding NRI deposits grew steadily from US$14.0 billion at end-March 1991 (constituting 16.7 percent of total external debt) to US$28.5 billion at end-March 2003 (25.3 percent of total external debt). However, there has been a significant policy-induced shift in the composition of NRI deposits to ensure their stability, with the proportion of local currency-denominated deposits increasing from around one-fourth in end-March 1991 to over two-thirds by end-March 2003. The short-term component of NRI deposits also declined sharply during the corresponding period. More recently, to prevent arbitrage-driven inflows on rupee-denominated NRI deposit, short-term flows (less than one year) have been discontinued and interest rate paid made subject to a ceiling of 25 basis points over LIBOR.

Short-term debt

Apart from annual ceilings on long-term ECB, short-term borrowing is under severe quantitative restrictions, excepting those strictly related to trade. These ceilings are applied in consonance with the outlook for the balance of payments. The differential treatment in favor of trade-related flows is accorded due to its stable source of financing and also to the leads and lags in trade-related payments that affect the level of short-term debt. The tight control on short-term debt resulted in an absolute decline from US$8.5 billion in end-March 1991 (10.2 percent of total debt) to US$5.8 billion in end-June 2003 (5.3 percent of total debt). This has led to a significant improvement in liquidity indicators, with short-term debt as a proportion of foreign currency assets declining sharply from 382.1 percent in end-March 1991 to 7.4 percent in end-June 2003.

Government account debt

External borrowing by the Government of India till now has been limited to borrowing from official sources—that is, credit from bilateral and multilateral sources. Such debt flows are characterized by their long maturity and high concessional element. As part of prudent debt management, the Government has not contracted any short-term debt. At the same time, state governments are not allowed to directly access any form of external borrowing. In recent years, as part of the Government of India's active management of the external debt portfolio, it has prepaid some of its high cost debt (US$3.1 billion in 2002/03). With reduced reliance on external borrowing, external debt of the Government declined steadily from US$50.0 billion in end-March 1991 to US$45.8 billion at end-December 2002. Given this and the rise of private debt, the share of public debt in the total external debt declined accordingly from 59.6 percent in end-March 1991 to 43.7 percent in end-December 2002.

12.4.5   Management of nondebt-creating inflows

Foreign direct investment

Since the 1980s, there has been a gradual liberalization of norms governing the operation of companies under foreign collaboration. This process gathered momentum and took definite shape during the 1990s. The Industrial

Policy Statement (1991) effected significant liberalization in the context of foreign collaborations—both financial and technical. Two specific routes for foreign collaborations were specified—the automatic route and case-by-case approval. Initially certain specific sectors were identified where foreign collaborators could approach the RBI for setting up new units under the automatic route. By and large, the maximum permissible foreign equity participation under the automatic route was at 51 percent.

In the course of the 1990s, sectoral coverage of FDI under the ambit of automatic route approval was significantly enhanced. The automatic route is no longer limited to the manufacturing sector. There are major thrusts in allowing foreign collaborations in infrastructure-related and technology-intensive sectors through the automatic route. Since 2000, all industries, except a small list, have been brought under the purview of the automatic route.[18] In addition, there is a negative list of only six industries where the Government prohibits FDI.[19] All other cases of FDI, including collaborations and takeovers of existing Indian companies require case-by-case approvals from the Government. The Foreign Investment Promotion Board (FIPB), set up by the Government of India, acts as the nodal agency for case-by-case approvals of foreign collaborations.

The automatic route is currently divided into four different categories. Key sectors where 100 percent foreign ownership is allowed under the automatic route include power, roads and highways, ports and harbors, mass rapid transport system, drugs and pharmaceuticals, the hotel and tourism sector, advertising, and mining. Another major area where up to 100 percent FDI has been permitted under the automatic route is in Special Economic Zones for most manufacturing activities. The major sectors where less than 100 percent FDI is permitted under the automatic route are the defense industry (26 percent) telecommunications sector (49 percent), and airports (74 percent). The financial sector has also been gradually opened for FDI in tune with the gradual liberalization initiated since the early 1990s. Currently, FDI is allowed in private sector banks (49 percent), nonbanking financial companies (NBFCs) (100 percent), and insurance sector (26 percent).

In addition to sectoral policy reforms, other measures have been initiated to facilitate FDI flows. The disinvestment process for public sector enterprises is open to FDI finance, subject to sector guidelines. Measures have also been introduced to allow foreign companies to set up wholly owned subsidiaries (WOSs) in India or to convert joint ventures (JVs) into them. Furthermore, the percentage of FDI through merger and acquisition route has also been increased from around 10 percent in 1999 to around 30 percent at present. Apart from equity participation, various terms and conditions relating to technical collaborations have also been brought under the automatic route. Under this approach payment to foreign collaborators on account of trademark, brand name, lump sum fees, and so on are allowed under the automatic route up to certain threshold limits.

Gross FDI flows, which were barely US$0.6 billion in 1992/93, increased sharply over the ensuing decade to US$6.2 billion in 2001/02, but fell back to US$4.8 billion in 2002/03. These flows still remain low in comparison to other emerging market economies. As part of adopting international best practices in compiling FDI statistics, data on FDI for both inward and outward flows was revised in June 2003 and is now based on a new methodology that includes reinvested earnings and other direct capital (in particular inter-corporate debt transactions between related entities) in FDI.

Portfolio investment

Investment by foreign institutional investors (FIIs) has been permitted since the early 1990s. Portfolio investments are restricted to select players—mainly for approved institutional investors. A single FII can invest up to 10 percent in any company, while FIIs together can invest up to the sectoral caps in both the primary and secondary markets. Two classes of FIIs exist—the first one is the equity route, including investment up to 30 percent in debt instruments (including holdings of government securities and units of debt-oriented mutual funds) and the second one is the debt route, or investment of 100 percent in debt instruments (subject to an overall cap of US$1.75 billion in 2003/04, up from US$1 billion during the previous year). The cap on investment by debt securities is based on the consideration of controlling short-term debt flows as part of the strategy for external debt management. Moreover, premature opening up of FII investment in debt securities, particularly in short-term government securities, could increase vulnerability to a liquidity crisis and speculative attack, as evidenced from the Russian crisis in 1998.[20]

There are no restrictions on repatriation of portfolio investment unlike stipulation of a minimum lock-in period imposed in some countries. However, taxes on short-term gains are higher than on long-term gains. In tune with the priority accorded to liberalize inflows, corporations are allowed to raise funds through ADRs/GDRs. While FPI has increased substantially over the years, it has also shown much greater year-to-year variations, ranging from a net inflow of US$3.3 billion in 1996/97 to a net outflow of US$61 million in 1998/99. In 2002/03, net portfolio investment amounted to US$1.0 billion.

12.4.6   Liberalization of capital outflows

The major issues with respect to liberalization of capital outflows include lifting of controls on convertibility of domestic assets by residents, the dollarization of domestic assets, and internationalization of local currency. While some measures are being taken to liberalize overseas investment, particularly in the recent years, the stance on dollarization and internationalization of the rupee has been quite conservative, based on appropriate prudential consideration for ensuring financial stability.

Overseas investment

Overseas investment in JVs or WOSs has been recognized as important instruments for promoting the global business of Indian companies. At present, the complete use of ADR/GDR proceeds and the export earner foreign currency account balances for this purpose is permitted. As a result of liberalization of the policy framework for Indian investment abroad, FDI flows from India increased from negligible levels in early 1990s to US$1.4 billion in 2001/02, before declining marginally to US$1.1 billion in 2002/03. Facilitated by the burgeoning reserves, overseas investment was further liberalized in 2003. Indian companies can now invest abroad in a JV or 100 percent WOS up to US$100 million without any prior approval. Similarly, an individual as well as a listed Indian company can invest abroad in listed shares and debt securities of any company that holds at least 10 percent equity in a listed Indian company. Further, a registered mutual fund, subject to an overall cap of US$1 billion, can invest in debt securities and listed shares of companies with at least a 10 percent equity stake in a listed Indian company. All of these measures are expected to make Indian companies globally competitive.

The hierarchy followed with regard to liberalization of outflows has been in the order of corporations, financial intermediaries, and individuals. This is, however, in contrast to the Tarapore Committee recommendation of preferring the liberalization of flows on individual accounts earlier in the hierarchy. It would be reasonable to expect some further liberalization on outflows with regard to companies in the near term, and for banks and other financial intermediaries with further progress in financial sector reforms.

Convertibility of domestic assets

A crucial element in capital account liberalization is allowing free convertibility of domestic assets by residents. In the event of any external shock, there could be expectations of an imminent depreciation of the local currency. An anticipated depreciation of the local currency could lead to a large number of residents to simultaneously decide to convert their domestic assets, which could be self-fulfilling, thereby making a severe external crisis inevitable. For India, the possible impact on the exchange rate could be gauged by the fact that domestic stock of the bank deposits in rupees was close to US$290 billion at the end of March 2003, more than four times the level of foreign exchange reserves. However, for industrial countries with international currencies like the US dollar or the euro, this kind of eventuality is less likely to occur since these currencies are held internationally by banks, corporations, and other entities as part of their long-term global asset portfolio. In contrast, for emerging market currencies, banks and other intermediaries normally take a daily long or short position for purposes of currency trades. Thus, for India, convertibility of domestic assets is expected to be lower down in the agenda toward capital account convertibility.

Dollarization and internationalization of rupee

A related issue that arises with capital account liberalization is allowing domestic residents to open foreign currency-denominated accounts. A highly conservative approach is adopted with reference to both dollarization of domestic economy and internationalization of domestic currency. On dollarization, it has been generally recognized that large-scale dollar-denominated assets within a country can disrupt the economy by creating potential destabilizing flows. As a result, no dollar-denominated transactions have been generally allowed between residents in India.[21]

The counterpart of dollarization is internationalization of a currency, which is characterized as the officially traded currency outside the country without any underlying trade or investment transactions. When a currency is held increasingly outside the country, any expectation of currency depreciation could lead to a widespread sell-off, resulting in a very sharp fall in the currency's value, especially when the local markets are not well developed. Keeping this concern, India does not permit the rupee to be transacted offshore; that is, the rupee is not allowed to be officially used as international means of payment or store of value.[22]

12.4.7   Opening of the financing sector

The opening of the financial sector is a crucial element of capital account liberalization due to its implications of systemic risks on macroeconomic and financial stability, and thus needs to be carefully sequenced and timed. The Indian financial sector was steadily opened up to FDI in the 1990s. The issue of foreign investment in the Indian financial sector could be viewed from the twin angles of the signaling impact and market discipline. First, in case of emerging market economies, such as India, the liberalization of foreign investment in the financial sector is often taken to be a benchmark of the reform process itself. Second, the introduction of foreign players typically imparts a degree of market discipline to the domestic industry. Foreign banks in India, for example, have typically enjoyed higher profitability with wider interest spreads as well as better asset quality. In order to provide a level playing field, the FDI in private sector banks was raised from 49 percent to 74 percent of their paid-up capital under the automatic route in 2004 (inclusive in the new limit are investments through portfolio schemes by FIIs and NRIs). In case of public sector banks, FDI and FPI are allowed up to 20 percent. However, FDI in Indian banks remains relatively low mainly for two reasons. First, most leading international banks already have a presence in India through their subsidiaries; and second, voting rights of foreign shareholders in Indian private banks are capped at 10 percent.

In addition to banks, other financial intermediaries have also been opened for foreign investment. FDI in NBFCs is permitted up to 100 percent subject to minimum capital norms. In the insurance sector, even though foreign companies are not allowed to operate directly, they are permitted to enter into a JV arrangement with an Indian company up to 26 percent stake in the paid-up equity capital of the company (foreign capital of Rs 6.3 billion, or approximately US$140 million, was invested in new private insurance companies as of end-March 2002). With the announcement of the new pension scheme by the Government of India, pension funds are also being opened up to the private sector with access to foreign funds.

12.4.8 Reserves management

Reflecting liberalization measures, India has attracted considerable private inflows, primarily in the form of FDI, FPI, ECB, and NRI deposits. In the process, capital flows have also undergone a major compositional change in favor of nondebt flows as well as longer maturity debt flows (Table 12.5). The surplus in India's capital account increased from US$3.9 billion during the 1980s to US$8.8 billion during the 1990s (1992/93–2001/02) and further to US$12.8 billion in 2002/03, with an increasing share in investment versus debt flows. As a proportion of GDP, total capital flows increased from 1.6 percent during the 1980s to 2.3 percent during the 1990s and further to 2.4 percent in 2002/03, in line with India's absorptive capacity given its growth performance during the 1990s.

With the current account deficit averaging a modest 1 percent of GDP in the 1990s, private capital flows have generally appeared adequate, leading to comfortable reserve build up. However, given a current account surplus each of the last three years, there has been a sharp build up in reserves. In absolute terms, foreign exchange reserves increased from US$5.8 billion at end-March 1991 to US$76 billion at end-March 2003, and further to US$113.0 billion at end-March 2004. However, rapid reserves accumulation has been viewed by some as a costly measure for the economy. It is, therefore, appropriate to examine in some detail the relevance of such concerns in the context of the overall approach pursued by India for opening its capital account in particular and the external sector in general.

While India's foreign exchange reserves increased sharply during the last three years, it needs to be noted that the bulk of the accretion to reserves has been on account of nondebt creating flows. For instance, out of the total reserves accretion of US$20.8 billion during the 2002/03, the major nondebt creating sources, namely the current account surplus, foreign investment and valuation changes, together accounted for 60.1 percent of the increase. Further, net drawdown in foreign assets of banks, which are also nondebt creating flows, contributed to an increase in net banking capital by US$4.9 billion, thereby accounting for another 23.6 percent of reserves accretion.[23] So far as nondebt creating flows are concerned (i.e. FDI and FPI), such inflows bear the same risk-return profile as any domestic investment and therefore the cost to the economy of such flows is the same irrespective of whether they accrue to foreign reserves or are matched by equivalent foreign currency outflow due to higher imports by India or investment abroad

Table 12.5 India: pattern of capital flows and their use[a] (in millions of US dollars, unless otherwise indicated)

Period	Net capital flows							Reserves (End-March)	Increase (+) decrease (−) in reserves[c]	Current account balance (in percent of GDP)	Debt stock	Short-term debt[d]	Debt service[e]
	Current account balance	Foreign investment	External borrowing	NRI deposits	External aid	Other capital[b]	Total capital inflows						
1990/91	−9,680	103	2,248	1,536	2,210	1,091	7,188	5,834	−1,278	−3.1	10.2	28.7	35.3
1991/92	−1,178	133	1,456	290	3,037	−1,139	3,777	9,220	3,385	−0.3	8.3	38.7	30.2
1992/93	−3,526	557	−358	2,001	1,859	−1,123	2,936	9,832	698	−1.7	7.0	37.5	27.5
1993/94	−1,158	4,235	607	1,205	1,901	1,747	9,695	19,254	8,724	−0.4	3.9	33.8	25.4
1994/95	−3,369	4,922	1,030	172	1,526	1,506	9,156	25,186	4,644	−1.0	4.3	30.8	25.9
1995/96	−5,910	4,902	1,275	1,103	883	−3,474	4,689	21,687	−2,936	−1.7	5.4	27.0	24.3
1996/97	−4,619	6,153	2,848	3,350	1,109	−2,048	11,412	26,423	5,818	−1.2	7.2	24.5	21.2
1997/98	−5,500	5,390	3,999	1,125	907	−1,410	10,011	29,367	3,893	−1.4	5.4	24.3	19.0
1998/99	−4,038	2,412	4,362	960	820	−294	8,260	32,490	3,829	−1.0	4.4	23.6	17.8
1999/2000	−4,698	5,191	313	1,540	901	3,155	11,100	38,036	6,142	−1.0	4.0	22.1	16.2
2000/01	−3,590	6,789	3,732	2,317	427	−3,819	9,446	42,281	5,830	−0.8	3.6	22.4	17.2
2001/02	782	8,151	−1,579	2,754	1,204	445	10,975	54,106	11,757	0.2	2.8	21.0	13.9
2002/03	4,137	5,639	−2,353	2,976	−2,428	9,009	12,843	75,428	16,980	0.8	4.4	20.1	14.7

[a] Net inflows into the capital account (excluding IMF) and the accretion to the foreign exchange reserves. Since 2000/01, data on foreign direct investment have been revised with expanded coverage to approach international best practices.
[b] Includes errors and omissions.
[c] Not adjusted for valuation effects.
[d] In percent of total external debt.
[e] In percent of total exports.

Sources: Reserve Bank of India and author's estimates.

by residents. Further, NRI deposits, which accounted for 14.4 percent of the reserves accretion in 2002/03, are now paying interest rates in line with those prevailing overseas, and external assistance, as concessional flows, continue to be contracted at much lower interest rates. Thus, the cost of additional reserves is not an area of concern given its present structure.

12.4.9 Monetary and exchange rate management and liberalization

Reflecting the policy imperatives, as highlighted by Jalan (2003), the main pillars of exchange rate management in India can be characterized as follows:

- The RBI does not have a fixed "target" for the exchange rate, which it tries to defend or pursue over time;
- Rather, the RBI pursues a managed float and, as such, is prepared to intervene in the market to dampen excessive volatility as and when necessary;
- The RBI's purchases or sales of foreign currency are undertaken through a number of banks and are generally discreet and smooth; and
- An attempt is made to ensure that foreign exchange operations and exchange rate movement are transaction oriented rather than being purely speculative in nature.

Reflecting these objectives, the RBI must balance the need to contain the monetary (and hence inflationary) effect of capital flows on the one hand and maintain the export competitiveness of the economy on the other. In order to strike the desired balance, starting in the 1990s, it has controlled the domestic liquidity impact of foreign inflows through timely monetary management. In the process, the RBI has moved monetary control away from direct instruments (cash reserve requirements) to indirect ones (open market operations, including repo). Given the large inflows in recent years, the ability of the RBI to successfully manage their impact on domestic liquidity has led to some replenishment of the RBI's stock of government securities, most recently through issue of market stabilization bonds by the Government of India to the RBI for monetary management purposes.

12.5 Conclusion

In terms of the standard indicators of effectiveness of capital controls, one could view that controls have been effective in India because: (i) despite strong inflows there has been no major real appreciation of the exchange rate; (ii) monetary independence has not been lost and a wedge between domestic and foreign interest rates has been successfully created and maintained; and (iii) the black market premium on the exchange rate has declined drastically to negligible levels with concomitant decline in capital flight. The emphasis on preconditions and a policy of gradual liberalization have enabled India to reap the benefits of opening up while avoiding the sources of vulnerability. Inadequate absorption of foreign capital has weakened the contribution of foreign capital to growth; however, the current policy of maintaining an adequate level of foreign exchange reserves and the associated prevention of exchange rate appreciation, both of which provide a cushion to financial stability, should not be abandoned in favor of a more flexible exchange rate and more open capital account just to deal with recent current account surpluses. If the capital account liberalization fails to increase absorptive capacity, such a policy can also represent a recipe for disaster. Given the trade-off between efficiency and stability associated with capital flows, India's preference has strongly been in favor of avoiding instability. Such an approach has imparted stability not only to the financial system but also to the growth process. The relative weights of efficiency versus stability need to be constantly reviewed with reference to both domestic and foreign developments. While realizing that growth performance could be augmented with foreign capital, it is imperative to ensure that liberalization of the capital account responds to the requirement of the overall economy in an appropriate, gradual, and cautious manner. Inflows have been substantially liberalized in India with a preference for companies versus individuals, which is expected to continue, but if the momentum of capital flows persists, it may be possible that with limits to sterilization, more capital account liberalization on outflows could be forthcoming, particularly for corporate entities and financial intermediaries. The pace of liberalization, particularly for the latter, would, however, continue to depend not only on domestic factors, especially the progress in the financial sector reform and fiscal consolidation, but also taking into account the evolving international financial architecture.

Notes

1. Principal adviser and chief economist, Department of Economic Analysis and Policy, Reserve Bank of India. The chapter states the author's personal views and not necessarily those of the institution to which he belongs. The author is grateful to Shri Sitikantha Pattnaik and Shri Arindam Roy for assistance. However, the usual disclaimer applies.
2. Rodrik (1998).
3. Quirk and Evans *et al.* (1995).
4. In his open letter to Prime Minister Mahathir on the capital controls in Malaysia, however, Krugman (1998) emphasized that (i) controls should disrupt ordinary business as little as possible; (ii) distortions associated with controls are serious and tend to grow over time, suggesting that controls must be used as a temporary measure; (iii) controls may do most damage when the intention is to defend an overvalued exchange rate; and (iv) controls must aid reforms and should not be viewed as the alternative to reform.
5. Growth in base money fell from 25 percent in 1997 to minus 15 percent in 1998, and the domestic lending rate hardened by close to 3 percentage points.

6. The one-year holding period requirement was replaced by a 0–30 percent graded exit levy on outflow of principal and 10–30 percent levy on profit repatriation, depending on the period over which profits were realized.

7. After the introduction of the controls, short-term interest rates fell by close to 5 percentage points and as a matter of policy the fiscal deficit widened from 3.7 percent of GDP in 1998 to 6.1 percent in 1999.

8. According to Edwards (1999), capital controls in Chile were effective on short-term inflows on an original maturity basis, but not on a residual maturity basis.

9. The reserves were to be maintained with the central bank for a minimum period of three months.

10. While some suggest the imposition of a tax on a permanent basis on all inflows, Tobin suggested a "throwing sand in the wheels" approach under which countries must appropriately raise the "threshold limit on capital inflows." As per a modified two-tier Tobin tax, a country could impose a transaction tax to increase the cost of foreign exchange trading and an exchange surcharge with the rate progressively increasing with the deviation from the equilibrium exchange rate.

11. Neither the volume nor composition of capital flows (in terms of residual maturity rather than original maturity) altered drastically in response to controls. The real exchange rate appreciated by 28 percent during April 1991–September 1998. The interest rate differential (adjusted for the expected change in the exchange rate) was small and disappeared quickly.

12. The Committee on Capital Account Convertibility was chaired by the then Deputy Governor of the RBI S. S. Tarapore.

13. The Fiscal Responsibility and Budget Management Law, which stipulates the elimination of the revenue deficit of the Central Government by end-March 2008, is expected to create an environment conducive for fiscal consolidation.

14. The ongoing efforts of banking sector reforms, which focus on better credit risk management and asset recovery measures (including the recent Securitization and Reconstruction of Financial Assets and Enforcement of Security Interest (SARFAESI) Act, 2002 are expected to provide banks with additional avenues for the disposition of their NPAs.

15. Previously, companies could only borrow up to US$50 million through the automatic route and up to US$100 million with prior approval of the RBI.

16. Total prepayment by corporates, which amounted to US$1.1 billion during April 2001 to December 2002, is estimated to have saved interest cost of US$90 million for these companies.

17. As part of the rationalization of NRI deposits, nonrepatriable rupee denominated (NRNRD) deposits (which amounted to US$7.1 billion at end-March 2002), on which only interest payments were freely repatriable, were discontinued effective April 1, 2002. At the same time, as part of the gradual move toward capital account convertibility, the maturity proceeds of outstanding NRNRD deposits were eligible to be reinvested in fully repatriable NRI deposits. Accordingly, the outstanding NRNRD deposits declined steadily to US$2.8 billion by end-July 2003, with the bulk of such deposits being reinvested in the nonresident (external) account of NRI deposits.

18. The small list of industries that require case-by-case approvals from the FIPB include domestic airlines, the petroleum sector (except private sector oil refining), print and broadcast media, postal and courier services, development of integrated township, tea plantations, defense and strategic industries, atomic minerals, the

establishment and operation of satellites, and investment companies in infrastructure and the services sector.

19. The negative list includes retail trading; atomic energy; the gaming, betting, and lottery business; the housing and real estate business; and agriculture (excluding floriculture, horticulture, seed development, vegetable and mushroom cultivation under controlled conditions, animal husbandry, pisiculture, and services related to agriculture and allied sectors) and plantations (other than tea).

20. By late 1997, the year when nonresidents were allowed to invest in government securities, roughly 30 percent of the GKO (a short-term government bill) market was accounted for by nonresidents.

21. However, to provide foreign exchange earners with greater flexibility, their foreign currency accounts could be used only for external payments. If such balances are to be used for local payments, they have to be converted into Indian rupees. Further, since November 2002, resident individuals have been allowed to open domestic foreign currency accounts only when they acquire foreign exchange through normal banking channels.

22. Moreover, Indian banks are not permitted to offer two-way quotes to NRIs or nonresident banks.

23. Out of the US$8.4 billion increase in net banking capital flows, the net drawdown in foreign assets of banks contributed to an increase in banking capital by US$4.9 billion. The remaining portion of the increase in banking capital was due to net increase in foreign liabilities of banks, comprising mainly NRI deposits (US$3.0 billion).

References

Ariyoshi, Akira, Karl Habermeier, Bernard Laurens, Inci Ötker-Robe, Jorge Iván Canales-Kriljenko, and Andrei Kirilenko, 2000, *Capital Controls: Country Experiences with Their Use and Liberalization*, IMF Occasional Paper No. 190 (Washington, DC: International Monetary Fund).

CEIC Economic Database, CEIC Data Company Ltd. (Hong Kong).

Cooper, Richard N., 2001, "Should Capital Controls be Banished?" in *Global Financial Crises and Reforms*, ed. by B.N. Ghosh (London: Routledge).

Edwards, Sebastian, 1999, "International Capital Flows and Emerging Markets: Amending the Rules of the Game," paper presented at the Federal Reserve Bank of Boston conference on *Rethinking the International Monetary System*, Boston (June).

Eichengreen, Barry, 1999, "Capital Controls: Capital Ideas or Capital Folly?," *Milken Institute Review*, Vol. 1.

Frankel, Jeffrey, 1999, "Proposals Regarding Restrictions on Capital Flows," *African Financial Journal*, Vol. 1, Part 1 (Bellville, South Africa: African Centre for Investment Analysis).

Gilbert, Christopher L., Gregor Irwin, and David Vines, 2000, "International Financial Architecture, Capital Account Convertibility and Poor Developing Countries," paper presented at an Overseas Development Institute seminar on *Capital Account Liberalisation: The Developing Country Perspective* (June), London.

Gourinchas, Pierre-Olivier and Olivier Jeanne, 2002, "On the Benefits of Capital Account Liberalization for Emerging Economies," unpublished (Washington, DC: International Monetary Fund).

Gruben, William C. and Darryl McLeod, 2001, "Capital Account Liberalization and Disinflation in the 1990s," Center for Latin America Working Paper No. 0101 (February) (Federal Reserve Bank of Dallas).

International Monetary Fund, *World Economic Outlook*, 2001 (October) (Washington, DC).

——, 1998 (May) (Washington, DC).

——, 1997 (October) (Washington, DC).

Jalan, Bimal, 2003, "Exchange Rate Management: An Emerging Consensus," paper presented at the 14th National Assembly of the Forex Association of India, Mumbai (August 14).

Johnston, R. Barry and Natalia T. Tamirisa, 1998, "Why Do Countries Use Capital Controls," IMF Working Paper 98/181 (Washington, DC: International Monetary Fund).

Kim, Woochan, 2003, "Does Capital Account Liberalization Discipline Budget Deficit?," *Review of International Economics*, Vol. 11, No. 5 (November), pp. 830–44.

Krugman, Paul, 1998, "An Open Letter to Prime Minister Mahathir," available via the internet (www.mit.edu/krugman/www/mahathir.html) (September 1).

McKinnon, Ronald, 1973, *Money and Capital in Economic Development* (Washington, DC: Brookings Institution).

—— and Huw Pill, 1996, "Credible Liberalization and International Capital Flows: The Overborrowing Syndrome," in *Financial Deregulation and Integration in East Asia*, ed. by Takatoshi Ito and Anne O. Krueger (Chicago: University of Chicago Press).

Neely, Christopher J., 1999, "An Introduction to Capital Controls," *Federal Reserve Bank of St. Louis Review* (November), pp. 13–30.

Panagariya, Arvind, 1998, "Full Convertibility: Must We Have It?," *The Economic Times* (October 26) (College Park: University of Maryland).

Quirk, Peter and Owen Evans *et al.*, 1995, "Capital Account Convertibility: Review of Experience and Implications for IMF Policies," IMF Occasional Papers No. 131 (Washington, DC: International Monetary Fund).

Reddy, Y.V., 2000, "Operationalising Capital Account Liberalization: Indian Experience," *RBI Bulletin* (October) (Mumbai: Reserve Bank of India).

Reserve Bank of India, 2003, *Report on Currency and Finance 2001–02* (Mumbai).

——, 1997, *Report of the Committee on Capital Account Convertibility*, S.S. Tarapore (Chairman) (Mumbai).

Rodrik, Dani, 1998, "Who Needs Capital Account Convertibility?" in *Should the IMF Pursue Capital-Account Convertibility?*, Essays in International Finance No. 207 (June) (Princeton, NJ: Princeton University).

Virmani, Arvind, 1999, "Capital Account Convertibility: Timing and Phasing," Policy Paper No. 16 (New Delhi: Chintan).

Yoshitomi, Masaru and Sayuri Shirai, 2000, "Policy Recommendations for Preventing Another Capital Account Crisis," paper presented at the Asian Development Bank's *Asian Policy Forum*, Manila (July 7).